STEVE WIDE &
MICHELLE MACKINTOSH

日本

JAPAN

A curated guide to the best
regions, food, culture & art

plum. Pan Macmillan Australia

Contents

Introduction 4

BEFORE YOU GO

The eras of Japan 13
Seasonal Japan 52
Places to stay 86
Train journeys 96

CULINARY JAPAN

Savoury 114
Sweet 139
Drinks 144

JAPAN BY REGION

Kantō 161
Tōhoku 193
Chūbu 213
Kansai 233
Chūgoku 263
Hokkaidō 277
Shikoku 291
Kyūshū 307

CULTURE

Beliefs & religion 332
Cultural icons 338
Historical building styles 342
Castles 344
Garden styles 346
Contemporary architects 352
Libraries 358
Museums 359
Traditional art & craft 366
Antique & flea markets 373
Contemporary art & artists 374
Fashion 376
Music 378

FAVOURITE THINGS

· History of Japanese fashion 26
· Enduring national symbols 36
· Pop culture icons 50
· What to pack 70
· Kids' Japan 78
· Ryokan mini break 95
· Ō-bentō 98
· Omiyage 109
· Vegetarian & vegan Japan 134
· Zen & the art of wagashi 142
· Brewery tastings & tours 148
· Food markets 154
· Playtime 168
· Vending machines 175
· UNESCO World Heritage Sites 181
· Mount Fuji 222
· Sacred sites & pilgrimage trails 228
· Power spots 267
· Unique places 299
· Cycling adventures 314
· Manhole art & station stamps 356
· Japanese arts 363

Thank you 382
Index 383

RICH HISTORY,
DEEP CULTURE,
UNFORGETTABLE
ADVENTURES

Introduction

Japan is a small country by most standards, but it packs a lot into its modest frame. Its history is steeped in mystery and intrigue: eras of unrest and upheaval followed by times of peace and growth; centuries of enforced solitude contrasted with decades of openness and rapid change. Japan has a transcendent sort of majesty and grandeur, but also an air of modesty and deference that belies its epic origins. The storybook clichés hold clues to reality: geisha, with their dedication to the arts; samurai, with their intense discipline and code of valour; sumo wrestlers, with their skilful devotion to a sport – and way of life – built on centuries of tradition. The history books may give you the impression that the country was built on dynasties, but its true foundations rest on the backs of its people.

——— No matter how many times we visit Japan, it always has something new to offer. Japan is world-renowned metropolises with towering skyscrapers, legendary landmarks and superbly designed structures overlooking networks of tiny alleys and enclaves: a thriving microcosm of activity and invention learning from the lessons of the past. It is small villages brimming with character, carved out by artisans whose skills have been built through generations of training. It is the old perfectly coexisting with the new: impossibly crowded urban clusters giving way to vast swathes of cultivated and uncultivated land.

Japan is train journeys – the longer the better – that carry you across an extraordinary network of rail lines through some of the most striking places on the planet. Cities teeming with people are just an easy train ride from areas with great natural and spiritual beauty, jaw-dropping history, truly ancient shrines and temples, and a slower, more meaningful pace of life. Depending on where you are, you might find rice paddies, tea plantations or apple orchards surrounding villages full of generations of specialty growers, makers and hands-on creators. With the Shinkansen (bullet train), even a quick daytrip from a major city can take you to places with their own unique landscapes, iconic natural symbols, mythologies, festivals, local delicacies, crafts and even styles of tea.

From daytrips out of town and extended explorations of outlying areas, to long-haul jaunts into the most remote regions, Japan's trains make intrepid adventures comfortable and interesting. Getting from one amazing place to another is fast, efficient and a major part of the fun. Within a day or less you can find yourself out of the big city and in a remote forest, staying in a centuries-old *ryokan* (traditional inn) with a history that is displayed proudly on its walls. The arresting views along the way (Mount Fuji on a clear day en route from Tokyo to Kyoto is a sight you won't forget in a hurry) are a highlight of anyone's visit. We've taken train rides that have lasted seven hours or more – and loved it! Just grab a *bentō* (boxed lunch) and a bottle of sake and you are off on an unforgettable adventure. →

OPPOSITE PAGE: Festival in Shibuya, Tokyo, Kantō
ABOVE LEFT: Shōwa-era toys RIGHT: Fashion advertising

For the first-time visitor, Japan is an endless delight. For the pop-culture fanatic, it's the holy grail: a nonstop party of flashing neon, crazy costumes, huge queues for the latest fad foods and character toys, and shelves of manga well beyond most collectors' capacity to store. For the contemplative, sinking into an *onsen* (hot spring), practising calligraphy, participating in a meditation session or even just walking into a shrine and smelling the wafting scent of incense will have you feeling at peace with yourself and with the world.

In our book *Tokyo*, we spoke of the mash-up of high culture and pop culture in Japan's biggest city, and the same goes for the rest of the country. You can go to the most far-flung regions and find cute cartoon characters representing a city or township alongside deep, intricate histories and local legends populated with serious shogun and samurai, comical drunkards and buffoons, powerful, towering gods and an oddball assortment of talking animals and objects come to life.

As is the case with most countries, every region in Japan has its own unique charm. Crossing the invisible borders that divide the country into prefectures and municipalities, you will notice both a real and a symbolic shift in the agriculture, food, fashion, behaviour and history that you encounter, with the differences most marked when you are travelling between the islands. Honshū is most travellers' first port of call (and some travellers' only destination), encompassing as it does the main cities of Tokyo, Kyoto and Osaka, as well as major tourist towns like Hiroshima and Nara.

Venture north to Hokkaidō and you'll find a distinct change in the kinds of foods you eat, the sights that you see and the history that you experience. Produce in particular is a big marker of an area's identity, and in Hokkaidō you'll discover local delicacies that you can't enjoy anywhere else, such as fish from the local waters or sweets made from the region's amazing dairy. The ramen is rich and thick with miso and curry soup is a moreish delight. The convenience stores in Hokkaidō stock many different brands to the main island, with designs and ingredients that reflect the emblems of the area.

Crossing the southern divide and travelling down to Shikoku, Kyūshū or Okinawa, you will find that the atmosphere becomes distinctly more relaxed and summery. The land is very volcanic and the waters vibrant, giving rise to some great bathing and hot-springs opportunities. The food down south is bigger and bolder, with huge fruits growing from the volcanic soil and an interesting array of delicacies being imported from the surrounding islands, Okinawa's American military bases and neighbouring countries, such as Korea and China. →

RIGHT: Daigo-ji, Kyoto, Kansai

In these pockets
of old-world Japan,
mists drift lazily
over mountains;
rivers wind
timelessly through
glades and chasms;
wildlife plays in
thicket and glade;
and autumn leaves
settle gently on
the ground as new
buds reach out into
the spring air.

Modern, urban Japan is a high-tech wonderland of gadgets, gizmos and invention, a pop-culture playground where colour and sound explode into the everyday. Once you branch out into Japan's further reaches, however, there is so much more to discover. Much of Japan's history might be forged within Honshū's furnace, but stepping outside of the country's urban centres can take you to Ainu communities, artisan villages, cavernous basins embracing thundering waterfalls, and mountainous regions with candy-floss clouds and centuries-old temples.

When we travel, we usually find that the further out you go from major cities, the more you find of the old world: the old ways, the manners, the lifestyle. This is certainly true of Japan, and you can imagine how much more an intrepid adventurer has to discover from the less-trodden reaches of the country.

In these pockets of old-world Japan, mists drift lazily over mountains; rivers wind timelessly through glades and chasms; wildlife plays in thicket and glade; and autumn leaves settle gently on the ground as new buds reach out into the spring air. Here you can get a real sense of 'magical' Japan, where familiar seasons take on a new resonance and are given meaning as they merge with local food and culture. Experience the artisan crafts and local knowledge that are part of daily life, and catch a glimpse of a truly delicate and elaborate world.

So let's travel together across the Land of the Rising Sun. For anyone seeking wonder, spirit, harmony and the perfection of simplicity, you've definitely come to the right place. Japan is all that you expect, and hope, that it would be. A journey to Japan is one that will thrill you, entertain you, teach you and, ultimately, change you.

OPPOSITE PAGE: Nadeshiko Hotel Shibuya, Tokyo, Kantō

行く前に

BEFORE YOU GO

The eras of Japan

Japan has a long and fascinating history that has intrigued the rest of the world for centuries. Castles with 'nightingale floors' (p. 242), scheming courtesans, warring shoguns – for a small island, this country has a big history. Luckily, it's ordered into periods and eras that correspond to the reign of various rulers, major historical events or cultural paradigm shifts.

Since 645 AD, Japan's periods and eras have borne the name of the seat of power or the dynasty that ruled over it. The semblance of 'society' was first glimpsed during the Nara period (710–794 AD) and has continued to develop until the current Reiwa era (2019–ongoing). Along the way, periods and eras came and went, dictated by rulership, battling shoguns, emperors and foreign influence. Styles that remained static for centuries suddenly became mutable as ports opened to foreign trade. Change didn't come often, but when it did, it happened swiftly. Chinese influence shaped the early periods, and later American styles would be in vogue, but all along, traditional Japanese beauty, fashion, food and manners would remain steadfast, no matter the outside influences. Japan's main periods and eras can be roughly divided into Nara (710–794), Heian (794–185), Kamakura (1185–1333), Muromachi (1338–1573), Azuchi-Momoyama (1573–1600) and Edo (1603–1868) periods, followed by the Meiji (1868–1912), Taishō (1912–1926), Shōwa (1926–1989), Heisei (1989–2019 and Reiwa (2019–ongoing) eras.

OPPOSITE PAGE: Traditional dress at Ginkaku-ji (Silver Pavilion), Kyoto, Kansai

EARLY JAPAN

PLACES TO VISIT

JŌMON PERIOD

Kizukuri Station's Jōmon sculpture exterior, Tsugaru, Tōhoku

Komakino archaeological site, Aomori, Tōhoku

Pottery displays at Korekawa Jōmon-kan and the Korekawa archaeological site, Hachinohe, Tōhoku

Sannai-Maruyama archaeological site, Aomori, Tōhoku

Tsugaru Jōmon-kan and the Kamegaoka archaeological site, Tsugaru, Tōhoku

AINU PEOPLE

Hokkaidō Museum, Sapporo, Hokkaidō

Hokkaidō Museum of Northern Peoples, Abashiri, Hokkaidō

Irankarapute sculpture at Sapporo Station, Sapporo, Hokkaidō

Kawamura Kaneto Ainu Museum, Asahikawa, Hokkaidō

Lake Akan Ainu Kotan, a living Ainu settlement, Kushiro, Hokkaidō

Sapporo Ainu Culture Promotion Centre, Sapporo, Hokkaidō

YAYOI PERIOD

Izumo Taisha, thought to be the oldest shrine in Japan, Izumo, Chūgoku (pp. 271, 335)

Kotai Jingū (4 BC), the inner shrine of Ise Jingū (Ise Grand Shine) and one of the most important shrines in Japan, Ise, Kansai (p. 334)

Shinto shrines (pp. 334–335)

Sumiyoshi Taisha (211 AD), Osaka, Kansai

Yoshinogari Historical Park, Yoshinogari, Kyūshū

The Jōmon period (1000–300 BC) is known for its pottery, thought to be some of the oldest examples of the craft in the world. A giant replica sculpture of the most popular Jōmon pottery piece – Shakoki-Dogu – looms large at Kizukuri train station in Aomori (p. 101), near where it was excavated. Japan's first people were the Ainu – a hunter-gatherer culture.

During the Yayoi period (1000 BC–30 AD) it is believed that the hunter-gatherers were overwhelmed by farmers from other Asian countries, known as the Yayoi people. The earliest examples of the Yayoi people can be found in Kyūshū. It was in this period that Japanese culture as we know it today originated, including the introduction of the Shinto religion.

Northern Japan, in particular Hokkaidō, is still home to more than 25,000 Ainu people. To this day, the Ainu have a creative and intricate culture, with amazing embroidery, pottery, dance, festivals and parades. There are so many places in Hokkaidō to see ancient Ainu art and craft, partake in festivals and learn about their history.

ABOVE: Ainu village in Hokkaidō
OPPOSITE: Deer in Nara, Kansai

NARA PERIOD
(710–794)

——————— The documented history of Japan began with the Nara period in 710 AD. Empress Genmei set up the capital in what is now known as Nara, a popular travel destination just out of Kyoto, famous for its roaming deer and the temple Yakushi-ji. At the time the capital was Heijō-kyō (relocatied from the previous capital, Fujiwara-kyō), a mostly rural population presided over by an upper class who had taken their cues from Chinese society, including adopting the system of writing (kanji), the religion (Buddhism) and the fashion. This even extended to the look and feel of the capital, which was modelled on the Chinese Tang Dynasty capital Chang'an.

The arts and artisan crafts began to flourish. Literature and poetry of the time produced some important texts, such as the *Kojiki* (*Records of Ancient Matters*; 712 AD) and the *Nihon Shoki* (*The Chronicles of Japan*; 720 AD), Japan's oldest and second-oldest book respectively, and the *Man'yōshū*, a compendium of highly influential poetry (known as *waka*), which inspired the name of the era that began in 2019, Reiwa. Despite the capital shifting around a little, Nara was still the main focus of urban growth and soon reached a population of 200,000 people, most of whom were agrarian, although around 10,000 worked in government jobs. It was at this time that Buddhism was established as the predominant religion of Japan. Stunning temple Tōdai-ji was completed in 752 AD and remains one of Nara's principal tourist drawcards, especially its Great Buddha Hall (Daibutsuden), which was, until 1998, the world's largest wooden building. Strolling the streets of Nara, flanked by ambling deer and snap-happy travellers, you can still get a sense of the ancient capital, and the peaceful lifestyle many would have led there. Traditional artisan handicrafts still flourish, and specialty foods deliciously reflect the area's history. Many structures have been rebuilt, but their faithful recreation and long history still make Nara one of Japan's leading travel destinations. The area's history can be experienced today in the many artefacts and scrolls housed in Shōsō-in, the treasure house at Tōdai-ji.

ARCHITECTURE
Influenced by the architecture of the Tang Dynasty in China

Wood, painted in gold, black and red, with blue tile roofing, was the material of choice

ART
Buddhist paintings

Intricate bronze sculpture

Key works: The Yakushi Triad at Yakushi-ji, Nara, Kansai; sculptures at Sangatsu-dō, Kyoto, Kansai; the seated image of Birushana Buddha at Tōshōdai-ji in Nara, Kansai

CRAFT
Aizome, traditional indigo-dyeing

Akahada pottery

Carved bamboo products, including exceptional tea whisks

First *furoshiki* wrapping cloth

Flat paper fans with intricate fretwork

Fude, brushes used for calligraphy

Handmade *washi* paper

Joufu, hand-woven hemp cloth

Kaya-fukin, tea towels made of mosquito netting

Porcelain

Sumi, ink sticks used for calligraphy

Tenugui, thin hand towels

CULTURE
Kasuga Wakamiya On-Matsuri, a winter festival in Nara, Kansai

Setsubun, a festival marking the start of spring, involving throwing beans to drive away evil spirits (p. 74)

Uchiwa Maki, a fan-throwing festival in Nara, Kansai

Uneme Matsuri, a festival with lantern-lit boats meant to calm the soul of a lady-in-waiting who drowned in Sarusawa Pond in Nara, Kansai

FOOD

Chagayu, rice and green tea porridge

Deer biscuits (to feed deer, not you!)

Kakinohazushi, pressed sushi wrapped in persimmon leaves

Kuzumochi, kuzu-starch cakes served with black sugar syrup and toasted soy flour

Narazuke, vegetables pickled in sake lees

Sake

Somen noodles made with the waters of Mount Miwa

GARDENS

Isui-en, Nara, Kansai

Nara Kōen, Nara, Kansai; a park where deer roam freely. You can pat them, they are up for a selfie and you can even feed them with special biscuits purchased from nearby vendors (p. 250)

Yoshiki-en, Nara, Kansai

LANDMARKS

Stone lanterns on the steps of Kasuga Taisha (Kasuga Grand Shrine; p. 251), Nara, Kansai

The Seven Great Temples: Tōdai-ji, Daian-ji, Gangō-ji, Kōfuku-ji, Saidai-ji and Yakushi-ji in Nara, Kansai; and Hōryū-ji in Ikaruga, Kansai

Tōshōdai-ji, Nara, Kansai

LITERATURE

Kojiki (*Records of Ancient Matters*; 712), Japan's oldest book

Man'yōshū (*Collection of Ten Thousand Leaves*; 759), one of Japan's oldest volumes of collected poetry

Nihon Shoki (*The Chronicles of Japan*; 720), Japan's second-oldest book

Kojiki (*Records of Ancient Matters*; 712), edited by Ō no Yasumaro

MUSEUMS

Nara Craft Museum, Nara, Kansai

Nara Prefectural Museum of Art, Nara, Kansai

Shōsō-in, the treasure house at Tōdai-ji, Nara, Kansai (p. 251)

MUSIC

Musical instruments strongly influenced by Chinese music, including the *biwa* (short-necked lute), *kin* (seven-stringed zither), *shakuhachi* (vertical bamboo flute) and *ryūteki* ('dragon flute')

ABOVE: *Kakinohazushi*, pressed sushi wrapped in persimmon leaves OPPOSITE PAGE: *Genji Monogatari* artwork, Uji, Kansai

HEIAN PERIOD
(794–1185)

——— As the Nara period came to a close, many changes were taking place in Japan. The capital moved to Kyoto (Heian-kyō) in 794 AD, Buddhism and Taoism were firmly established, and political manoeuvrings were at their most Machiavellian. On the surface, power lay with the imperial family, but they were controlled by the Fujiwara clan, a wealthy aristocratic family who had married into their ranks and eventually became acting regents. Despite all the machinations, and the swift rise of a powerful military class, Heian is translated as 'peace', and Japan enjoyed a period of prosperity and cultural and artistic development at this time. It is often referred to as the 'golden era' of Japan. The scripts *katakana* and *hiragana* started to develop into their modern form. There was a strong interest in a 'literature of the people' and, in contrast, very 'graceful poetry'. Poetry was a way to gain status in the imperial court: reputations could be made and destroyed on the strength of a haiku.

A notable feature of this era was the development of 'Japanese beauty'. It was considered important to be 'beautiful', which was achieved by powdering your face and blackening your teeth for women and men. The men adopted a goatee and a sprinkle of hair under the nose that would pass as a wispy moustache. The women plucked or shaved their eyebrows and painted them back on, but higher up on their foreheads. They also made their mouths smaller, like a red rosebud. Geisha style echoes elements of this today. Women's robes became elaborate, multi-layered and intricately patterned.

Power struggles, the rise of the military class and a decentralisation of government made this era a vibrant time of intrigue, manipulation and deceit. It's no wonder *Genji Monogatari* (*The Tale of Genji*) — Japan's first true novel, a court soap opera populated by more characters than *Game of Thrones* – was written in this period. This weighty tome would have lasting and incalculable impact on Japanese and world literature.

ARCHITECTURE

First *minka*, 'houses of the people' with thatched roofing (p. 343)

First *machiya* (wooden townhouses; p. 342)

Red-painted wood was the material of choice, with wooden or green tile roofing featuring upturned edges

Shinden-zukuri, an architectural style developed for the aristocracy, featuring groups of buildings and a central garden

Shinto shrines, previously left with a natural wood finish, now painted red

ART

Early *raigō-zu*, religious paintings featuring Amida Buddha arriving on a cloud

Kakemono, hanging scrolls, and *emakimono*, picture scrolls that tell a narrative

Kara-e ('Chinese painting'), a style of painting influenced by Chinese art, depicting landscapes and legendary figures

Temple murals (especially at Daigo-ji, Kyoto, Kansai)

Yamato-e ('Japanese painting'), a style of painting that illustrated Japanese life, especially in rural areas

BUILDINGS
Kyoto Heian Hotel, Kyoto, Kansai
Kyoto Imperial Palace, Kyoto, Kansai

CRAFT
Detailed bamboo carving
Elaborately handcrafted fashion
Intricate gold, silver and copper enamelwork
Silk embroidery

CULTURE
Development within the high arts
First appreciation of cherry blossom recorded in *Genji Monogatari* (*The Tale of Genji*; c. 1008)
First reference to Hina Matsuri (Doll's Day or Girls' Day; p. 82) in *Genji Monogatari*, as well as poetry and haiku
Patronage of shrines and temples
The start of religious pilgrimages

EXPERIENCES
Kamakura, Kantō, the first seat of shogun rule (p. 177)
Kyoto, formerly known as Heian-kyō (p. 234)
Pilgrimages, including the Kumano Kodō (p. 230) and the Shikoku Henro (p. 229)
Uji, Kansai, where the final chapters of *Genji Monogatari* take place (p. 249)

FOOD
Chestnuts
Dried fish
Fruit, especially persimmons
Jelly
Pheasant
Pickles
Salted salmon
Sashimi
Simmered and steamed food
Soup with chopped vegetables
Tea

Vegetarian cuisine rather than meat-based dishes (except for seafood)
Widespread use of seaweed

GARDENS
Kyoto Gyoen, the gardens of the Imperial Palace, Kyoto, Kansai (p. 347)

LANDMARKS
Byōdō-in, Uji, Kansai (p. 249)
Enryaku-ji (early Heian), Ōtsu, Kansai
Heian Shrine and its gardens, Kyoto, Kansai (p. 239)
Kiyomizu-dera, Kyoto, Kansai (pp. 239, 337)
Nijō Castle, Kyoto, Kansai (p. 242)
The earliest form of Fushimi Inari, Japan's main shrine dedicated to the Shinto deity Inari, relocated to its present-day location in 816 AD, Kyoto, Kansai (p. 243)
The murals of the five-tiered pagoda at Daigo-ji, Kyoto, Kansai

LITERATURE
Development and adoption of *hiragana* and *katakana*
Genji Monogatari (*The Tale of Genji*; c. 1008) by Murasaki Shikibu
Haiku
Nikki bungaku, poetic diaries
The lyrics of 'Kimigayo', the Japanese national anthem

MUSEUMS
Costume Museum of Japan, Kyoto, Kansai
Kyoto Museum of Traditional Crafts, Kyoto, Kansai

MUSIC
Gagaku, or court music was the prevailing musical style, characterised by wind, string and percussion instruments played by an ensemble

RIGHT: Byōdō-in, Uji, Kansai

KAMAKURA PERIOD
(1185–1333)

——————— With the military classes slowly gaining power throughout the early Heian period, the Kamakura shogunate, led first by Shogun Minamoto No Yoritomo, began to control Japan. The samurai warrior class established a feudal rule that would last some 240 years until defeat and destruction in 1333 at the hands of Emperor Go Daigo, who temporarily re-established imperial rule. The period was marked by two Mongol invasions (led by Kublai Khan), both repelled by the onset of typhoons ('divine wind') but both reinforcing a distrust of China within Japan and an insular approach to governance. Buddhism continued in popularity, and old and new styles of Buddhism became widely practised.

The Japanese writing system (*kana*) began to develop, and although Chinese 'Kanbun' was still spoken in the courts, Japanese literature started to really come into its own. *Monogatari* (novels) and essays on Buddhism (only the court and Buddhist monks were literate) led to some important Japanese historical works of literature.

ARCHITECTURE

Buke-zukuri, an architectural style developed for military families, featuring groups of buildings, large kitchens and guard towers

Simple, earthy styles utilising more modern techniques: new technologies changed the way buildings were made, while natural disasters and war meant there was less money for lavish architecture

Unadorned tea houses made from simple materials, where people from all walks of life could unwind and meditate through the simplicity of a cup of tea

ART

A new emphasis on realism and dynamism

Art influenced by cultural exchange with the Chinese Song dynasty, in particular detailed ink paintings and sculpture

Kei school of Buddhist sculpture

Key artists: Jōchō, Kōkei, Unkei

Religious paintings featuring mandalas and calligraphy

CRAFT

Calligraphy influenced by Zen Buddhism (p. 336)

Carved wooden furniture

Lacquerware

Metalwork

Pottery

Textiles

The start of papercraft

CULTURE

Bonsai

Literature, including novels, religious tracts and essays

Martial arts influenced by Zen Buddhism

Nichiren, Rinzai and Ji-shū schools of Buddhism

Pure Land Buddhism

Zen Buddhism

Zen gardens (p. 348)

FOOD

Dried abalone

Jellyfish

Mandarins

Oranges

Pears

Samurai banquets

Seasoned rice

Umeboshi, pickled plum

LITERATURE

Court poetry

Hōjōki (An Account of My Hut; 1212) by Kamo no Chōmei

Military stories

Renga, a genre of collaborative poetry

Shin Kokin Wakashū (New Collection of Poems Ancient and Modern; 1205)

Tanka, short poems with thirty-one syllables

Tsurezuregusa (Essays of Idleness; c. 1330) by Yoshida Kenkō

MUSEUMS

Kamakurabori Museum, Kamakura, Kantō

MUSIC

Military music

Yōkyoku, the choral music of *Noh* theatre (p. 363)

TEMPLES & OTHER BUILDINGS

Danjō-garan Fudo-dō, Mount Kōya, Kansai (p. 259)

Koyurugi Jinja, Fujisawa, Kantō

Nanzen-ji, Kyoto, Kansai

Sanjūsangen-dō, Kyoto, Kansai

The Great Buddha at Kōtoku-in, Kamakura, Kantō (pp. 177, 337)

The Sanmon Gate at Tōfuku-ji, Kyoto, Kansai (p. 243)

The *shariden* (relic hall) at Engaku-ji, Kamakura, Kantō; the only building designated a National Treasure in Kanagawa prefecture (p. 177)

OPPOSITE PAGE: The Great Buddha at Kōtoku-in, Kamakura, Kantō

MUROMACHI (1338–1573) & AZUCHI-MOMOYAMA (1573–1600) PERIODS

——— When shogun power moved to Kyoto from Kamakura in 1338, the Ashikaga shogunate took up residence and started a push-pull struggle for control of the country. Ruler Yoshimitsu managed to get a bit closer to establishing a power base, some of which was achieved by developing the arts – in particular the tea ceremony, *Noh* theatre, ikebana, Zen Buddhism and the further development of *Sumi* ink painting. Civil war continued; in fact, the period became known as *sengoku jidai* or 'the age of war'. Think instability, overlapping civil wars and working-class uprisings, and you get a picture of the times. Structures that made a statement became popular, and the original versions of iconic Kyoto buildings Kinkaku-ji (the Golden Pavilion) and Ginkaku-ji (the Silver Pavilion) were constructed.

The Azuchi-Momoyama period takes its name from Momoyama Castle, seat of legendary samurai and political leader Toyotomi Hideyoshi. Known as one of Japan's 'great unifiers', Hideyoshi's rule eventually led to the establishment of the peaceful Tokugawa shogunate. Some of Japan's most impressive castles, including Himeji, Matsumoto and Kumamoto, were built during this time.

ARCHITECTURE

Architecture with a completely Japanese aesthetic

Decorative castle architecture

Shoin-zukuri, a style of building centred around a *shoin*, or study

Use of gold leaf in buildings

ART

Intricate paintings of town scenes; nature; strong, dominant animals; and with gold- or silver-leaf backgrounds

Kanō school of painting

Key artist: Eitoku Kanō

Raigō-zu, religious paintings featuring Amida Buddha arriving on a cloud

Suiboku-ga, a style of monochromatic ink-wash painting

Key artists: Josetsu, Sesshū Tōyō, Kaō Ninga and Sesson Shukei

Zen painting and gardens (p. 348)

CASTLES

Himeji Castle, Himeji, Kansai (p. 345)

Zeze (or Sekiroku) Castle ruins, Lake Biwa, Kansai

Matsumoto Castle, Matsumoto, Chūbu (pp. 219, 345)

Matsue Castle, Matsue, Chūgoku (p. 345)

Kumamoto Castle, Kumamoto, Kyūshū (p. 329)

CRAFT

Ikebana, flower-arranging

Kintsugi, the practice of repairing broken pottery with gold (p. 368)

Lacquerware

Leatherwork

Metalwork

Printed books

The rise of the tea ceremony led to simple new pottery styles, including Mino ware, Shino ware, Raku ware and Karatsu ware

ABOVE: Dry gardens at Taizō-in, Kyoto, Kansai

CULTURE

Edo (now Tokyo) founded as
a castle town
Government instability
Japan open to foreign trade, with
Portuguese traders and missionaries
arriving in Kyūshū
Markets and regional products
Noh (p. 363) and *kyōgen* theatre
People from all walks of life mixing
Tea ceremonies as an art form, tea
houses and tea masters
Zen Buddhism

FOOD

Pop-up eateries around shrines
The start of *washoku*, what we
recognise today as Japanese cuisine

GARDENS

Konchi-in, Kyoto, Kansai
Saihō-ji, Kyoto, Kansai (p. 337)
Taizō-in, Kyoto, Kansai
Tōfuku-ji, Kyoto, Kansai
(pp. 243, 348)

LITERATURE

Heike Monogatari (*The Tale of the
Heike*; c. 1371)
Renga, a genre of collaborative poetry
Travel literature and diaries
Key works: *Fuji Kikō* (*Journey to
Fuji*; 1432) by Masayo Asukai and
Tsukushi Michi no Ki (*A Record of the
Road to Tsukushi*; 1480) by Iio Sōgi

MUSEUMS

Tokyo National Museum, Tokyo

MUSIC

Hayashi, *Noh* theatre musical
ensembles consisting of three
drummers and a flautist
Yōkyoku, the choral music of
Noh theatre (p. 363)

TEMPLES

Engaku-ji, Kamakura, Kantō (p. 177)
Ginkaku-ji (the Silver Pavilion),
Kyoto, Kansai (p. 337)
Kinkaku-ji (the Golden Pavilion),
Kyoto, Kansai (p. 337)
Ryōan-ji, Kyoto, Kansai

LEFT: Ginkaku-ji, Kyoto, Kansai
TOP: Tenryū-ji, Arashiyama, Kansai
BOTTOM: Koke-dera (Saiho-ji), Kyoto, Kansai

History of Japanese fashion

NARA PERIOD

Fashion was dictated by law.

Men: *Agekubi* robes – a two-piece outfit, usually in one dark colour with a gold belt, hair parted in the middle in an almost slicked-back arrangement.

Women: *Tarikubi* robes – a two-piece outfit with long sleeves and and apron, floral patterns and a variety of accessories, hair in a bun and heavy make-up.

HEIAN PERIOD

Birth of the kimono and what we now consider traditional Japanese fashion. As Japan looked away from China and into itself for inspiration, this was a time of incredible creativity. To this day, imperial family coronation and wedding dress is high Heian.

Men: Red was reserved for men of a high rank, and other bright colours depicted place in society. Working-class men wore an outfit (*hitatare*) that was the predecessor of samurai dress. Powdered face, blackened teeth, a goatee and an ever-so-faint moustache were the fashion of the day.

Women: High-born ladies wore twelve layers of silk garments (*jūnihitoe*), although some wore as many as thirty to forty layers and others wore just a few; long straight hair worn almost to the ground, heavy white make-up with red lips and blackened teeth, eyebrows shaved and redrawn. (In Heian society men could not look upon a woman's face, so instead layers of silk sleeves were seen as very romantic.)

KAMAKURA PERIOD

Samurai fashion.

Men: *Hitatare* – the common men's outfit of the Heian era. Kamakura men identified with the working class rather than the aristocracy, but their version was decorated with brocade and had more practical sleeves.

Women: Up to five layers, in a pared-back version of aristocratic rather than working-class dress.

MUROMACHI PERIOD

Men: Muromachi men still wore the *hitatare* but it had become highly decorative. A new variant called the *kataginu* was the outfit of the day.

Women: The *kosode* (an inner layer for Kamakura ladies) worn as an outer layer. *Katsugu* (headwear) and *uchikake* (layers) were established as the styles of this period, while the *hakama* (apron) slipped out of favour. Beautiful patterns and colours made this period distinct.

EDO PERIOD

Men: Fashion laws and restricted dress codes were followed throughout the Edo period. Men's fashion favoured long sleeves, a wide obi, more embellishments and a longer garment. Obi were tied at the back and men took many of their fashion cues from their heroes in the kabuki acting world. Men's fashion dictated darker outer colours, with detail and colour on the inner garment.

Women: Edo laws also determined women's fashion, and were often changed. A new, more modern type of *kosode* appeared, with bold, larger patterned fabrics made by the new highly skilled breed of craftspeople. Artists painted onto silk, dyeing techniques including *shibori* (resist dyeing) were invented, and artisans experimented with gold and brocade. A woman's social standing, age and marital status determined how her garments were made and how long her sleeves were.

OPPOSITE PAGE: Taishō Era women with bobbed hair

MEIJI ERA

The start of Western influence in fashion for both men and women.

Men: The Emperor ditched fashion laws and was seen out and about in Western clothing. He then passed a new law that his officials should wear Western dress to important meetings. After the Emperor cut off his topknot, men had the go-ahead to try out Western hairstyles too. A military-style suit and hat were also popular for men.

Women: After the Empress was seen wearing a Western dress, the stylish and educated followed suit. Initially, Western dress was reserved for special occasions, as the Victorian outfits were not suitable to everyday life in a Japanese house. There was a transition period from Eastern to Western dress.

TAISHŌ ERA

Japanese fashion experienced a creative burst. Fashion was heavily influenced by the Art Deco and Art Nouveau styles of the 1920s. The sailor-style school uniform (*seifuku*) was introduced in 1920 and is still the uniform style to this day. A more military style was first adapted in the Meiji era, but the current uniform (based on European royal children's outfits in the Victorian era), designed by educator and poet Utako Shimoda, was a pure Taishō creation.

Men: Taishō men mixed and matched a straw boater or military-style hat with a simple stylish kimono, or a Western suit and bowtie, or suit, waistcoat, hat, shirt and tie exactly as their European counterparts would have worn.

Women: *Moga* (modern girl) – bob haircuts, drop-waisted dresses and cloche hats teamed with bold new colour combinations. Kimono designs and striking Art Deco prints were readily available in large department stores and snatched up by a new class of women who worked, frequented European-style cafés and loved jazz music. The *yukata* (casual summer kimono) also became popular.

SHŌWA ERA TO PRESENT

Experimentation on the world stage – Issey Miyake, Junya Watanabe, Comme des Garçons

Japanese streetwear – key brands: A Bathing Ape, Evisu Jeans, Beams, Onitsuka Tiger, Undercover, and global dominators Uniqlo and Muji; women's brands: Tsumori Chisato, Cosmic Wonder, Minä Perhonen

Harajuku – an umbrella term for Japanese street fashion, made famous by *Harajuku* girls

Cosplay – a style involving dressing up like characters from anime, manga, movies or video games

Decora – an over-the-top style featuring rainbow outfits (and hair) and dozens (or even hundreds) of accessories

Dolly kei – a style based on European fairy tales

Ganguro – a style featuring tanned skin, bleached hair and brightly coloured outfits

Gyaru – an ultra-feminine style based around glamorous outfits, wigs, false eyelashes and elaborate manicures

Lolita – a style (despite its name) influenced by the Victorian and Edwardian eras

Mori girl – a soft and natural style utilising layers and floaty fabrics.

EDO PERIOD
(1603–1868)

Edo samurai complexes and *karesansui* (Zen or dry landscape) gardens and strolling gardens created at this time remain some of Japan's most popular attractions.

——— This era is all about the shogun Tokugawa Ieyasu. Given the dissatisfaction and disarray of the previous periods, it's no surprise that the Edo period and Ieyasu's rule have become so important in Japanese history. Ieyasu managed to do the impossible: unite a warring and disparate Japan. Considering there were around 300 different *daiymo* or regions, this was no easy task, but in 1603 Japan entered a phase of unification and consolidation that would shape its international reputation and representation.

The seat of power shifted from Kyoto to Edo, now known as Tokyo, which, despite a few minor twists and turns, would remain Japan's capital from that day forward. The isolationist policies of the Ieyasu shogunate ensured Japan was cut off from Western influences. The rise of a new middle class, keen to play as hard as they worked, made for new strides in culture and leisure. Handicrafts and trading thrived, and familiar techniques and skills in Japanese handcrafting, such as dyeing fabric or preparing exquisitely delicate but simple food, became a staple of Japanese culture. This period of both enlightenment and restriction was brought to a close by the Meiji Restoration in 1868, when Edo forces were defeated by armies loyal to the Emperor, continuing the ongoing struggle between the army and ruling classes that had dominated Japanese history.

ARCHITECTURE

Blackened exteriors on houses, storehouses and buildings

Gassho houses (p. 343)

Refined *machiya* houses (p. 342)

Sukiya style

Two-storey houses

ART

Modern Rinpa, a vibrant, colourful and decorative revival of the classical Japanese style of painting known as *yamato-e*, drawing on Japanese literature like *Genji Monogatari* (*The Tale of Genji*) and *Ise Monogatari*, and influencing Japanese and world art Key artist: Sakai Hōitsu (p. 219)

Ukiyo-e ('pictures of the floating world'), woodblock prints that captured the goings-on of Japan's pleasure quarters Key artist: Katsushika Hokusai

Wedding pictures

CRAFT

Aizome indigo-dyeing and experimental textile techniques

Ceramics

Elaborate sword smithing

Fans

Glassware, including Satsuma *kiriko* (p. 322)

Kokeshi dolls

Maneki neko (lucky cat) figurines

Nambu Tekki ironware (Morioka; p. 202)

Origami (also known as *orisue* or *orikata*)

Screens

Scrolls

Shodō, the art of calligraphy (p. 336)

Vibrant lacquerware

CULTURE

Kabuki theatre (p. 363)

Major developments in architecture and painting

Noh theatre (p. 363)

Poetry

Rangaku ('Dutch learning'), the study of Western science, medicine and technology permitted during *sakoku*, the country's period of national isolation

Sentō, man-made bathhouses

Sumo wrestling (p. 363)

Tattoos

Ukiyo ('the floating world'), escaping the everyday through pleasure, beauty and art

Ukiyo-zōshi ('books of the floating world'), literature centred around life during the Edo period

EXPERIENCES

Edo-yu, an Edo-themed bathhouse, Tokyo, Kantō

Hanayashiki, an Edo-period amusement park, Tokyo, Kantō

Nakasendō Way, Kiso Valley, Chūbu (p. 231)

FOOD

Castella cake

Edo ryōri (Edo cuisine), which would influence *kaiseki ryōri* (Japanese haute cuisine; p. 127) and *shōjin ryōri* (temple cuisine; p. 126)

Edomae sushi, a dish of seafood on rice and a precursor to *nigiri* sushi, or modern-day sushi

Fish and seafood became a staple of Japanese cuisine

Horse meat

Inari sushi, fried tofu pockets with sweet rice

Japanese breakfast (fish, rice, tofu and beans)

Soba noodles

The beginnings of tempura

Tsukemono, pickles

Unagi, eel

Vegetables such as daikon, spinach, bamboo shoots, ginger and pumpkin

Yatai, street-food stalls. Street food became the norm for workers

GARDENS

Chaniwa (tea), *tsukiyama* (hill) and *karesansui* (Zen or dry landscape) garden styles (pp. 347, 348)

Imperial Palace East Gardens, Koishikawa-Kōrakuen, Rikugi-en and Shinjuku Gyo-en (all Tokyo, Kantō)

Ritsurin Kōen, Takamatasu, Shikoku (p. 301)

Kōraku-en, Okayama, Chūgoku (p. 268)

Sengan-en, Kagoshima, Kyūshū (p. 322)

LITERATURE

Chikamatsu Monzaemon, *bunraku* (puppet theatre) and kabuki (p. 363) dramatist, considered by some to be Japan's Shakespeare

Fukuda Chiyo-ni, a great haiku poet, who paved the way for other female poets with her uncanny mastery of haiku's structure and simple beauty

Jippensha Ikku, Japan's great tragicomic novelist, often compared to Mark Twain Key work: *Tōkaidōchū Hizakurige* (*Shank's Mare*; 1802–1822)

Kaitai Shinsho (*The New Book of Anatomy*; 1774) by Genpaku Sugita

Matsuo Bashō, Japan's master of haiku, was a roaming rhymester who seemed to have been at every destination you go to. He composed beautiful words to commemorate his journeys in his famous travel diaries

OPPOSITE PAGE: *Maneki neko* at Gōtoku-ji (cat temple), Tokyo, Kantō

MUSEUMS

Edo-Tokyo Open Air Architectural Museum, Tokyo, Kantō

Kamakurabori Museum, Kamakura, Kantō

Tokyo National Museum and the Kuromon ('black gate'), Tokyo, Kantō

MUSIC

Biwa, a short-necked lute

Koto, a thirteen-stringed zither

Melodic hand-flute soundscapes in minor keys

Shakuhachi, a vertical bamboo flute

NEIGHBOURHOODS

Samurai and geisha districts, Kanazawa, Chūbu (p. 214)

Ya-Ne-Sen, the Yanaka, Sendagi and Nezu neighbourhoods, Tokyo, Kantō

TEMPLES & OTHER BUILDINGS

Asakusa Sensō-ji, Tokyo, Kantō (p. 172)

Chiran Samurai Residence Complex, Kagoshima, Kyūshū

Edo Wonderland Nikkō Edomura, Nikkō, Kantō

Gokoku-ji, Tokyo, Kantō

Izumi-Fumoto Samurai Residences, Izumi, Kyūshū

Kitsuki Castle Town, Kitsuki, Kyūshū

Nakasendō Way, Kiso Valley, Chūbu (p. 231)

Nikkō Tōshō-gū, a Shinto shrine and Tokugawa Ieyasu's mausoleum, Nikkō, Kantō (pp. 178, 335)

Shimadzu Satsuma Kiriko Glassworks, Kagoshima, Kyūshū

Shōrinzan Daruma-ji Temple, Takasaki, Kantō (p. 189)

RIGHT & TOP RIGHT: Ritsurin Kōen, Takamatsu, Shikoku BOTTOM RIGHT: Sengan-en, Kagoshima, Kyūshū

MEIJI ERA
(1868–1912)

———— Otherwise known as the Meiji Restoration, the 1860s to the early 1900s marked a move away from shogun rule towards a more modern Japan. The shogunate was based in Edo but its official capital had been Kyoto. Edo was now renamed Tokyo and became the centre of things, a combination of the political – the power base shifting away from Kyoto, and to a more populist approach – and of the explosion of creativity from the new 'middle classes', which would shape the future of Japan's culture, arts, food and lifestyle. Emperor Mutsuhito (Meiji the Great) was a very modern ruler; most crucially, he opened Japan to the West, which made for some startling 'Japanese-only' creations in food and architecture. Japanese people had dressed in almost the same way, with some fluctuations, for centuries (see also p. 26). The influence of Western culture now meant the style changed dramatically, and this was reflected in the silhouettes of kimono, less intricate and more graphic fabric patterns, and women no longer blackening their teeth or shaving their eyebrows (which never came back into fashion, strangely). Deep-fried foods and even pizza became popular, as did women's fashion magazines.

Tokyo's Yamanote Line hits most of the Meiji hotspots. Places like Shiseido in Ginza still channel the spirit of the age. Try the restaurants here for Western-inspired food of the era, such as omelettes and rice or beef curry. Wander Ginza's main streets and its alleyways, and take in the kimono-clad lunching ladies and old-world stores making a stand against modernisation.

ART

European-style oil paintings

Nihonga, traditional Japanese-style paintings that became popular in response to increasing Western influence on art. Many *Nihonga* artists, however, used Pre-Raphaelite and Renaissance techniques in their paintings – an example of the push and pull between Western culture and Japanese tradition that can still be seen today

Key artists: Hishida Shunsō, Takeuchi Seihō and Tomioka Tessai

Yōga, Western-style painting

CRAFT

Carved wooden furniture

Lacquerware

Metalwork

Textiles

CULTURE

Introduction of Western sports, such as baseball, soccer and rugby

Japan's first universities established

FOOD

Bīfu suteiki, steak

Bread

Chocolate

Coffee

Croquettes

Kare, curry (p. 138)

Katsu, breaded and fried meat (p. 136)

Pizza

Taiyaki, fish-shaped waffle with sweet fillings (p. 128)

GARDENS

Kenroku-en, Kanazawa, Chūbu (p. 214)

Murin-an, Kyoto, Kansai

Namikawa-ke, Kyoto, Kansai

OPPOSITE PAGE: Dessert at Shiseido in Ginza, Tokyo, Kantō THIS PAGE: *Taiyaki* being made in Kichijōji, Tokyo, Kantō

LITERATURE

Feminist writer Yosano Akiko

Japanese naturalism

Masaoka Shiki's new take on haiku

Realism

The 'Japanese Voltaire' Yukichi Fukuzawa (*Meiji Six Journal*)

Wagahai wa Neko de Aru (I Am a Cat; 1905) by Natsume Sōseki

MUSEUMS

Museum Meiji-Mura, Inuyama, Chūbu

Natural Museum of Nature and Science, Tokyo, Kantō

Toyama Education Museum, Toyama, Chūbu

MUSIC

Experimental journeys using the rhythms and scales of Western classical music

Military-style marches

Renewed interest in traditional Edo-style Japanese music

TEMPLES & OTHER BUILDINGS

British Embassy Villa Memorial Park, Lake Chūzenji, Kantō (p. 179)

Former Niigata Customs House, Niigata, Chūbu

Kabuki-za theatre building, Tokyo, Kantō (p. 166)

Kaichi School Museum, Matsumoto, Chūbu

Kimuraya – Meiji bakery in Ginza still making bread using recipes from the 1800s, Tokyo, Kantō

Kobe City Museum of Literature, Kobe, Kansai

Lake Biwa Canal, Lake Biwa, Kansai (p. 256)

Meiji Shrine, Shibuya (top end of Omotesandō shopping street), Tokyo, Kantō

Mitsukoshi department store, Tokyo, Kantō

Nara National Museum, Nara, Kansai

Shiseido parlour, Tokyo, Kantō (p. 32)

RIGHT: Kenroku-en, Kanazawa, Chūbu

Enduring national symbols

CHERRY BLOSSOM (SAKURA)

The emergence of the pink *sakura* flower from the end of March to early May across Japan begins Hanami (p. 80), one of the most popular events in the Japanese calendar. At its core, it's a celebration of life, a riot of vibrant colour, a gathering of the clans and a reflective moment where the true, intense beauty of nature can be appreciated. *Sakura* reminds the viewer of both the beauty of nature and the ultimate transience of such beauty – cherry blossom flowers last for a week at best before fluttering down and smothering the earth in *sakura* snow. It's a melancholy but triumphant metaphor – a life lived well is not defined by its length. Families and friends picnic in parks under the canopies of brightly coloured flowers, with the clink of sake cups, flurries of heartwarming laughter and joy in the air. It's something to anticipate and something to savour.

GOURD (HYŌTAN)

The humble gourd, first mentioned as far back as 720 AD in the *Nihon Shoki* (*The Chronicles of Japan*), symbolises the legendary samurai ruler Toyotomi Hideyoshi (p. 22). Hideyoshi chose it as one of the symbols on his heraldic flags, as a sign of his humble birth. The gourd was often used as a 'replacement' for the deceased figure of a famous actor or musician in wood-block prints. It can also be used to carry sake. Several characters in Japanese mythology carry the gourd, most notably the racoon dog or *tanuki* (p. 341). Gourd shapes also appear regularly in art and made objects. Hyōtan ('Gourd') Onsen in Beppu is so named because the male bathing area features a gourd-shaped bath.

LOTUS (RŌTASU)

A potent symbol for Hindus and Buddhists (and the ancient Egyptians), the lotus signifies purity and beauty, an unblemished white flower springing from caliginous waters. The pink lotus is considered the true lotus of the Buddha, a sign of achieving enlightenment, whereas the white lotus in Hinduism symbolises more than just purity – it also stands for spirituality, prosperity, fertility and eternity. Use of the lotus extends to graphic design, art, literature and even food – the roots, leaves, flowers and seeds are all edible.

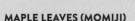

MAPLE LEAVES (MOMIJI)

The name for the maple tree, *momiji*, has come to symbolise the maple leaf – a revered shape that features in many of Japan's south-western towns and villages. Maples, said to represent balance and calm, herald autumn. The shape is used primarily in the famous *momiji wagashi*, a delicious Japanese sweet lightly flavoured with maple syrup. Often, as is the case in Miyajima or Nara, the *momiji* will be paired with the symbol of the deer – or served where actual deer roam. Momijigari, viewing the beauty of the red maple leaf, is a popular event. The name comes from *momiji* meaning 'red leaves' and *gari* meaning 'hunting'. Momijigari is especially popular in Nikkō (especially Kegon Falls), Arashiyama, Mount Takao, Daisetsuzan Asahi-dake, Kirishima and Kyoto (especially Ryōan-ji).

PLUM BLOSSOM (UME)

Although it doesn't enjoy the celebrity status of its cherry cousin, the plum blossom is having its moment in the sun. Now part of Hanami (p. 80), viewing of the white plum blossom happens in mid-February and is gaining widespread appreciation. The beautiful white flowers signify that spring is on the way, marking the end of stark winter. Plum blossoms are more fragrant than cherry blossoms – an added bonus as they go head to head with their archnemesis – but the real defining factor might be the deep darkness of the plum tree's bark set against the white petals of its blossoms, which makes for a truly spectacular sight.

OTHER SYMBOLS

bamboo (*take*)

cedar (*sugi*)

chrysanthemum (*kiku*)

great purple emperor butterfly (*omurasaki*)

green pheasant (*kiji*)

koi (*koi*)

pine (*matsu*)

plover (*chidori*)

rising sun (*asahi*)

TAISHŌ ERA
(1912–1926)

———— When Emperor Meiji died on 30 July 1912, he was succeeded by Prince Yoshihito, who reigned as Emperor Taishō for fourteen short years before his death in 1926 at the age of forty-seven. Complications from pneumonia and a subsequent heart attack were the result of lifelong problems stemming from a bout of cerebral meningitis as a child. He was kept out of the public eye and his son Hirohito served as the visible regent. Despite its brevity, the Taishō era made an indelible mark on Japanese history, in particular society and architecture. Often called 'Japanese Deco', the era was chic and modern. 'Moga', or modern girls, adopted the European bob hairstyle and opted for more casual kimono with simpler graphic prints. Jazz became the music du jour – starting a Japanese obsession that shows no signs of abating to this day. It became popular to learn French and voting became universal (for men). Traditional arts merged with international styles to create new forms. Known colloquially as Taishō Roman or European romanticism, Taishō represented an era of freedom and boundless possibility.

Most of the stylistic change was felt in the thoroughly modern capital of Tokyo, where relics of Taishō-era architecture sprinkle the landscape. The original Tokyo Station structure, the Yamagata Building (no longer with us), the University of Tokyo's Yasuda Auditorium, and a multitude of modern *ryokan* (Japanese inns; p. 87) were echoed further afield. But deco forms, arched windows, domed roof structures and red-brick facades framed by white woodwork are also found in towns like Morioka, Hakodate, Nikkō and Yamagata. Short-lived though the period was, it saw one of Japan's greatest historical disasters, the Great Kantō Earthquake of 1923, whose quake and subsequent tsunami and fires killed more than 100,000 people and destroyed some 570,000 homes.

ABOVE: *Two Girls By the Sea*, Kafu (mid-1920s) OPPOSITE PAGE TOP: Tokyo Metropolitan Teien Art Museum, Tokyo, Kantō
OPPOSITE PAGE BOTTOM: Daimaru Shinsaibashi, Osaka, Kansai

ART

Blending traditional Japanese art with Western techniques

Key artists: Yumeji Takehisa, Taikan Yokoyama, Shinsui Itō, Goyō Hashiguchi

CRAFT

Meisen silk, bold patterns and new colours used on kimono

Sōsaku-hanga and *Shin-hanga*, creative new print movements

Widespread use of porcelain

CULTURE

Advances in film and photography through the *bunka* (culture) boom

The Amakasu incident (in which Sakae Ōsugi, his wife and his six-year-old child were beaten to death for open activism by Lieutenant Masahiko Amakasu, who served only a few years in prison for the murders)

The 'Oriental Exclusion' Act banned Japanese immigration to the United States

FOOD

Kare raisu, curry rice

Katsu, deep-fried cutlets (p. 136)

Kissaten, European-style coffee houses (p. 152)

Korokke, croquettes

Omuraisu (or *omurice*), omelette and rice (p. 138)

Steak with a 'demi-glace' sauce

Western-influenced food (p. 138) no longer just for the wealthy, but a staple for everyone

LITERATURE

Jingoistic and propaganda-based manga

Naoya Shiga, known as 'the god of the novel'

Seito (*Bluestocking*) feminist magazine, edited by Raichō Hiratsuka

MUSEUMS

Kasho Takabatake Taishō Roman Museum, Ehime, Shikoku

Shitamachi Museum, Tokyo, Kantō

Taishō Glass Museum, Fukushima, Tōhoku

Taishō Roman Museum, Ena, Chūbu

The Museum of Kyoto, Kyoto, Kansai

Tokyo Metropolitan Teien Art Museum, Tokyo, Kantō

Yumeji Art Museum, Okayama, Chūgoku

MUSIC

Jazz

TEMPLES & OTHER BUILDINGS

Daimaru Shinsaibashi, Osaka, Kansai

Ginzan Onsen (stunning Taishō-era village; p. 208), Tōhoku

Hibiya Public Hall, Tokyo, Kantō

Japanese Industry Club Hall, Tokyo, Kantō

Jiyū Gakuen Myōnichikan (attributed to Frank Lloyd Wright), Tokyo, Kantō

Koraibashi Nomura Building, Osaka, Kansai

Mengyo Kaikan Hall, Osaka, Kansai

Mitsui Honkan, Tokyo, Kantō

Naniwa Church, Osaka, Kansai

Nichieiyu Bathhouse, Nagasaki, Kyūshū Old Courtrooms, Nagoya, Chūbu

Osaka Gas Building, Osaka, Kansai

Ran Hotei Tea House, Kyoto, Kansai

Saitama Resona Bank and some buildings on Taishō-Roman Street, Saitama, Kawagoe, Kantō

Shuhouen Hall, Akita, Tōhoku

Taishō Roman Tea Room, Hirosaki, Tōhoku

Tokyo Station, Tokyo, Kantō

Uchiko-Za (Taishō-era kabuki theatre; p. 305), Matsuyama, Shikoku

LEFT: Ginzan Onsen, Tōhoku

SHŌWA ERA
(1926–1989)

———— Taishō regent Hirohito went on to rule over both the early and late Shōwa eras, taking in the Second World War and the fastest paced and most prolific stages of Japanese cultural change. Early in the era the effects of the Great Kantō Earthquake were still being felt, and the harsh realities of the Great Depression of 1929 hit home, leading to a decade of austerity that also saw an extensive rebuilding of Japan, including a rail network, roads and public services in general. The idea of moving the capital from Tokyo reared its head again but never took hold. Typhoid was rife, leading to improvements in the healthcare system.

A fear of disaster and catastrophe became ingrained in the Japanese psyche, still felt by residents and visitors to this day. This led to a system of ingenious disaster-prevention and construction techniques that have been adopted the world over. Japanese 'stoicism' and their respectful ways of mourning great tragedy and loss of life was established, and was used to good effect during the Fukushima earthquake and nuclear disaster of 2011.

Although Japan's official entry into the Second World War on the side of the Axis powers came when they bombed the US naval base at Pearl Harbour in Hawaii in December 1941, they had been following an aggressive expansionist policy in the Asia-Pacific throughout the 1930s. Facing defeat, Japan refused to surrender until the Allies dropped atomic bombs on Hiroshima and Nagasaki in August 1945, causing horrific destruction in both cities. Hirohito, the Shōwa Emperor, capitulated; the subsequent American military presence in Japan led to the popularity of Americana, which continues to this day.

The second part of the long era is the iconic Western vision of modern Japan: an explosion of manga, Godzilla, Astro Boy, bullet trains, robots, consumerism and construction. Modern Japan stills lives in Tokyo's Shibuya, Akihabara or Shimokitazawa, in hubs like Ome and Yamanashi, down south in Bungotakada (Ōita), in the emerging late-1900s culture in Hiroshima, and up north in Aomori, Hakodate and Sapporo. Lovers of Japanese retro will find an abundance of collectibles from this boom in pop culture. Trainspotters can marvel at the unparalleled growth of the rail system, still the fastest, most dynamic and most efficient in the world. *Izakayas* (small bars), standing sushi bars, station hubs, toys, mass consumerism – everything we relate to modern Japan was cemented in the late Shōwa era.

ART

Ero-guro-nansensu movement (eroticism, grotesquery, nonsense)

Fluxus, an international experimental art movement

Key artists: Ay-O, Yoko Ono, Yayoi Kusama

Metabolism, an architectural movement exploring new ways to inhabit spaces and environments

Mono-ha, an artistic movement exploring the interplay between natural and industrial materials

Tarō Okamoto

Tetsumi Kudo

The Gutai group, Japan's first radical postwar artistic movement, which rejected traditional art styles

CRAFT

Blue porcelain

Creativity with *kokeshi* dolls (p. 340)

Folk craft

Potters Yanagi Sōetsu and Kawai Kanjirō

CULTURE

Architect Isamu Noguchi (examples of his work can be found across Sapporo and in Tokyo, especially in Midtown)

Atari, Sega and Nintendo video games

Gachapon (capsule toys; p. 168) and vending machines (p. 175)

Manga

Osamu Tezuka, manga artist

Key texts: *Kimba the White Lion* (1950), *Astro Boy* (1952), see also p. 50

Sony Walkman

OPPOSITE: Seats in Morioka, Tohōku
TOP: Building near Tsumago, Chūbu
BOTTOM: Sato Pharmaceutical mascot, Sato-chan and family

FOOD
Boiled egg on toast

Chewing gum and sweets with collectable cards

Dagashi (retro sweets)

Doughnuts

Hanbāgu, hamburger (p. 138)

Hot dogs

Kare raisu, curry rice (p. 138)

Omuraisu (omurice), omelette (p. 138)

Pasuta naporitan (Neopolitan pasta)

Taco rice (p. 138)

Torys whisky

Wafu pasuta (Japanese-style pasta)

Western-style coffee (p. 152)

LITERATURE
Asakusa Kurenaidan (*The Scarlet Gang of Asakusa*; 1930) by Yasunari Kawabata

Haru no Yuki (*Spring Snow*; 1966) by Yukio Mishima

Manga (comics and graphic novels)

Suna no Onna (*The Woman in the Dunes*; 1960) by Kōbō Abe

Tetsujin 28-go (*Gigantor*; 1956–1966) manga by Mitsuteru Yokoyama

MUSEUMS
Fukui Prefectural Museum of Cultural History, Fukui, Chūbu

Hakone Open-Air Museum, Hakone, Kantō (p. 185)

Kyoto Manga Museum, Kyoto, Kansai

MoMAK, Kyoto, Kansai

National Museum of Western Art, Tokyo, Kantō

National Shōwa Memorial Museum, Tokyo, Kantō

Nebuta Museum Wa-Rasse, Aomori, Tōhoku (pp. 198, 361)

Retro Museum of Packaging from the Shōwa era, Ome, Kantō

Shōwa Museum of Art, Nagoya, Chūbu

Takayama Shōwa Museum, Takayama, Chūbu

MUSIC
Cuban music

Kayōkyoku (pop tune), the Westernisation of Japanese music and the basis for modern J-pop

Idol kayō: a style with solo artists singing intensely emotional songs

Mood kayō: atmospheric pop influenced by jazz and Latin music

Metal and hardcore

Rock'n'roll

Shōwa poppusu, pop music

The birth of Japanese electronica and experimentation

Key artists: Yellow Magic Orchestra, Ryuichi Sakamoto

'Ue O Muite Aruko' (1961) – also known as 'Sukiyaki' – by Kyu Sakamoto, the first Japanese song to go to number one on the American charts

TEMPLES, BUILDINGS & STREETS
Bunkamura, Tokyo, Kantō

Harmonica Yokochō, Tokyo, Kantō (p. 175)

Hiroshima Peace Memorial Museum, Hiroshima, Chūgoku (pp. 265, 361)

Hotel Okura, Tokyo, Kantō

Isetan Department Stores, Tokyo, Kantō; Kyoto Station, Kyoto, Kansai

Nonbei Yokochō, Tokyo, Kantō

Osaka Ekimae Building, Osaka, Kansai

Rohm Theatre, Kyoto, Kansai

Shinjuku Golden Gai, Tokyo, Kantō (p. 165)

St Mary's Cathedral (Kenzō Tange, p. 353), Tokyo, Kantō

Takimi-Koji, Shin Osaka Station, Osaka, Kansai

The Italian Embassy, Nikkō, Kantō (p. 179)

Wako department store, Tokyo, Kantō

Yanaka Beer Hall, Tokyo, Kantō

Yurakocho, Tokyo, Kantō

LEFT: The Italian Embassy, Nikkō, Kantō
TOP: Yoyogi Stadium, Tokyo, Kantō
BOTTOM: British Embassy, Nikkō, Kantō

HEISEI/REIWA ERA (1989–ONGOING)

——— Heisei and Reiwa have fostered a culture of knocking down the prefab buildings of modern twentieth-century Japan and rebuilding its cities into thriving contemporary mega-cities, lorded over by extraordinary towering skyscrapers, unparalleled museums and galleries, seemingly endless shopping centres, and cultural hubs and train stations you could actually live in if you needed to. Just as the Tokyo Olympics of 1960 introduced the nation to the world, new development and change mark the Reiwa era, showcasing a vibrant and international Japan to the world for the 2020 Olympics.

Dystopian visions of a neon metropolis with cramped living and harsh working conditions have given way to a complex network of hubs boasting small makers, craft coffee, traditional craft revival and small-scale contemporary technological innovation living side by side with fast-paced new development, towering metropolitan growth and competitive and international businesses – all connected by an ever-growing network of intricate rail lines.

Lifestyles have changed. Young Japan is not happy to sit back and become the salaryman or housewife – new opportunities created by technology mean new ways for the Japanese to invent and reinvent commerce, no matter the scale. Personal taste and obsession are poured into art, shopping, food and all manner of boutiques, music enclaves and bars. Repurposing has extended not just to recycling things, but recycling ideas – traditional Japanese know-how has been redefined and reshaped for a vibrant and brilliant future.

ABOVE: 21_21 Design Sight in Roppongi, Tokyo, Kantō **OPPOSITE PAGE:** Opening Ceremony in Harajuku, Tokyo, Kantō

ART
Hiroshi Sugimoto
Kohei Nawa (p. 375)
Takashi Murakami, founder of the Superflat movement (p. 375)
Yayoi Kusama (p. 375)
Yoko Ono
Yoshitomo Nara

CRAFT
Eco-friendly techniques
Minimal and new decorative pottery from Arita and Mashiko (pp. 310, 183)
Rebirth of handicrafts and young makers using traditional techniques with repurposed materials

CULTURE
A Bathing Ape clothing brand
Animal cafés
Blythe/Junie Moon 1970s Americana dolls
Kubrick and Bearbrick toys
Nagano Winter Olympics
Pokémon (p. 50)
Re-emergence of traditional food prepared in traditional ways with locally sourced ingredients
Sailor Moon manga series
Uniqlo's Heattech and AIRism
Washi tape and craft culture

FILM & TELEVISION
Battle Royale (2000), dir. Kinji Fukasaku
Dare mo Shiranai (*Nobody Knows*; 2004), dir. Hirokazu Kore-eda
Death Note (television series; 2006–2007), dir. Tetsurō Araki
Hana-bi (*Fireworks*; 1997), dir. Takeshi Kitano
Ringu (*Ring*; 1998), dir. Hideo Nakata
Studio Ghibli and Hayao Miyazaki
Key films: *Mononoke-hime* (*Princess Mononoke*; 1997), *Sen to Chihiro no Kamikakushi* (*Spirited Away*; 2001), *Hotaru no Haka* (*Grave of the Fireflies*; 1988), *Hauru no Ugoku Shiro* (*Howl's Moving Castle*; 2004)
Tetsuo: The Iron Man (1989), dir. Shinya Tsukamoto

FOOD
Craft beer and coffee

Junk food (KFC for Christmas, burgers, pizza)

Traditional food with new ingredients

LITERATURE
Banana Yoshimoto

Key text: *Kitchen* (1988)

Cell-phone novels and manga: literary works written on mobile phones, usually sent direct to readers via SMS

Haruki Murakami

Key texts: *Noruwei no mori* (*Norwegian Wood*; 1987), *Nejimaki-dori kuronikuru* (*The Wind-Up Bird Chronicle*; 1994), *1Q84* (2009–2010)

MUSEUMS
21_21 Design Sight, Tokyo, Kantō (p. 167)

Aomori Museum of Art (featuring Yoshimoto Nara's *Aomori Dog*), Aomori, Tōhoku (p. 199)

Cup Noodles Museum, Yokohama, Kantō (pp. 191, 361)

D47 Museum, Tokyo, Kantō

Gallery MoMo, Tokyo, Kantō

Ginza Graphic Gallery, Tokyo, Kantō

Glion showroom (car museum), Osaka, Kansai

Koji Kinutani Tenku, Umeda Sky Building, Osaka, Kansai

Matsumoto City Museum of Art (Yayoi Kusama permanent exhibition), Matsumoto, Chūbu (p. 219)

Miho Museum, Shiga, Kansai (p. 257)

Mint Museum, Osaka, Kansai

Mizuma Gallery, Tokyo, Kantō

Mori Art Museum, Tokyo, Kantō (p. 167)

Mori Digital Art Museum (teamLab Borderless), Tokyo, Kantō (p. 171)

National Art Center, Tokyo, Kantō (p. 167)

National Museum of Modern Art, Osaka, Kansai

National Museum of Modern Art, Tokyo, Kantō

Osaka Museum, Osaka, Kansai

Osaka Museum of History, Osaka, Kansai

Taka Ishii Gallery, Tokyo, Kantō

Yayoi Kusama Museum (2014), Tokyo, Kantō

MUSIC
J-indie

Key artists: Shonen Knife, The 5.6.7.8's

J-pop and J-rock

Key artists: AKB48, Kairi Pamyu Pamyu, Perfume

Japanese minimalist pop

Key artists: Lullatone, Cornelius

Kawaii metal

Key artist: Babymetal

Shibuya-kei ('Shibuya style'), a music scene inspired by 1960s culture, French pop and kitsch, among other things

Key artist: Pizzicato Five

TEMPLES & OTHER BUILDINGS
Chloé (2006), Tokyo, Kantō

Comme Des Garçons, Tokyo, Kantō

Fujiya Ryokan, Ginzan Onsen, Tōhoku

Kyoto Station rebuild, Kyoto, Kansai (p. 236)

Reversible Destiny Lofts, Tokyo, Kantō (p. 92)

Ribbon Chapel, Onomichi, Chūgoku (p. 354)

Shoji Ueda Museum of Photography, Saihaku, Chūgoku (p. 274)

SunnyHills, Tokyo, Kantō (p. 353)

Tokyo Midtown shopping centre, Tokyo, Kantō (p. 167)

Tokyo Skytree (2012), Tokyo, Kantō

Unicorn Gundam Sculpture, DiverCity, Tokyo, Kantō (p. 171)

RIGHT: Michelle and a Yayoi Kusama sculpture, Matsumoto City Museum of Art, Matsumoto, Chūbu

Pop culture icons

Sure, Japan is shrines and temples, art, nature, geisha, spirituality, exquisite food, etc. – but it's also pop culture. Manga, cartoons, characters, toys, games, cuteness, pop, pop and more pop. It's fun, it's joyous and it's essential to understanding what Japan is all about. One of the most commonly used words in Japan is *kawaii*, meaning cute. Importantly, it explores the emotion that something cute stirs within you. And there is plenty of that in Japan.

CUTE & CLASSIC CHARACTERS

ASTRO BOY

Astro Boy, AKA Mighty Atom, was a popular manga created by Osamu Tezuka and serialised by publishing house Kobunsha between 1952 and 1968. The spin-off TV series saw Astro Boy become the first Japanese manga character to gain popularity outside Japan and bring the concept of anime to the world. The robot boy with human emotions remains hugely popular today. Fans should head to Takadanobaba Station in Tokyo (p. 100) – Tezuka lived and worked here, and as trains are about to leave, the station loudspeakers play the Astro Boy theme song.

DOMO-KUN

This angry block of fur is Japanese television channel NHK's official mascot. His square head displays a permanently visible range of sharp teeth. His favourite food is *nikujaga* stew, but he hates apples. Domo-kun began appearing in short animations screened in-between NHK shows. He lives in a cave with Mr. Usaji (a rabbit), although rumour has it he has demanded his own trailer.

GODZILLA

Gojira – a blend of the Japanese words for gorilla and whale (which sounded like Godzilla to the Americans) – first appeared in 1954. The dinosaur/sea dragon/lizard-like movie monster (made of wobbly latex and bubble wrap) became hugely popular worldwide. It was easy to see Godzilla, whose power was born of nuclear radiation, as a symbol of Hiroshima and Nagasaki. Godzilla has since starred in thirty-two films, with no sign of his popularity waning. He has fought Mothra, Megalon, Gigan, Mechagodzilla and even King Kong and the Fantastic Four. Godzilla figurines remain popular in Japan and older models (especially with movable parts) are highly collectible.

HELLO KITTY

It's fair to say that Sanrio's Hello Kitty is one of the most popular Japanese characters with Westerners. 'Kitty White' (her full name) was designed by Yuko Shimizu in 1974. Her first product was the still-popular Hello Kitty coin purse, launched in 1975. By 2014, Hello Kitty was worth US $8 billion a year.

KIMBA THE WHITE LION

Ultra-cute and melancholy Kimba is a manga character created by Astro Boy inventor Osamu Tezuka and serialised from 1950 to 1954. The television show was broadcast from 1965 to 1967 on Fuji TV and became popular around the world.

POKÉMON

These adorable 'pocket monsters' were created by Satoshi Tajiri for Nintendo in 1995. An instant hit, Pokémon have maintained constant popularity, and had a major relaunch in 2016 with the Pokémon Go game, which brought the characters into the real world through the use of smart phones and augmented reality. To date, Pokémon is the highest-grossing media franchise in history.

TOTORO

The star of 1988 Studio Ghibli animation *My Neighbor Totoro* has become one of Japan's most beloved characters. A woodland sprite, Totoro looks a bit like an owl, rabbit or cat – but is wholly its own species. Despite making few appearances outside of the film, Totoro can still be seen everywhere in Japan in various forms of merchandise.

OPPOSITE: Mori Art Museum, Tokyo, Kantō

OTHER POPULAR
JAPANESE CHARACTERS

- Anpanman
- Doraemon
- Goku (Dragon Ball Z)
- Gundam (the titular robot of the popular media franchise)

- L (Death Note)
- Monkey D. Luffy (One Piece)
- Motoko Kusanagi (Ghost in the Shell)

- Sailor Moon
- Shokupanman
- Shotaro Kaneda (Akira)
- Speed Racer
- Ultraman

Seasonal Japan

Japan is heavily influenced by the seasons, and each change is eagerly awaited. It can also be dreaded, as it brings extreme temperatures and some frankly quite alarming weather events. The seasons influence almost every aspect of Japanese culture, including food, fashion, art, events, shopping – weather has worked its way deep into the very fabric of the every day. The extremes of seasonal weather can be harsh on the Japanese (and we hapless visitors). From the biting cold, thick snows and icy winds of winter, to the relentless blazing heat of summer and its suffocating, sweat-inducing humidity, to the downpours of the rainy season, when heavy clouds unburden their loads in a seemingly never-ending deluge, choking gutters and drains and soaking everyone below. If you're not prepared, you can get into real trouble.

But Japan makes it all worthwhile, with wonderfully practical ways to combat the weather. When the rain begins, sturdy and affordable dome-like umbrellas emerge magically in almost every store, a welcome purchase for the unprepared traveller. There are 'hot pockets' (small packets of heat you can carry in cold weather), cold patches for the heat, raincoats that pack down into tiny parcels, clothing made from protective fabrics, and items to tackle even the most aggressive weather conditions. In summer, Tokyo locals will escape to the cooler climes of the north or hit the beaches around Tokyo (p. 176), the cool forests of Yakushima (p. 325) or Shikoku (p. 291) or the distant shores of the islands of the deep south – Ibusuki (p. 329), Kagoshima (p. 320) or Okinawa (p. 326). In winter, people choose not to escape the snow but to embrace it: winter illuminations, steaming onsen (hot spring) baths, Sapporo's world-famous ice sculptures (pp. 74, 281) or Mount Fuji's snow-capped majesty (p. 222). Cherry or plum blossom in spring, flaming autumn red and gold, vibrant summer festivals – no matter what the seasons throw at Japan, the country meets it head on.

OPPOSITE PAGE: Garden near the Hara Museum, Ikaho Onsen, Kantō

Summer

The Japanese summer is hot, but it's not just the heat, it's the unbelievable humidity, which brings on serious *natsubate* (summer heat fatigue). Add the midsummer rains, and you have a season to be reckoned with. That's summer in Japan, and it doesn't deviate from its malicious schedule.

Luckily there are parts of the country where summer is a little more forgiving and others that truly come alive in the warmer months. When in doubt, go north. Tōhoku (p. 193) and Hokkaidō (p. 277) are still very warm, but you can escape into the mountains or a have an *onsen* (hot spring) bath while watching dragonflies flit through the undergrowth or colourful butterflies duck and weave around thickly flowered hedges. If you're thinking of travelling in summer, deep countryside, forest bathing (*shinrin-yoku*), temple retreats or a shady mountain sanctuary will make you forget about the unforgiving sun and relentless humidity of the big cities. You would think Kyoto's surrounding mountains would keep it cool, but in fact they keep in the heat, making it one of the hottest cities.

At Hokkaidō's northernmost tip, people swear by the gentleness of the summer climate, which offsets the harshness of the northern winter. Conversely, the southern island of Kyūshū (p. 307) also offers an escape – especially in Kagoshima (p. 320), where the summer temperature is relatively mild, albeit quite rainy. Okinawa (p. 326) is cooler and dryer than most of the capitals, but the humidity gives it a tropical feel. Okinawan islands such as Kume, Miyako, Amami and Ishigaki (all p. 327) are also perfect for summer beach escapes. Beach towns like Enoshima (p. 177), Izu (p. 226), Shirahama (p. 261), Bōsō, Jōdogahama and Tottori (p. 275) are great places to visit. Shikoku (p. 291) is temperate in summer.

There are plenty of places with pools, waterslides, wave pools or cold-water *onsen* – for example Spa World in Osaka; Suginoi Hotel in Beppu; Spa LaQua, Summerland, Yomiuriland or Aqua City in Tokyo; Spa Land in Nagashima (Nagoya); Rusutsu Jumbo Pool; Hokkaidō Spa Resort; and Hawaiians in Fukushima. Many *onsen* have cold-water pools or blood-temperature pools, and you can always have a cool shower. →

OPPOSITE PAGE: Outdoor bathing *onsen*, Ikaho Onsen

SUMMER IN JAPAN AT A GLANCE

—

FLORA

Hydrangeas

Irises

Lavender

Roses

Sunflowers

—

FOOD & DRINK

Coffee jelly and iced coffee

Edamame (boiled and
salted soybeans)

Grilled salted *ayu* (sweetfish)

Grilled *unagi* (eel)

Kakigōri (shaved ice dessert with
syrup and toppings)

Mugicha (iced roasted-barley tea)

Onigiri (rice balls) and beer

Sofuto kurīmu (soft-serve
ice cream)

Sushi and sashimi, especially *uni*
(sea urchin)

White asparagus

Zaru soba (chilled soba noodles
with dipping sauce)

—

FRUIT

Cherries

Peaches

Rockmelon

Watermelon

—

IN A WORD

Shinrin-yoku – 'forest bath':
taking a walk in the forest for
its restorative benefits

In a big city like Osaka or Tokyo, air conditioning is a lifesaver: usually icy cold, especially in department stores, it sets you up for a few more hours outside. Keep hydrated – convenience stores and drink machines offer a ridiculous range of chilled options – and always remember that you can duck inside somewhere interesting if the heat and humidity get too much for you. Try a *kakigōri* (shaved ice; p. 140) dessert for a true Japanese experience and a cold green tea will give you the antioxidants you need to keep walking. Or do what the Japanese look forward to in summer: line up to have a delicious *unagi* (eel) lunch or dinner or a *zaru soba* (cold soba with dipping sauce).

Japan has brilliant sunscreen products, a range of stylish hats and neck scarves (pop in a life-saving ice pack) and flannels to mop the profuse sweat from your brow. Techy fabrics that you can wet and throw around your neck have the dual benefits of cooling you down while protecting the back of your neck from the sun. We always take a paper fan each, and Michelle uses a summer umbrella as well, an essential form of portable shade. Tokyu Hands, Loft convenience stores, Donki and pharmacies are one-stop shops for these summer necessities.

One of our favourite parts of summer in Japan is seeing groups of girlfriends and women lunching in brightly coloured *yukata* (casual summer kimono). If you're visiting an *onsen* (hot springs) town you'll see both men and women *onsen*-hopping and floating around in *yukata*, carrying cute little bags with a towel (*yukata* will be provided in a country *ryokan*, or inn; p. 87). You can join in on this too! If your Western clothes seem too heavy and restrictive for the Japanese summer, both men's and women's summer dress are available at all price points in all the stores.

The Japanese have fifty words for rain, which tells you everything you need to know about the rainy season. The downpour can start in the morning and not let up all day. Its relentless presence may make you feel like it is trying to 'dampen' your spirits, but a patterned umbrella or lightweight raincoat will brighten the cloudiest of days.

Rainiest areas? The Kii Peninsula, Shikoku and Kyūshū's mid-southern region are subject to some frightening typhoons and monsoons. Japan has typhoons from May to October, with peak season running from August to September. Expect heavy rains and also winds that can reach 100 kilometres per hour. Okinawa sits right in the 'typhoon alley', and Kyūshū and Shikoku are also in the path. That said, a typhoon can strike any city in Japan (although Hokkaidō has no rainy season), so if you're travelling in typhoon season, check the news daily for storm warnings. Check train and plane schedules if you're caught up in a typhoon, and shop hours too – a lot of them will close. If somewhere you expected to be busy seems deserted, chances are everyone else has got wind – pun intended – that a typhoon is on its way.

Seasonal note: Late July to late August is school holiday time in Japan – be prepared; trains, attractions, hotels and restaurants will be more crowded. →

ALL IMAGES: Tokyo Midtown, Roppongi, Tokyo, Kantō

BEST BEACH ESCAPES

Atami Sun Beach, Izu, Chūbu

Enoshima (Fuji views), Tokyo, Kantō

Izu Peninsula, Chūbu

Miho (Fuji views), Chūbu

Naha and Ishigaki, Okinawa, Kyūshū

BEST FOREST & MOUNTAIN ESCAPES

Arashiyama, Kyoto, Kansai

Arashiyama Bamboo Forest, Arashiyama, Kansai

Bijinbayashi woods, Chūbu

Kiso Valley, Chūbu

Kōyasan, Wakayama, Kansai

Minakami, Gunma, Kantō

Nachi Falls, Wakayama, Kansai

Nikkō, Kantō

Shikoku

Shōdoshima Island, Shikoku

Yakushima Island, Kyūshū

SUMMER FESTIVALS

There are many colourful and vibrant summer festivals, or *natsu matsuri*, in Japan, always featuring incredible street food. If you time your travels to coincide with a festival, you'll not only experience something unique, but also glean some valuable insights into Japanese culture. If you have a Japan Rail (JR) Pass (p. 97), you could spend a week visiting all manner of interesting cities during their main festivals. Here are some of our favourites.

TOKYO

HARAJUKU–OMOTESANDŌ GENKI MATSURI SUPER YOSAKOI

Traditional Dance Festival
Late August

Expect a riot of colour, costumes, singing, dancing, some very enthusiastic musicians and a general party vibe. Anyone wanting to immerse themselves in traditional Japanese dance will find this festival endlessly fascinating.

HOZUKI-ICHI

Lantern Plant Festival
9–10 July

The lantern plant, with its brightly coloured pods hanging in clusters, is so beautiful it deserves its own celebration. Various summer fairs – most notably the one at the Sensō-ji temple in Asakusa (p. 172) – honour lantern plants by displaying bunches of them, showing off their vibrant colours and, later, their skeletal, decaying beauty. Florists also stock lantern plants and allow them to slowly wither: another potent symbol of the transience of life.

SHITAMACHI TANABATA MATSURI

Shitamachi Star Festival
Five days around 7 July

In Tokyo's old quarters (p. 172), on a long stretch of road between Asakusa and Ueno, the Shitamachi Tanabata Matsuri is celebrated with street parades, singing and dancing, street food and general frivolity. Tanabata, which has its roots in the Chinese Qixi Festival, is celebrated across Japan. It commemorates the story of celestial lovers Orihime and Hikoboshi, who were forbidden from meeting by the Sky King except on the seventh night of the seventh month, when they can cross a bridge over the Milky Way and unite (as long as it's not raining). This festival is our favourite, with its colourful and beautiful decorations that flutter in the wind. With the Skytree and temples as its backdrop – a hybrid landscape of old and new – the festival feels like a true Tokyo tradition. Ask your hotel front desk or host for their favourite Tanabata celebration in the city.

Tanabata also has its own specific *wagashi* (traditional sweets; p. 140) shaped like leaves, representing the old custom of writing a wish on mulberry or bamboo leaves. These days, people write their wishes on strips of paper called *tanzaku*.

SUMIDAGAWA HANABI TAIKAI

Sumida River Fireworks Festival
Last Saturday in July

This famous fireworks festival takes place in Sumida, one of Tokyo's traditional areas. It has roots in the Edo period, dating back to 1732, but the current incarnation has been a Tokyo festival fixture since 1978. Nearly a million people congregate to see the stunning fireworks display on the banks of the Sumida River. It's a family-friendly event, with the fireworks starting at 7 pm and lasting a little over an hour. Wearing a *yukata* (casual summer kimono) to the festival is popular, and a really fun way to get into the spirit of things.

KYOTO

GION MATSURI

Gion Festival

17 July

One of Japan's main festivals, happening over the whole of July, Kyoto Gion Matsuri is a celebratory affair dating back to 869 AD, with a procession of intricately designed and striking giant floats (*yamaboko junko*) called *yama* and *hoko*. The floats can take around two weeks to build, often on closed-off main streets of Kyoto. They feature high platforms and a towering tree motif, and are filled with people dressed in the traditional skimpy summer blue-and-white outfit.

GOZAN NO OKURIBI DAIMONJI FESTIVAL

Five Mountain Send-off Fire

From 16 August

Marking the end of Obon (p. 61), Kyoto's Daimonji is an astounding festival where the hills are literally set alight to guide the spirits on their way. If you've ever seen kanji characters 'shaved' into the mountains around Kyoto, they are the funeral pyres. The kanji are lit and viewed from various points in Kyoto (*daimonji* means 'large character'). The festival starts at 8 pm and the burning runes can be seen from most places in the city. The characters are lit in order and burn for under an hour: *dai* (大 – one/first), *myoho* (妙法 – excellent law of the Buddha), *funagata* (舟形 – 'boat-shaped'), *hidari daimonji* (左大文字 – large) and *toriigata* (鳥居形 – bird-shaped). Around 8.30 pm, all of the fires are alight at the same time, speeding the spirits to heaven. Great places to view the fires include private restaurant spaces, the banks of the Kamogawa – especially around Imadegawa and Demachiyanagi – and the Kamo delta.

AOMORI

NEBUTA MATSURI

2–7 August

Another of Japan's major festivals, the Nebuta Matsuri celebrates Nebuta, a mythical local warrior, in a series of stunning illuminated floats that roll through the city, surrounded by merriment, dancing and celebration. It seems likely that the genesis of the vibrant floats goes all the way back to the ninth century AD, when General Sakanoue-no-Tamuramaro possibly used them to scare his enemies. Constructed from fabric on a bamboo frame, the floats have remained incredibly popular to this day and make for a breathtaking procession. If you miss the event itself, don't despair; the Nebuta Museum Wa-Rasse (p. 198) features some of the best floats, lit up and spread out in a large hall. When you turn the corner and see the display, you will definitely gasp.

MIYAGI PREFECTURE

SENDAI TANABATA MATSURI

The Star Festival

7 July

Tanabata celebrates Orihime and Hikoboshi (see Shitamachi Tanabata Matsuri). In Sendai, streamers flow from myriad poles, making a bright, colourful procession that is attended by thousands of people every year. The Sendai Tanabata Matsuri is one of the three great festivals of Tōhoku, with Aomori's Nebuta Matsuri (above) and Akita's Kantō Matsuri. →

ABOVE: Nebuta Museum, Aomori, Tohoku

OBON
Festival of the Dead
13–15 August

Obon is a Buddhist festival where the spirits of the dead revisit the world to commune with their descendants – a poignant opportunity to address any misgivings, settle any disputes and express your feelings (see opposite). It's a family affair, so anyone who lives away returns to the fold and lights lanterns for the dead (this has become particularly symbolic for soldiers who have died on active duty).

The celebrations can take on an almost riotous joy. Kimono-clad families participate in *rokudō mairi*, attending shrines and temples and calling for deceased family members. At Obon festivals you'll find fun, colourful food, costumes and rituals: equal parts celebration and deep spiritual respect. Dusk and night-time events have incredible lighting displays, and often host over-the-top parades and spectacles, too. Dancers in bright costumes perform *Bon odori* ('Obon dance'), a circular dance accompanied by traditional drums and music. Watching bystanders can be called up onto the stage – a stunning sight, as most people also wear *yukata* (casual summer kimono) for this festival. Many businesses close for Obon holidays, usually for a few days around 15 August. As it's such a popular time of year for travel, plan your movements carefully if you're in Tokyo during Obon.

Okinawa is a great place to experience Obon in a different way. The warm climate and beach setting make it perfect to engage in Eisa festival dancing, a folk dance unique to Okinawa. The celebrations often go on well into the early hours, singing and beating drums for departed ancestors, an important part of mourning and marking the end of Obon.

MEDIA ARTS FESTIVAL
Mid-June

Held all over Japan, this arts festival showcases (and awards) new innovations in Japanese media (both digital and non-digital), art, video games, entertainment, animation and manga. Leaving aside 1997, when they chose computer game *Kage* over the legendary and influential *Final Fantasy VII*, the festival is a pivotal point in judging the standards of new media. →

INSIDER'S GUIDE
アンサイダーガイド

Obon in Ōita

COCO TASHIMA, EDITOR AT PAUMES BOOKS, TOKYO, KANTŌ

Can you quickly explain Obon?

Obon is the traditional Japanese Buddhist event to welcome the spirits of our ancestors. It's from August 13 to 16 (although in some areas like Tokyo, Hakodate and Kanazawa, it's sometimes held in July).

We know you visit your home town in Ōita, Kyūshū (p. 329), for Obon. How important is this festival to you and your family?

Japanese people often take Obon holidays and go back to their parental home to spend time with their family. It's an old tradition, but nowadays many people take holidays just for fun and to relax. I was the same, but I changed my mind when I lost my grandparents recently. Hatsubon, the first Obon after the death of a family member, is the most important for the family, and now I've been to my home town for Obon the past three years. I think the Obon holiday is a precious way to spend time with family, sharing our memories and enjoying daily life with each other.

What kind of schedule do you have for the holiday?

There are various customs for Obon depending on the region and Buddhist sect. In my family, in preparation to welcome the spirits of our ancestors, we clean up the Buddhist altar and our family grave. We display lanterns, and lay the *uchishiki*, a special cloth for the Buddhist altar, and flowers. We often use chrysanthemums, sakaki plants and especially Chinese-lantern plants for Obon. We put out sweet offerings like seasonal fruits and *wagashi* (traditional sweets), too. A monk visits our home, and we recite a sutra with the monk and other relatives. I wasn't interested in the sutra at all when I was a child, but I enjoy it now. Then we all have dinner together. The menu isn't anything special, but it's a familiar meal for me and always enjoyable.

What's your favourite part of the festival?

Many fireworks displays and Obon dance festivals are held across the country during July and August. A lot of people who go to these festivals will dress up in *yukata*, the traditional summer kimono. I get so excited just seeing it all.

Does Ōita have a special take on Obon that differs to the rest of Japan?

In Ōita, we value Hatsubon (the first Obon after a family member dies). One of our customs is preparing the special basket for Hatsubon. We call it a 'basket', but it's actually a plate full of food and offerings attached to a stand, which is then decorated with a wreath of artificial flowers and the sender's name. Some of them have a lantern under the plate too. *Yaseuma* is Ōita's local food specialty, and we always make it for Obon and put it on the Buddhist altar, too. *Yaseuma* is a kind of dumpling in a narrow, flat shape like a noodle. We serve it with soy flour and sugar according to taste. I've also heard that old-style dances and customs for Obon still exist even now in Ōita.

OPPOSITE PAGE: Bon Odori dance, Tokyo, Kantō **ABOVE:** Coco-san's family Obon traditions at her grandmother's in Ōita, Kyūshū

SUMMER EXPERIENCES

Two of Tokyo's (and the world's) best music festivals take place in summer, offering a huge array of national and international bands, events, food and general abandon. No music-festival obsessive can say they've done it all until they've included these two major events on the global music calendar. The Fuji Rock Festival happens at the Naeba Ski Resort in Niigata on the last weekend of July. Summer Sonic in Chiba (also in Osaka) is a two-day festival that takes place in mid-August.

Kyoto (p. 234) is replete with festivals in summer, and has the best spots for viewing or partaking in them. At night the heat subsides (slightly), giving you a great chance to get amongst the action.

Beer (and sake) festivals are dotted around the country to help people through the warmer months. The best sake festivals are saved for the new year and the new rice, but beer is a summer drink. Tōhoku's Jibiru Festival is a craft beer festival in Akita (p. 194) in the northern part of Honshū, bringing together Japan's best craft beer makers in one riotously tasty weekend in mid-June.

On Hokkaidō, the Furano Lavender Fields (p. 287) are well worth a summer visit.

TOP: *Kakigōri* café in Naoshima, Shikoku
BOTTOM: Setouchi Retreat Aonagi, Matsuyama, Shikoku **OPPOSITE PAGE:** Girls wearing *yukata* (casual summer kimono) in Kyoto, Kansai

Autumn

There's a phrase in Japan, *shokuyoku no aki*, which means 'autumn appetite', hinting at the delicious fruit and produce the season brings. This season is all about the gentle whispers of the fading summer and approaching winter, but most particularly about the fiery colours of the trees, whose leaves start to change colour in late October, depending on where you are. By mid-November everyone is out exploring the most beautiful spots to view them. Photography becomes an extreme sport – intense focus on each wonderful nuance of the autumn leaf is practised by smartly dressed men and women everywhere.

The flaming red and yellow of the autumn leaves can be viewed all over Japan, but Kyoto's (p. 234) mid-country climate and positioning – not to mention its stunning temple backdrops – make it a hotspot for autumn leaf viewing. *Sakura* (cherry-blossom; pp. 36, 80) season is probably the most pivotal moment in Japan, but autumn leaves definitely make an impression, and in some cases the multicoloured foliage might trump the single pink of the cherry blossom (don't tell anyone we said that).

Over the years, Japan has planted deciduous trees and nurtured them so we can enjoy their intense beauty in perfectly placed arrangements. Or you can experience them growing wild around jaw-dropping sites. Autumn is also the time of harvest, so expect delicious fresh fruit and produce. Persimmons are hung up and dried – you'll see them hanging from the eaves of houses and shops – and chestnut is used to flavour everything. But the *momiji* (maple leaf) reigns supreme, and Japanese maple leaf shapes dominate gifts, chopstick holders, sweets and snacks – and maple syrup flavours biscuits and cakes. Yellowy-orange pointy ginkgo trees are another delightful sign of autumn, especially on Tokyo's Icho Namiki Avenue, which comes alive in late November, drawing crowds of admirers. →

AUTUMN IN JAPAN AT A GLANCE

FLORA

Chrysanthemums

Cosmos

Ginkgo

Kochia

Maple (*momiji*)

Pampas grass

Red spider lilies

Roses

FOOD & DRINK

Anything shaped like *momiji* (maple leaf) – *wagashi, manju* – and anything maple flavoured

Kabocha (Japanese pumpkin)

Kuri (chestnuts)

Matsutake mushrooms

Oden (fish cakes) and daikon simmered in broth and served with ginger–miso sauce

Sanma (Pacific saury fish)

Shinmai (new rice)

Yaki imo (roasted sweet potato)

FRUIT

Apples

Kaki (persimmon) – hung and dried

Nashi

Yuzu

IN A WORD

Koyou – leaves changing colour

Momiji – red leaves or maple tree

Rakuyou – fallen leaves

RIGHT: Kiyomizu-dera Seiryu-e Dragon Festival, Kyoto, Kansai OPPOSITE PAGE: Jizō at Enkō-ji, Kyoto, Kansai

AUTUMN FESTIVALS

KYOTO

JIDAI MATSURI
October

One of the three best known Kyoto festivals, this mesmerising event features a parade of local *geiko* (Kyoto's geisha) and people dressed in traditional outfits making a spiritual pilgrimage from the Kyoto Imperial Palace to Heian Shrine. The end destination, Kurama, features the Kurama Fire Festival that evening.

KURAMA NO HI MATSURI KURAMA FIRE FESTIVAL
22 October

In this follow-up to summer's Daimonji (p. 59), large burning effigies and torches are carried through the streets by local men wearing loincloths and braided-rope skirts.

KIYOMIZU-DERA SEIRYU-E DRAGON FESTIVAL
Mid-September

For lovers of spectacular costumes and set design, Seiryu-e is a visual treat with a party atmosphere. A giant dragon tended by monks winds its way from Kiyomizu-dera through the main street surrounded by music, dancing, street-food stalls and general frivolity. For design and film buffs Emi Wada (*Ran*, *Hero*, *House of Flying Daggers*) is responsible for the amazing costumes and sets. Join in and wear a *yukata* (casual kimono).

TOCHIGI CITY

AUTUMN FESTIVAL
Mid-November

This three-day festival features the towering *ningyo dashi*, detailed Edo-period (p. 28) illuminated floats with powerful robed figures.

TAKAYAMA

AUTUMN FESTIVAL
9–10 October
This festival is regarded as one of Japan's three most beautiful, alongside Kyoto's Gion Matsuri(p. 59) and the Chichibu Yomatsuri. It features a celebration of the Hachiman Shrine (a festival in its own right called the Hachiman Matsuri) in a variety of impressive floats. There are performances of *karakuri ningyō*, intricate and elaborate puppets, a *mikoshi*, or portable shrine procession, and at night colourful and illuminated floats are pulled through the streets. Expect dancing and celebration.

IZUMO

KAMIARI FESTIVAL
Mid-September
This takes place at Japan's 'first shrine', the spectacular Izumo Taisha (p. 271). All the gods from each Shinto shrine (tens of thousands) visit Izumo Taisha for one night of communion with the people. It's a great opportunity to gain the grace of as many gods as possible. Keep your prayers internal as this is a silent festival – the gods should not be disturbed. All construction in the area stops and there is no music or dancing. One of the gods' duties during this melancholy mass silence is to 'match-make' any single people within the crowd, and nuances of attendees' lives are decided without them ever knowing – such is the will of the gods.

SAPPORO

AUTUMN FEST
September
Sapporo celebrates the autumn harvest with vigour, enjoying the quality produce in a series of events that make the most of the new season seafood, vegetables, wine and sake.

JAPAN-WIDE

TSUKIMI MOON-VIEWING FESTIVAL
Second Friday in September
The moon-viewing tradition goes back thousands of years. Great viewing spots include Tokyo Tower, Tokyo Skytree, Himeji Castle, Sankei-en garden and Ise Shrine. Don't miss the 'Moon Viewing Platform' at Ginkaku-ji (the Silver Pavilion) in Kyoto (although you can't stand on it). Festival food includes *tsukimi* (egg dishes), taro, *tsukimi dango* (rice dumplings) and *usagi* (rabbit). The Japanese don't have a 'man in the moon' but a rabbit pounding *mochi* (glutinous rice cakes), so rabbit-shaped *mochi* cakes are popular.

DANJIRI MATSURI
CART-PULLING FESTIVALS
These festivals (dates vary) feature the pulling of large ornate floats or 'carts'. The Kishiwada Danjiri Matsuri in Osaka is the most famous. →

AUTUMN EXPERIENCES

AUTUMN LEAVES & GINKGO TREES

KYOTO

· Eikando
· Enko-ji
· Enri-an
· Hojo Garden, Tōfuku-ji (p. 348)
· Imperial Palace Gardens
· Kitano Tenmangu (p. 240)
· Kurama/Kibune (p. 240)
· Nanzen-ji
· Ruriko-in

TOKYO

· Icho Namiki (Ginkgo Avenue)
· Imperial Palace East Gardens
· Koishikawa-Kōrakuen
· Mount Takao (p. 176)
· Rikugi-en
· Shinjuku Gyo-en
· Shōwa Memorial Park
· Yoyogi Park

OSAKA

· Expo Memorial Park
· Hoshida Park Suspension Bridge
· Katsuō-ji, Minoo
· Midōsuji (avenue of ginkgo trees)
· Minoo
· Mount Inunaki
· Osaka Castle Gardens
· Settsukyo Park
· Ushitakiyama (Daiitoku-ji)

ELSEWHERE

· Befukyo Canyon, Shikoku
· Daisetsuzan National Park, Hokkaidō (p. 285)
· Fuji Five Lakes, Chūbu (p. 221)
· Hiraizumi, Iwate, Tōhoku
· Hokkaidō University, Sapporo, Hokkaidō
· Kirishima, Kyūshū (p. 324)
· Kōsetsu-en, Hakodate, Hokkaidō
· Kunenan, Kyūshū
· Meigetsu-in, Kamakura, Kantō
· Mount Asahidake, Hokkaidō
· Mount Kōya, Kansai (p. 259)
· Mount Nasu, Fukushima, Tōhoku (p. 191)
· Naruko Gorge, Miyagi, Tōhoku (p. 204)
· Nyūtō Onsen, Akita, Tōhoku (p. 196)
· Ōhori Park, Fukuoka, Kyūshū
· Oze National Park, Nikkō, Kantō
· Saito Villa, Niigata, Chūbu

ABOVE: Tea in Kanazawa, Chūbu
OPPOSITE TOP RIGHT: Steve at Fuji Five Lakes, Chūbu MIDDLE: Seasonal sweet potato snacks BOTTOM: Kyorinbo Temple, Lake Biwa, Kansai

芸術の秋
Autumn,
the season
for art

FLOWER FESTIVALS

Autumn is not just about leaves – the colour of flowers is also a big deal during autumn, and there are plenty of top spots and amazing festivals where you can enjoy nature in full bloom.

· Akabori Kogiku no Sato (Chrysanthemum Park), Isesaki, Kantō
· Kinchakuda Red Spider Lily Festival, Saitama, Kantō
· Kochia Carnival, Hitachi, Kantō
· Kyu-Furukawa Gardens (Rose Festival), Tokyo, Kantō
· Sengokuhara (pampas grass fields), Hakone, Kantō
· Yamanakako Hananomiyako Park (cosmos fields), Chūbu

What to pack

When you are packing, remember that the south will be warmer and the north will be cooler. Typhoon season is from June to October (mostly July and August) so take care when planning your trip. Check your dates online to see when the rainy, blossom and snow seasons are expected.

WHAT TO PACK FOR SUMMER

Humid, June–July rainy season

Average daytime temperature: Sapporo Jun 21°C, Jul 25°C, Aug 26°C Tokyo Jun 25°C, Jul 25°C, Aug 31°C Takayama Jun 26°C, Jul 29°C, Aug 31°C Osaka Jun 27°C, Jul 31°C, Aug 33°C Fukuoka Jun 27°C, Jul 31°C, Aug 32°C

· bathers
· clothing made from new tech cooling fabrics
· fan
· flannel
· hat
· light cotton or linen clothing (don't show too much skin!)
· necktie with icepack
· reusable water bottle
· sandals
· sun umbrella
· sunglasses
· sunscreen
· *yukata* (casual summer kimono)

Rainy season

· rain boots
· raincoat
· umbrella

WHAT TO PACK FOR AUTUMN

November, leaves start to change

Average daytime temperature: Sapporo Sep 22°C, Oct 16°C, Nov 8°C Tokyo Sep 27°C, Oct 22°C, Nov 17°C Takayama Sep 26°C, Oct 20°C, Nov 13°C Osaka Sep 29°C, Oct 23°C, Nov 17°C Fukuoka Sep 28°C, Oct 23°C, Nov 18°C

· light jumper
· light scarf
· mid-weight jacket and clothing
· mostly long sleeves
· sunglasses
· thermal singlets to wear under lighter tops
· trainers or comfortable walking shoes
· umbrella

WHAT TO PACK FOR SPRING

Cherry blossoms late March to early April

Average daytime temperature: Sapporo Mar 4°C, Apr 11°C, May 17°C Tokyo Mar 13°C, Apr 18°C, May 23°C Takayama Mar 9°C, Apr 17°C, May 22°C Osaka Mar 13°C, Apr 20°C, May 24°C Fukuoka Mar 14°C, Apr 19°C, May 24°C

· light coat
· light scarf
· long sleeves and short sleeves
· spring shoes and socks
· sunglasses
· thermal singlet to wear under lighter top

WHAT TO PACK FOR WINTER

Sunny and dry, snow if you are in the mountains or up north, end of autumn leaves, February start of plum blossom season

Average daytime temperature: Sapporo Dec 2°C, Jan -1°C, Feb 0°C Tokyo Dec 12°C, Jan 10°C, Feb 10°C Takayama Dec 6°C, Jan 3°C, Feb 4°C Osaka Dec 12°C, Jan 9°C, Feb 9°C Fukuoka Dec 13°C, Jan 10°C, Feb 11°C

· gloves or mittens
· 'hot pocket' hand warmers
· sturdy waterproof shoes
· thermals
· warm coat
· warm scarf
· waterproof jacket if you are going country
· woolly layers
· woolly socks
· woolly winter hat

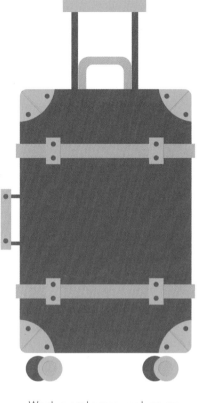

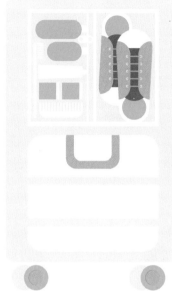

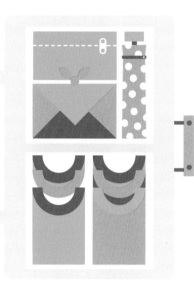

- We always take carry-on lugguage only (for trips up to a month)
- Inside our carry-on bag, we take a fold-down bag so we can bring back a few treasures

- Pack a zero-waste kit with a water bottle, reusable food container and reusable cutlery, and *furoshiki* (reusable cloth wrapping)
- Pack a waterproof bag and umbrella
- Packing cubes are your friends
- Put your liquids in a clear reusable bag and pop in your handbag to get through customs
- Take a thermal singlet or tee or a warm scarf for the plane

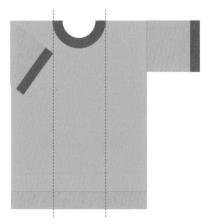

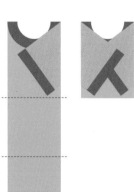

- Fold your clothes into thirds, then thirds again, and pack neatly into packing cubes. Check out YouTube for some addictive packing content

Winter

Winter can be as relentless as summer across Japan – hard to escape, constantly disrupting travel plans, bleak, unforgiving, aggressive. However, Tokyo (p. 162) and Kyoto's (p. 234) average temperatures of around 8–12 degrees with crisp blue skies also make it one of our favourite seasons to travel in. For a milder winter, head to Kagoshima (p. 320) or Okinawa (p. 326): the tropical feel of the deep south-west will warm the most frozen of hearts, and you might even find yourself in short sleeves.

It's worth rugging up and braving the elements though, because Japan is one of the world's best places to visit in winter. Imagine sitting in an *onsen* (hot spring) looking out over snow-whitened fields or at ancient buildings bejewelled with hanging icicles. There's little better than coming in from the cold and sitting in a warm room drinking sake and ladling out bowls of thick, hearty *nabe* (hotpot; p. 119); piping-hot winter stews; or steaming, nourishing curry. In the capitals, shopping in warm department stores is a must. Further out, the skiing is considered some of the best in the world.

Niseko and Hakuba are favourite areas for visitors, but lesser known spots like Zaō (p. 209) and Manza (p. 187) are also recommended and have some stand-out *onsen*. Northern Hokkaidō's Asahi-dake is one for the intrepid and boasts great-quality snow. Akita's Tazawako has incredible views and Aomori's Hakkōda has what skiing experts (which we are not) describe as some of the best deep-powder skiing in Japan. Yamanouchi (p. 227) is a triple threat. It's a great spot to ski, but if you don't (like us) there are two other major drawcards: monkeys with their own *onsen* (p. 78); and two excellent *onsen* towns, Shibu and Yudanaka.

Major cities offer myriad things to do in the winter months. Around New Year things can get quiet as people head home for the holidays. Even bustling Tokyo or Kyoto become eerily silent, and there's much less in the way of big, loud parties, as New Year is a spiritual, family time in Japan. (If you're looking for a mad, dress-up, noisy-people fest, Halloween in autumn might be more your thing.) New Year is a great time to be there as long as you know what's open and what's on offer. You can beat the tourist rush and often find yourself in shops or iconic landmarks with few people to get in your way. Just make sure you're fortified against the cold! Of course, it's not long before the sales start, and Japanese sales are manic, fun, colourful and offer some serious bargains. →

OPPOSITE PAGE: Shisho Shrine, Kinosaki Onsen, Kansai

WINTER IN JAPAN AT A GLANCE

FLORA

Buttercups

Camellias

Irises

Magnolia

Moss

Plum blossom

Silver birch trees

Snowbells

Tiger lilies

Wisteria

FRUIT

Grapes

Melons

Oranges

Peaches

Plums

Strawberries

Yuzu

IN A WORD

Aisu – ice

Yuki – snow

WINTER FESTIVALS

SAPPORO

SNOW FESTIVAL
4–11 February

The Sapporo Snow Festival is popular with Japanese and international visitors, primarily for the gigantic and intricate ice sculptures that appear across the city. Various satellite areas of Hokkaidō also get involved, and some of the outlying festivals have attracted strong patronage of their own. One of the main drawcards is the illumination of the ice carvings, which usually begins at sunset and continues throughout the night.

ASAHIKAWA

WINTER FESTIVAL
Early to mid-February

The Asahikawa Winter Festival, less than two hours from the Sapporo festival, also features ice sculptures and illuminations, along with a spectacular fireworks display. The Asahiyama Zoo is also a major attraction in this area, famous for its penguin parade.

JAPAN-WIDE

SETSUBUN (SPRING EVE)
3 February

Setsubun (Risshun) is celebrated on the day before the beginning of spring. Most people do their 'spring' cleaning the new year, so think of this as a spiritual 'spring' clean. Roasted soybeans (*fukumame*) are thrown at *oni* (monsters or demons; actually people in demon masks) in the bean-throwing ritual called *mamemaki*, which wards off evil spirits and clears out the darkness of winter to allow in the new growth of spring. The head male of the household usually throws the beans at demons outside the door, then the family chants, '鬼は外! 福は内! *Oni wa soto! Fuku wa uchi!*' 'Demons out! Luck in!' In Kansai the main food for Setsubun is *futomaki* – long sushi rolls. Kids love this fun

festival; it's very popular at shrines across the country, where beans, money and gifts are often thrown at parading *oni*. Decorations are sardines and holly, and the customary drink is ginger sake. Sensō-ji in Asakusa, Tokyo (p. 172), draws 100,000 people a year. Other popular places to experience Setsubun are Yasaka-ji in Kyoto (where geisha throw beans at the *oni*; p. 239) and Rozan-ji in Uji (p. 249), where three demons, red, blue and green, battle it out while onlookers hurl beans in their direction.

Aomori, Tōhoku **BOTTOM RIGHT:** Jigokudani Monkey Park, Yudanaka, Chūbu

OTHER WINTER FESTIVALS

Yokote Kamakura Festival is held in Yokote, Akita (p. 194), in the north of Honshū (not in the more famous Kamakura near Tokyo). A stand-out feature is the small 'igloos' or *kamakura* huts where you can sit and eat seasonal foods like *mochi* (rice cakes). A major part of the festival are the flotillas of small snow lanterns that float down the river. The Kakunodate Fire and Snow Festival, celebrated in mid-February, features large bonfires and the spectacular sight of participants spinning large fireballs over their heads (you are invited to participate). The Urasu Naked Man Pushing Festival (we're sure we have your attention now), which dates back 1200 years and takes place at the Bishamon-do temple in the East Mountains of Kyoto (p. 239), features men in a uniform of loincloth and sandals who essentially wrestle each other to be first in line to worship the ancient deity Bishamonten. It's fun to watch, especially when you're all rugged up. Festival food and events happen all around the main event. Zaō Snow Monster Festival (p. 209) features the 'snow monsters', a natural formation of 'alien sculptures' that appear in the snowscape. The forest of white monstrous humanoid figures makes for great photographs and a truly eerie sight at dusk. →

'Although there is the road, the child walks in the snow.'

MURAKAMI KIJO
(1868–1938)

HATSUMŌDE
New Year's Day

One of Japan's most important festivals is the first Shinto shrine visit of the new year, which often takes place at sunrise. Many people go on subsequent days as well, so expect shrines to be busy; many also choose to visit Buddhist shrines. The crowds flow respectfully, and various tents and stands are set up for food and prayer/temple items. Areas with a high concentration of temples and shrines like Kyoto will be busy, especially at important Shinto shrines. Book accommodation ahead, but don't miss this life-affirming experience.

FOOD & DRINK

Amazake (hot fermented
rice drink)

Hokkaidō hotpot

Hokkaidō stew

Hot tea

Karaage (fried chicken)

Kare (curry)

Nabe (variety of hotpot dishes)

Nikumon (Shūmai-style
steamed buns)

Oden (fish cakes and daikon
simmered in broth and served
with ginger–miso sauce)

Osechi-ryōri (New Year
tiered *bentō* feasts)

Ozoni (clear soup)

Ramen

Shabu-shabu (hotpot with thinly
sliced meat)

Soba and udon noodle soups

Warmed sake

Yakitori

Yudōfu (tofu simmered
in kelp broth)

TOP: Steve at a *kotatsu* table at Tocen
Goshoboh, Arima Onsen, Kansai
BOTTOM LEFT & RIGHT: Sengan-en
garden's Iso Residence, Kagoshima, Kyūshū

WINTER
EXPERIENCES

NEW YEAR'S EVE DECORATIONS

· *Shimekazari* – these rope wreaths, often decorated with paper fans, flowers, messages and fruits, start appearing on doors in the lead-up to New Year. Every prefecture has a different style of *shimekazari*.

· *Kadomatu* or *Kadomatsu* – a mini 'pine gate' of two thin pine fronds arched together and placed in front of houses, used to welcome spirits and a new spring harvest.

· *Kagomi-mochi* (mirror rice cake) – glutinous rice balls placed on top of each other topped with a small Japanese orange (*daidai*) with attached leaves. Look out for them (and souvenir versions) around New Year.

WINTER FOODS

In some ways winter food in Japan is the highlight of its many culinary delights – hotpots, udon soups, warm sake, chunky nabe, deep rich ramen, curry nanban – and you should most definitely travel to enjoy the subtle regional variations.

Chankonabe (p. 119), a thick hearty hotpot, is the perfect dish in winter – Toyko's Sumida has many specialist restaurants, and many sumo stables in Osaka have establishments that excel in this fortifying dish. Whatever your taste, pop into an *izakaya* (pub) in any city or town, order a beer and warm up with a range of incredible dishes, from yakitori (p. 128) and *karaage* (fried chicken; p. 118) to *agedashi dōfu* (p. 133) and tasty *oden* (p. 119).

A major part of winter is *osechi-ryōri*, the New Year *bentō* feast. Around the end of the year you'll see these *bentō* pop up in every department store – expensive tiered boxes with all manner of delights, often with high-end seafood or delicious pickles. They differ from region to region, often depending on the local produce. *Ozoni* is another New Year specialty, a simple clear broth made of dashi with *mochi* (rice cakes) and vegetables.

New Year is also a major time for sake. The new rice sake appears in food halls, shopping centres and temples. For a few days in some food halls you can often try the new sake straight from the barrel, a special experience. On the New Year's Eve (*Ōmisoka*) celebration, soba noodles are eaten (symbolising longevity).

Kids' Japan

Kids will be in sensory overload in Japan just from walking around the streets. Vending machine *gachapon* (capsule toys; p. 168); conveyor-belt sushi; giant character sculptures like Gundam in Odaiba, Tokyo, or Gigantor (Iron Man) in Kobe. Mizuki Shigeru Road in Sakaiminato, Tottori, is strewn with manga legend Mizuki Shigeru's quirky creations.

CHIBIKO NINJA MURA (KIDS' NINJA VILLAGE) (NAGOYA, CHŪBU)

For the small ninjas in your family, the village of their dreams awaits! Ninja costumes are available to hire for the day (and then buy). One hour by bus from Nagoya Station then a fifteen-minute walk. *ninjamura.com*

CHURAUMI AQUARIUM (NAHA, OKINAWA)

Considered one of the best in the world, this aquarium has a magnificent coastal location and is known for its giant tank with whale sharks and manta rays (see also p. 327). *churaumi.okinawa*

DEER AT NARA PARK (KANSAI) OR MIYAJIMA ISLAND (CHŪGOKU)

Feeding wild-roaming deer will be one of the highlights of your small person's trip to Japan (see pp. 250, 272). *nara-park.com*

EKIBEN (TRAIN BENTŌ) (ALL OVER JAPAN)

Any major station in Japan will have the most amazing train *ekiben* (train *bentō*; p. 98), which your kids will love. Lunch can come in the shape of a train, Hello Kitty, a piece of fruit, a snowman and even a *daruma* (p. 339).

JIGOKUDANI MONKEY PARK (YUDANAKA, CHŪBU)

Yudanaka is around three-and-a-half hours by train from Tokyo Station. Kids can choose a *bentō* box for the Shinkansen then ride the Snow Monkey Express train from Nagano to Yudanaka. A bus to the start of the Snow Monkey Park is followed by quite a long walk (1.6 kilometres) for little ones. But if you think your family can manage this, you'll be rewarded with the once-in-a-lifetime sight of fluffy, cheeky, woolly snow monkeys bathing in *onsen* (hot-spring) water. *snowmonkeyresorts.com*

LEGOLAND JAPAN RESORT (NAGOYA, CHŪBU)

Lego heaven, including robot workshops, themed areas, food and a hotel. *legoland.jp*

MOOMINVALLEY PARK (HANNŌ, KANTŌ)

A seventy-minute train journey from Tokyo Station, then a fifteen-minute bus (or taxi) ride, this is an achievable daytrip from Tokyo if your children are fans of Finland's Moomintrolls. *metsa-hanno.com*

ŌKUNOSHIMA ISLAND (RABBIT ISLAND, CHŪGOKU)

An island-hopping experience for bunny lovers (see also p. 296). Take the Shinkansen to Mihara, then a train to Tadanoumi Station, then a short ferry ride from Tadanoumi Port. *rabbit-island.info*

SANRIO PUROLAND (TOKYO, KANTŌ)

Pink and pretty theme park devoted to Hello Kitty (p. 50) and friends. *en.puroland.jp*

TOTORO BUS STOPS (KYŪSHŪ)

Yes, you can stand at and even catch a bus from a Totoro (p. 50) bus stop in a few places around Kyūshū! *saiki-kankou.com* *discover-nagasaki.com*

ZAŌ KITSUNE MURA (ZAŌ FOX VILLAGE) (SHIROISHI, TŌHOKU)

Yes, it's a village of foxes (see also p. 209). It's tricky to get to on public transport (there's a bus from Shiroishi Station on Tuesdays and Fridays, but only twice a day), but worth it for fox fans. Check the website for more information. *zao-fox-village.com*

Jigokudani Monkey Park, Yudanaka, Chūbu

Spring

Spring is the promise of new growth, the end of a barren, relentlessly cold winter, the excitement of the coming *sakura* (cherry-blossom) season and the joy of fresh spring food: new ginger, rapeseed shoots, spring vegetables and *sakura*-flavoured everything. Spring brings flower-viewing festivals and intense interest in the new growth, plants, buds and shoots that appear in parks, at temples and on streets. It marks the new financial and school year, and one of Japan's major holidays, Golden Week, where everyone gets a whole week off work. Fresh strawberries and persimmons fill markets and stores.

Moss phlox blooms right after *sakura* in Japan. From early May, it flowers in a variety of colours across the mountain slopes of Higashimokoto Shibazakura Park in Ozora town in Hokkaidō or at Fuji Shibazakura Festival (mid April to late May) in Fujikawaguchiko, creating a stunning pink field. Festivals are held during the season, and at night illuminations highlight the beauty of the pink 'moss'.

In the end though, spring in Japan is all about the delicate, temporary perfection of *sakura*. Hanami (flower-viewing) takes place in parks and gardens across Japan, the first opening of the blossoms closely followed by the falling of the petals (*sakura* snow), which forms a pink carpet on the ground. It's summed up in one phrase: *mono no aware* (literally 'the bitter-sweetness of fading beauty') – the tender beauty and melancholy of transient things. Predicting the exact opening of the first cherry blossom and where it will happen takes over the public consciousness in the lead up. The first appreciation of cherry blossom is recorded in *Genji Monogatari* (*The Tale of Genji*), written in Uji, between Kyoto and Nara, in around 1008. Okinawa is the first place for the flowers to open (usually in February), and to the north the blossoms open last, with most of Hokkaidō's flowers appearing in May. Tokyo, Kyoto and Osaka bloom anywhere between mid March and early April, and are the focus of much of the festivities and picnics. →

OPPOSITE PAGE: Inokashira Park, Tokyo, Kantō

SPRING IN JAPAN AT A GLANCE

FLORA

Lilies

Moss phlox

Nanohana (rapeseed shoots)

Poppies

Sakura (cherry blossom)

FOOD & DRINK

Bonito

Broad beans

Cabbage

New potatoes

New tea

Spanish mackerel

Wasabi

Young bamboo shoots

FRUIT

Cherries

Peaches

Persimmons

Strawberries

IN A WORD

Sakura-fubuki (桜吹雪)
(cherry-blossom snowstorm)

ABOVE: *Sakura* soft-serve ice cream
(only available in cherry-blossom season)

SPRING FESTIVALS

JAPAN-WIDE

HINA MATSURI

Doll's Day or Girls' Day

3 March

Dating back to the Nara period (p. 15), this festival is about praying for the health and happiness of girls. Homes across Japan display two *hina* dolls, representing the Emperor and Empress, on red velvet a few days before 3 March, coinciding with peach blossom around the country, and put them away soon after. Hina Matsuri features girls' parties, kimono, *amazake* (a hot, sweet drink made from fermented rice) and sweets, including green or three-coloured *hishi-mochi* (rice cakes) and *ichigo daifuku* (strawberry *mochi*). You can also view wonderful vintage doll collections.

Places to enjoy Hina Matsuri, try the food and view vintage dolls:

· Saitama – Bikkuri Hinamatsuri, 18 February–3 April
· Shima Onsen – Mayahime Matsuri (Princess Maya Festival), mid-February to mid-March department stores and public places
· Tokyo – Hotel Gajoen, Meguro, 3–4 Mar 2020; Doll Floating Ceremony, Asakusa, mid-February to mid-March
· Wakayama – Awashima Shrine, late February–early March
· Yamanashi – Saiko Iyashi no Sato (display and doll-making), 3 March

TOKYO

JINDAI-JI YAKUYOKE GANZAN JIE DAISHI SAI
Jindai-ji Temple Daruma Doll Fair
Early March

Steve likes to collect *daruma* (p. 339), red, bearded figures modelled on the founder of Zen Buddhism, Bodhidharma. A symbol of good luck, they're a perfect gift for any facial-hair-obsessed loved ones. Go early to festivals and pick your favourite from one of hundreds of stalls. You can spend a day taking your chosen doll to different stalls for inscriptions and hoping for good luck. At Jindai-ji temple in Chōfu you can buy dolls and participate in *daruma* festivities.

Other good *daruma* festivals are the Takasaki Daruma Festival and Kawagoe Daruma Festival.

NEW FINANCIAL AND SCHOOL YEAR
1 April

The first day of both the financial year and the school year in Japan is 1 April. It represents new beginnings and is a day of hope and anticipation for the year ahead. It can also coincide with Hanami (flower-viewing) – when it does, it takes on a truly festive and joyous atmosphere.

GOLDEN WEEK
Late April to early May

Japanese people don't get much annual leave, but they do have a lot of public holidays. The phrase 'Golden Week' was coined in the 1950s to mark a week full of public holidays, and it is one of the busiest travel times in Japan. The public holidays are Shōwa Day (29 April), Constitution Memory Day (3 May), Greenery Day (4 May) and Children's Day (5 May). Some businesses shut completely during this week, and many workers take days off between the public holidays to spend time with family. Trains and airports are crowded as people leave home to visit families in other prefectures, so you may find the big cities a little less crowded than usual.

KOINOBORI
Children's Day koi streamers
Late April to early May

The tradition of *koinobori* ('carp streamers'), when families would display a windsock shaped like a carp at the entrance of their homes for any young boys living there, is now part of Kodomo no Hi, or Children's Day (see Golden Week). The Koinobori Matsuri (festival) of Tsuetate Onsen in Kumamoto prefecture (the birthplace of the festival) is the most incredible example, set around the river in Kumamoto.

Koinobori Village Festivals are held in:
· Higashi Matsuhima, Tōhoku
· Kazo Shimin Heiwa Matsuri (Kazo Citizens' Peace Festival), Kantō
· Tatebayashi, Kantō
· Takatsuki, Kansai
· Tokyo Tower – More than 300 colourful carp streamers floating around Tokyo Tower is a sight to behold if you're in Tokyo for Golden Week.

KANAMARA PENIS FESTIVALS
Early April

This parade of giant phallic symbols, which happens in Yokohama (p. 191) at the Kanayama Shrine, apparently helps ward off STIs, among other things. The shrine has long been popular with sex workers, who often pray to be 'protected'. Kanayamahiko and Kanayamahime, the gods of smithing and mining, are enshrined within. Legend has it that they tended Shinto goddess Izanami after she gave birth to a fire god. People have since prayed to them regarding STIs, childbirth, and so on because of this myth.

OMITZUTORI
Fire Festival/Water-drawing Festival
1–14 March

This festival, based around Buddhist rituals of repentance, is most popular in Nara (p. 250) and Okinawa (p. 326).

SPRING EVENTS

· Anime Japan – late March
· Tokyo Rainbow Pride – 28 April–6 May
· Design Festa – mid-May
· Sumo Grand Tournament – mid-May

SPRING SAKURA

Hanami, from the words *hana*, meaning 'flower', and *mi*, meaning 'to see', is one Japanese custom you can't miss in spring – and if you time your travel right you could even catch it in different places across the country. When the blossoms arrive, everything suddenly takes on a festive, enchanting atmosphere. Friends gather under the pink boughs to catch up, have picnics and drink sake. Paper lanterns threaded through the trees light up the evening, illuminating the beauty of the flowers into the night. It's a happy celebration where people absorb the joy of nature through the bright, beautiful pink of the cherry blossom. Expect laughter – more laughter than you're likely to have heard in any public place in Japan – and festive treats and delights aplenty: pink champagne, pink sake, *sakura* soft-serve ice cream, *sakura* flowers and flower shapes in food, pink *dango* (dumplings) and *sakura umeshu* (plum liqueur). A truly magical time made all the more so by the fact that the flowers only bloom for a week.

SAKURA-VIEWING TRAINS

· Sagami Line Sobudaishita Sakura, Kantō
· Sagano Scenic Railway, Kansai
· Tsugaru Railway, Tōhoku
· Yosan Line, Shikoku →

SAKURA MOCHI

This *sakura*-flavoured rice cake, wrapped in pickled cherry-blossom leaves, is delicious. We head to our favourite stores (Higashiya Man in Tokyo, and Toraya or Kagizen Yoshifusa in Kyoto) and line up early so as not to miss out. Pop-up stalls inside stations, around shrines or anywhere festive are a great way to try a more rustic version. *Ichigo daifuku* (strawberry *mochi*), a chewy rice cake wrapped around sweet red-bean paste and a juicy strawberry is another must-try. Just one more reason to visit Japan in springtime. *Oishii*!

BEST PLACES FOR SAKURA-VIEWING

- Fukuoka Castle, Kyūshū
- Himeji Castle, Kansai (p. 345)
- Hirosaki Castle, Tōhoku (p. 211)
- Japan Mint Tunnel and Yodogawa Riverside Park, Osaka, Kansai
- Mount Fuji, Shizuoka, Chūbu (p. 222)
- Mount Yoshino, Kantō
- Shinjuku Gyo-en, Ueno Park, Nakameguro Canal, Inokashira Park, Yanaka Cemetery, Yoyogi Park and Kitanomaru Park, Tokyo, Kantō
- Takayama City, Takayama, Chūbu
- The Philosopher's Path, Ninna-ji and Todai-ji, Kyoto, Kansai

SPRING FOODS

- Bamboo shoots
- Clams, mussels and sardines
- Hanami *dango*, sweet dumplings – typically eaten at Hanami picnics, and always served in threes: one pink, to symbolise cherry blossoms; one white, to symbolise snow; and one green, to symbolise grass
- Limited *sakura*-themed packaging for chocolate, beer, candy ... and everything else!
- Pink sake and pink champagne
- *Sakura* Kit Kats
- *Sakura onigiri*, rice balls with embedded *sakura* flowers
- *Sakura* soft-serve ice cream
- *Sakura wagashi*, extraordinarily detailed and artistic sweets with a *sakura* theme
- Stir-fried cabbage
- *Umeboshi*, pickled plums from the previous season's harvest

ABOVE: Stylish women at Kyoto Station, Kansai RIGHT: *Sakura* treats in Inokashira Park, Tokyo, Kantō OPPOSITE PAGE: Aoyama Cemetery, Tokyo, Kantō

ACCOMMODATION
IN JAPAN COMES IN
ALL SHAPES & SIZES

Places to stay

Accommodation that includes bed, bath, hospitality, dinner and breakfast has been a part of Japanese culture since 700 AD. Nishiyama Onsen Keiunkan in Yamanashi, which opened in 705 AD, has been owned by fifty-two generations of the same family and is still in operation today (*keiunkan.co.jp*).

STAYING IN A RYOKAN

When arriving at a *ryokan* you are typically served tea and *wagashi* (traditional sweets). You will then be shown to your room, and around the facilities (bath, garden, common areas). Your room will most likely have a tatami floor and *shōji* screens, although many modern versions now put a twist on the old ways.

The *ryokan* will set a breakfast and dinner time with you and let you know the bathing hours. In some *ryokan* you can reserve a private bath, others have male and female baths and some mixed-sex bathing. If you find your *ryokan* has mixed-sex baths, there will always be a ladies hour for those not group-naked inclined. When we stay in a *ryokan*, Michelle will always have three baths (depending on the baths): one on arrival, one after dinner and one in the morning, or sometimes up to five! Your room will have a *yukata* (casual summer kimono) and a *haori* (warm jacket) in winter.

If you're staying in an *onsen* (hot springs) town you may wear your *yukata* around town and visit some of the local bathhouses (we highly recommend this).

Dinner will be a myriad of small, delicious, beautifully presented courses. If you have any dietary requirements *ryokan* staff will try their best to accommodate you. Dinner can be served either in your room or in a common area along with sake or beer. After you eat, a walk around the *ryokan* grounds or the town before a bath is a perfect way to unwind. When you head back to your room, staff will have set up futon beds on the tatami floor.

Staying in a *ryokan* in an *onsen* area is one of life's highlights. Each trip to Japan we stay in a new *ryokan* in a country setting. Sometimes we'll spurge on a famous building with an amazing bath, then stay at inexpensive places for the rest of our trip, or we may choose a rustic *ryokan* that doesn't break the bank, perhaps with shared bathrooms in a difficult place to reach by public transport. The memories of *ryokan* stays are some of our most treasured, so whatever your budget, please spend a night in a *ryokan* and discover why this tradition has been around for more than 1300 years.

For other *onsen*, see 'Japan by Region', pp. 157–329. →

MEMORABLE RYOKAN

ARAI RYOKAN
Izu, Chūbu
arairyokan.net

HOSHI ONSEN CHOJUKAN
Hoshi Onsen, Kantō
hoshi-onsen.com

HOSHINOYA TOKYO
Tokyo, Kantō
hoshinoya.com/tokyo

IWASO
Miyajima, Chūgoku
iwaso.com

LAMP NO YADO
Noto Peninsula, Chūbu
lampnoyado.co.jp

RYOKAN SANGA
Kurokawa Onsen, Kyūshū
sanga-ryokan.com

SHOKINKAN
Yasugi, Chūgoku
japanican.com/en/hotel/detail/7318A02

YUEN BETTEI DAITA
Tokyo, Kantō
https://www.uds-hotels.com/en/yuenbettei/daita/

ALL IMAGES: Ryokan Sanga, Kurokawa Onsen, Kyūshū

LUXE SPECIAL-OCCASION EXPERIENCES

THE HOSHINOYA BRAND

When it comes to beautiful contemporary hotels, *ryokan*, glamping and *onsen ryokan*, no one does it better than the HOSHINOYA and Kai brands (*hoshinoya.com*). Every time we've stayed at one of their venues we've had a unique experience we'll remember forever. Whether it's your honeymoon, anniversary, or just the occasion of taking a holiday to Japan, booking a night (or five) at any of their fine establishments will give you both a deep cultural experience and a glimpse into *omotenashi* (Japanese hospitality). The *onsen* at Kai Hakone, the boat ride to HOSHINOYA Kyoto, bathing with a view of a Nebuta float at Aomoriya, glamping at HOSHINOYA Fuji, or the vast ceiling in the deep dark *onsen* at HOSHINOYA Tokyo Ryokan are all incredible experiences.

SEVEN STARS IN KYUSHU

The romance of train journeys is alive and well on Seven Stars in Kyushu (*cruisetrain-sevenstars. jp*; pp. 102 and 106). If you're looking for a luxury journey with a difference, Seven Stars has meticulously researched and designed a total experience encompassing interior design, cuisine showcasing local ingredients, the very best sights and more.

GLAMPING & YURTING

If you like a bit of a romp in the outdoors with only a thin piece of fabric between you and the elements, then glamping/yurting might be just the Japan experience you're looking for. They're located all over the country, and more and more are popping up each year. →

THIS PAGE: Seven Stars in Kyushu, Kyūshū
OPPOSITE PAGE: Steve at Takaragawa Onsen Osenkaku, Gunma, Kantō

CIRCUS OUTDOOR TOKYO
Tokyo, Kantō
circusoutdoor.com

FIELD SUITE HAKUBA KITAONE KOGEN
Hakuba, Chūbu
fieldsuite-hakuba.com

GLAMP ELEMENT
Yubinbango, Kansai
glamp-element.jp

HOSHINOYA FUJI
Yamanashi, Chūbu
hoshinoresorts.com/en/ resortsandhotels/hoshinoya/fuji.html

NAMEGATA FARMERS VILLAGE
Namegata, Kantō
farmglamping.namegata-fv.jp

RUGU ISLAND RESORT
Kurima Island, Okinawa
rugu.co.jp

TSUTSUJISO
Naoshima, Shikoku
tsutsujiso.com

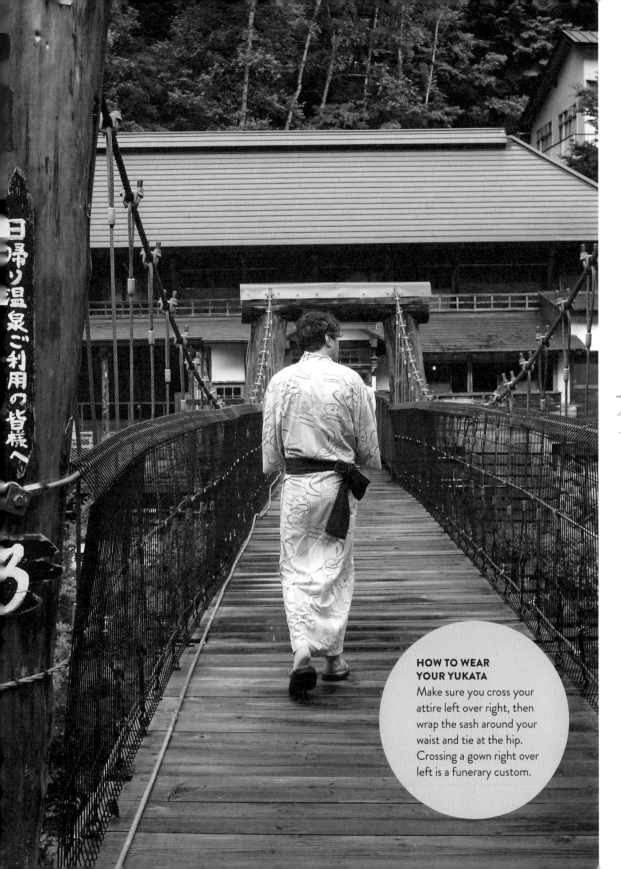

HOW TO WEAR YOUR YUKATA

Make sure you cross your attire left over right, then wrap the sash around your waist and tie at the hip. Crossing a gown right over left is a funerary custom.

CAPSULE HOTELS

BOOK AND BED
Tokyo and Kyoto
bookandbedtokyo.com/tokyo

CAPSULE HOTEL CITY CABIN BY NIKOH REFRE (MEN ONLY)
Sapporo, Hokkaidō
citycabin.info

CAPSULE INN
Sapporo, Hokkaidō
capsuleinn.com

FIRST CABIN
Tokyo and Tokyo Airports, Osaka and Osaka Airports, Kyoto, Fukuoka, Nagasaki, Niseko, Kanazawa, Nagoya and Wakayama
first-cabin.jp

NADESHIKO HOTEL SHIBUYA (WOMEN ONLY)
Tokyo, Kantō
nadeshiko-hotel.jp

NINE HOURS
Tokyo and Tokyo Airports, Osaka and Osaka Airports, Kyoto, Fukuoka, Sendai
ninehours.co.jp

WELLCABIN NAKASU
Fukuoka, Kyūshū
wellcabin.info/english.html

TEMPLE STAYS IN MOUNT KŌYA (SHUKUBO)

Mount Kōya or Kōyasan (p. 259), founded as a religious mountain in 816 AD, is the home of Shingon Buddhism and the gateway for religious pilgrimages. It's the perfect place to experience the simplicity of life at a temple, with *shōjin ryōri* vegetarian cuisine (p. 126), dawn meditation sessions, calligraphy classes, contemplation and a quiet atmosphere with mythical surroundings. If you're looking for a spiritual or wellness experience, the whole of the Kōyasan area has an atmosphere unlike anywhere else.

INFORMATION ON TEMPLE STAYS, SIGHTS AND ACTIVITIES
http://eng.shukubo.net/

HOMESTAYS

For a real insight into Japan, a homestay is a wonderful opportunity to talk to locals, ask questions and get advice on things that are off the tourist grid. It's also a great way to travel if you're on your own and want to dive head-first into the culture from an insider's perspective.
homestay.com/japan
homestay-in-japan.com/eng

HOSTELS

ARK HOSTEL
Osaka, Kansai
ark-osaka.jp

HOMEIKAN
Tokyo, Kantō
japaneseguesthouses.com

K'S HOUSE ITŌ ONSEN
Ito, Kantō
kshouse.jp/ito-e/index.html

THE PAX HOSTEL/ RECORDS/MORE
Osaka, Kansai
thepax.jp

THEMED HOTELS

ESPORTS HOTEL E-ZONE CYBERSPACE
Gaming floors and themed rooms, Osaka, Kansai

HENN NA HOTEL
Robot-staffed hotel, Tokyo, Kantō
h-n-h.jp

HOTEL GRACERY
Godzilla theme, Tokyo, Kantō
gracery.com/shinjuku

KEIO PLAZA HOTEL
Hello Kitty–themed rooms, Tokyo, Kantō
www.keioplaza.com

SUPERSTAR ARCHITECT HOTELS

GARDEN TERRACE NAGASAKI
NAGASAKI, KYŪSHŪ
By Kengo Kuma
gt-nagasaki.jp

HOTEL KEYFOREST
Hokuto, Kobuchizawa, Chūbu
By Atsushi Kitagawara
kob-art.com/hotel

KYOTO PIECE HOSTEL
Kyoto, Kansai
By Highspot Design
piecehostel.com

SETOUCHI RETREAT AONAGI
Matsuyama, Shikoku
Tadao Ando gallery-turned-hotel overlooking the magnificent Seto Inland Sea.
setouchi-aonagi.com

SKYE NISEKO
Niseko, Hokkaidō
By Koichi Ishiguro/ISA Architects and Architectus
skyeniseko.com

→

ABOVE LEFT: Setouchi Retreat Aonagi, Matsuyama, Shikoku RIGHT: Nadeshiko Hotel Shibuya, Tokyo, Kantō OPPOSITE PAGE: Clare and Michelle at Nadeshiko Hotel Shibuya, Tokyo, Kantō

REVERSIBLE DESTINY LOFTS

The colourful and unusual architecture of the Reversible Destiny Lofts (*www.rdloftsmitaka. com*) in suburban Mitaka, Tokyo, was conceived in dedication to Helen Keller by architects Shusaku Arakawa and Madeline Gins. With floors that dip and rise and a roof and surfaces that subtly slant, it has spaces where children may feel more at home than adults, a blind person can experience more than a sighted person and an older person is more comfortable than a teenager. You'll think about your body in a new way after staying here – it will awaken all of your senses. If you're a fan of Escher or Hundertwasser, here's another chance to enter an artwork. With a colour palette to delight the senses, each zone showing a new way to see the everyday and mundane, this is the perfect Tokyo Airbnb accommodation for the curious at heart. Oh, and this is where Shoshanna lived in her Tokyo episode of *Girls*, and it's close to the Ghibli Museum! Two apartments are available through Airbnb – the rest are long-term rentals.

AIRBNB

Airbnb has some wonderful and interesting accommodation options around Japan: it's a way to get to know a city with the help of your host rather than follow the tourist track. Under 'More filters' click 'Unique stays' to find accommodation in barns, airstreams and campervans, campsites and boats.

ART STAYS

BENESSE HOUSE
Naoshima, Shikoku
Tadao Ando–designed hotel on Naoshima art island (p. 292).
benesse-artsite.jp/en/stay/ benessehouse

ECHIGO-TSUMARI ART FIELD
Niigata, Chūbu
Sleep in an artwork.
echigo-tsumari.jp/eng/facility/stay

PARK HOTEL TOKYO
Tokyo, Kantō
Has artist-themed rooms.
parkhoteltokyo.com/ja

LOVE HOTELS (RABUHO)

Japan has more than 30,000 love hotels, designed for couples to get 'cosy'. These intimate spaces can range from quirky and eclectic to straight-up utilitarian. If you're not a couple in need of 'couples time', a hotel charging by the hour is a great place to rest (*shukuhaku*) or even stay the night.

Love hotels are typically grouped together in big cities, so head to one of the designated areas and take your pick. Many come with a big bath, kooky interior design, colour themes, anime themes, karaoke facilities, vending machines, and so much more. Some love hotels are now included on international hotel booking sites.

TOKYO LOVE HOTEL AREAS
Around Kabukicho, Shinjuku, Love Hotel Hill Dogenzaka, Shibuya, Roppongi and Ikebukuro. Stand-outs include Hotel Zebra, Hotel Sara Sweet and Hotel & Spa J-mex.

OSAKA LOVE HOTEL AREAS
Osaka opened Japan's first love hotel, Hotel Love, in the 1960s. The best *rabuho* clusters are around Umeda, east of Namba Nankai Station, Nipponbashi and Tennoji. Hotel Love is still in operation, although in a revamped format.

AROUND JAPAN
Hotel Princess Cinderella, Kyoto, Kansai; Hotel Fairy Iwatsuki, Saitama, Kantō.

SUPER SENTŌ OR DAY-RATE ONSEN

Day-rate super *sentō* (man-made hot-spring baths) or *onsen* (natural hot springs) will often be open twenty-three hours (shutting sometime between 8 and 11 am for cleaning). They have great relaxation spaces with big cosy seats, restaurants, vending machines and more, so why not stretch out and stay the night? Look for big complexes and check the opening hours and the late-night fee. They can be great places to crash after a messy night out – just make sure you're sober when you arrive.

HEIWAJIMA ONSEN
Haneda, Kantō
heiwajima-onsen.jp

OOEDO ONSEN MONOGATARI
Tokyo, Kantō
daiba.ooedoonsen.jp

SPA LAQUA
Tokyo, Kantō
www.laqua.jp

SPA WORLD
Osaka, Kansai
spaworld.co.jp

TERIHA SPA RESORT
Fukuoka, Kyūshū
terihaspa.jp

OPPOSITE PAGE: Reversible Destiny Lofts, Mitaka, Tokyo, Kantō ABOVE: Shibuya love hotel district, Tokyo, Kantō

THIS PAGE: HOSHINOYA Kyoto, Arashiyama, Kansai **OPPOSITE PAGE:** Naoshima art island, Shikoku

Ryokan mini break

MICHELLE AND HER FRIENDS CLARE AND ARMELLE TAKE A GIRLS' OWN TRIP TO JAPAN

We organised to stay at HOSHINOYA Kyoto in Arashiyama (p. 245) after researching its remote location, Zen garden, riverside views and beautiful rooms. We were looking for a Japanese cultural and wellness experience, but what we actually got was so much more. After staying overnight at the airport due to a rogue typhoon, we arrived having had no sleep and feeling a little bit the worse for wear.

Our magical transformation started at the boat terminal, where we enjoyed tea and *wagashi* (traditional sweets; p. 140) in the waiting area while the staff relieved us of our bags ahead of the much-anticipated journey. A small wooden boat arrived, and we boarded and took our seats for the slow tranquil journey down the Ōigawa River to the *ryokan* (traditional inn; p. 87). The building itself is more than 100 years old; Rie Azuma's sensitive modernisation of the buildings has kept many of the original features intact. Upon arrival a staff member was playing Buddhist musical instruments in time with the waterfall behind her.

We were shown around the property, then collapsed in our room, taking a shower and putting on the room wear (my favourite thing about travelling to Japan!). The room's wide window overlooking the river gave us a soundtrack of rustling trees and temple bells, and a view of the mountains and a small scenic railway. We drifted around the grounds, having tea on the deck or balcony, reading books in the floating tea room, and enjoying sake and *wagashi* in Salon & Bar Kura. Our favourite time of day was when the afternoon light made beautiful shadows on our room's bright-blue walls, the twisty-turning pathways started to light up with lanterns, and the smell of the forest and the river calmed our senses.

Dinner was of course sublime, and after a heavenly sleep the incredible in-room Japanese breakfast was a favourite moment of our whole trip. A dawn meditation and mid-morning incense appreciation class gave us a deeper understanding of Japanese culture. This was such a memorable experience to have with friends, time away from everyday life and work pressures.

The ease and politeness of the staff ensured our every question and need was answered and exceeded. When we hopped back on the boat for the fifteen-minute ride back to reality, we were already plotting our next visit.

MORE THAN
JUST 'A TO B'

Train journeys

Densha, or *den* for short, is train in Japanese. The wonderful world of *densha* has something for every personality: kooky character rides, large scenic windows, luxury sleepers. Riding on a train has so many joys built in. First, *ekiben* or train *bentō* are nothing short of incredible, and drinking alcohol on a longer train ride is definitely a thing. For local commutes there are female-only carriages, incredibly fast and efficient subways, and stations with amenities as extensive as small cities.

ABOVE: Osaka Station, Osaka, Kansai **OPPOSITE PAGE:** *Tamago sando* and vitamin drink

SOME TIPS BEFORE WE START

THE SCHEDULE

We always book trains at least a day ahead of our journey. Allow at least half an hour at the station (with a booked ticket) for *ekiben*, drink and *omiyage* (regional souvenir; p. 109) purchasing.

THE STATIONS

Large Shinkansen (bullet train) stations will have all your needs (and more) covered. Small stations can be so charming you'll wonder how your hometown could acquire some of this magic (Naruko-Gotenyu and Randen-Arashiyama stations are favourites).

EKIBEN

These train *bentō* boxes are one of our favourite Japanese experiences and something we try and recreate at home on a weekly basis. Compartmentalised boxes with all five food groups represented, plus all the regional specialties, make a delicious lunch, dinner or snack. It's one of the true joys of Japanese train travel.

Each region has its own specialties, so for a very low price you can travel the country with your JR Pass and sample the country's varied cuisine through *bentō*. For a traditional local *bentō*, look on the packaging for sights of the city you're visiting. Spending a few extra yen on your *bentō* is highly recommended, especially in towns known for their fish or beef products. →

GENERAL RAIL-TRAVEL TIPS

Reserve your seat – it's free if you have a JR Pass. There are non-reserved carriages, but you're not guaranteed a seat.

Ask to sit on the side with Mount Fuji views if you are travelling from Tokyo to Kyoto (or vice versa).

Consider getting off the train at one of the connecting stations on your journey and popping your luggage in storage for a few hours. An unexpected adventure awaits!

Stations typically open at 5–5.30 am and close around midnight.

ONLINE SCHEDULING

Enter your A to B stations into your search engine and choose a website to help you make plans. Screen-grab the best connections (yes there are good and bad ones), then take them with you to the ticket counter or machine to book your ride.

EXITS

If you get off a train with a destination in mind, make sure you've researched the exit you need to take. Or find a large map inside the station before you leave; if you can pinpoint your destination you can find the right station exit. Some stations like Shinjuku in Tokyo have 200 exits. If you're at a smaller station, look for north (*kita* 北), south (*minami* 南), east (*higashi* 東) and west (*nishi* 西).

BAGGAGE LOCKERS

All stations have lockers to store your bags for the day. Lockers come in three sizes on a sliding price scale. Larger stations have multi-day baggage services and also lockers you can use for up to three days. See Tokyo Station's website for an example. Remember to do your research and find out the locker situation before you travel. Many busy stations are popular places to store bags and luggage (think Shibuya Station in Tokyo, Namba in Osaka or Shijo in Kyoto), so it's a good idea to arrive early to find an empty locker if you're leaving your bags for the day.

TIP

If you're not sure, get a *bentō* with many compartments. There'll be things you like there as well as a few discoveries.

Ō-bentō

Bentō and *ekiben* (train *bentō*) are an essential part of Japanese
food culture and an amazing experience for any traveller in Japan.

Kyoto Station's seasonal *ekiben*

A *bentō* is a segmented box featuring a variety of small tasty dishes in each compartment. Climbing aboard a train with a few hours' journey ahead of you, clutching a colourful *bentō* and a can of booze, is a great joy. Opening the *bentō*, discovering what's inside and how it's laid out, then tucking in while Japan's spectacular vistas roll past your window – what could be better?

Bentō boxes are many and varied, depending on which part of the country you are in, featuring fantastic-shaped packaging or regional icons. A good tip to ensure you get the regional specialty is to buy the *bentō* with the prominent feature of the area you're in on the cover.

Ekiben stores can be found in stations and often on station platforms, so have a look around and see what appeals. Shop around main station hubs, particularly in Kyoto and Tokyo, where there is a wealth of choice. It could be delicious, it could be unusual, but it will always be an experience! Ekiben-ya Matsuri ('Train Bentō Festival') at Tokyo Station now has English descriptions of their *bentō* for those who are hesitant to take a risk ... *Bentō* can also be bought in department stores or specialist shops, and enjoyed for lunch or dinner.

STEVE'S TOP EKIBEN

AJI OSHIZUSHI (ŌFUNA STATION, KANTŌ)
The local *oshizushi* (pressed sushi) horse mackerel *ekiben* is an all-time Japanese favourite and dates back more than 100 years.

DARUMA EKIBEN (TAKASAKI, KANTŌ)
A *bentō* shaped like a *daruma* (p. 339) filled with delicious vegetables. As an added bonus, it has a money slot and gets a second life as a piggy bank.

EBI SENRYOU CHIRASHI (NIIGATA STATION, CHŪBU)
Niigata's bestseller, this *bentō* is a seafood overload. It's not subtle – slabs of omelette cover prawns (*ebi*), grilled eel, shredded kelp, spotted shad, sashimi and squid.

KAISEN EZO-SHOMI (SAPPORO STATION, HOKKAIDŌ)
Sushi rice with crab, salmon, *ikura* (fish roe) and *uni* (sea urchin) make this *ekiben* one of Japan's top sellers.

KYOTO GYUZEN (KYOTO STATION, KANSAI)
Kyoto's delicious *suguki* pickles and black *shichimi* rice are added to teriyaki beef and shredded omelette. Look for the image of the Toji Pagoda on the box.

MEAT YAZAWA KUROGE WAGYU HAMBURG BENTŌ (TOKYO, KANTŌ)
One of Tokyo Station's most popular *bentō*. You can try a selection of patties from the famed 'Blacows' restaurant in Yuzawa.

RED SNOW CRAB BENTŌ (SHIN-HAKODATE-HOKUTO STATION, HOKKAIDŌ)
Sweet morsels of the famous local crab in the shell on rice with egg, pickles, crab miso and crab butter. Hakodate is known for its *bentō*.

SABU SUGATAZUSHI BENTŌ (KYOTO STATION, KANSAI)
Nara's sushi specialty is vinegar and salt mackerel wrapped in persimmon leaves, and Kyoto Station has it presented in a jewel-like box. Michelle's favourite.

SELF-HEATING BEEF BENTŌ (ALL OVER JAPAN)
The prefectural beef specialty in a *bentō* with a string attached that you pull for instant steaming heat.

SHAMOJI KAKIMESHI (HIROSHIMA STATION, CHŪGOKU)
At Hiroshima Station you can get this delight from Ajiroya, one of Japan's oldest *ekiben* businesses. Shaped like a *shamoji* (rice scoop), it features many of Hiroshima's specialties, such as oysters in citrus miso, omelette and rice cooked in oyster soup.

SHINKANSEN E7 KEI BENTŌ (TOKYO STATION, KANTŌ)
Tokyo Station's children's *bentō* is a replica of the Shinkansen. The kids will enjoy an East-meets-West selection that includes a frankfurt and two *onigiri* (rice balls) among other treats. Keep the pack afterwards as your own *bentō* bullet train!

TAN TON BENTŌ (SENDAI STATION, TŌHOKU)
Grilled beef tongue is a feature of this *ekiben*, which also includes pork over rice – and it's self-heating!

TOGE NO KAMA-MESHI (KARUIZAWA STATION, CHŪBU)
With a fifty-year history, this *ekiben* is cooked and sold in a ceramic bowl and features chicken, burdock, shiitake, bamboo and quail eggs on rice, cooked in a rich soup (the recipe is a long-guarded secret).

TOSHIE GOZEN (KANAZAWA STATION, CHŪBU)
Toshie Gozen are immaculate two-tiered *ekiben* that showcase Kanazawa's flavours, packaged as an irresistible train feast. Expect Kanazawa staples like fresh seafood, croquettes, rice and even *wagashi* (traditional sweets).

TOILETS

Shinkansen and some fast trains have toilets on board, while train stations (like Shinagawa in Tokyo) have incredible set-ups with powder rooms and all the latest mod cons. Some rural and older stations just have 'Japanese toilets' in the floor for women – with a bit of trickery and agility you can balance over it (tough if you're wearing stockings). Okay, this is already too much information! What you need to know is the toilet door will often have signs for Japanese or Western so you can wait in line for the Western version. Many toilets will have instructions and flush buttons in Japanese: 大 for a 'big flush' and 小 for a 'small flush'. Other type that means flush is 流す and ながす.

SOME POPULAR TRAIN PASSES

Japan Rail owns most of the large routes throughout the country, but many subway systems and smaller lines are owned by private companies. If you have a JR Pass it will be valid in large cities on a few lines but most of your daily travel will be through private lines. Kyoto, Tokyo and Osaka, for example, have subways where you cannot use your JR Pass. These local lines will have discounted day or multi-day passes.

SUICA OR PASMO IC CARD

Buy a Suica or Pasmo card from train station machines. Load it up with yen whenever you're running low and use it on one of the many private train lines or on buses anywhere in the country. You can even use it to buy snacks in a convenience store and many other places throughout Japan.

ZERO-WASTE TIPS

Sonno mama de ii in Japanese means 'as it is': without the plastic bags and extra packaging. To ask for 'without chopsticks', use the phrase *o hashi nashi*.

QUIRKY STATIONS

RANDEN-ARASHIYAMA STATION, KYOTO, KANSAI

This gorgeous little private station has a path lit by kimono patterned poles (come at night) to the tracks and a small foot *onsen* (*ashiyu*) on the actual station.

DOAI STATION, MINAKAMI, KANTŌ

This unattended kind-of-brutalist-triangular-looking station requires a ten-minute walk inside a mountain tunnel to reach the platform. One of the most unique experiences you can have in Japan – it's definitely about the destination, not the journey.

KEIO TAKAOSANGUCHI STATION, TOKYO, KANTŌ

This station houses an incredible *onsen*, designed by architect Kengo Kuma (p. 353). Train timetables are displayed from the baths, so you'll never miss your ride (or just miss it and plan for the next one).

www.takaosan-onsen.jp/english

TAKADANOBABA STATION, TOKYO, KANTŌ

This Tokyo area near Shinjuku is the home of Astro Boy (p. 50). You can find a mural at the entrance, and the theme song plays as trains arrive and depart.

KIZUKURI STATION, AOMORI, TŌHOKU

At the tip-top of Honshū, the exterior of this station, built in 1924 (the Taishō era; p. 38) is home to Shako-chan, a nearly eighteen-metre, sturdy, almost brutalist figure – a replica of the Jōmon period's most famous piece of pottery (see also p. 14) – whose eyes light up when trains are approaching (or whenever she mysteriously feels like making a statement). The architect also threw in a triangular window (a reference to the pyramid craze of the 1920s, no doubt).

THE TRAINS

LOCAL TRAINS

Many local lines are run privately, and some boast the most charming and comfortable rides. In Kyoto, for example, Steve loves the Keihan Main Line and Michelle loves the Eizan Line. Other private lines are Hankyu, Kintetsu, Tobu, Odakyu – the list goes on.

EXPRESS TRAINS

In big cities like Tokyo, Osaka and Kyoto, there are limited-express and express trains for commuters to get to the outer city a little bit faster. In Tokyo, the Sōbu Rapid, Inokashira Rapid and Tōkyū Tōyoko Rapid are just a few that may make your day travel that little bit faster.

SHINKANSEN (BULLET TRAINS)

Developed for the 1964 Tokyo Olympics to transport citizens around the country at unparalleled speeds, Shinkansen have been much copied and admired – and gone from strength to strength. A bullet train journey will be a highlight of your Japanese adventure. →

JR PASS

If you're thinking of doing a bit of travelling, the seven-, fourteen- or twenty-one-day pass will save you both time and money. Buy before you leave from a travel agent or online (or pay a bit more and buy in Japan). All seats are reserved, so line up at a large JR office at the airport or one of the main stations in the area you're travelling and book a few trains in advance. Make sure you keep your JR Pass close: it's non-refundable and you must show it whenever asked. It does not allow travel on the fastest Shinkansen Nozomi or Mizuho rides, so look out for Hikari, Sakura, Tsubame and Kodama for your fast rail travel.

japan-rail-pass.com.au/common-questions/where-to-activate-japan-rail-pass

TOKYO WIDE PASS

Use this three-day pass to visit areas such as Hakone, Mount Fuji, Nikkō, Karuizawa, Takasaki, and Narita and Haneda airports.

www.jreast.co.jp/e/tokyowidepass

REGIONAL PASSES

Check Japan Rail's website for fantastic regional passes at great prices, including Kyūshū, Kansai, Shikoku, Hokkaidō and Tōhoku. Many of these passes are flexible (e.g. can be used for any four days within a ten-day period), which makes for a leisurely trip.

GREEN CAR

For an extra fee, the green car provides comfort and sometimes a seat when the main train carriages are full to the brim. JR Green passes are also available and recommended if you're travelling in Golden Week (p. 83), or need to be comfortable when travelling. Trains in Japan are clean and efficient, so going green is not mandatory; it just provides that little extra level of comfort.

OPPOSITE PAGE: Tama train, Wakayama, Kansai ABOVE: Naruko-Gotenyu Station, Tōhoku

The romance of rail

KEITARO OSAJIMA, KYUSHU RAILWAY COMPANY
WWW.CRUISETRAIN-SEVENSTARS.JP

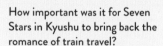

How important was it for Seven Stars in Kyushu to bring back the romance of train travel?

Our company's chairman, Koji Karaike, came up with the idea of a cruise train, and with designer Eiji Mitooka made the idea come true. Together they pondered the meaning of luxury, and decided they wanted to create a modern yet classic atmosphere that retained its appeal over time. The Seven Stars concept is 'A journey to discover a new way of life, to discover the beauty of Kyūshū'. We want to give guests the opportunity to meet new people, to think about their partner and family, to look back on their lives, to find rich emotions inside. We think romance has an important part to play in this.

Tell us about your designer and the reason he was chosen for this important job.

The designer, Eiji Mitooka, has worked with the Kyushu Railway Company for years. He has designed many other unique trains for our company, such as the A-train, Umisachi Yamasachi, Ibusuki no Tamatebako, and so on. They are

ingredients and who have an emotional connection to Kyūshū. We serve not only Japanese cuisine, but also Western cuisine, such as a French full-course menu, or Western fusion-style Japanese food. Each room has an Arita pottery washbasin, made by the late Sakaida Kakiemon XIV, a National Treasure. Some of the interiors were made by Imaizumi Imaemon XIV, a Living National Treasure, and traditional handcrafted Kumiko latticework can be seen throughout the train. They are all impeccable works.

How important is the service? From our experience, service and kindness are some of the reasons we fell in love with your country.

As you say, the level of hospitality seems to be quite high in Japan, but we want the service on Seven Stars to be the best in the world. Staff have extensive team training before becoming official crew members, as their hospitality is the most important aspect of Seven Stars. Some guests come back to Seven Stars again and again because they love those crew members like their own family and enjoy their hospitality throughout the journey so much.

What kind of unique Japanese experiences would Seven Stars offer a design- and food-focused international traveller?

For design-lovers, the train itself is appealing. Once you step inside, you will notice the dedication and attention to detail of the people who made this train. And yet it's very functional. For food-lovers, they will find that even the French cuisine we serve has a Japanese and historical influence. The sushi and Japanese cuisine is also creative and authentic. All of our food uses Kyūshū's local ingredients, because Kyūshū has the best of the best when it comes to produce. Many restaurants in Tokyo use Kyūshū's ingredients. Why not enjoy them even fresher and tastier on board?

very popular trains and unique selling points for our company. So he was really the only one who could make this happen. Seven Stars would be the culmination of his work for us.

Are international travel agents able to book for their customers?

We already have several travel agents working for us internationally, and we've been welcoming international

guests since we launched. Really, Seven Stars was built to promote not only our company but Kyūshū island to the world.

We're huge fans of Kyūshū food and crafts. Tell us about the Kyūshū cuisine and local artists' work on board.

We selected the finest chefs in Kyūshū, who are proud of local

CHARACTER TRAINS

ANPANMAN TRAIN

Ride this beloved character train on the island of Shikoku.

Takamatsu to Matsuyama, Shikoku
shikoku-railwaytrip.com/railinfo.html

GEGEGE NO KITARO

A super-popular character in Japan, this train will be full of locals and serious fans making a pilgrimage.
Sakaiminato, Chūgoku
en.japantravel.com/tottori/gegege-no-kitaro/1563

HELLO KITTY TRAIN

Check timings when planning your trip to avoid disappointment – this train is very popular.
Shin-Osaka Station, Kansai, to Hakata Station, Kyūshū
jrailpass.com/blog/hello-kitty-shinkansen

KINTETSU IKOMA CABLE LINE (DOG, CAT AND CAKE CARRIAGES)

This cute and colourful train journey takes you to an incredible temple or an amusement park built in 1928, past beautiful scenery.

Ikoma Station to Hozan-ji, Kansai
visitnara.jp/venues/A00947

KUMAMON TRAIN

This cute bear-themed train travels around Kumamoto. The yellow train is particularly kawaii (cute)!

Kumamoto, Kyūshū
kumamotodentetsu.co.jp

LIMITED EXPRESS ASO BOY

Each carriage has its own fun theme on this stylishly designed train. On your trip, visit the library, café and children's play area featuring a play pool filled with small wooden balls.

Kumamoto to Miyaji, Kyūshū (weekend service only)
www.jrkyushu.co.jp/english/train/asoboy.html

POKÉMON

Ride the Pokémon-themed train in Tōhoku. Board two and half hours from Tokyo at Ichinoseki Station.

Ichinoseki to Kasennuna, Tōhoku
www.jrailpass.com/blog/pokemon-with-you-train

WAKAYAMA ELECTRIC RAILWAY (CAT TRAIN, 'TAMA DENSHA')

A cat station master and cat-themed train and station (see also p. 107). The Tama train has a cat-themed library on board and also has ears – as does the station!
Wakayama to Kishi, Kansai
wakayama-dentetsu.co.jp/en

ABOVE: Slurping noodles at the station
OPPOSITE PAGE LEFT: Yufuin No Mori interior RIGHT: Matsuyama Station, Shikoku

LANDSCAPE & NATURE TRAINS

ENODEN

This lovely local train weaves in and out of tiny streets and neighbourhoods with view of the sea, the Enoshima Sea Candle (p. 177) and Mount Fuji (p. 222) on a clear day.

Kamakura to Fujisawa, Kantō
enoden.co.jp/en/train

HISATSU LINE

From Kaiji Station, Kyūshū
hisatsusen.com/01history/index_e.html

KUROBE GORGE

Unazuki Station, Japanese Alps, Chūbu
www.kurotetu.co.jp

LIMITED EXPRESS YUFUIN NO MORI

A beautifully designed mountain train with a fantastic forest-themed on-board library, delicious *bentō* and amazing forest textiles on the seats. We caught this stunning green train from Yufuin to Beppu after a day soaking in hot springs.

Hakata to Beppu via Yufuin, Kyūshū
www.jrkyushu.co.jp/english/train/yufuin_no_mori.html

TRAIN AROUND LAKE BIWA

A great Kyoto daytrip in a gorgeous, newly designed train.

From Kyoto, Kansai
kyotostation.com/jr-biwako-line-for-otsu-omi-hachiman-hikone-the-hokuriku-region

WIDE VIEW HIDA TRAIN

Nagoya to Takayama, Chūbu (p. 213)
nagoyastation.com/the-limited-express-hida-for-gifu-gero-takayama-toyama

SUMMER TRAINS

FURANO BIEI NOROKKO TRAIN (LAVENDER EXPRESS)

Sapporo to Furano, Hokkaidō
July to mid-October
jprail.com/trains/sort-by-type/limited-express

HIMI LINE (TOYAMA)

Takaoka Station to Himi Station (Toyama), Chūbu
japan-rail-pass.com.au/japan-by-rail/travel-tips/himi-line

AUTUMN TRAINS

EIZAN RAILWAY TO KURAMA MAPLE LEAF TUNNEL

Demachiyanagi to Yase-Hieizanguchi or Kurama, Kyoto, Kansai
eizandensha.co.jp

JR RIKUU-TO LINE

Furukawa to Naruko Onsen (and bus to Naruko Gorge), Tōhoku
tohokuandtokyo.org/spot_31 →

WINTER TRAINS

GONO LINE, AKITA
Aomori to Akita, Tōhoku

www.jreast.co.jp/e/joyful/shirakami.html

TŌHOKU EMOTION
Hachinohe to Kuji, Tōhoku

www.jreast.co.jp/e/joyful/tohoku.html

WIDE VIEW HIDA TRAIN
Nagoya to Takayama, Chūbu (p. 105)

SPRING TRAINS

CHERRY BLOSSOM TRAINS
Japan Rail recommends: Tsugaru
Railway (Tōhoku); Mooka Railway
(Kantō); Oigawa Railway (Chūbu);
Sagano Scenic Railway (Kansai);
Yosan Line (Shikoku).

HANWA LINE
Osaka to Wakayama, Kansai
osakastation.com/the-jr-hanwa-
line-kishuji-rapid-service-for-otori-
hineno-wakayama

KOMINATO RAILWAY
Chiba, Kantō
kominato.co.jp/satoyamatorocco/
index-e.html

GLAMOROUS & HIGH-END EXPERIENCES

SEVEN STARS IN KYUSHU
Travelling the seven prefectures
of Kyūshū in style, this incredible
train has a luxe vintage feel, with a
nostalgic nod to the age when train
travel was glamorous and romantic
(see also pp. 88, 102). Stopping
at the very best cultural sites and
cities, with beautiful scenery,
exquisite food and so much more,
this overnight train only takes
applications in certain months
online. Options include two days,
one night or four days, three nights.

www.cruisetrain-sevenstars.jp

SHIKI-SHIMA
Designed by revered industrial
designer Ken Okuyama, the Shiki-
shima varies in its routes, so check
online for the latest information.

Ueno, Tokyo, Kantō, through the
Tōhoku region
Options include four days, three
nights or two days, one night.
www.jreast.co.jp/shiki-shima

SUNRISE SETO & SUNRISE IZUMO
You can use you JR Pass on these
sleeper trains for the Nobi Nobi
Seat, a partitioned carpeted area
where you can lie down, have a
shower and enjoy one of the last
sleeper trains in Japan. There are
more private rooms for an extra
fee. Both trains visit areas of Japan
that are a little off-the-grid but
definitely worth your time. Izumo
and its surrounding prefectures
hold some of our dearest memories
of travelling in Japan.

Overnight train from Tokyo, Kantō,
to Takamatsu, Shikoku, or
Izumo, Chūkogu
jprail.com/trains/sort-by-type/
limited-express/sunrise-seto.html

TŌHOKU SHINKANSEN GRAN CLASS
This is first-class train travel at
its finest. If you have a regular
or Green JR Pass you can pay to
upgrade to Gran Class. All food
and drinks are included.

Tokyo to Shin-Aomori
jrailpass.com/blog/shinkansen-
gran-class

TWILIGHT EXPRESS MIZUKAZE
An Art Deco–inspired train
travelling along the coast.

Kyoto Station, Kansai, to
Higashihama, Matsue and
Okayama, Chūgoku
twilightexpress-mizukaze.jp/en/
cars/index.html

TRADITIONAL CULTURE TRAINS

HANAYOME NOREN
The interior of this poppy red train
showcases the traditional crafts of
the Hokuriku area, including gold
leaf, lacquerware and silk-dyeing.

Kanazawa Station to Wakura
Onsen, Chūbu
www.westjr.co.jp/global/en/train/
hanayomenoren

KYO TRAIN GARAKU
The Hankyu Line's stylish
traditional train from Osaka to
Kyoto. Each carriage has a different
design (we love cars 3 and 4).

Hankyu Umeda (Osaka) to Kyoto,
Kansai (weekends and holidays only)
hankyu.co.jp/global/en/
characteristic/special_specification_
train/index.html

STYLISH & DESIGNER TRAINS

LIMITED EXPRESS SONIC (883 AND 885 SERIES)
This is one of our all-time favourite
train rides. There are metallic-blue
and white versions of this tilt train,
so you'll need to book two trips
to try both! We book green car
(p. 101) seats for this journey, then
sink back and relax in the leather
'Mickey Mouse ear' seats.

Hakato to Oita via Beppu, Kyūshū
www.jrkyushu.co.jp/english/train/
sonic.html

LIMITED EXPRESS UMISACHI YAMASACHI
This train along the island coast
has an incredible wooden-and-
patterned-textile interior (with
cabinets featuring local toys).

Miyazaki to Nichinan, Kyūshū
www.jrkyushu.co.jp/english/train/
umisachiyamasachi.html

TOKYO DAYTRIP ROMANCE

FUJI EXCURSION TRAIN

A new direct service between Shinjuku and Mount Fuji. All the changeovers usually render this journey extremely unromantic, so this direct route provides welcome relief. It's partially covered by the JR Pass – ask at the station for the additional fee.

Shinjuku, Tokyo, Kantō, to Mount Fuji, Chūbu
jrailpass.com/blog/fuji-excursion-train

LIMITED EXPRESS SPACIA

We pay an extra surcharge for a 'compartment room' on this lovely journey. The train also has a kiosk on board.

Asakusa (Tokyo) to Nikkō and Kinugawa Onsen, Kantō
www.tobu.co.jp/foreign/en/using/express/spacia.html

THE ROMANCECAR

Hakone itself is a romantic destination, but we're still trying to find the 'romance' in the Romance train (Steve says bring your own romance)! Lack of romance is made up for with the *kawaii* mini Romancecar-shaped *bentō*.

Shinjuku to Hakone
odakyu.jp/english/romancecar

LOOK OUT FOR

The new earthquake-proof Alfa-X Shinkansen will travel at speeds of around 400 kilometres per hour. The new Maglev (magnetic levitation) train hovers above the tracks and is even faster! Hold onto your hat at the station when this new train pulls into town.

jrailpass.com/blog/alfa-x-shinkansen-bullet-train

SL GINGA

A steam locomotive themed around Kenji Miyazawa's novel *Night on the Galactic Railroad*, this vintage-looking train has an optical planetarium, galleries, cosy vintage seats and many other wonders!

Hanamaki to Kamaishi, Tōhoku
visitiwate.com/article/4799

WAKAYAMA ELECTRIC RAILWAY

Wakayama pulls out all the stops with its wonderful cat (Tama I and II; p. 104), *omoden* (toys), *umeboshi* (sour plum) and *ichigo* (strawberry) themed trains. The Umeboshi train is one of the most stylish trains we've ever seen – we talked about getting a tiny house made in its image. Please visit! At Wakayama Station you need to find platform 9 (almost 9¾).

Wakayama to Kishi, Kansai
wakayama-dentetsu.co.jp

ABOVE: Shinkansen train station

Omiyage

Buying omiyage (regional souvenirs) for friends and family is a serious tradition in Japan. Airports and train stations will have favourite city and prefecture handicraft, food and drink products. If you're taking presents home for loved ones, regional omiyage come with built-in stories.

CHŪBU

- Echizen – Washi paper
- Fuji Five Lakes (p. 221) – Mount Fuji souvenirs
- Kanazawa (p. 214) – Gold-leaf sake
- Kiso Valley (p. 231) – Kiso rice buckets
- Shizuoka (p. 227) – Matcha
- Takayama (p. 224) – *Ittobori* yew-wood carving (small wooden carvings of seed pods and animals)
- Yamanaka (p. 227) – Lacquerware

CHŪGOKU

- Hiroshima (p. 264) – Kumano *fude* (painting, calligraphy and make-up brushes)
- Tottori (p. 275) – *Hakota Ningyo* handmade paper dolls

HOKKAIDŌ

- Sapporo (p. 281) – Packaged soup curry and ramen

KANSAI

- Kinosaki Onsen (p. 261) – Bath salts
- Kyoto (p. 234) – *Wagashi* (traditional sweets; 140), incense, Yojiya facial papers, geisha make-up brushes
- Nara (p. 250) – tea whisks
- Osaka (p. 252) – *Randoseru* (school bags)
- Uji (p. 249) – Matcha

KANTŌ

- Mashiko (p. 183) – Pottery and indigo-dyed fabric
- Takasaki (p. 188) – *Daruma* everything

- Tokyo (p. 162) – Tokyo Banana
- Hakone (p. 184) – *Yosegi* marquetry

KYŪSHŪ

- Beppu (p. 316) and Ōita (p. 329) – *Kobosu* (Japanese citrus) products, woven baskets
- Hita – *Geta* sandals

SHIKOKU

- Naoshima (p. 292) – Yayoi Kusama keyrings

TŌHOKU

- Morioka (p. 200) – Nambu Tekki ironware, grass brooms
- Naruko Onsen (p. 204) – *Kokeshi* dolls

ALL IMAGES: Regional omiyage including premium fruits and *kokeshi* dolls, Naruko Onsen, Tōhoku

CULINARY JAPAN

Food is one of the best reasons to travel to Japan. It is a thrill to discover new tastes and new flavours, to see unique ingredients combined with the attention to detail and consummate cooking skills in which the chefs and home cooks of Japan take pride. This is a place where the art of food and drink has been perfected over hundreds of years, and it's this constant culinary exploration that has led to some true classics. Eating in Japan you'll find new loves, some challenges and plenty to learn. Some dishes will be familiar; some will be startlingly different. Many are healthier than their Western counterparts.

When it comes to dining (and drinking) out, classic Japanese options include sushi and sashimi (p. 130), ramen (a Japanese take on Chinese noodle soup; p. 122), *gyōza* (another twist on a Chinese classic, this time 'potsticker' dumplings; p. 116), tempura (p. 132), *donburi* (rice bowls), yakitori (grilled and skewered meat, usually chicken; p. 137), *wagashi* (traditional sweets; p. 140), sake (p. 146) and tea (p. 151). Western influence has led to popular choices like *omuraisu* (a soft omelette filled with fried rice), *hiyashi raisu* (beef with demi-glace sauce over rice), coffee, craft beer, pizza and pasta (albeit with a Japanese flair; see *yōshoku* p. 138). The typical Japanese home, however, still operates on rice (p. 115), *tsukemono* (pickles), miso soup and grilled extras: simple, delicious fare that can be cost-effective and healthy – a diet from which we can all learn something.

If you're a culinary adventurer looking to taste the ultimate version of your favourite food, Japan is filled with cities – and entire regions – that specialise in your dish of choice. Ramen is everywhere, but it has delicious variations in Sapporo (p. 281), Fukuoka (p. 308) and Tokyo (p. 162). Tempura can be found all over the country, but many areas have their own specialties; Beppu (p. 316), for instance, offers chicken tempura – a real delight. Truly superb sushi and sashimi can be had anywhere, but in Kyoto (p. 234) and elsewhere in Japan, sushi takes different forms and features unique ingredients, with local seafood delicacies varying from one place to the next. Just an hour or two on the Shinkansen can carry you to wildly different flavours and experiences. Osaka (p. 252) excels in street food – quick and delicious. Ancient Kyoto (p. 234) and Wakayama's Mount Kōya (p. 259) make *kaiseki ryōri* (p. 127): small, perfect dishes presented beautifully in a feast to remember and treasure. The northern cities – Sapporo (p. 281), Hakodate (p. 278) and Aomori (p. 198) – are known for seafood: snow crab, fresh fish, prawn curries and tempura scallops. The southern island of Kyūshū (p. 307) is home to exceptional volcanic waters; here, food is simmered in hot springs or cooked in steam that comes from deep beneath the earth. Kobe (p. 261) prides itself on its beef; the northern capitals on their whisky and apples; Uji (p. 249) and Kagoshima (p. 320) both lay claim to early tea production. For anyone with even a passing interest in food, Japan is unmissable.

LEFT: Setouchi Retreat Aonagi's Japanese breakfast, Matsuyama, Shikoku

SAVOURY
OISHI

—————— Without *gohan*, or rice, Japan would cease to operate. Infrastructure would shut down and governments would crumble. Hyperbole? Maybe – but not by much. A side dish, a meal, a religion: rice has been grown and perfected in Japan for more than 2000 years, and has played an important part in Japanese culture for just as long. In the early days, up to the twelfth century, rice was used as a commodity currency. Today, rice is a major part of the Japanese diet, and the word *gohan* is also used to refer to a meal of any kind.

Japanese rice is a short-grain variety and comes in different grades. It's used as a base for rice bowls, as an addition to lunch sets, and in one of Japan's great snack foods, *onigiri* (rice balls). Rice flour is an ingredient in tempura and *katsu* (breaded and fried meat), and is even used in sweets like *mochi*, a kind of glutinous rice cake. Sake is fermented from rice, while *shōchū* is distilled from it. There are regional festivals for planting and harvesting rice, and the release of *shinmai* ('new rice') is celebrated yearly.

Rice paddies are an amazing sight: rectangles of water crisscrossing and segmenting the landscape. As the rice matures, the colours change from green to gold. Certain regions are feted for their rice production and are the best places to take in spectacular rice paddy–filled landscapes. Check out the town of Noto in Ishikawa, Chūbu (p. 226); Shōdoshima (p. 297), which lies between Shikoku and Chūgoku; and Echigo Tsumari in Niigata, Chūbu (p. 226). For true lovers of rice and rice production, Yamagata prefecture in Tōhoku (p. 193) is where the real rice magic happens: in Sakata, along with many historical rice storehouses, you will find the Shōnai Rice History Museum, housed in a beautiful old storehouse overlooking the water.

ACCOMPANIMENTS & CONDIMENTS FOR JAPANESE FOOD

GOMA
(sesame seeds)

SANSHŌ
(Japanese pepper)

SHIO
(salt)

SHISO
(perilla leaf) seasoning

SHŌYU
(soy sauce)

TARE
(soy-based dipping sauce)

TSUKEMONO
(pickles)

UME SŌSU
(plum sauce)

UMEBOSHI
(pickled plum)

THIS PAGE: *Onigiri* in Tokyo, Kantō **OPPOSITE PAGE TOP:** Miso ramen, Sapporo, Hokkaidō **BOTTOM:** Breakfast at HOSHINOYA Kyoto, Arashiyama, Kansai

GYŌZA

餃子

——— This dumpling (based on the Chinese *jiaozi*) is one of Japan's best-known ramen side dishes and beer soakers. *Gyōza* are usually filled with meat, most often pork with cabbage. (Nowadays, vegetarians may be able to find *gyōza* they can eat, but they will be rare, a bit like vegetarian ramen.) There are two varieties: boiled or the more popular version, which is pan-fried and steamed at the same time. The mark of a quality dumpling is all about the seasoning and filling – seafood (prawn), meat (pork), mushroom or spinach, they all work well – and its ratio to wrapper thickness. Some *gyōza* are similar to a perfect *xiao long bao* (soup dumpling); it's the juice inside that makes it so good. Part art form, part street food, if you get *gyōza* wrong you can forget it – but get it right and you'll have a line snaking out of the door.

Find them in ramen shops as a side dish, at some festival street-food stalls and in bars. *Gyōza* can be ordered as a side of three or six dumplings, or as a large connected ring of dumplings held together with a thin, crispy pastry webbing. If you are a fan of the dumpling, this could be the food pilgrimage of your trip.

GYŌZA HOTSPOTS & REGIONAL VARIETIES

AOMORI, TŌHOKU

Katsu (breaded and fried meat) in Aomori (p. 198) is often served with a side dish of apple *gyōza* made from the region's premium fruit.

HAKATA, KYŪSHŪ

Japan's 'food of the people' capital (p. 308) obviously has to have its own style of *gyōza*: *tetsunabe*. It's all about volume here, with the seriously chunky *gyōza* held together by 'plates' of crispy dough cooked and served in iron pans.

HAKODATE, HOKKAIDŌ

This northern city (p. 278) features a dish of *gyōza* floating in a *shio* (salty clear broth) ramen. You can also try the famed and rare squid-ink *gyōza* here.

KANAZAWA, CHŪBŪ

Kanazawa (p. 214) is famed for its white *gyōza* (named after their Chinese creator, whose surname Hak means 'white'). The selling point of these *gyōza* is their thicker layer of dough and the intensity of the garlic in their filling.

KYOTO, KANSAI

Kyoto (p. 234) is home to Gyōza Chao Chao, twice winner of Japan's national *gyōza* competition. If queues are too much for you, try Gyozadokoro Takatsuji Sukemasa near Shijō Station, where you can try true Kyoto-style *gyōza* made with local ingredients.

UTSUNOMIYA, KANTŌ

Utsunomiya (p. 191) is the *gyōza* capital of the world and home to 200 *gyōza* eateries. Try Minmin, Menmen, Gyōtendo, Umaiya, Masashi or Satsuki Tokujiromachi. Utsunomiya even has a *gyōza* statue ... a female figure encased in a *gyōza* dumpling. The *Venus de Gyōza*?

IZAKAYA FOOD

居酒屋

——— An *izakaya* is a Japanese pub and casual eatery – in the sense that you go there to drink and food is provided (so it looks like you're not just going there to drink). That's not to say that the food is just an accompaniment; there's normally a range of small dishes on offer, similar to tapas, that make for a great meal. The atmosphere is rambunctious: at the end of a long, hard week of work a Japanese *izakaya* is a thing to behold, so get amongst it.

The best areas to find *izakaya* are in and around train stations – sometimes in tunnels under the rail lines – in areas with lots of salarymen and women, and in older buildings (*machiya* houses). Look upstairs, downstairs, down laneways and through hidden doors. If in doubt, ask a shop owner, local or someone working at your hotel for their favourite.

Izakaya across Japan have a number of staple dishes, though menus will vary from one to another. Seasonal and local produce will feature heavily on the menus of the cities you are visiting.

To single out the best *izakaya* would be a fool's errand, as there are so many, each with their own unique charm. A rule of thumb is to look for the red lantern, or *akachōchin*, as it denotes a non-chain *izakaya* (although chain *izakaya* can also be passable). Drinks are cheap and plentiful, so chances are it won't matter *too* much about the food, but if you get an *izakaya* with great drinks and great food, it's hard to beat it.

Always try the local specialties wherever you are: seafood if you're staying by the sea; Hida beef and Hoba miso in Takayama (p. 224); Kantō-style sushi; *kurobuta* (black pork) in Kagoshima (p. 320); *unagi* (eel) in Matsuyama (p. 302). Check the 'Japan by Region' chapter (pp. 157–329) for each region or prefecture's specialties. We always order one thing we've never tried before – it's a great way to find out about the local area and test your tastebuds at the same time!

BELOW: Local *izakaya* (pub), Kyoto, Kansai

IZAKAYA DISHES

SMALL DISHES TO START
Edamame (boiled salted soybeans), *tsukemono* (pickles), *aji o kuri* (miso cucumber)

SALADS
Cabbage salad, potato salad, seasonal salads with local vegetable specialties

VEGETABLE DISHES
Nasu dengaku (grilled miso eggplant), sesame spinach, *imo furai* (fried potato), vegetable tempura

TOFU DISHES
Agedashi dōfu (fried tofu), *hiyayakko* (chilled tofu with bonito flakes)

FISH
Sushi and sashimi (raw seasonal fish and seafood of the region), *zakana* (fried, grilled or crumbed fish dishes)

EGG DISHES
Oden tamago (egg cooked in oden broth), *tamagoyaki* (rolled omelette)

GRILLED & FRIED DISHES
Karaage (fried chicken), *tempura* (battered and deep-fried vegetables and seafood), yakitori (grilled skewers of meat or vegetables), *kushikatsu* (deep-fried meat skewers)

RICE
Gohan (plain rice, often served with miso soup), *chazuke* (rice topped with salmon, pickles or other seasonal ingredients in stock or water), *ochazuke* (rice with green tea), *yaki onigiri* (grilled rice balls)

WESTERN DISHES
Pizza, tacos and pasta can pop up on izakaya menus!

KARAAGE

からあげ

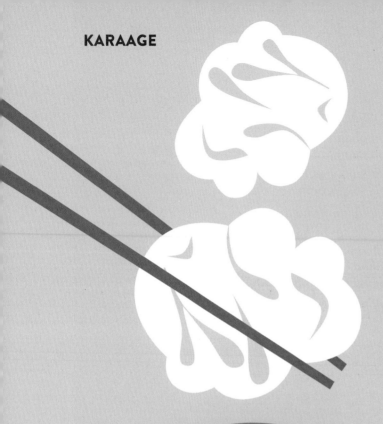

—— Japan's answer to fried chicken is a perennial favourite with visitors. The lighter coating of potato starch makes it a little healthier and even tastier than its Western counterparts. Found in many small eateries, especially as part of a lunch set, *karaage* (or, more accurately, *tori karaage* – *tori* means 'bird' and *karaage* is the method of cooking) is most commonly served with Japanese-style mayonnaise and a small salad or rice. Similar dishes include *tatsutaage*, where the chicken is marinated before being coated and deep-fried; *tebasaki*, chicken wings deep-fried with or without a thin coating; and *hanmi-age*, a deep-fried halved chicken. Certain cities and regions also have their own takes on *karaage*. Being cheap and fast, *karaage* doesn't have many high-end restaurants dedicated to it, but there are many places that make the perfect example of this dish.

KARAAGE HOTSPOTS & REGIONAL VARIETIES

CHŪBŪ

Nagoya is known for *tebasaki* – deep-fried chicken wings tossed in a flavourful glaze and scattered with sesame seeds. Toyama's (p. 226) black *karaage* is seasoned with local soy sauce and is deep, dark and salty (Steve's favourite).

HOKKAIDŌ

Zangi is Hokkaidō's (p. 277) take on *karaage*. Chicken pieces are marinated in a soy-based seasoning, then coated, fried and served with a spicy dipping sauce. Delicious.

KANTŌ

Tokyo (p. 162) is *karaage* central. Try Nakameguro Sai in Kamimeguro, Nakatsu Karaage Kei in Shinagawa or Yakiton Mako-chan in Shinbashi (it's a chain, but irresistible). Speaking of chains, Tenka Torimasu joined forces with teen idol group Kamen Joshi to create two *karaage* sauces that were meant to taste like the band members' sweat and feet. True story.

KYŪSHŪ

In Ōita (p. 329), the local fried chicken dish is *toriten*, often paired with udon noodles. *Toriten* uses wheat flour not of potato starch, resulting in a deeper golden-brown coating. In Miyazaki prefecture, chicken *nanban* is king: *karaage* is coated in a tangy vinegar sauce after frying and served with tartare sauce.

OKINAWA

The Okinawan (p. 326) specialty is *gurukun no karaage*. *Gurukun*, also known as the banana fish, is a local delicacy. It's lightly coated in starch, fried and served whole with lemon.

NABE

鍋

A *nabe* is a cooking pot, traditionally made of clay or cast iron, and the word has come to describe a variety of dishes, typically one-pot specials that feature a bubbling broth packed with tasty bits and pieces. *Nabe* (or *nabemono*, 'pot things') comes in many forms and is one of Japan's must-try dishes. *Chankonabe* is the meal of choice for the sumo wrestler: a dense, fortifying and irresistible feast-in-a-pot packed with meatballs, seafood balls, tofu, noodles and a whole range of vegetables. *Shabu-shabu* is a popular hotpot dish where you swish thinly sliced meat and other ingredients in boiling broth, cooking it quickly – a tasty and fun communal-dining experience. *Yosenabe* is the true one-pot dish, with all kinds of ingredients – meat, seafood, vegetables, tofu – cooked together in a dashi-based broth. You might be surprised to learn that *sukiyaki*, the dish of simmered thinly sliced beef and vegetables commonly seen in Japanese restaurants in the West, is also a kind of *nabe*.

Kimchi *nabe* is another popular choice; the ultra-spicy Korean pickled cabbage works perfectly in this kind of soup. For vegetarians, *yudōfu* is the perfect *nabe*: tofu simmered in a savoury kelp broth. Finally, no list of *nabe* staples is complete without *oden*. A simple dish traditionally comprising fish cakes, boiled eggs, daikon and konjac in dashi broth, this is one of the healthiest and tastiest things you can eat in Japan. *Oden* is as ubiquitous as it is flexible, and you will find it being served out of street-food carts, in the bain-marie at convenience stores, and in high-end restaurants.

NABE HOTSPOTS & REGIONAL VARIETIES

CHŪBŪ

Nagoya lives up to its miso-mad reputation with *dotenabe*, a one-pot dish of meat and vegetables simmered in a miso broth, and Kantō-*ni* or miso *oden*, with *oden* ingredients cooked in, you guessed it, local miso.

KANSAI

Kansai specialties include *botan nabe*, a wild-boar hotpot, and *hari-hari nabe*, an Osakan *nabe* featuring whale meat. *Oden* in Kansai, known as Kantō-*daki*, is darker and heavier than usual. In Kyoto (p. 234), the *oden* bar Takocho has been going for more than 100 years. For a more modern experience, try Sho. Visit the sumo neighbourhood of Namba in Osaka (p. 252) to try *chankonabe*.

KANTŌ

For sumo specialty *chankonabe* head to Tokyo's Sumida. Tokyo (p. 162) is also home to numerous century-old *oden* hotspots, such as Otafuku in Asakusa and Otako in Ginza. Also try Samon in Nakameguro, Esaki in Shinjuku and Owariya in Akihabara.

KYŪSHŪ

Fukuoka (p. 308) is home to *motsunabe*, a deep, dark dish of beef or pork offal simmered with garlic chives and cabbage in a soy-based broth.

SHIKOKU

Kagawa prefecture's local *nabe* is Benkei *no najiru* ('Benkei's vegetable soup'), which, contrary to the name, contains several different kinds of meat. Shikoku (p. 291) has its own style of *oden*, with broths flavoured with soy sauce or beef stock and ingredients presented on skewers.

Noodles are as important to the Japanese people as rice – and that's saying something. Unlike rice, which is used mainly as an accompaniment, noodles are used as the foundation of a range of dishes. The three most common types of noodle are ramen (p. 122), udon (p. 124) and soba (see opposite), but these can vary in size and use. We differ on our noodle of choice. Michelle goes for the delicate soba noodle, a thin buckwheat noodle that can sit alone or with very little accompaniment – perhaps a piece or two of tempura – in tasty soups. Steve opts for the udon, often the thickest one going, with unctuous toppings and robust accompaniments. (A curry udon is one of life's great pleasures.)

TOP LEFT: *Tonkotsu* ramen, Hakata, Kyūshū **OTHER IMAGES:** 'Ramen street', Kyoto Station, Kansai **OPPOSITE PAGE:** Sobanomi Yoshimura, Kyoto, Kansai

Soba noodles are often enjoyed in a dish called *tensoba*: a thin, tasty broth with tempura (p. 132) placed delicately on top and little else except for some spring onions and a few vegetables. A light, simple and inexpensive dish, it's a worker's staple and a delicious meal. Soba is also served chilled – all year round, but particularly good in summer – with a simple soy-based dipping sauce instead of broth. This dish, *zaru* soba, can quickly become an obsession, especially in hot weather. It's a good option for pescetarians and more flexible vegetarians (there will most likely be dashi, made from bonito, in the dipping sauce). Soba salads – tangy, tasty bowls of soba with sliced vegetables – are also a blessing in summer.

SOBA HOTSPOTS & REGIONAL VARIETIES

CHŪBŪ

Nagano prefecture's Shinshū soba is one of the most highly valued in the country. Shinshū soba bears the former name of Nagano prefecture and must contain more than 40 per cent buckwheat flour. Many notable soba eateries can be found in Nagano City and around Kurohime and Togakushi, which are closest to the prefecture's soba-producing areas.

HOKKAIDŌ

Most of Japan's buckwheat is produced in Hokkaidō (p. 277), so it's not surprising that the northern island is known for its soba. Newly made soba is known as *shin* soba and is considered a delicacy, as it is sweeter and has a more complex flavour.

KANSAI

Osaka (p. 252) has its own specialty soba: *tanuki* soba. *Tanuki* are raccoon dogs, fox-like animals native to Japan (see also p. 341), but don't worry, *tanuki* soba contains no actual *tanuki* – just crispy bits of tempura batter scattered over soba noodles in tasty soup. If you want to glimpse a little bit of soba history, visit Kyoto's (p. 234) Honke Owariya, which is more than 550 years old.

KANTŌ

Tokyo (p. 162) is home to a plethora of famous soba houses, which have been family-run for centuries. Tokyo's Sarashina Horii in Azabu-jūban is one such place; more than 230 years old, it's currently run by the eighth generation of the Horii family.

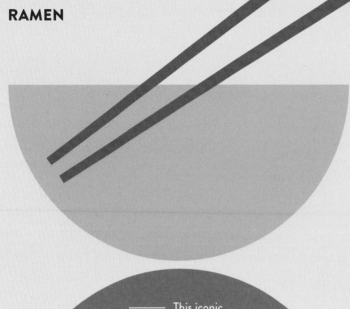

—————— This iconic noodle dish can vary not only from island to island and region to region, but also from town to town. No ramen lover's trip to Japan is complete without hitting up a few of the country's famous ramen cities to try their regional variations. The city of Fukuoka (p. 308), Kyūshū, is famous for its deep, rich and creamy *tonkotsu* ramen, made with pork-bone broth that is cooked for hours to extract the most flavour. Up north, *shio* (salt) ramen from Hakodate (p. 278) and miso ramen from Sapporo (p. 281) should be on your culinary list. *Shōyu* (soy) and *kare* (curry) ramen are must-try specialties in Tokyo (p. 162) and Yokohama (p. 191); in fact, Chinatown in Yokohama can lay claim to the earliest variants of the irresistible bowl. Another Tokyo dish, *tsukemen* ('dipping ramen'), is a deconstructed ramen where the noodles, soup and accompaniments are kept separate, allowing diners to add them at their leisure or to suit their tastes.

True noodle fanatics will want to visit the Shin-Yokohama Ramen Museum and the Cup Noodles Museum (both located in Yokohama, Kantō; pp. 191, 361) or head to the Cup Noodles Museum in Osaka, Kansai (p. 252).

RAMEN HOTSPOTS & REGIONAL VARIETIES

HOKKAIDŌ

Sapporo (p. 281), Japan's northernmost capital, gets very cold in winter and stays that way for quite some time. So what better way to get through the chilly months than with ramen? Ganso Ramen Yokochō, a tiled laneway girded by tiny, picturesque eateries that dispense different varieties of superb ramen, is world-famous. It's the birthplace of miso ramen, the type that Sapporo is best known for. The miso broth is slightly lighter, and for vegetarians, a pork-free ramen is best when it is miso-based. For others, the miso-based ramen gives Sapporo soup masters a chance to diversify, and taste-testing the many kinds of miso ramen – light, dark, burnt, red, white – is the realm of the enthusiast. If you only have a limited amount of time, pick what appeals to you most; you won't be disappointed. If you're all in for trying every variety Sapporo has to offer, Sapporo Station has its own ramen alley, the cute and cheerful Sapporo Ramen Republic, and it's home to mini versions of Hokkaidō's best ramen shops. As they say in Hokkaidō, when the temperature drops below zero, the hearty hot broth of Sapporo ramen is essential.

KANSAI

Jump into one of Wakayama's famous ramen taxis (p. 261) and take a tour of the city's best noodle shops with a driver who has to pass a ramen exam in order to get the job. If you're not sure you can eat more than one bowl, forego the taxi and visit Ide Shoten, a renowned shop that has been trading for more than 30 years (you can also grab an Ide Shoten–branded ramen kit from local food outlets so you can make it at home). Wakayama's main style of ramen, or *chūka* soba as it is often referred to in this southern city, is similar to Fukuoka's *tonkotsu* (pork-bone) ramen: deep and dense, with a rich pork flavour.

In Kyoto, Kyoto Station has its own ramen street, Kyoto Ramen Kōji, way up on the tenth storey of the station building (p. 234). An unmissable destination for the ramen devotee, it showcases some of the most notable ramen stores from regions across Japan. Sapporo, Tokyo, Nagoya, Osaka, Fukuoka and more are all represented in this reconstructed old-school alleyway where you can drop your money into a machine and sample the delicacy of your choice. Being Kyoto, the machines also have English translations, so you can decipher the flavours you would like to explore – or the region whose ramen you would most like to become an expert in. It's fun, sure, but it's also a serious business and a great way to get in touch with what it is to be a regional ramen specialist. Or you can just get a fantastic bowl of noodles.

KANTŌ

Let's not forget the nation's capital. Maybe Tokyo (p. 162) doesn't have the cred of being a distant city with its own local charm and specialty ingredients, but it has more hungry workers than most places in the world and the number of noodle shops that cater to their every need is prodigious. Noodles submerged in extraordinarily tasty soups are served up in an astounding array of establishments, all of which take great pride in what they do – good news for your tastebuds. Akihabara, Shinjuku, and Jimbōchō – any place, really, that has a lot of students and workers – are reliable ramen neighbourhoods. Akihabara has some premium ramen eateries hidden among the fast-food joints, *otaku* shops and electronics retailers. Some of the ramen chains are actually excellent, like Afuri in Ebisu, which caters to those who prefer a lighter broth (in this case, chicken-based with a yuzu citrus twist). In Ginza, visit Ginza Kagari, whose *tori paitan* ramen, a creamy chicken broth–based ramen, is a must for those who don't eat red meat (and anyone else, really). For more adventurous eaters, the *niboshi* ramen served up in the Golden Gai has a legendary and intense sardine broth.

KYŪSHŪ

The city of Fukuoka (p. 308) is the gateway to Kyūshū, and is closer to South Korea than it is to Tokyo or Osaka. The ferry from the South Korean port city of Busan to Fukuoka takes around five-and-a-half hours, and there is a long history of Korean workers making the trip to work and set up a life in the canal city. Fukuoka has a unique feel as a result: a city of shopping and street food, with *yatai*, or street-food stalls, lined up along the canals – an immensely popular attraction, especially in summer. If you are a street-food fan, Fukuoka should be one of your top destinations.

The thing about ramen is that the tastier it is, the more irresistible it becomes. In Fukuoka, particularly the areas of Hakata (formerly Fukuoka's twin city, since absorbed into the city) and Tenjin (downtown Fukuoka, around the canals), the ramen is so densely packed with flavour that it has to be one of the tastiest – and thus most irresistible – in Japan. Fukuoka is known for its *tonkotsu* (or Hakata) ramen. Thick, creamy, deeply complex pork-bone broth; firm, pale noodles; and filling ingredients like roasted or braised pork belly make for the perfect worker's ramen. Once bitten, twice obsessed in this case: the rich broth and meltingly tender pork is a dish for the ages. Order some sides, but be warned: even the traditionally more delicate extras come with extra oomph here. The *gyōza* (dumplings; p. 116) are a hefty version of the Japanese staple, while the mound of crunchy battered chicken pieces you receive when you order *karaage* (fried chicken; p. 118) will make you question whether you can finish both your *karaage* and your ramen.

UDON

Udon noodles are thicker than soba and ramen and stand up well to richer sauces and soups, like those flavoured with Japanese curry or tangy miso. You will also find these noodles in thinner soups with tempura, vegetables or thin slices of meat, or stir-fried in a tasty soy-based sauce that clings to the noodle. Udon come in all shapes and sizes, from thinner, lighter varieties like *inaniwa* udon, all the way up to wide noodles like lasagne sheets called *himokawa*. Like soba, udon can be eaten quite simply, to enjoy the noodle for who it is, not the company it keeps. *Kamaage* udon, for instance, serves the noodles in hot water with a simple dipping sauce, so that you can taste the udon in all its glory. *Karē nanban*, a dish of udon (and often tempura or sliced duck) in a lip-smacking curry soup, is the opposite: a chance to see how well the noodle plays with others. Udon is not limited to hot dishes, either: *zaru* udon, *hadaka* udon ('naked udon') and *bukkake* udon are all delicious examples of chilled udon dishes.

UDON HOTSPOTS & REGIONAL VARIETIES

CHŪBŪ

Miso-nikomi udon is a specialty dish in the city of Nagoya, which has a reputation for its local variety of miso, *hatchomiso*. A must-try if you are visiting, *miso-nikomi* udon features thick udon in a rich *hatchomiso* or red miso broth.

KANSAI

Osaka (p. 252) is the birthplace of a delicious udon dish popular all across Japan, *kitsune* udon ('fox udon'), which features the noodle in a hot soup topped with sweetened deep-fried tofu pockets known as *aburaage*. As for the name, legend has it that fried tofu is a favourite food of Japanese foxes and fox spirits (see also p. 339).

SHIKOKU

Kagawa prefecture (p. 291) is famous for udon, in particular Sanuki udon, a thick variety of udon noodle with square edges. In Kagawa prefecture alone there is an estimated 600 udon eateries; if that's too much choice, you can hire an udon taxi that will take you to the restaurant (or restaurants) serving up the best version of your favourite udon dish, similar to Wakayama's ramen taxis (p. 261).

LEFT: Sanuki udon, Takamatsu, Shikoku
OPPOSITE PAGE: *Okonomiyaki*, Hiroshima, Chūgoku

OKONOMIYAKI

—————— No ordinary pancake, *okonomiyaki* is a meal in itself: an eggy batter fried on a hot plate with extras such as bean shoots, meat, seafood, herbs and noodles, then topped with mayonnaise, Worcestershire or tomato sauce. (Actually, it is best with all three.)

Evolving from early pancake dishes like *funoyaki* (a sweet crepe) and *gintsuba* (crepes with sweet bean paste), *okonomiyaki* became popular out of necessity. In times of scarcity, such as after the 1923 Great Kantō earthquake and around the Second World War, the simple dish was used to fill the void, with few realising that it would become a signature Japanese dish.

Okonomiyaki can easily become an obsession. There are many variations, the two main types being Osaka-style and Hiroshima-style; the key differences between them is the way they are put together (and the inclusion, or not, of noodles). The rivalry between Osaka and Hiroshima is legendary. Of course, we are the winners: we get to try both!

OKONOMIYAKI HOTSPOTS & REGIONAL VARIETIES

CHŪGOKU

We're on team Hiroshima (p. 264): there's something about the way the ingredients are layered that we find appealing. The noodles add an extra dimension to the dish and the extra cabbage is a plus, piled high and squashed down to make a delectable, dense package. Hiroshima natives are so proud of their version that they call it Hiroshima-*yaki* (or *modanyaki*,

'modern *yaki*'). In Hiroshima, hit up Micchan, Nagataya, Fumichan and Chibo. If you're only visiting Tokyo, Sometaro in Asakusa, Sakura-tei in Harajuku and Ushio in Roppongi all dish up Hiroshima-style *okonomiyaki*.

HOKKAIDŌ

Sapporo's (p. 281) cold climate and proximity to the ocean makes it the perfect place to tuck into a seafood-based okonomiyaki. Try Macca, Enami or Tanokyu.

KANSAI

Osaka (p. 252) can probably claim bragging rights for the origin of *okonomiyaki*. Ingredients are mixed together rather than layered onto the grill, and the pancakes are thinner, with spring onion, pork belly, squid, shrimp and cheese common inclusions. Areas to enjoy Osakan variants of the dish include the entertainment district Namba, where *okonomiyaki* originally took off. Here, Osaka Botejyu still makes the original recipe. Also try Mizuno, Yukari, Kurochan, Kiji or Tengu.

KANTŌ

Tokyo's (p. 162) *monjayaki* is similar to *okonomiyaki*, but its batter is far runnier – the texture of the pancake is more like béchamel sauce – and it is eaten straight from the grill, usually after cooking it yourself.

OKINAWA

Hirayachi, made with leek or spring onions, is Okinawa's (p. 326) version of *okonomiyaki*. Thinner and crispier than *okonomiyaki* from other regions, it is usually eaten with a Worcestershire-based sauce.

SHŌJIN RYŌRI

精進料理

—— The Buddhist cuisine of Japan, *shōjin ryōri* (devotion cuisine) has a simple splendor. It is similar in presentation to *kaiseki ryōri* (see opposite), but may have fewer courses, sometimes just one platter. Flavours are subtle; dishes are simple yet inventive and use natural ingredients often gathered from the surrounding region. It is almost always vegetarian or vegan (dashi may be used but it is often vegan dashi rather than fish-based). Expect an assortment of delicacies including clear soup, tempura vegetables, tofu, agar, konjac, rice porridge and pickles, all of which will be artfully prepared, arranged and presented.

SHŌJIN RYŌRI HOTSPOTS

Anywhere with Buddhist temples will offer *shōjin ryōri*. Kyoto (p. 234) has many places; Mount Kōya (p. 259) in Wakayama prefecture has an array of Buddhist temples that are well worth the stay and serve delicious *shōjin ryōri* meals. Osaka (p. 252), Nagoya and Tokyo (p. 162) all have specialist *shōjin ryōri* restaurants.

KAISEKI RYŌRI

From its humble early origins as simple food to accompany a tea ceremony, *kaiseki ryōri*, Japanese haute cuisine, has been elevated to high art. *Kaiseki ryōri*, or simply *kaiseki*, refers to a multi-course meal where every dish is exquisitely considered, beautifully presented and perfectly balanced. A typical *kaiseki* meal might consist of an amuse-bouche or appetiser, followed by a selection of sashimi, *nimono* (simmered or stewed vegetables), *yakimono* (grilled meat or vegetables), *agemono* (deep-fried food), *chawanmushi* (steamed savoury custard) and *tsukemono* (pickles). Rice and miso soup accompany these seasonal delicacies, and the meal is finished with a sweet course that is almost always simple and modest – more like a palate cleanser than heavier Western-style desserts.

Kaiseki ryōri is inextricably linked to *ryokan*, or Japanese inns (p. 87). In the days of yore, travellers, merchants and pilgrims on the road would need a place to stay and eat (and bathe – hence the wonders of the *onsen*, or hot springs). Many of these places still exist today with little adjustment (yes, you can get wi-fi and television, but when you settle into a *ryokan* you quickly forget about those things), and pride themselves on their exceptional food. A *kaiseki* meal at a *ryokan* is one of life's true highlights.

KAISEKI RYŌRI HOTSPOTS

The nature of *kaiseki ryōri* means that it can be quite expensive, but it is worth it as a once-in-a-lifetime experience. We recommend saving up and booking a dinner, not just for the food, but for the magical sight of seeing a *ryokan* lit up at night, for being able to dine in a serene private dining room in a beautiful old *machiya* (traditional wooden house), and for the best service in the world. If you want the meal without the price tag, lunch deals are the way to go. Many places offer a (relatively) cheaper version of their *kaiseki* feast for lunch. Another good way to have a memorable *kaiseki* experience is to shell out for accommodation in a posh *ryokan* and factor in the food. If dinner and breakfast are included in the price, you might even come out on top. Besides *ryokan*, *kaiseki ryōri* is also served at specialty *kaiseki* restaurants called *ryōtei*, but these establishments are often highly exclusive.

Most *onsen* (hot springs) towns and locations with many old-style houses or *ryokan* will be *kaiseki* hotspots. Kyoto (p. 234) is pretty much your go-to for premium *kaiseki ryōri*; venture into the surrounding hills, south to Nara (p. 250) or west to Arashiyama (p. 245), and you'll find some of Japan's best. Elsewhere, places like Iwaso in Miyajima (p. 272), Chūgoku, or Hoshi in Minakami, Kantō, are unforgettable examples.

LEFT: *Kaiseki ryōri* dish
OPPOSITE PAGE: *Shōjin ryōri* at Mount Kōya, Kansai

STREET FOOD 屋台の食べ物

———— You'll find some of the world's best street food in Japan – on temple streets, during festivals, in parks on holidays, in *onsen* (hot spring) towns and in most built-up areas. Fast, cheap, tasty and often healthy, Japanese street food has been shaped over time into a staple for the person on the go, so it's perfect for the traveller who gets a bit peckish while exploring. There are many new things to try, twists on familiar snacks and entirely unique options.

TAIYAKI MANIA

Taiyaki – a crispy waffle pastry shaped like a seabream (*tai*), stuffed with sweet fillings made of sweet red-bean paste, custard or sweet potato – is one of our favourite Japanese street foods. There are vendors all over the country serving up every variety you can imagine. In Tokyo (p. 162), you can find Naniwaya, the original *taiyaki* house, in Azabu-Jūban, or watch the *taiyaki* being made in the window of Kurikoan in Kichijōji, on the fringes of the warren of bars and eateries known as Harmonica Yokochō. (Try the purple sweet potato filling.) If you want to try *taiyaki*'s cousin *imagawayaki,* which is cylindrical rather than fish-shaped, the Mr Bean franchise can be found all over Tokyo and sells a version enriched with soy milk.

In Kyoto (p. 234), Naruto Taiyaki Honpo serves up premium *taiyaki* out of a beautiful old-school frontage. Hakata Hiiragi in Fukuoka (p. 308) is popular for its *taiyaki*, which can be had for around 200 yen. The best part is that the regular and *mochi* varieties are vegan.

The city of Goshogawara in Aomori prefecture, Tōhoku, is the home of *age taiyaki,* or deep-fried *taiyaki*. The deep-frying adds extra crunch and chew to the waffle exterior. Meanwhile, in Sapporo (p. 281), they have panda *taiyaki*. Yes, *taiyaki* shaped like a panda. As you were.

OTHER TYPES OF STREET FOOD

CREPES
Instead of being a subtler version of its European counterpart, Japanese crepes are deliciously overstuffed and over the top.

DANGO
Mochi (rice cake) balls on skewers. There are many variations, including *chadango* (green-tea flavoured), *botchan dango* (tri-coloured) and *mitarashi dango* (drizzled with syrup). Most *dango* are sweet, but some are slightly savoury.

TAKOYAKI
Fried dough filled with chopped octopus, topped with bonito flakes and drizzled with a special Worcestershire-based sauce.

YAKI IMO
Roasted sweet potato.

YAKI TOMOROKOSHI
Grilled corn on the cob.

YAKISOBA
Stir-fried wheat noodles with vegetables, a tangy sauce and sometimes meat.

YAKITORI
Skewered and grilled meat (traditionally chicken, p. 137).

ABOVE: Street-food stall in Shinsekai, Osaka, Kansai **OPPOSITE PAGE:** Pop-up food stall at a festival in Shibuya, Tokyo, Kantō

——— These quintessentially Japanese dishes are similar but different. Sashimi is straightforward: the freshest fish, carefully sliced and served raw with soy and wasabi. Sushi is generally raw fish on a bed of vinegared rice, but it can also feature cooked seafood, omelette and vegetables.

Both sushi and sashimi are deceptively simple. The fish must be prepared and cut just right; the rice, if used, must be perfectly seasoned. The dishes have few ingredients or extras to hide behind. Fresh sashimi is in a class of its own: delicate, melt-in-the-mouth morsels that are as healthy as they are delicious. *Maguro* (tuna), *sake* (salmon), *katsuo no tataki* (lightly seared tuna) and even *ebi* (prawns) and *hotate* (scallops) can be served as sashimi.

Sashimi can sometimes be suitable for vegetarians – you might come across avocado and radish preparations – or the complete opposite, with horse or whale being served in some regions. One common piece of sashimi that you will encounter is *aji*, or horse mackerel. Don't worry: this is a type of fish and not a type of horse.

Sashimi can stand alone as a pricey feast, or accompany more casual *shokudō* (home-style eatery) or *izakaya* (pub) food. Like sashimi, sushi can be extremely high-end, or it can drift past you on a conveyor belt. An expensive sushi *omakase* ('I'll leave it up to you') meal prepared by a master is one of life's best dining experiences. Sushi trains are a cheap and cheerful roundabout of deliciousness: fun for kids, great for adults, always tasty and at times intriguing. Both experiences embody the essence of Japanese food.

Sushi toppings can include *maguro*, *sake*, *tamagoyaki* (rolled omelette), *tobiko* (flying fish roe), *toro* (belly tuna), *ebi* and *hotate*. We often see chive-topped sushi – perfect for vegetarians.

Nigiri is the most popular kind of sushi: small portions of rice with simple toppings. *Gunkanmaki* ('battleship rolls') are a version of *nigiri* wrapped in nori to keep ingredients like *uni* (sea urchin) or *tarako* (cod roe) secure. *Chirashizushi* is a sashimi-topped bowl of vinegared rice with various vegetables, and is a staple dish in Japanese homes. *Temaki* are cone-shaped hand rolls. *Makizushi* or *norimaki* are sushi rolls, the kind that we associate with California rolls in the West. *Futomaki* are extra-large sushi rolls, while *hosomaki* are thinner ones; you'll often find them with a tuna or cucumber filling. Convenience stores sell fresh, cheap and delicious *makizushi*, *futomaki* and *hosomaki* – a great takeaway lunch. The nori is often wrapped in a separate plastic sheet so that it stays fresh and crunchy.

HOTSPOTS & REGIONAL VARIETIES

KANTŌ

For high-end sushi in Tokyo (p. 162), visit Sukiyabashi Jiro in Ginza (of *Jiro Dreams of Sushi* fame; bookings must be made through a hotel concierge), Komuro in Shinjuku, Uoshin Nogizaka in Akasaka and Sushi Nakamura in Roppongi. If 'sushi for the people' is more your style, try Genki Sushi, Uobei, Nemuro Hanamaru and Sushi no Midori, all with multiple locations across the city.

KANSAI

Shiga prefecture (p. 256) is one of the few places in Japan where *narezushi* and *funazushi*, two variations of fish fermented with salt and raw rice, are still common. *Narezushi* is the earliest form of sushi and is something of an acquired taste.

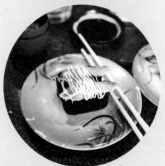

THIS PAGE TOP: Sashimi at Setouchi Retreat Aonagi, Matsuyama, Shikoku BOTTOM & OPPOSITE PAGE: Conveyor-belt sushi at Heiroki Sushi in Harajuku, Tokyo, Kantō

Then there is *inari* sushi: pockets of *aburaage* (fried tofu) filled with sweetened rice. You can get *inari* sushi everywhere, but Kyoto's (p. 234) plethora of shrines dedicated to Inari (a Shinto deity associated with foxes and rice) means that you will see it all over the temple city. Kyoto also has sushi specialties, such as *sabazushi*, made with lightly pickled mackerel, and *nigiri* with *unagi* (freshwater eel) or *anago* (conger eel).

Osaka's (p. 252) specialty, *oshizushi*, is a variety of sushi where ingredients are layered and then pressed into a wooden mould, known as an *oshizushihako*. The ancient town of Nara (p. 250) also has its own type of pressed sushi, *kakinohazushi*, which is wrapped in persimmon leaves.

HOKKAIDŌ

Most places close to the sea or with a renowned seafood market, like Sapporo (p. 281) and Hakodate (p. 278) in Hokkaidō, will offer a variety of sashimi that you might not be able to try in bigger cities. Hokkaidō is famous for *amaebi* (sweet shrimp), which is enjoyed as sashimi. The city of Niigata (p. 226) in Chūbu is also an *amaebi* epicentre.

TŌHOKU

Hotate – scallop sashimi – is popular in the northern port town of Aomori (p. 198), and is quite common as you head north into Hokkaidō. Aomori also excels in tuna sashimi, including *katsuo no tataki*: skipjack tuna that is lightly seared before it is sliced.

OKINAWA

The smallest of Japan's main islands (p. 326) is known for some pretty out-there sashimi, including trumpet fish, giant clam, parrot fish, and a giant sea slug that lives in a cone-like shell.

———— The Portuguese missionaries who settled in Nagasaki in the sixteenth century brought the technique of dipping ingredients in batter and frying them, and we are all forever grateful. Tempura is one of most recognisable Japanese dishes in the West, and for good reason: the combination of crispy, lighter-than-air batter covering fresh seafood and vegetables is irresistible. The magic of a good tempura is that the batter never overpowers the perfectly cooked ingredient inside, just enhances it.

Popular options are fish and seafood (especially prawns), asparagus, sweet potato, eggplant, pumpkin, mushrooms or *kakiage*, a mixture of shredded vegetables and occasionally seafood fried together in a delicious cluster. A vegetarian temple *shōjin ryōri* (Buddhist meal; p. 126) might feature bracken, *shiso* (perilla) leaves and the region's mountain vegetables. In *shokudō* (casual home-style eateries), tempura can be an accompaniment to a whole meal; you'll often get a delicious mini-feast of miso soup, rice, sashimi and pickles with a small plate of tempura. Tempura is also a popular topping for rice bowls (a dish called *tendon*) and noodle soups (*tensoba* and tempura *udon*).

Casual *shokudō* tempura and *tendon* are usually cheap, but tempura-*ya* (specialty tempura restaurants) can be very high end. Here, tempura will usually be served as part of a set menu, starting with lighter ingredients and moving towards richer flavours. You'll be given various salts, a light sauce of soy and sesame, and daikon as an accompaniment.

TEMPURA HOTSPOTS & REGIONAL VARIETIES

HOKKAIDŌ
Places near mountains or the sea are usually good spots to get tempura. Sapporo (p. 281) and Hakodate (p. 278) fit the bill, and both do good seafood tempura. Try Ebiten or Tsunahachi in Sapporo.

KANSAI
Kyoto (p. 234) is surrounded by mountains and temples, and as a result the local tempura often features delicious mountain bracken and root vegetables, especially if you are eating at a temple (a good choice for vegetarians). For special occasions, visit a tempura-*ya* (specialty tempura restaurant) like Tempura Endo. If you're in Osaka (p. 252), try Shunsaiten Tsuchiya, whose tempura has been deemed worthy of two Michelin stars.

KANTŌ
On the subject of Michelin-starred tempura, Tempura Kondo in Tokyo (p. 162) is also the recipient of two. Tsunahachi, also in Tokyo, is another great stop on the tempura trail, and has been serving tempura since 1923.

KYŪSHŪ
Tempura's origins are in Nagasaki (p. 329), so it's not a surprise that tempura eateries are plentiful there. Elsewhere in Kyūshū, the port town of Moji is a good place to hunt out seafood tempura. In Ōita prefecture, the regional specialty is chicken tempura; it's rare to get meat in tempura, so this rustic variety is a real treat and quite unusual.

LEFT: Tempura Endo Yasaka, Kyoto, Kansai
OPPOSITE PAGE: *Shōjin ryōri* (vegetarian banquet), Mount Kōya, Kansai

TOFU

豆腐

—— Introduced to Japan from China as far back as the Nara period (710–794 AD; p. 15), tofu is another Japanese staple with a rich culinary tradition: one recipe book from the Edo period (1603–1868; p. 28) documents 100 ways to prepare tofu. *Shōjin ryōri*, the vegetarian cuisine of Buddhist monks (p. 126), features tofu as a primary ingredient in many of its dishes. Tofu comes in many forms: as silken additions to miso soup; as *agedashi dōfu*, a delicious dish of coated and lightly fried tofu with a dashi sauce; as *ganmodoki*, fried fritters studded with vegetables; as fried pouches filled with vinegared rice called *inarizushi*; or as *yuba* (tofu skin) cut into strips and added to rice dishes. Tofu skin might sound strange, but it is a tasty addition to many dishes and can even be a dish on its own. Kyoto (particularly Arashiyama; p. 245) in Kansai and other temple towns are your key destinations if you want to try tofu in its many forms. The *yuba* feasts at both Senmaruya and Seike in Kyoto (p. 234) are unforgettable.

TYPES OF TOFU

ABURAAGE
Fried pouches of tofu, the basis of *inarizushi*

ATSUAGE
Thick fried tofu

GOMA DŌFU
A kind of 'mock tofu' made from sesame seeds and *kudzu* (Japanese arrowroot) starch

KINUDOSHI DŌFU
Delicate silken tofu, often served as-is with soy sauce

MOMEN DŌFU
Tofu with a firmer texture, suitable for *nabe* (p. 119) and *sukiyaki*

TOFUYO
Fermented tofu with a strong cheese-like flavour; an Okinawan specialty

YUBA
Tofu skin made from boiling soy milk

Vegetarian & vegan Japan

Michelle is a pescetarian but mostly eats vegetarian, so like many people these days she has specific food needs! We always ask for vegetarian recommendations at the tourist information centre, at the station in the town we're visiting or at our accommodation.

CAFÉS

Many new cafés have at least one veggie option, or if the lunch is in compartments, you can leave the meat element, but more and more vegetarian cafés are popping up all over Japan, serving delicious fixed-price lunch plates.

· Fil Gyoza and Coffee
(Tokyo, Kantō)
Vegetarian *gyōza*
Instagram @fil_gyoza.and.coffee
· Yoshiya Restaurant
(Arashiyama, Kansai)
yosiya.jp/okunoniwa
· Thallo (Kobe, Kansai)
thallo.jp

DEPARTO (DEPARTMENT STORES)

· Breads and baked goods
· Fruit and vegetables
· *Onigiri* (rice balls) and plain rice
· Salads

FESTIVALS

· Chocolate-coated bananas
on skewers
· *Dango*: sweet rice dumplings
on skewers
· *Goheimochi*: soy-glazed rice cakes
on skewers

· *Kushikatsu*: crumbed and deep-fried food on skewers – try lotus root, mini capsicums, mushrooms or egg
· *Taiyaki*: fish-shaped pastry filled with sweet red-bean paste or custard
· *Yaki imo*: baked sweet potato
· *Yaki tomorokoshi*: soy-glazed grilled corn cob on a skewer
· *Yakiguri*: roasted chestnuts

IZAKAYA

· Cucumber with miso
· Edamame: green soybeans served in the pod either chargrilled or cold
· *Hiyayakko*: chilled tofu dishes (ask for no bonito)
· *Nasu dengaku*: eggplant and miso
· *Onigiri*: rice balls – plain, *umeboshi* (pickled plum,) mountain vegetable or grilled
· Plain rice and miso soup (ask if there are clams or pipis in the soup)
· Potato salad (ask if it comes with ham or seafood)
· Salad dishes (check ingredients)
· *Tamagoyaki*: rolled omelette
· *Tsukemono*: pickles
· Yakitori vegetables: grilled vegetable skewers, mushrooms, green peppers

KARE (JAPANESE CURRY)

· *CoCo Ichibanya* – With options such as tomato and asparagus, spinach, vegetable and eggplant, this inexpensive chain may be your vegetarian saviour in Japan; *ichibanya.co.jp*

KOMBINI (CONVENIENCE STORES)

· *Anin dōfu*: almond dessert
· Boiled eggs
· Edamame, broad beans and corn
· Egg sandwiches
· *Furutsū sando*: fresh fruit sandwiches
· Fruit and jelly (made with agar)
· *Onigiri* (rice balls) with *umeboshi* (pickled plum), seaweed or adzuki beans
· Plain soba noodles with vegetable tempura on the side
· Rice crackers
· Salads
· Veggie and yuzu chips

RAMEN

Some ramen restaurants do a great veggie option so it's worth checking.

Many have good salads or cucumber and miso. Most ramen joints are inexpensive, with a machine at the door to order, so it's hard to ask for extras or to omit ingredients. You can, however, ask for extra toppings, so if you get your noodles on the side you can customise a delicious dish.

- Afuri (Tokyo, Kantō)
  afuriramen.com
- Shinjuku Gyo-en Ramen Ouka (Tokyo, Kantō)
  m-ouka.com
- T's Tan Tan (Tokyo Station, Kantō)
  ts-restaurant.jp/tantan
- Yuniwa Vege Ramen (Osaka, Kansai)
  vegewa.com

REGIONAL CUISINE

HOBA LEAF AND MISO

Ask for tofu with mountain veg.

- Suzuya (Takayama, Chūbu)
  suzuyatakayama.ec-net.jp/top_
  english.html

OKONOMIYAKI

Ask for vegetable fillings and no bonito on top.

- Mizuno (Osaka, Kansai)
  mizuno-osaka.com/index2.html
- Nagataya (Hiroshima, Chūgoku)
  nagataya-okonomi.com

SANUKI UDON

Ask for shōyu broth (not dashi).

- Ippuku Machinaka Ten (Takamatsu, Shikoku)
  udonippuku.com/en/info-english

SOUP CURRY

Vegan or vegetarian with egg.

- Garaku (Sapporo, Hokkaido)
  s-garaku.com

TACO RICE (NAHA, OKINAWA)

- Ukishima Garden (Naha, Okinawa)
  ukishima-garden.com

WANKO SOBA (MORIOKA, TŌHOKU)

- Azumaya (Morioka, Tohoku)
  Wanko soba restaurant with à la carte soba and vegetable options.
  wankosoba.jp/en/alacarte

SUSHI RESTAURANTS

- Nori rolls with cucumber, natto, pickles, avocado or umeboshi (pickled plum)
- Tamagoyaki: rolled omelette

TEMPLE FOOD (SHŌJIN RYŌRI)

Shōjin ryōri (p. 126) is multi-course Buddhist cuisine, an artfully presented full Japanese breakfast, lunch or dinner that's 100 per cent plant-based. Breakfasts and lunches may seem pricey, but it will probably be the best meal and cultural experience of your life. Dinners can be on the more expensive side, but if this sounds like something you'd love to try, check below and try booking online or getting your hotel to book for you. The temple setting, food presentation and general atmosphere will transport you to a place you'll need to store away in a memory chamber to relive once you're back home.

- Hakuun-an, Manpuku-ji (Uji, Kansai)
  hakuunan.com
- Ikkyu, Daitoku-ji (Kyoto, Kansai)
- Hanabishi (Wakayama, Kansai)
  hanabishi-web.jp
- Isuzen, Daiji-in (Kyoto, Kansai)
  kyoto-izusen.com
- Kakusho (Takayama, Chūbu)
  kakusyo.com
- Shigetsu, Tenryu-ji (Arashiyama, Kansai)
  tenryuji.com
- Ukishima Garden (Naha, Okinawa)
  ukishima-garden.com
- Yakuo-in (Mount Takao, Kantō)
  takaosan.or.jp

GREAT RESOURCES

- happycow.net/asia/japan
- vegietokyo.com

LEFT: Vegetarian lunch in Kyoto, Kansai

TONKATSU

とんかつ

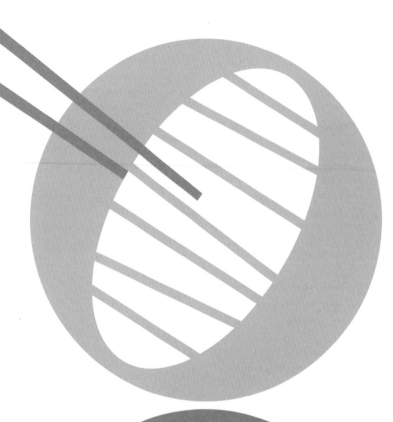

KATSU HOTSPOTS & REGIONAL VARIETIES

CHŪBŪ
The Japanese often joke that people from Nagoya will put miso on anything, and *katsu* doesn't escape the miso treatment. The local *hatchomiso* sauce gives miso *katsu* its unique flavour.

KANSAI
The cities of Kobe (p. 261) and Osaka (p. 252) are situated in a region well known for its beef, with Kobe lending its name to the legendary wagyu. So it's only natural that you should find *gyūkatsu*, or beef *katsu*, here.

TŌHOKU
Katsu gets its own special side dish in Aomori (p. 198): apple *gyōza* (dumplings) made with the area's famous fruit. It's an irresistible combination.

——— *Tonkatsu*, or simply *katsu*, is technically a *yōshoku* ('Western food'; p. 138) meal, but it has been ingrained in the Japanese psyche for so long that it has essentially become a classic *washoku* ('Japanese food') dish. Breaded and fried pork cutlet is the usual mode for *katsu*, with rice, shredded cabbage and a fruit- and vinegar-based sauce the typical accompaniments. Ubiquitous, filling and available at a price point for the people, *katsu* is a good all-rounder (and a reliable fallback for picky eaters). Variations include *katsu sando* (a sandwich often found in *ekiben*, train-station *bentō*; p. 98), *katsudon* (*katsu* over rice, topped with egg and onions), *katsu* curry (often served as a *donburi*, or rice bowl – yum!), *menchikatsu* (breaded and fried meat patties) and *hamukatsu* (made with ham rather than pork cutlet). The technique of breading and deep-frying can also be applied to other meats, including prawns (*ebikatsu*) and chicken (*torikatsu*).

YAKITORI

焼き鳥

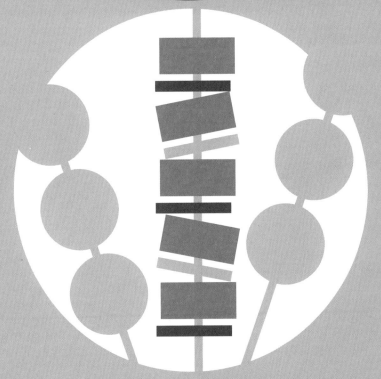

—— Meat threaded onto skewers and grilled over an open flame: a staple of the *izakaya* (Japanese pub; p. 117) and the ideal food for the worker on the go. What can be skewered varies from simple chicken thigh or breast to offal and offcuts, to quail eggs, mushrooms and green peppers. (The term yakitori can be used interchangeably with the word *kushiyaki*, except when referring to specific items, in which case yakitori only refers to cuts of chicken, while *kushiyaki* can describe food grilled on skewers in general.) Yakitori is served with *shio* (salt) or *tare* (sauce). Favourites include *negima* (chicken thigh paired perfectly with spring onion), *tsukune* (chicken meatballs) and *momo* (chicken thigh). *Kawa*, or crispy chicken skin, is also delicious, though not for everyone. Real culinary adventurers might want to try *ikayaki* (grilled cuttlefish), *hāto* (chicken hearts), *shiro* (chicken small intestines) or *gyūtan* (beef tongue).

YAKITORI HOTSPOTS & REGIONAL VARIETIES

As one of the main accompaniments for booze, yakitori is most often found in cities. The best place to experience it is in old-school alleyways and dive-ish *izakaya*: hit up Tokyo's (p. 162) Yūrakuchō, where there are plenty of small eateries that do great yakitori (and excellent drinks) under the train tracks. Shinjuku's Omoide Yokochō ('Memory Alley', although it's also known by the affectionate title of Piss Alley), is picturesque and full of great yakitori joints. The beauty is that you can have a drink and some skewers, then move on to the next one until you find your favourite (usually the one you end up at when you are the most drunk). The Nakasu entertainment district in Fukuoka, Kyūshū (p. 308), is famed for yakitori (almost as much as it is for ramen). As a street-food hotspot, Osaka (p. 252) has many good yakitori joints: try Ichimatsu, Sumiyaki Shoten Yo Namba, Tsuki no Odori or Akiyoshi.

YŌSHOKU

———— *Yōshoku* is the word used to describe any Japanese version of a Western dish imported from France, America, Italy and beyond and given a Japanese spin. The Meiji Restoration (p. 32) was a liberating time for the Japanese, and their newfound freedoms and a burgeoning interest in the outside world extended to food. Often the information would be incomplete or lost in translation and, as a result, the dishes took on a flavour and look of their own. These dishes became so popular that many of them are now considered to be Japanese by the general public. A desire to emulate the chic style of the French led to 'parlour'-style eateries that sold upmarket versions of hamburgers or croquettes. Moneyed-up towns like Ginza (p. 166) in Tokyo and specialist beef cities like Kobe (p. 261) continue to excel at this. Taco rice, Okinawa's (p. 326) greatest export, took the concept of a taco and deconstructed it. Spaghetti, beefsteaks with sauce, curry and potato salad were all adapted to the Japanese palate – giving us delicious new versions of well-known dishes to try.

BELOW: Potato salad at a ramen joint in Hakata, Kyūshū

HANBĀGU (HAMBURGER)
The Japanese-style hamburger comes with rice and salad rather than a bun, often with a French demi-glace sauce.

HAYASHI RICE (BEEF AND RICE)
Usually made up of beef, onion and mushroom on rice, *hayashi* originated in Hyōgo prefecture, home of the prized Kobe beef. It is also very good made with Hida beef in Takayama (p. 224).

KARE (CURRY)
Served with rice or noodles, Japanese curry is rich and mild in flavour. Regional specialties include scallop curry in Aomori (p. 198), black pork in Kagoshima (p. 320), bitter melon in Okinawa (p. 326) and oyster in Hiroshima (p. 264).

MENTAIKO PASTA
Mentaiko (spicy cod roe), butter, olive oil, nori, mushroom and shiso leaves on pasta – a true Japanese flavour profile for an Italian staple.

OMURAISU (OMELETTE RICE)
A pillowy omelette served on or filled with rice, served with tomato or demi-glace sauce. Popular lore says it was invented in Ginza in Tokyo (again), but Osakans made it their own.

POTATO SARADA (POTATO SALAD)
Japanese potato salad is pretty similar to the Western dish, but with Japanese mayonnaise and wasabi. An easy first dish for a Japanese food newbie.

TACO RICE
Tacos have been popular in Okinawa (p. 326) since 1956, thanks to the US forces barracked there. In 1984, Matsuzo Gibo took away the shell and invented this delicious new dish, with traditional taco fillings served on rice.

JAPAN

日本

138

CULINARY JAPAN – SAVOURY

SWEET
OKASHI

RIGHT: *Kakigōri* from Maruzen Tea Roastery, Shizuoka, Chūbu BELOW: *Wagashi* from Zen Kyoto, Kansai

WAGASHI 和菓子

———— *Wagashi*, or traditional Japanese confectionery, is an intricate art form – often way too exquisite to bite into, although curiosity (and hunger) will get the better of you eventually. *Wagashi* is seasonal; flavours match whatever is blooming, ripening or being harvested at the time: cherry blossom, plum, peach, yuzu citrus, lime, apple ... the range is extensive, and often the *wagashi* will be shaped, in the most delicate and creative way, like its flavouring. *Wagashi* are generally less sweet than you would expect, but the flavour is very easy to get used to. No trip to Japan is complete without trying *wagashi*.

TYPES OF WAGASHI

ANMITSU
Cubes of agar jelly topped with sweet red-bean paste and syrup.

DAIFUKU
Glutinous rice cakes with a sweet filling.

DANGO
Rice-flour dumplings on skewers.

DORAYAKI
Sweet red-bean paste sandwiched between pancakes.

KAKIGŌRI
Shaved ice drizzled with syrup – perfect in summer.

KONPEITŌ
Tiny, colourful, confetti-like hard candies popular in Kyoto.

MANJŪ
Steamed buns with a sweet filling.

MOCHI
Glutinous rice cakes.

MONAKA
Sweet red-bean paste sandwiched between crisp wafers.

SENBEI
Sweet or savoury rice crackers in various shapes.

WARABI MOCHI
A chewy jelly made from bracken starch, topped with roasted soybean flour.

YŌKAN
Jelly traditionally made with sweet red-bean paste, sugar and agar.

YŌGASHI

洋菓子

——— In contrast to *wagashi*, *yōgashi* refers to Western-influenced desserts with a Japanese twist. French classics like Mont Blanc or crème brûlée are popular. A matcha (green-tea) éclair or cheesecake is a new taste sensation. *Kissaten* (European-style coffee houses; p. 152) and food halls are great places to go to discover Japan's extensive range of sweet delights.

TYPES OF YŌGASHI

CASTELLA
A starch-syrup sponge cake with a hint of vanilla. Often sold as a gift, boxed beautifully, to give away with a subtle implication: 'This is good to share with the person who is giving it to you.'

CHIFFON CAKE
Fluffy cake similar to a sponge cake.

CHEESECAKE
Sometimes called 'cotton-soft' cheesecake; pillowy and light as a feather in comparison to its Western counterparts.

CREPES
An over-the-top collision of French-style crepes and Belgian waffles. Expect cream, ice cream, fruit, sweet red-bean paste and so much more.

DOUGHNUTS
Lighter and healthier than regular doughnuts. Japanese doughnuts are mostly made from soy or tofu pulp, and the reduced sweetness but fluffier texture makes them easy to inhale.

FURŪTSU SANDO
Sandwiches filled with fruit – strawberries, kiwi fruit, mandarin and more – and cream, mostly found in convenience stores or food halls.

HONEY TOAST
Hollowed-out loaves of bread filled to the brim with fruit, cream and honey. Fun for you and your friends – you can't eat it on your own ... surely.

KITTO KATTO (KIT KAT)
Hugely popular in Japan and comes in a range of flavours, including sake, soy sauce (2010's best-selling chocolate bar), cheese, blueberry, adzuki bean and roasted corn.

MATCHA (GREEN-TEA) ÉCLAIR
The classic French pastry with a Japanese spin.

MELON PAN
A sweet, melon-shaped bread with a crispy topping.

PARFAIT
A take on the French delight that layers sponge cake and cream with Japanese ingredients like *mochi* (rice cakes), sweet red-bean paste and matcha ice cream.

ROLL CAKE
Like a swiss roll. Japan usually sticks to the classic flavours here but try the matcha.

SOFUTO KURĪMU
Soft-serve ice cream in a cone that is a little lighter and less sweet than what you may find at home. Delicious flavours include black sesame, yuzu, matcha (green tea) and edamame (soybean). Soy-based soft-serve is also available – so if you're vegan you won't have to miss out.

THIS PAGE: Matcha soft-serve ice cream
OPPOSITE PAGE: Toraya Akasaka Main Store, Tokyo, Kantō

Zen & the art of wagashi

An incredible selection of *wagashi* (traditional sweets; p. 140) can be found in the basement food halls (*depachika*) of large department stores. Isetan and Mitsukoshi in Tokyo (p. 162), Takashimaya and Daimaru in Kyoto (p. 234), and Hankyu in Osaka (p. 252) are our favourites for their curation. You'll get an overview of the styles, shapes, flavours and packaging of the sweets, and maybe a sample or two. Train stations and airports also have great selections, as *wagashi* are a favourite *omiyage* (regional souvenir; p. 109) to take home to friends and loved ones. Below are some of our personal favourites. Remember, Japanese sweets are not like Western sweets – the textures and flavours will be a completely new sensation. They're not as 'sweet' and use many seasonal ingredients. Wooden *wagashi* moulds (*kashigata*) are beautiful collectables from flea and vintage markets (p. 373). We buy them to display in our home – the woodcarving is impeccable.

CHŪBU
- **Ame-no Tawaraya** (Kanazawa)
  Rice and barley Japanese sweets, some with a thick sauce.
  ame-tawaraya.co.jp
- **Kinseiken Daigahara** (Yamanashi)
  Mizu shingen mochi (raindrop *mochi*).
  fujisan-pref.jp/en/article/46
- **Minatoseika** (Niigata)
  Delicious *daifuku*, *mochi* and *dango*.
  niigata-minato.co.jp/en/index.html
- **Murakami Wagashi** (Kanazawa)
  Kintsuba, *warabi mochi* and brown sugar *fukusa mochi* with gold leaf.
  wagashi-murakami.com

CHŪGOKU
- **Keigetsu-do** (Matsue)
  Famous for *izumo zanmai*.
  keigetsudo.jp

HOKKAIDŌ
- **Marui Sakaemochihonten** (Hakodate)
  Masters of *bekomochi* (leaf-shaped *mochi* for boys' festival).
  tabelog.com/en/hokkaido/A0105/A010501/1021161

KANSAI
- **Hourandou** (Arashiyama, Kyoto)
  Warabi mochi and adzuki bean sweets.
  hourandou.net/wp
- **Mochisho Shizuku** (Osaka)
  Beautiful store, beautiful *wagashi*.
  nichigetsumochi.jp
- **Nakamuraken**
  (Arashiyama and Kyoto city)
  Sublime *mochi*, *dango*, *kakigōri* and more.
  nakamuraken.co.jp
- **Toraya Karyo** (Ichijō, Kyoto)
  global.toraya-group.co.jp
- **Umezono Sabo** (Nishijin, Kyoto)
  Our favourite place for *wagashi*.
  umezono-kyoto.com/nishijin

KANTŌ
- **Ginza Akebono** (Tokyo)
  One of Tokyo's best-loved *mochi* specialists.
  ginza-akebono.co.jp
- **Higashiya Ginza** and **Higashiya-man Aoyama** (Tokyo)
  Manjū, *monaka*, *rakugan*, castella and other seasonal sweets.
  higashiya.com

- **Sugamo-en** (Tokyo)
  Shio (white) *daifuku*.
  sugamoen.com
- **Toraya Akasaka Main Store** (Tokyo)
  Artful adzuki-bean sweets.
  global.toraya-group.co.jp
- **Usagiya** (Tokyo)
  Incredible *dorayaki* (sweet adzuki-bean-filled pancakes).
  ueno-usagiya.jp

KYŪSHŪ
- **Kitagawa Tenmeido** (Kumamoto)
  230-year-old *wagashi* specialist known for koi-shaped *wagashi*.
  kitagawa-tenmeido.com

SHIKOKU
- **Kinosaki Onsen Minatoya** (Kinosaki)
  Edo period *ryokan* that is a now a *wagashi* shop specialising in *dokosui* (sweet bean paste).
  kinosaki-miyage.com

TŌHOKU
- **Sakuranbo** (Yamagata)
  Famed regional cherry *wagashi*.
  sakuranbo-shop.co.jp

WAGASHI MUSEUM

· Kyoto Confectionary Museum
  (Kyoto, Kansai)
  *www.kyoto-museums.jp/en/museum/
  north/3929*

WAGASHI-MAKING CLASSES

· Ishikawa Local Products Center
  (Kanazawa, Chūbu)
  kanazawa-kankou.jp

· Kanazawa Museum of Wooden
  Japanese Sweet Molds
  (Kanazawa, Chūbu)
  *Morihachi wagashi—making classes.
  kanazawa-experience.com/program/
  japanese-confectionery-molding/*

· Kanshundo (Kyoto, Kansai)
  *kanshundo.co.jp/museum/make/
  annai_e.htm*

· Karakoro Art Studio
  (Matsue, Chūgoku)
  *accessible-travel-san-in.com/
  karakoro-art-studio*

ABOVE: Kanazawa Museum of Wooden Japanese Sweet Molds, Kanazawa, Chūbu
BELOW: Umezono Sabo, Kyoto, Kansai

DRINKS
NOMIMONO

BEER

ビール

——— We've considered Japanese beer to be the best in the world for a long time now. Endless variety, rich flavours, ready availability (in both vending machines and convenience stores) and strikingly inexpensive ... and perhaps there's just something in the water. The big brands – Sapporo, Kirin, Yebisu and Asahi – will be familiar, but the beers you might know are usually brewed under license by third-party breweries in the West. In Japan, the corporate breweries produce a large range of different styles, and these beers are perfect when paired with *yakitori* or *izakaya* (pub; p. 117) food – especially on a sweltering summer's day.

Craft beer has taken off as well, leading to some amazing regional varieties. Hitachino Nest, Suiyoubi no Neko, Yona Yona, Minoh and Swan Lake are all worth a try. There are also plenty of places to sample the beers without going direct to the makers: Kyoto (p. 234), Tokyo (p. 162) and Osaka (p. 252) in particular have craft beer venues aplenty.

CRAFT BEER HOTSPOTS & REGIONAL VARIETIES

CHŪBU
Baird Beer, Shizuoka
Fujizakura Heights Beer, Yamanashi
Oriental Brewing, Kanazawa
Try the matcha beer ... or don't!
Outsider Brewing, Yamanashi
Swan Lake, Niigata
Yo-Ho Brewing, Nagano

CHŪGOKU
Miyashita, Okayama

HOKKAIDŌ
Abashiri Beer, Abashiri
Famous for their Okhotsk Blue Draft, which is made with melted ice from the Sea of Okhotsk and gets its distinctive blue colour from seaweed extract)
Okhotsk Beer, Kitami
SOC Brewing, Ebetsu

KANSAI
Minoh, Osaka

KANTŌ
Kiuchi Brewery, Ibaraki

KYŪSHŪ
Fukuoka Craft, Fukuoka
Suginoya, Hakata

TŌHOKU
Sekinoichi Shuzo, Iwate
Shinken Factory, Miyagi
Tono Zumona Beer, Iwate

LEFT: Sake explained at Setouchi Retreat Aonagi, Matsuyama, Shikoku **OPPOSITE PAGE TOP:** Tea with a lovely local, Kyoto, Kansai **BOTTOM:** Shibuya bar, Tokyo, Kantō

SAKE

酒

Despite the rising popularity of whisky, beer and even wine, sake, or Japanese rice wine, still remains the drink of choice in Japan. You will find it offered as an accompaniment to all traditional dishes, as well as in many contemporary drinking and dining establishments. The taste is slightly acidic and a little bit sweet; paired with a *kaiseki ryōri* feast (p. 127), it is perfection. After a beer or two in an *izakaya* (pub; p. 117), it can't be beaten. Like tea, it can be served in a special ceremony where it is lightly warmed. We prefer drinking sake chilled or at room temperature, but the right sake, when heated – especially in winter – can be a real treat. Exploring the many facets of sake could take a lifetime – in fact, many Japanese people have dedicated themselves to just that.

Buying sake outside of Japan can prove expensive, even for an average sake, whereas cheap sake in Japan is generally a pleasure. It's worth it, however, to shell out just a little more; you'll quickly notice the difference. Craft sake has become popular in recent years. Considering that the tipple was handmade for centuries, it should come as no surprise that people would go back and discover the true roots of how to make sake. The intricacies in the process are many: rice selection, polishing ratio, filtration, ageing ... in fact, there are so many variables that there are many different types and grades of sake, each with their own name.

As a side note, the word 'sake' in Japan refers to alcohol in general, while *nihonshu* refers to the drink we know in the West as sake. To avoid confusion, it is usually best to ask for *nihonshu*.

TYPES OF SAKE

AMAZAKE
Sweet, low-alcohol sake made with sake lees. A non-alcoholic version can be made with fermented rice

GENSHU
Undiluted sake, higher in alcohol

KUROSHU
Unpolished (brown) rice sake, similar to Chinese rice wine

NAMAZAKE
Unpasteurised sake that must be refrigerated

NIGORI
Unfiltered (*nigori* means 'cloudy') sake containing rice sediment

TEISEIHAKU-SHU
Sake made with highly polished (up to 80 per cent) rice, with a distinct rice flavour

梅酒

REGIONAL SPECIALTIES

KANSAI
Kinpaku Iri Umeshu Hamada (premium *umeshu* with gold leaf)

Make your own *umeshu* at specialty shop Choya in Kyoto

Wakayama Prefecture is known for its delicious *umeshu* made from Nanko plums

KYŪSHŪ
Black sugar *umeshu*, Okinawa

Purple sweet potato *umeshu*, Okinawa

SHIKOKU
Yuzu *umeshu*, Shikoku

UMESHU

This Japanese plum liqueur is sweet and delicious. Unripe plums are steeped in alcohol (usually *shōchū*, see opposite) and sugar for at least nine months, resulting in one of Japan's most popular drinks, especially when served with soda. An *umeshu* soda is perfect on a summer's day. The best-known brand is Choya, but there are other favourites.

SHŌCHŪ

——— Distilled from rice, buckwheat, sweet potato, barley or brown sugar, *shōchu* is comparable to vodka – or possibly moonshine! Drinking it straight is hardcore, although people do drink it on the rocks. When mixed with fruit juice and soda water to make a *chūhai* (short for *shōchū* highball), however ... oh, the heaven that awaits! *Chūhai* made with *kabosu* (a sour citrus fruit) from Kyūshū is particularly excellent. *Chūhai* is often sold in cans as Chu-Hi, with common flavours being lemon, peach, grapefruit or plum (yuzu citrus Chu-Hi is one of Michelle's all-time favourites). Be wary when knocking back canned Chu-Hi, as new variants can be as high as 9 per cent alcohol by volume – you can get smashed on one. There's an interesting reason for this: in Japan, beverages containing up to 8 per cent alcohol by volume are taxed quite heavily, but above that the tax is quite low; expect this loophole to be closed soon. Another interesting and delicious use of *shōchū* is *sobayuwari*: *shōchū* blended with the water left over from cooking soba noodles, offered by some soba restaurants. It's unique and highly recommended.

REGIONAL SPECIALTIES

CHŪBU
Rice *shōchū*, Niigata

KANSAI
Soba (buckwheat) *shōchū*, Kyoto

KYŪSHŪ
Awamori crushed rice *shōchū*, Okinawa
Barley *shōchū*, Ōita
Brown sugar *shōchū*, Amami Islands
Iichiko Shōchū (brand), Ōita
Shōchū infused with kabosu (citrus)
Ōita Sweet potato *shōchū*, Kagoshima

WHISKY

——— Scotland has long held the distinction of being home to the world's best whisky. Centuries of tradition and pure Highland waters make for award-winning spirits. Given Japan's obsession with whisky – and its own plentiful high-quality waters – it makes sense that Japanese distillers would not only want to make their own superior whisky, but also to compete on a global scale ... and win.

With this in mind, it shouldn't come as a surprise that Japan is an excellent place to indulge in the legendary spirit. *Haibōru* ('highballs'), mixed drinks typically made of whisky and soda (but sometimes more), are one of the most popular drinks among salarymen, and are a great way to finish off a night of eating and drinking. If you're wanting a bottle or two to take home, look for sales in food halls; you can pick up a bargain on great whisky.

Japanese whisky has taken out many of the top honours in recent years, and drops of note include Nikka, Nikka Coffey (which is not made with coffee, but rather named after nineteenth-century Irish distiller Aeneas Coffey) and Yoichi, from Sendai, Tōhoku; Ohishi, an award-winning whisky made with rice in Kumamoto, Kyūshū; and Suntory's many offerings, including Hakushu (distilled in Hokuto, Chūbu), Yamazaki (distilled in Osaka, Kansai), Chita (distilled in Chita, Chūbu) and Hibiki (made from a blend of Hakushu, Yamazaki and Chita whiskies).

REGIONAL SPECIALTIES

CHŪBU
Fuji Gotemba Distillery, Gotemba
Karuizawa whiskies
Suntory Hakushu Distillery, Yamanashi

HOKKAIDŌ
Akkeshi Distillery, Akkeshi
Yoichi Nikka Distillery, Yoichi

KANSAI
Suntory Yamazaki Distillery, Osaka/Kyoto
White Oak Distillery, Akashi

KANTO
Ichiro's Malt, Chichibu Distillery, Saitama

KYŪSHŪ
Mars Tsunuki Distillery, Minamisatsuma

TŌHOKU
Miyagikyo Distillery, Sendai

Brewery tastings & tours

SAKE

FUKUMITSUYA SAKE BREWERY (KANAZAWA, CHŪBU)
The oldest sake brewery in Kanazawa.
fukumitsuya.co.jp

FUSHIMI SAKE BREWERS' ASSOCIATION (KYOTO, KANSAI)
Tours and tastings close to Fushimi Inari Shrine and Kyoto Station.
fushimi.or.jp/sake_guide/tasting

HELIOS DISTILLERY (NAGO, OKINAWA)
This classic all-rounder brewery in a picture-perfect building makes sake, craft beers, *awamori*, *shōchū* and whisky. Tours and tastings available.
helios-syuzo.co.jp

ISHIKAWA BREWERY (TOKYO, KANTŌ)
Tours in English – reserve ahead.
tamajiman.co.jp

KAMOIZUMI SAKE BREWERY (HIROSHIMA, CHŪGOKU)
Established in 1912, Kamoizumi strives to preserve the finest sake-making methods, working with local farmers to grow the very best rice for sake – called *yamada nishiki*. It offers tours and tastings in beautiful buildings. Hiroshima is a sake hotspot, so check the website for more tastings and tours if this is your bag.
sake-hiroshima.com/en/kura/kamoizumi.php

NADA SAKE DISTRICT (KOBE, KANSAI)
The world's number-one sake area has been brewing since the 1700s. Complete with a Sake Museum, tastings and tours, for the sake connoisseur it's a perfect day out.
hakutsuru.co.jp
www.kikumasamune.com
sakuramasamune.co.jp
enjoyfukuju.com

TAIHEIZAN BREWERY (AKITA, TŌHOKU)
Akita prefecture's sake is famous throughout Japan, and this 140-year-old brewery makes some of the finest. Check online for tour details.
www.kodamajozo.co.jp/en/visit-us

TONOIKE SAKE BREWERY (MASHIKO, KANTŌ)
Dating back to 1937, this award-winning sake brewery is a wonderful daytrip from Tokyo (sample Mashiko's famous crafts while you're at it).
tonoike.jp

SHŌCHŪ

IICHIKO HITA FACTORY (HITA, KYŪSHŪ)
A famous *shōchū* name with some of the most beautiful packaging you'll ever see. Only accessible by car and surrounded by incredible nature, this hidden treasure is beloved by the residents of Kyūshū. The factory shows nostalgic vintage commercials that tug at the heartstrings of Japanese people who grew up watching them.
iichiko.com

SHŌCHŪ IN KAGOSHIMA (KYŪSHŪ)
Kagoshima calls itself the kingdom of *shōchū*, so if you're a fan, this is your prefecture to explore. We love Kiccho Houzan, Satsuma Black and anything from the Nishishuzo brewery. Steve likes his *shōchū* with kabosu lime, while Michelle likes hers with cold green tea, soda water or Calpis (Japanese soft drink)!
kagoshima-kankou.com/s/for/highlights/shochudistillerytour/kuraguide
satsuma.co.jp/english
nishi-shuzo.co.jp

WHISKY

CHICHIBU DISTILLERY (SAITAMA, KANTŌ)

If you're looking for one of the best up-and-comers, Chichibu, the face of Japan's new boutique distilleries, should be on your radar. If you're in luck, your tour may be given by the maker, Ichirō Akuto.
Instagram @chichibudistillery

KIRIN FUJI GOTEMBA DISTILLERY (GOTEMBA, KANTŌ)

Whisky and beer tours – a must if you're visiting Mount Fuji for a few days and love the dark alcoholic arts.
www.kirin.co.jp/entertainment/factory/english/whisky

NIKKA (YOICHI, NEAR OTARU, HOKKAIDŌ)

The crisp mountain air and brutally cold climate make for some of the best whisky in the world. Plan a day in the area, with a visit to Otaru before or after your whisky odyssey.
nikka.com/eng/distilleries/yoichi

SUNTORY HAKUSHU DISTILLERY (YAMANASHI, KANTŌ)

Tours, tastings, a restaurant and even a bird sanctuary make this a wonderful day out.
suntory.com/factory/hakushu

SUNTORY YAMAZAKI DISTILLERY (OSAKA, KANSAI)

Online tour reservations are available in this happily situated distillery between Kyoto and Osaka.
suntory.co.jp/factory/yamazaki

BEER

ASAHI FACTORY SUITA (OSAKA, KANSAI)

Only forty-five minutes from central Osaka, this is one of the best beer factories with tours and tastings.
osaka-info.jp/en/page/asahi-beer-suita-factory

SAPPORO BEER FACTORY (SAPPORO, HOKKAIDŌ)

A red-brick megaplex in the middle of Sapporo with a giant beer hall, gardens, food, tours and tastings (see also p. 283).
sapporobeer.jp

YEBISU BEER FACTORY (EBISU, KANTŌ)

A great tour in the middle of Tokyo, with one of Japan's best beers.
sapporobeer.jp/english/brewery/y_museum

CRAFT BEER

KIUCHI BREWERY FOR NEST BEER (IBARAKI, KANTŌ)

Kiuchi has a lot of brews on the go, but it's Japan's darling beer of the moment, and Nest beer is a must try.
hitachino.cc/en/brewery

YOHO BREWING (TOKYO, KANTŌ)

The adorable cat packaging for Sui Youbi no Neko makes Michelle wish she was a beer-drinker. The taste is similar to a Belgium white.
yonayonabeerworks.com
yohobrewing.com

TOP LEFT: Fukumitsuya Sake Brewery, Kanazawa, Chūbu MIDDLE & RIGHT: Sapporo Beer Factory, Sapporo, Hokkaidō

TEA

——— Tea – *ocha* – is much more than just a drink in Japan. Steeped in tradition, it's closer to an art form or ritual. The Japanese tea ceremony, *sadō* ('the way of tea'), is calming and spiritual, and a cultural experience that you shouldn't miss. A proper tea ceremony will be expensive, and typically takes place in a location of great beauty, such as a temple, Japanese garden or *ryokan* (inn; p. 87). Entry was traditionally via a small door that people could only enter by taking off any armour or finery and crouching or crawling – making all participants equal in status. A tea-maker immaculately dressed in gorgeous kimono will whisk *matcha* tea in a bowl and serve it with *wagashi* (traditional sweets; p. 140). Bowls will be rotated just so; tea will be whisked to perfection; and sometimes stories will be told. Some ceremonies let you get involved, clumsily whisking your own tea in the bowl, trying to get it to froth in the same perfect way that the experts do. Kyoto, Uji and Kagoshima are great places to experience a proper tea ceremony, but there are many others dotted all over the country. If the ceremony sounds like a little too much for you, you can just have the tea. Many places will whisk tea for you and serve it with *wagashi*. It's particularly wonderful when experienced in a garden or temple ground in Kyoto, particularly Arashiyama, which often serve properly made *matcha*.

TEA HOTSPOTS & REGIONAL VARIETIES

KAGOSHIMA, KYŪSHŪ

Located on the southern tip of Kyūshū and a waypoint on your journey down to Yakushima and Okinawa, Kagoshima (p. 320) is presided over by a spectacular volcano. This town is home to many unique delicacies, one of which is tea – in fact, Kagoshima is one of two places in Japan that lays claim to being the birthplace and main source of tea and tea leaves. Brews here are diverse, intricate and delicious. Buy some to take home.

SHIZUOKA, CHŪBU

Although Kagoshima and Uji are regarded as the country's oldest tea-growing areas, Shizuoka (p. 227), the green-tea capital, has its own claim to fame. Its tea fields produce the most tea in Japan and its teas are known for their excellent quality.

UJI, KANSAI

The other home of tea in Japan, Uji (p. 249), celebrates the beverage in many ways. Matcha (powdered green tea) is the main product here, and you can find it not only in tea ceremonies, but also as a flavouring for soft-serve ice cream and biscuits – and even soba noodle soups and curry. The main street is a shrine to tea and tea boxes; tea-related statues and lore can be found throughout the city. A must for tea fanatics.

TEA TYPES

GENMAICHA

Green tea and roasted rice mixed together. It was invented at the Nishiki market in Kyoto (p. 238).

HŌJICHA

Late-season tea made by roasting the stems and leaves of the tea plant. Delicious hot or cold.

MATCHA

A finely ground green powder used in most tea ceremonies. The tea is made from plants grown in the shade, the leaves of which have had the veins and stems removed after picking and before air-drying. The prepared leaves are then ground with a mortar and pestle to create matcha.

MATCHA LATTE

A combination of matcha powder and milk served as a hot drink or cold with ice cream in a 'soda' glass.

SENCHA

Japan's favourite tea type is made from the first of the season's tea, which has been grown in full sunlight, then steamed and dried. Delicious hot or cold.

TEA MADE FROM OTHER PLANTS

Sobacha is made from roasted buckwheat kernels, *mugicha* from roasted barley, *gobocha* from roasted burdock root and *kombucha* from kelp.

OPPOSITE PAGE: Tea house in Kōraku-en, Okayama, Chūgoku

JAPAN

日本

152

CULINARY JAPAN – DRINKS

————— Japanese coffee can be approached from two different directions. The first, contemporary coffee, is a masterclass in craft brews. Beans are selected with investigative precision and styles like stovetop, syphon (which is like a delicious science project), percolator and drip have been explored and studied, extracting the most out of the coffee-making process – to the point where Japan can take Italy on in coffee the same way it has taken Scotland on with whisky. If you want a perfect contemporary brew, then you can now find it in Japan – quite the feat, considering a good latte or café au lait was very hard to come by as recently as ten years ago.

The other side of the coin is the coffee that Japan has been brewing for half a century: the coffee of the kissaten, unique European-inspired coffee dens full of flavour and character that are some of Japan's must-try experiences. Coffee is often pricey, but it will be served up with care and dedication. Kissaten are usually mom-and-pop affairs (although these days the kids have taken over, keeping the nostalgic spirit alive while adding a touch of the new) and will be accompanied by treats like chiffon cake, coffee jelly (yes please!) and sponge cake and cream. Be adventurous, coffee lovers. There's a whole world of coffee out there, and Japan has it well and truly covered.

COFFEE TYPES

AMERICAN DRIP
The staple coffee in most eateries in Japan, served with a tiny jug of milk and sugar on the side.

BARISTA MADE
Most big cities will have chic designer cafés serving coffee made from premium beans in a variety of ways.

CHAIN-STORE COFFEE
Fast, inexpensive and can be dubious in quality. Lattes, cappuccinos and seasonal flavours are on the menu.

COFFEE BEER
We've tried it at Fuglen in Tokyo, and seen it pop up around the country!

COFFEE COCKTAILS
Spotted at cheap and cheerful *izakaya* (pubs; p. 117) in unusual forms, and as the classic espresso martini in some of the finest cocktail bars.

COFFEE IN A CAN
It's coffee, it's in a can – hot or cold, black or milky. It's coffee, but not as you know it.

COFFEE JELLY
A dessert we always order at a classic *kissaten*. A little bit of alcohol can be added and a dollop of cream and a mint leaf are often used to garnish.

KISSATEN COFFEE
Made in front of you by the *kissaten* owner, usually in a dark room with a jazz soundtrack.

POUR-OVER AND SYPHON
If you love it in your home town, you'll be taken to the next level in Japan.

REGIONAL FOOD & DRINKS

RAMEN
Ramen was perfected in Yokohama; miso ramen (Sapporo); *tonkotsu* ramen (Fukuoka, Hakata); *shio* ramen (Hakodate); *shōyu* ramen (Tokyo); Onomichi-style seafood ramen (Hiroshima); Tokushima ramen (Shikoku); miso milk curry ramen (Aomori)

SUSHI, SASHIMI AND SEAFOOD
Oysters (Kanazawa, Hiroshima); crab (Kinosaki, Hakodate); fish cakes – Satsuma *age* (Kagoshima); sashimi (Sapporo); sushi (Tokyo, Okinawa, Kyoto, Osaka); eel (Matsuyama)

RICE
Rice porridge (Nara); Koshihikari rice – the best rice in Japan (Kanazawa, Niigata); taco rice (Okinawa)

SWEETS
Wagashi (Kyoto, Kanazawa); cheesecake (Hokkaidō); *manjū* – sweet steamed buns (Nara); *purin* – egg custard (Yufuin); *dango* – rice dumplings (Shikoku)

NOODLES
Wanko soba (Morioka, Ise); Udon: (Ise); Sanuki udon (Takamatsu); Inaniwa udon (Akita); Hippari udon (Yamagata); *chūka* soba (Wakayama); pasta (Takasaki)

MEAT
Beef (Takayama, Morioka, Beppu, Kobe); pork (Kagoshima); chicken (Beppu); Spam (Okinawa)

SAKE AND SHOCHU
Shōchū (Kyūshū); sake (Kyoto, Niigata, Akita, Hiroshima, Kanazawa)

BEER AND WHISKY
Beer (Sapporo, Osaka, Mount Fuji area, Shizuoka, Niigata); whisky (Osaka, Mount Fuji area, Chichibu, Nagano)

TEA
Uji, Shizuoka, Kagoshima

HOKKAIDŌ 北海道

SAPPORO

HAKODATE

AOMORI

AKITA

MORIOKA

YAMAGATA

TŌHOKU 東北

NIIGATA

NAGANO

TAKASAKI

CHICHIBU

KANAZAWA

TAKAYAMA

MOUNT FUJI

TOKYO

YOKOHAMA

KANTŌ 関東

KINOSAKI

CHŪGOKU 中国

KYOTO

UJI

NARA

SHIZUOKA

CHŪBU 中部

HIROSHIMA

OKAYAMA

KOBE

TAKAMATSU

OSAKA

WAKAYAMA

KANSAI 関西

FUKUOKA

MATSUYAMA

BEPPU

ŌITA CITY

YUFUIN

SHIKOKU 四国

KYŪSHŪ 九州

KAGOSHIMA

OKINAWA
↓

FAVOURITE THINGS

私たちのお気に入り

Food markets

Japan is not an early riser, so head to a food market for an early morning breakfast if you're up with the birds. Seafood, fruit, pickles and all manner of foodstuffs new to a Western palate are on show to be tried, tested and tasted.

HAKODATE ASAICHI MORNING MARKET (HAKODATE, HOKKAIDŌ)

Hakodate is famed for crab, and there's nowhere better to taste it. See also p. 278.
uu-hokkaido.com/corporate/hakodate-asaichi.shtml

KUROMON MARKET (OSAKA, KANSAI)

Pickles and fresh produce, seafood galore, Kobe beef skewers – find it all at this popular market in Osaka.
kuromon.com

NIJO MARKET (SAPPORO, HOKKAIDŌ)

You'll eat the freshest seafood here, and see why Hokkaidō is called Japan's kitchen. See also p. 283.
nijomarket.com

NISHIKI MARKET (KYOTO, KANSAI)

Historic market in the heart of Kyoto. Pickles, black sesame ice-cream, seafood and more. See also p. 238.
kyoto-nishiki.or.jp

OMICHO MARKET (KANAZAWA, CHŪBU)

A fish market famed for its salmon and salmon roe bowls (with gold leaf on top). See also p. 216.
ohmicho-ichiba.com

TAKAYAMA MORNING MARKETS (TAKAYAMA, CHŪBU)

Two morning markets for a leisurely stroll before starting your sightseeing in this beautiful part of the world.
hida.jp/english/touristattractions/takayamacity/historyandculture/4000162.html

TSUKIJI FISH MARKET (TOKYO, KANTŌ)

The world-famous Tokyo fish market, newly relocated. See also p. 166.
tsukiji.or.jp/english

YOBUKO MORNING MARKET (KARATSU, KYŪSHŪ)

Fish market in a country setting.
karatsu-kankou.jp

TOP LEFT: Kuromon Market, Osaka, Kansai
MIDDLE: Nijo Market, Sapporo, Hokkaidō
RIGHT: Nishiki Market, Kyoto Kansai
OPPOSITE: Omicho Market, Kanazawa, Chūbu

JAPAN BY REGION

地域別日本

MAIN JAPANESE ISLANDS

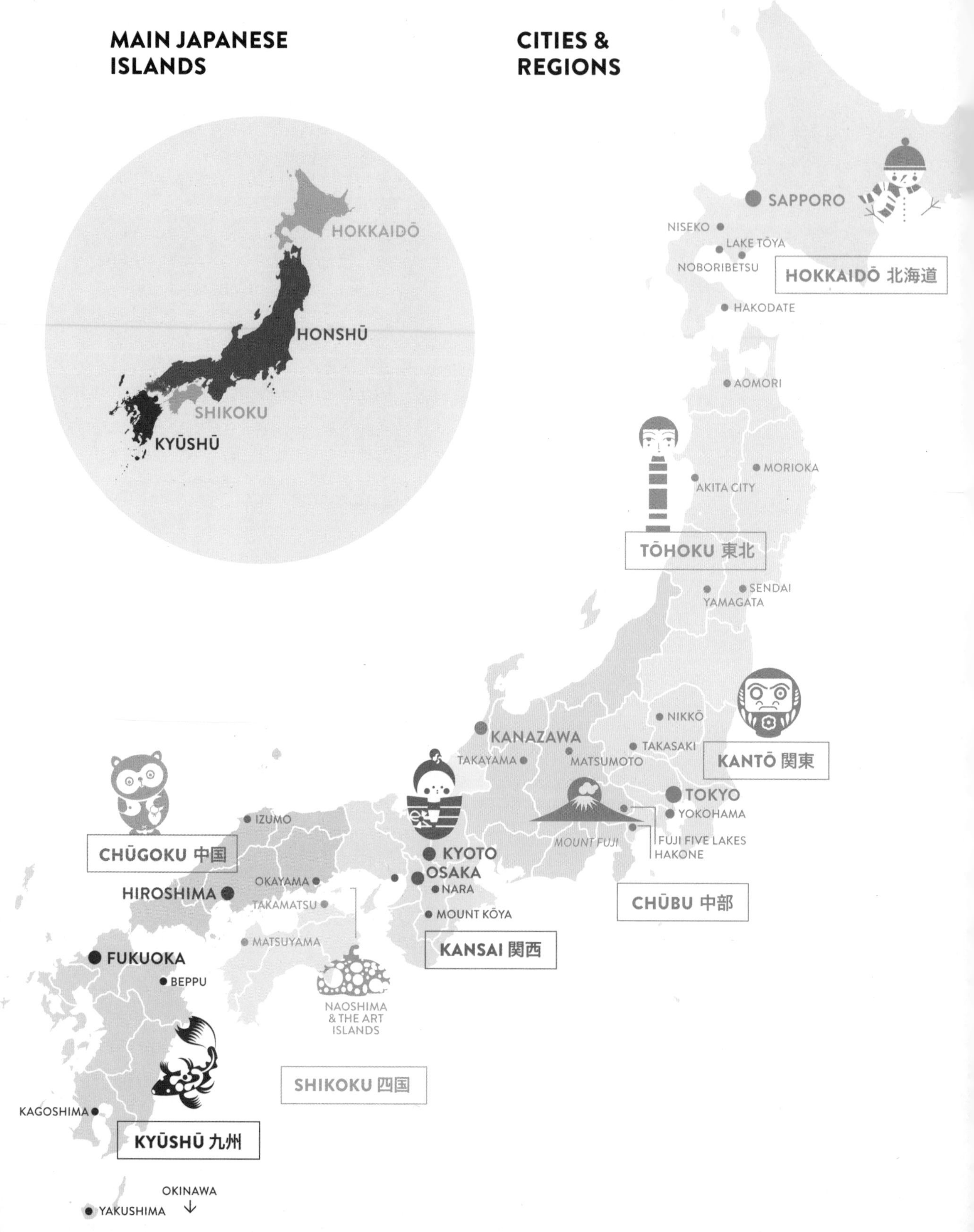

HOKKAIDŌ

HONSHŪ

SHIKOKU

KYŪSHŪ

CITIES & REGIONS

SAPPORO

NISEKO

LAKE TŌYA

NOBORIBETSU

HAKODATE

HOKKAIDŌ 北海道

AOMORI

MORIOKA

AKITA CITY

TŌHOKU 東北

SENDAI
YAMAGATA

NIKKŌ

TAKASAKI

TAKAYAMA

MATSUMOTO

KANAZAWA

KANTŌ 関東

TOKYO

YOKOHAMA

FUJI FIVE LAKES

MOUNT FUJI

HAKONE

CHŪBU 中部

IZUMO

KYOTO

OSAKA

NARA

CHŪGOKU 中国

OKAYAMA

HIROSHIMA

TAKAMATSU

MOUNT KŌYA

MATSUYAMA

KANSAI 関西

FUKUOKA

BEPPU

NAOSHIMA & THE ART ISLANDS

SHIKOKU 四国

KAGOSHIMA

KYŪSHŪ 九州

OKINAWA
↓

YAKUSHIMA

PREFECTURES
BY REGION

HOKKAIDŌ 北海道

1. Hokkaidō

TŌHOKU 東北

2. Aomori
3. Iwate
4. Miyagi
5. Akita
6. Yamagata
7. Fukushima

KANTŌ 関東

8. Ibaraki
9. Tochigi
10. Gunma
11. Saitama
12. Chiba
13. Tokyo
14. Kanagawa

KANSAI 関西

24. Mie
25. Shiga
26. Kyoto
27. Osaka
28. Hyōgo
29. Nara
30. Wakayama

CHŪBU 中部

15. Niigata
16. Toyama
17. Ishikawa
18. Fukui
19. Yamanashi
20. Nagano
21. Gifu
22. Shizuoka
23. Aichi

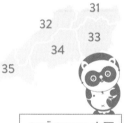

CHŪGOKU 中国

31. Tottori
32. Shimane
33. Okayama
34. Hiroshima
35. Yamaguchi

SHIKOKU 四国

36. Tokushima
37. Kagawa
38. Ehime
39. Kōchi

KYŪSHŪ 九州

40. Fukuoka
41. Saga
42. Nagasaki
43. Kumamoto
44. Ōita
45. Miyazaki
46. Kagoshima
47. Okinawa

↓
47

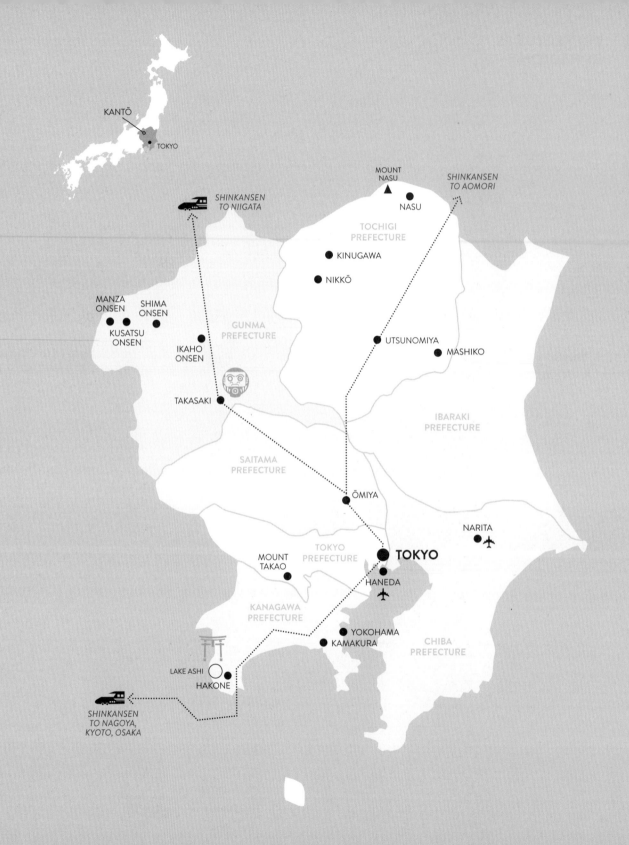

KANTŌ

TOKYO

SHINKANSEN TO NIIGATA

SHINKANSEN TO AOMORI

MOUNT
NASU

NASU

TOCHIGI
PREFECTURE

KINUGAWA

NIKKŌ

MANZA
ONSEN

SHIMA
ONSEN

KUSATSU
ONSEN

IKAHO
ONSEN

GUNMA
PREFECTURE

UTSUNOMIYA

MASHIKO

TAKASAKI

IBARAKI
PREFECTURE

SAITAMA
PREFECTURE

ŌMIYA

NARITA

MOUNT
TAKAO

TOKYO
PREFECTURE

TOKYO

HANEDA

KANAGAWA
PREFECTURE

YOKOHAMA

KAMAKURA

CHIBA
PREFECTURE

LAKE ASHI

HAKONE

*SHINKANSEN
TO NAGOYA,
KYOTO, OSAKA*

関東

KANTŌ

For many people, Honshū will be the only Japanese island they visit and where they will spend most, if not all, of their time. Encompassing the regions of Kantō, Tōhoku, Chūbu, Chūgoku and Kansai – and including the major tourist destinations of Tokyo, Kyoto, Osaka and Hiroshima – there is more than enough to fill any itinerary to the brim.

There's no doubt that the rapidly beating heart of the Kantō region is Tokyo (p. 162), capital city of Japan, a formidable, mesmerising metropolis with looming towers and hidden enclaves, startling new builds and pockets of deep history, noisy night-time alleys and moments of profound peace. But Kantō is much more than just the capital.

The region takes in seven prefectures – Gunma, Tochigi, Ibaraki, Saitama, Tokyo, Chiba and Kanagawa – each offering a unique experience and some startling discoveries. Tokyo's surrounds are striking enough: beautiful Hakone (p. 184); historical and magical Nikkō (p. 178); and bustling Yokohama (p. 191), Japan's second-largest city, to name a few. Head into the prefectures, however, and Japan's cultural riches and natural wonders really start to reveal themselves. Gunma (p. 186) is an area of mountainous forests and splendorous, historical hot-spring towns, as is Nasu (p. 191) in Tochigi. Chiba is a land of national parks and rugged coastlines. Kanagawa takes in Yokohama, Kamakura (p. 177) and Hakone. Ibaraki features lakes and gardens, including one of Japan's 'big three' landscaped wonders: Kairaku-en. So next time you're in the capital, make sure you venture out a little further and explore.

Tokyo

Japan's capital since Kyoto's power base officially shifted across in 1868, Tokyo is now one of the world's most striking cities, an absurdly expansive metropolis made up of many distinct, ever-moving parts. You can easily get lost in just one portion of the whole, a web-like network of jaw-dropping city centres, urban clusters and winding alleyways. Trying to navigate it all seems a daunting and overwhelming task to most people, even locals. It's best to identify a few areas you want to explore and start from there. Of course, getting lost isn't too much of a problem – you're sure to find something intriguing and exciting, and you'll never be too far from a train station, taxi rank or bus stop.

Part of the joy of Tokyo's many hubs is that each has its own unique flavour (and flavours – food specialties are often individual to one train stop or urban hub). You'll find towering neon wonderlands, the skyscraper city of *Akira*, department stores that seem to touch the clouds, and train stations that descend into endless networks of tunnels and boast some of the world's best underground shopping and eating. Areas can be traditional and historical with astounding architecture, museums and craft; or contemporary and arresting, with the latest art, technology and buildings.

World-famous monuments and experiences are scattered around the vast zone. They can be quiet and contemplative with beautiful gardens and paths, or busy, loud and chaotic. Shopping is outstanding. Eating can be high-end or cheap and cheerful, ranging from some of the world's best upscale restaurants to small, charming noodle houses.

Exploring Tokyo could easily be a lifelong pursuit – there really is too much to see and do – but whether you're cramming it in or taking it slowly, it's going to be an adventure like no other, and no two experiences will be alike. →

BELOW: Buildings in Shibuya **OPPOSITE PAGE:** Comme des Garçons in GYRE, Harajuku

▶ **TRANSPORT**

Haneda and Narita airports, JR and private trains, buses, bicycles, taxis

▶ **CLOSE BY**

Hakone, Kamakura, Yokohama, Nikkō

▶ **ATMOSPHERE**

Riotous, inspiring, contemporary, cutting-edge and thrilling or tranquil, traditional and contemplative

▶ **REGIONAL FOOD & DRINK**

You name it, they have it

▶ **OMIYAGE**

Hato Sabure (shortbread), Shiseido tins, Tokyo Banana (banana-filled sponge), NHK character toys, *uchiwa* (fans), crazy flavour Kit Kats, manga and anime figurines, *yukata* (summer kimono)

▶ **SIGHTS**

Senso-ji, Tokyo Tower, Tokyo Skytree, Meiji Jingumae Shrine

▶ **GARDENS & PARKS**

Shinjuku Gyo-en, Kiyosumi Teien, Happō-en, Koishikawa-Kōrakuen, Rikugi-en

▶ **MUSEUMS & GALLERIES**

Mori Art Museum, National Art Center, MOT Museum of Contemporary Art, 21_21 Design Sight, Nezu Museum, teamLab Borderless, Edo-Tokyo Museum, Mingeikan Japan Folk Crafts Museum, Meiji Jingu Museum

▶ **VIEWS**

Mori Art Museum, Tokyo Tower, Tokyo Skytree, Tokyo Metropolitan Government Building

▶ **FESTIVALS**

Asakusa Sanja Matsuri, Natsu Matsuri, Sumida River Fireworks, Eisa Festival, Tsukiji Honganji Temple Bon Odori Festival, Kōenji Awaodori Festival, Fukagawa Hachiman Festival, Azabu-Jūban Noryo Festival, Harajuku Omotesandō Genki Matsuri Super Yosakoi, Fuji Matsuri Wisteria Festival, Tenno Matsuri, Hatsumode, Design Festa, Setsubun

▶ **WEB**

gotokyo.org

BRIGHT LIGHTS, BIG CITY

If you're seeking the Tokyo of futurist dreams – long, wide streets and clusters of towering buildings bejewelled with neon, outrageously sized placards and television screens – it can be found in the city's most astounding, over-the-top mini-metros: Shinjuku, Shibuya, Harajuku, Aoyama, Ginza and Roppongi.

TOP: *Meiji Jingu Museum* BOTTOM: *Michelle in Shibuya*

SHINJUKU

A city of rebirth, Shinjuku offers the best of both urban worlds. The spiralling twentieth-century buildings, laneways, crumbling facades and Shōwa-era (p. 42) drinking alleys are offset by the striking new architectural builds – from the impressive Mode Gakuen Cocoon Tower to fresh-faced department stores like NEWoMan, which keeps things up-to-date as Japan moves ever forward.

Amongst it all, one of the world's oldest and most beautiful stores, Isetan, will astound you – the sweets section alone will have you browsing for hours. Huge music collectors' heaven Disc Union also has its main store here in Shinjuku. Maze-like, tottering, decidedly unsafe (both the buildings and the booze) drinking den Golden Gai will turn you into an instant local. Line up for a bathroom break at dubious outside stalls, order the pungent *niboshi* sardine ramen, or have a potent drink served by somebody standing next to some taxidermy or a pink rubber dildo. A truly unmissable relic of old Japan.

These tight-knit civic cells hide backstreets with long-established food stalls, alleys with stores that have been around for a century, and sleazy Kabukichō, the sex quarter, almost a theme park in itself and one of Tokyo's rare dark havens. All of this spirals out from a train station you can get lost in for days without even knowing or caring. Shinjuku Station is the world's most notorious travel hub, servicing millions of people a day, a *Guinness World Records* icon with recommended shopping and eating and endless tracks and corridors – make sure you know your platform! Getting lost (everyone does) has never been this much fun.

SHIBUYA

Energetic and youthful Shibuya is a shopping mecca where ideas come and go in the blink of an eye. Megastores entice you in and keep you locked in a vortex of consumerism. Shibuya has a great story, and one that spawned one of the world's most famous meeting places: Hachikō Square. This is where Hachikō, the golden Akita dog, reportedly waited for his master for nine years after his death, in the same spot he had waited patiently for him during his lifetime. Get your picture taken next to the modest statue of the faithful pooch.

From Hachikō Square, head over to the Shibuya Crossing (AKA the Scramble), a true Tokyo phenomenon. When the lights turn green you walk across a multi-street intersection – in any direction! All you have to do is dodge the endless photographers, video-takers, Instagram influencers and selfie-obsessed who pause midway to set up a tripod and snap some shots of the milling throng. An estimated 3000 people can cross at peak time. Enjoy the best of Tokyo's billboards, TV commercials blaring at you from massive screens and jingles filling the air. Snap some overhead shots of the manic marvel from the vertigo-inducing Sky Stage at the top of Shibuya Scramble Square.

Tokyu Department Store's 'Food Show', flashily revamped in 2021, is a vibrant clutch of food stalls in a train station basement. Outside is department store Hikarie ShinQs, featuring D&Department's design museum, which showcases Japanese regional specialties in design, craft and food – a must-visit.

Loft, Tokyu Hands and Muji may have opened many other superstores but somehow Shibuya feels like their spiritual home. Tokyu Hands is unmissable – a maze of DIY trinkets and tools, a mecca for all things Japanese, handy and clever. Nearby Tower Records keeps the musical heart of Shibuya beating, a sci-fi tower of retro futurism with new-release Japanese and international CDs, books and records.

HARAJUKU & AOYAMA

Omotesandō, an easy walk down Cat Street from Shibuya, features vibrant Harajuku at one end and chic Aoyama at the other. Harajuku's Laforet has five floors crammed with Tokyo's best indie fashion stores, where people-watching is in order. Takeshita Dōri has long been a rite of passage for teenage Tokyo. Snap a shot from the top of the street as you emerge from the station – the mad, seething crush of shoppers is a sight to behold.

Aoyama plays host to visually impressive upmarket fashion houses, such as Comme des Garçons and Issey Miyake, watched over by the many glass eyes of Prada's tower.

Both areas offer memorable chances to escape the bustle of the streets. In peaceful repose at the top of Omotesandō is the Meiji Jingumae Shinto Shrine. Housing the spirits of Emperor Meiji and his wife (now Shinto gods), it's a peaceful stroll through towering trees to a large shrine and impressive grounds, a major hub for new year festivities. Don't miss the new Kengo Kuma–designed museum on the approach to the shrine, a modern marvel in glass and dark and pale wood, which houses the shrine's many treasures.

At the southern end of Omotesandō in Aoyama, the Nezu Museum features one of Tokyo's most tranquil strolling gardens, spread out before a museum that exhibits beautiful and impressive historical artifacts in an atmospheric setting. →

GINZA

When the silver mint was established here in the Edo period (p. 28), Ginza rapidly became the first of the cashed-up areas of Japan. It played host to the sophisticates and socialites emerging as the new middle class in the Meiji era (p. 32), and catered to lunching ladies in the Shōwa era (p. 42). Such ladies still stroll the streets, resplendent in kimono or *yukata* (casual summer kimono), dropping into high-end eateries, old-school coffee houses and chopstick or *noren* curtain stores. It's also effectively the 'top end of town'. Big-name brands have built impressive monuments to their labels, proud towers that exhibit their wealth and excess, and by default some pretty spectacular architectural innovation. As a casual punter you can wind in and out of these stores and marvel at their lack of restraint, but no matter how hard they try they're all still competing with early adopter Mitsukoshi, one of the world's first department stores. Its cut-paper feather ceilings lead you into an atrium that will leave you breathless – with its 'celestial maiden' statue standing guard over an Art Deco–lover's dream of a staircase.

Like most of Tokyo, Ginza has been modernised for the 2020 Olympics and beyond. An interesting recent development has been the addition of luxe versions of Japanese superstores. Uniqlo kicked it off, their multi-storey power store bringing busloads (literally) of everyday travellers to the normally ultra-chic area. In response, Loft and Muji also shifted their flagships from nearby Yokochō and set up destination department stores that lack the rough-and-tumble spirit of the originals but make up for it in impressive shop design. The famed Tsukiji Fish Market (p. 154) is gone now, moved to an obscure bayside space and taking some of the heart of traditional Ginza with it. But you can still tour the outer markets of the original space and feast on some fresh seafood.

Kabuki-za Theatre continues to impress with its ornate facade. Take in a show, and don't forget to hit up the colourful and bustling basement for some souvenirs or satellite eateries. While the theatre itself has undergone extensive renovations, the surrounding bars, udon restaurants and coffee joints remain relatively unchanged, and provide some charming and delicious dining opportunities.

ROPPONGI

Tokyo's unruly child, Roppongi
had always been the up-all-night,
drunk-at-the-station, streets-
need-a-serious-clean kind of
town where expats and visitors
went to see how the Japanese
play. Recently, however, there has
been a noticeable lean towards the
upmarket which has changed the
landscape. The street cred is all
still there – you can't reinvent the
wheel without getting a puncture
or two – but despite still needing

a serious scrub on a Sunday
morning, Roppongi is now also
both Tokyo's art capital and a chic
shopping district.

With the three-pronged attack
of the Mori Art Museum (with
an unmissable Tokyo panorama
from the lofty perches of the
observation lounge and Sky Deck),
the National Art Center (with
multiple exhibition rooms, striking
curved metal facade, popular Joël
Robuchon café and standout gallery
shop) and the 21_21 Design Sight

(a contemporary space set in a
concrete bunker beneath the green
grass of the bountiful grounds of
Tokyo Midtown) – you have
a district with some serious new-
school acumen. The shopping zones
of Roppongi Hills and Midtown
offer floors of world-class shopping.

At night, Roppongi is illuminated,
bustling, manic and mad, the
enticing stuff of Tokyo neon dreams
and nightmares, now rolled up in
the cotton-wool promise of a new
sophistication. →

OPPOSITE PAGE: Mitsukoshi, Nihonbashi
ABOVE: 21_21 Design Sight, Roppongi

Playtime

THE JAPANESE ARE KNOWN FOR THEIR WORK ETHIC, AND AFTER A HARD WEEK AT THE OFFICE, THERE ARE PLENTY OF WAYS ALL OVER THE COUNTRY FOR PEOPLE TO LET OFF SOME STEAM.

Karaoke ('blank orchestra') is one of the best known worldwide. *Utago-kissa* were cafés in the 1950s–1970s where communal singing was all the rage. Karaoke built on that and now you can sing your heart out with your friends, with complete strangers (liquid courage will help) or even in a private booth on your own or with a loved one. The premise is simple: a backing track plays and you sing along. You can be a good singer or a bad one – it's all about the health benefits of belting out a tune. Bigger places will have a wide variety of choice for music styles or group numbers, so experiment. For visitors, closed captioning in English will usually be available. It can get pricey, so if you're budget conscious, happy-hour deals are the way to go.

Pachinko is a game where you drop small metal balls into what's best described as 'vertical pinball'. Pachinko is sometimes played for fun but mostly to gamble. While gambling is illegal in Japan, as is any game that exchanges money, pachinko circumvents this law by returning tokens or pay-offs of more balls to the winner. These can be exchanged for money. Pachinko is a major obsession in Japan, and you'll see (and hear) brightly coloured, migraine-inducing pachinko parlours all over the country.

Hobbies, card games, collecting and model-making are hugely popular in Japan and easily become a lifetime obsession. Even the most straitlaced businessman can have a secret penchant for collecting *gachapon* (capsule toys) or making intricate models of monsters or aeroplanes. These hobbies are well and truly catered for in Japan, and even if you're not a hobbyist yourself, visiting the stores and events centred around them can be a lot of fun. Battle-card games have been big business in Japan since the late 1980s and early 1990s, and collectors will go out of their way to get their next top-level card. Games like YU-GI-Oh and Dragon Ball Z have turned into franchises, including anime, manga and character toys. Capsule toys are another obsessive pastime for the collector (and great fun for the rest of us). They can range from cheap and cute to pricey but incredibly intricate – and in some cases rare, as many capsule toys are made as limited editions, to the endless frustration of completists. Toys include miniature food, tiny animals, office workers, robots, monsters, character toys and a whole odd assortment of fantastic things in between.

Arcade games are another way to shake out the work blues or celebrate a holiday, and you'll find them in cities all over Japan. Popular games include UFO Catcher (lower the claw and try to pick up a prize from the bubble), Purikura Photo Booth (take pics with your friends and add cute graphics like cat ears, noses, etc.), Taiko Drum (take your frustrations out on a large Japanese drum) and Dance Dance (follow the computer prompts and master the dance steps!).

Theme cafés are also big news – places where you get to sip tea or coffee, eat snacks and pet fluffy creatures. The types of animals in cafés so far include cats, owls, dogs, hedgehogs, rabbits and penguins ... there's even a much less cuddly-sounding snake café. Other themes for cafés and restaurants include trains, maids, vampires, Hello Kitty, Final Fantasy, Moomins, ninja ... the list goes on. We're sure that if you like it, there'll be a café for it.

ANIMAL CAFÉS

KYOTO, KANSAI
· Kyoto no Fukuro no Mori (owl café)
· Petton Dog Café

TOKYO, KANTŌ
· Cat Cafe Temari No Ouchi (Kichijōji)
· Calico Cat (Shinjuku)
· Fukuro Sabo Owl (Kokubunji)
· Hedgehog Café Cheese (Chiyoda)
· Hedgehog Café Harry (Harajuku)
· Nekobukuro (Ikebukuro)
· Rabbit and Grow fat (Ra.a.g.f) (Harajuku)
· Sakuragaoka Goat Café (Sakuragaoka)

ARCADE GAMES

OSAKA, KANSAI
· Video Game Bar Space Station (Nishi Shinsaibashi)
· Game Bar Continue – vintage (Higa Shishinsaibashi)
· Game Bar GeeBee (Shinsaibashi)

TOKYO, KANTŌ
· Club Sega (Akihabara)
· Mikado (Takadanobaba) – vintage game arcade
· Super Potato (Akihabara) – top floor
· Taito Station (Shibuya)

CAPSULE TOYS
· Gachapon Kaikan (Akihabara, Tokyo, Kantō)
· Super Position (Tokyo, Kantō; Osaka, Kansai)
· Village Vanguard (all over Japan)

HOBBYISTS
. Mandarake (all over Japan)
. Super Potato – retro computer games (all over Japan)
. Village Vanguard (all over Japan)
. Yellow Submarine (all over Japan)

KARAOKE
. Big Echo (all over Japan)
. Daichi Kosho (all over Japan)
. Karaoke-Kan (Tokyo, Kantō)
. Karaoke Manekineko (all over Japan)
. Shidax (all over Japan)
. Tetsujin (all over Japan)

PACHINKO
· Club-D (all over Japan)
· Omega (all over Japan)
· Maruhan (all over Japan)
· Starlight (all over Japan)

TOP LEFT: Gaming at a department store, Sapporo, Hokkaidō BOTTOM LEFT & RIGHT: Super Potato, Tokyo, Kantō

TOYS, TECH & TROUBLE
Maybe it's a little passé now, but the idea of a Tokyo nerd paradise, with all the new tech, toys, games and dubious maid cafés, still draws the crowds, and has taken on a kind of retro charm in recent years.

AKIHABARA

Anyone wanting to delve into Tokyo (or, for that matter, Japanese) 'nerd' culture, can still find what they're looking for in Akihabara. It singles itself out as a mecca for model shops, vintage video games, theme cafés, manga stores and general *otaku* (obsessive fandom). Long gone are the days when nerds had to take their revenge, though. Now they can shop the overpriced merchandise and afford to pay for it on their huge tech salaries. Mandarake, Yellow Submarine, Super Potato and Don Quijote all maintain their dork credentials as some of the finest toy, model, retro-gaming, doll and knick-knack stores in the world. Cat cafés, maids flipping flyers to unwary tourists on the street (no photos!), pachinko and game parlours, people dressed as Pikachu or Mario – it's all fun and games, veiling a very real showcase of some serious new gadgets and tech. As an added bonus, Akihabara has become a bit of a ramen hotspot. The fast-food capital of Tokyo has perfected the city's best fast food, and some of the most recommended ramen eateries are in and around this area.

IKEBUKURO

This transport hub could almost fall into the mega-city category all on its own. It's estimated its train station handles more than one million passengers a day, linking city and country. It's a built-up and brash area that plays off electronic giants Yamada Denki and Bic Camera in the battle for consumer hearts, and where train magnates Seibu and Tobu have created a kind of discount playground. After Akihabara, Ikebukuro has become a major *otaku* centre, a wonderland of manga, electronics, games, toys, books and music.

If you think geek and collector culture is limited to guys, head to Otome Road, a famous spot that caters exclusively to *otaku* girls. Sunshine City is one of Tokyo's first biospheres, a mega shopping complex built in 1978 that features indoor theme parks (Sanrio Puroland's ode to Hello Kitty and friends is here, as is Namco Namja Town for Pacman fanatics, all good retro fun). There's also an aquarium, museum and planetarium, and an absurd number of shops and restaurants. The sixty-metre-high Sunshine 60 Observation Deck Sky Circus has one of Tokyo's best city views. Outside at the base of Sunshine City, you can grab a bit of old-world Japan at Takamura paper shop, an absolute gem that sells elegant *chiyogami*, washi and origami paper. Impressively, they have been plying their trade for more than eighty years.

THIS PAGE: Chūō Dōri, Akihabara
OPPOSITE PAGE: teamLab Borderless, Azabudai Hills

ODAIBA

A bit of a mystery, Odaiba is an out-of-the-way bayside space that was meant to be the new go-to destination but instead fell by the wayside, becoming a spacious, man-made oddity full of office blocks, civic parks and wide roads. What better place for DiverCity, then, to set up one of Tokyo's unmissable attractions: the Unicorn Gundam statue. The Gundam robot statue stands a mighty 19.7 metres and actually moves – its armour shifts position at 11 am and 1, 3 and 5 pm. It's a must for kids, fans of the manga robot's many adventures (which inspired Transformers) and anyone into pop culture or comic art.

AZABUDAI HILLS

The new Azabudai skyscraper shopping complex meets multipurpose hub now features Tokyo's immersive digital art experience, teamLab Borderless. Momentous interactive spaces invite you to become part of their digital art landscape. Magical projected graphics turn rooms and corridors into light-, shape- and character-filled wonderlands, all with that knowing wink to online sharing culture that makes it one of the most 'now' experiences you can have in Japan.

OLD-WORLD CHARM & TRADITIONAL HEART

ASAKUSA

Anyone wanting to uncover the Tokyo of old should head to Asakusa, the 'low city' of Shitamachi, a place where the Edo period (p. 28) still flavours the food and the atmosphere. There are plenty of backstreets to explore, with old-school eateries specialising in everything from udon noodles to tempura, some for a century or more. Sensō-ji, Tokyo's oldest Buddhist temple, is undoubtedly the centrepiece, still ancient and resplendent despite many rebuilds over the years (including one after the Second World War).

For the perfect day out if you have limited time, stroll along Nakamise and Shin-Nakamise Dōri (and nearby Asakusa Underground Street), shopping the stalls along the way for street food, souvenirs, and a colourful and lively taste of how daily life was lived in old Edo. Approach via the impressive Kaminarimon Gate on your way to the interior Hōzōmon Gate and magnificent five-tiered pagoda. Chefs and budding cooks should make the short walk from here to Kappabashi Dōri (Kitchen Town), a lengthy street made entirely for foodies, where you can buy every gadget, pot, cookie cutter and kitchen device imaginable. If you're starting your own restaurant, the *noren* curtains, crockery and cutlery alone will be great inspiration. Nearby Marugoto Nippon is a mecca for products sourced from around the country. Not far away, the gentrified and contemporary streets of Kuramae offer some gems, including hidden cafés, independent stationery shops and rustic homeware stores.

UENO PARK & YANAKA

This serene park and the surrounding Yanaka streets are also a great place to discover classic Tokyo – partly because of surrounding shrines and buildings that can date back more than 100 years, but also because the park itself houses museums that tell of the history of old Edo, and the modern Tokyo that grew from it. You'll also find Tennoji Temple just near Nippori Station, and beautiful Nezu Shrine in Yanaka, as well as a five-tiered pagoda Tōeizan Kan'ei-ji Endon-in within the grounds of Ueno Park itself (the pagoda is actually on the grounds of the zoo). Six Tokugawa shoguns are buried here, and you can find various shrines and plaques dedicated to them. Ueno Station now stands at the gate to the park, so you'll be mostly moving through a ghost version of what was once a massive temple complex, but you can find a range of ruins that still tell the story. The Heiseikan (National Museum) and Shitamachi (Low Town) Museum give a detailed and fascinating insight into the area's past.

VINTAGE TOKYO

Tokyo is a treasure trove for retro shelf-shufflers and rack-wranglers. Stores stock vintage Japanalia as well as a fair amount of Americana and even some top European label clothing from yesteryear. One-stop vintage clothes shops like Ragtag in Shibuya and Harajuku or Chicago, Inc. have aisles and aisles of styles from the late twentieth century that, if put together just so, feel very relevant now (everything old is new again, right?).

SHIMOKITAZAWA

Long the haunt of visitors and locals looking for Tokyo vintage, Shimokitazawa has grown up – kind of. You can still osmose that hippie 1970s flavour, and the rabbit-warren backstreets still throng with locals and visitors looking for some premium pre-loved. People who live in the area are moving with the times and setting up cool coffee houses, eateries and vinyl record stores among the concentration of low-rise buildings and apartments. It has an inbuilt and ingrained charm, and as one of the closest stations to Shibuya and Shinjuku it has become the central point to get a feel for neighbourhood Tokyo in

OPPOSITE PAGE: Steve in Asakusa
ABOVE: Vintage store in Shimokitazawa

action – and a feel for the spaces that thrived in the late twentieth century. Haight & Ashbury, Flamingo, Garage Department and New York Joe Exchange are musts for the memory magpie.

Craft beer is big in Shimokita (get like a local and remove the 'zawa' to be cool). Check out beer haunts Tap and Growler, B&B (Book&Beer), Ushitora (beer brewed in Toshigi prefecture) and Tazawako Alt Beer (Akita's finest craft beer). Craft coffee has to accompany craft beer. For your lovingly barista-made bean fix, head to Coffea Exlibris, Kate Coffee, Moldive or City Country City, Bear Pond, etc. – there are options aplenty so get hopped up and hop into some trash and treasure.

Shimokita Station has slowly been refurbished to become a shiny new hub of activity, losing a little of its grubby charm in the process – but it was probably about time. The area will change with it ... although something tells us you just can't take the authentic out of Shimokita.

KOENJI

Another haven for vintage collectors, especially when it comes to vinyl, Koenji has kept its cool in twenty-first-century Tokyo. Rail-side eateries, second-hand record collectors' paradises, international and Japanese vintage clothing from the 1950s, 1960s and 1970s, charming *izakaya* (pubs) with great food and booze, and a network of rough-and-ready backstreets – you get it all. On top of that the area is a bit of an unknown ramen hotspot – check out the *wontonmen* at Hayashimaru, for example – a ramen with plump shrimp-and-

pork wontons is always going to fill the void. Try Ramen Yamatoki, Huuhuura-en and Ichizou. For *izakaya*, it's hard to go past Dizz. Its lemon *shiso*-leaf chicken skewers are just the spicing on the cake for this atmospheric old-school eatery, propped up by booze, faded posters and the laughter of happy post-work customers.

The old-school intellectual vibe of the 1970s and 1980s is still palpable at classic *kissaten* Poem – and the coffee is great. Or try Nelken for a real taste of old Japan, with its sixty-year history of great coffee, in a setting with classical music, statues, paintings and endless elegance. Drinks? Homemade honey *umeshu* (plum liqueur) at El Pato, craft beer at Koenji Beer Kobo, or hit the BnA hotel for Bar Frontdesk – placed, surprisingly, by the front desk.

We could list the plethora of vintage stores that you can find in and around the right-hand side of the station exit, but that would spoil the fun of wandering – stroll in and flip through the racks until you find that special vintage something. It's a day's worth of fossicking at least. Just one addendum: shoe fetishists might want to check out the absurdly extensive range of vintage footwear on offer at Whistler.

NISHI-OGIKUBO

Not far from Koenji, Nishi-Ogikubo takes vintage to the next level. Hit up the information centre for a free map that takes you on a tour of the vintage stores in the area. You can shop the deep mix of stunning repurposed ephemera, classic vintage furniture and bric-a-brac, and high-end antiques, all in a quiet backstreet setting. →

WEEKEND TOKYO

Weekends in Tokyo can get slightly hectic ... Shoppers, daytrippers, urban explorers and those with a bit of free time flood into the manic metropolis looking for, and usually finding, a treasure trove of experiences. If you want to get amongst it, head to Shinjuku (p. 165) on a Saturday or Shibuya (p. 165) on a Friday night and find out the true meaning of 'jam-packed'. It's great to be in the thick of it, if you don't mind the occasional elbow and jostle; you get a real feeling of being where the action is. But if you want to escape it all and take a bit more of a leisurely stroll along the byways and boulevards of Tokyo, there are a few other places you can head to.

DAIKANYAMA

Book, magazine and music behemoth Tsutaya set up T-Site here and it ranks as one of the world's all-time-best bookhops, making Daikanyama the classic weekend destination. Drop into Ivy Place on the grounds for an early breakfast or brunch before tackling Tsutaya's remarkable catalogue of books, magazines, music, CDs, DVDs and oddments. To cap it off there are study spaces, cafés and even a convenience store. Daikanyama is the perfect Sunday town. Stroll the back streets and lanes for excellent small-store shopping experiences.

MEGURO

Stroll down Meguro Dōri on a Sunday afternoon for some excellent furniture and bric-a-brac shopping. Mid-century, Japanese and European – Meguro Dōri has it covered in a long strip of excellent stores. Jyūgaoka and Gakugei-Daigaku should also be on your radar for a casual Tokyo weekend.

矢口書店
演劇・戯曲

FAVOURITE THINGS
私たちのお気に入り

Vending machines

TOKYO'S VENDING MACHINES ARE ICONIC AND GO BACK AS FAR AS THE 1964 OLYMPICS

A welcome sight on Tokyo streets, they can warm you up in winter with hot soup, hot green tea or coffee, and cool you down in summer with ice-cold green tea, water or iced coffee. Tokyo's vending machines also stock a variety of things from booze, junk food and soup or pasta in a can to a complete change of clothes.

Some of the more risqué vending machines you might have heard about will be hard to find these days, and you'll have to stalk the halls of the seedier areas like Tokyo's Kabukichō or Ameya-Yokochō, or Osaka's Shinsekai, for example. Vending machines can also be a great source of fun and cheap gifts for friends, similar to capsule-toy machines.

KICHIJŌJI

Combining some Kichijōji shopping with a stroll through lovely Inokashira Park is Tokyo perfection. Inokashira has plenty to offer: the lake is beautiful, it's a *sakura* (cherry-blossom) hotspot and it's a known haunt for birds (and bees, for that matter – there are bee sanctuaries on the grounds). It also houses the Ghibli Museum (p. 361), a pilgrimage site for animation and manga fans the world over. Start the day with a wander, taking in the park's sights, then head in to Kichijōji's Nakamichi Dōri, a quaint shopping street with design, homewares and vintage stores. Nearby Sunroute Plaza has premium tea, pickle and meat buys, while Harmonica Yokochō is a charming rabbit warren of old-school bars and eateries.

JIMBŌCHŌ

If you want to flip through 1960s and 1970s books on art and architecture, or colourful 1980s pop and rock mags, then a Sunday afternoon in Jimbōchō, the second-hand book capital of the world, is just the ticket. You can run the gamut from twentieth-century books to ancient scrolls and atlases on the same street (sometimes next door). Book-lovers will truly be in heaven – you'll trip over carts of books, admire towering walls of crammed bookshelves and flip through box after box, unearthing endless personal literary holy grails. Some stores have books stacked up on shelves outside, a wonderful and inspiring sight to photograph and a great chance to get in a bit of reading while you enjoy some fresh air, relax and decompress from the city's more extreme shopping experiences.

ABOVE: Vintage books in Jimbōchō
OPPOSITE PAGE LEFT: Harajuku crepes
TOP RIGHT: Harajuku on Sunday BOTTOM RIGHT: Daikanyama flower sculpture

NEAR TOKYO
JUST A STONE'S THROW TO SECRETS & SOLITUDE

Quick trips just beyond Tokyo's borders can take you out to some pretty special places. Not far from the capital you'll find temples, mountains, gardens, hot springs and museums, all accessed by some charming train journeys. A day out of the main city hubs will add history and depth to Tokyo's many charms, and will help give you an insight into the wonders of the Kantō region.

MOUNT TAKAO

Mount Takao makes for a perfect Tokyo day out and is only fifty minutes away (Keiō semi-limited-express train from Shinjuku Station to Takaosanguchi Station, or the JR Chūō Line to Takao Station then Keio Line to Takaosanguchi). The station was first opened in 1967, and has since had a complete makeover by hardworking architect Kengo Kuma (p. 353). Its looming wooden-beam roof uses local cypress and from below it looks like you're standing under a giant woodland mushroom. The station even has its own *onsen* (hot spring), so you can combine hiking with soaking – the perfect Tokyo escape.

Striking in any season, the mountain really shines in autumn and summer – and on clear days the views from the hiking trails are outstanding. Catch the quaint and perilous chairlift to the top (or back down, where views of distant Tokyo will impress) or ride the cable car. Bridges, stone lanterns, quaint souvenir stops and the 'Octopus Tree' (named for its tentacle-like root system) are just some of its treasures. Serious hikers, determined walkers or casual strollers will all find the perfect trail.

At the base of the mountain you'll find a wonderful wooden Niō-mon (guardian gate), which leads you into Yakouin Temple, home to a group of mystical monks called the Shugen-dō. These monks consider the mountain to be of great spiritual importance and draw power from it by meditating under a waterfall. The temple is dedicated to the crow-like *tengu* (p. 341), whose statues and images you'll find dotted around the extensive grounds. The shrine itself is ornate and colourful, and guarded by two fearsome *tengu* statues, one beaked, the other winged.

If you're hungry, Mount Takao has plenty of street food to offer. The grilled *dango* (rice dumplings on skewers) are vegetarian-friendly and delicious dipped in soy. Sweet potato comes in many forms, and can be found grated into soba noodle soups. Blueberries flavour many things, including ice cream (the 'Honeyberry' blends blueberry and honeysuckle). *Tengu* makes an appearance in the form of bean-filled pastries or *senbei* (rice crackers). Anyone wishing to share lunch with the monks can join in; they do a *shōjin ryōri* (small vegetable dishes; p. 126) lunch at the temple (book ahead).

ENOSHIMA

A coastal town, Enoshima is set on a tiny triangular island at the southern tip of Tokyo, just south-west of Yokohama (p. 191). As the quintessential beach-holiday escape, it holds a lot of deep memories for people brought up in Tokyo. Enoshima Station is a charming stop that deposits you in a small town set up for visitors – expect plenty of souvenir and street-food stalls. A long bridge from town leads to a somewhat touristy stretch of beach, popular with visitors and locals.

Lighthouse fanatics (we're sure there are some out there!) will be pleased to know that the world's most contemporary lighthouse is the Enoshima Sea Candle, a torch-shaped metal structure that is also an observation deck. You can find it in the Samuel Cocking English-style gardens, which are full of in roses and camellias. The lighthouse features some great sea views, and on clear days you can see Mount Fuji (p. 222), Sagami Bay and the Pacific Ocean. The lighthouse is the focus of New Year celebrations, when its illuminations are impressive and, of course, hugely popular.

KAMAKURA

Kamakura (ninety minutes by train from Shibuya to Fujisawa then the Eno-den), has amazing gardens; the Great Daibutsu (p. 337), Japan's second-largest cast Buddha; *sakura*

(cherry-blossom) hotspots; hiking trails; beaches; and an astonishing range of highly regarded temples. A major seat of power 100 years ago, it was a capital where Buddhism and political intrigue would often mix.

Engaku-ji is the second most important Zen temple in Japan (one of the Buddha's actual teeth can be found enshrined here) and the large *ōgane* bell is a must-see for temple obsessives. It was cast by Mononobe Kunimitsu in around 1301. The massive bell is the largest in the region and one of only two to be designated a National Treasure. The nearby *waniguchi* gong was made in 1540. It's also a beautiful spot for autumn colours. The Shariden hall of relics is the only building in Kanagawa to be designated a National Treasure. The impressive *sanmon* (gate), main hall, and Sembutsudo and Kojirin meditation halls add to an already perfect temple experience.

Tsurugaoka Hachimangū shrine, Kenchō-ji Temple, Hase-dera (the eleven-headed Kannon statue is particularly popular) and Zeniarai Benten are also spectacular. The Great Daibutsu can be found at Kōtoku-in; it comes second in height only to Nara's Buddha in Tōdai-ji (p. 251). It was built in 1252 and originally lived inside the temple, until the temple buildings were destroyed by tsunamis and typhoons. Kōtoku-in can be reached easily from Hase Station (third along from Kamakura Station).

The main street Komachi Dōri is packed with shops and eateries. The local *omiyage* (regional souvenir) is the famous Hato Sabure shortbread biscuit shaped like a pigeon – you'll see them everywhere and you can't miss the bright-yellow tin. Toshimaya Honten confectionery

shop, operating for more than fifty years, sells Hato Sabure and other Kamakura trinkets. For craft beer and sake head to Mikawaya Honten or The Bank. Dankazura Kozusu still hand-knead their *warabi mochi* (glutinous sweets). For coffee try Café Vivement Dimanche, Ishikawa Coffee or The Good Goodies.

A NOTE ON THE ENO-DEN

There are other ways to get to Kamakura, but the Eno-den is by far the most atmospheric. Established on Christmas Day 1900, the charming retro train runs on thin tracks through narrow lanes, often bypassing backyards; trundles along main streets; and passes wonderful local scenery. The Eno-den circles from Kamakura to Enoshima and Fujisawa, passing many smaller stations along the way, most of which exude country charm.

OPPOSITE PAGE: Enoshima
ABOVE: Eno-den and merchandise

Nikkō

As a daytrip (or take your time and stay over), Nikkō is a destination with some seriously jaw-dropping locations and local food specialties. Shrines, nature, lakes, waterfalls, hot springs – Nikkō has it all, and although it's well known, Nikkō's distance from Tokyo has ensured it hasn't become overrun with snap-happy visitors. The shrines of Tōshō-gū, Rinnō-ji, Futarasan-jinja and Taiyu-in are all in the same grounds or within walking distance of each other. Tokugawa Ieyasu (p. 28) spared no expense or pomp when it came to honouring himself, and the resulting Tōshō-gū Shrine (p. 335) is a colourful, intricate, elaborate and detailed mausoleum. The carvings (the three wise monkeys feature in the inner courtyard), the towering *torii* gates (p. 333), the ornate Ieyasu statue at the gate and the two mighty connected cedar trees of the Futasaran Shrine (representing eternal bliss and a potent symbol for anyone seeking out true love) are just some of the pleasures that await. Vermilion Shinkyo Bridge at the entrance to the grounds is a fitting welcome.

TRANSPORT

Tokyo Shinkansen to Utsunomiya Station; then Nikkō Line 'Yamabiko' or 'Nasuno' train to Nikkō Station, about 2 hours. Or the direct Tobu Skytree Line train, 2 hours (Spacia train 110 minutes). Around Nikkō: World Heritage Meguri Bus

ATMOSPHERE

Tranquil, historical, spectacular, inspiring

REGIONAL FOOD & DRINK

Soba noodles, Nikkō *yuba*, red pepper in *shiso* (perilla) leaf, pickles, *shōjin ryōri*, *kaiseki ryōri*, Tochi-Otome giant red strawberries, local mountain vegetables baked in a fire pit (Heike warrior cuisine), beef, fish, *maitake* mushrooms, *yōkan* (hard jelly sweets), shaved ice (made with Nikkō water), *manjū* (sweet steamed buns)

OMIYAGE

Three Wise Monkeys, samurai weapons (swords, *shuriken* – throwing stars), *yōkan*, sake (made with Nikkō water), sake *manjū*, Nikkō *jingoro* rice crackers, Tochi-Otome strawberry cheesecake

SIGHTS

Tōshō-gū, Rinnō-ji, Futarasan-jinja, Italian Embassy Villa Memorial Park, Kinugawa-Kawaji Hot Springs, Kegon Falls, Lake Chūzenji, Kanmangafuchi Abyss, Shinkyo Bridge, Tamozawa Imperial Villa, British Embassy Villa Memorial Park

FESTIVALS

Tōshō-gū Shrine Autumn Grand Festival, Tōshō-gū Shrine Spring Grand Festival, Togyo-Sai 1000 Samurai Procession, Yayoi Festival, Oyama Summer Festival, Yabusame Shinji

WEB

nikko-travel.jp

——— If you're hungry after all the shrine-hopping, Nikkō has an embarrassment of food riches. With its renowned soba and *yuba* (tofu skin) as well as local mountain vegetables, pickles and both rice and sake made with the area's abundant and pure water, you'll be feasting on some of Japan's most delicious fare. Top it off with a delicious matcha soft-serve in summer, or a sweet steamed *manjū* bun in winter. *Yōkan*, or hard jelly sweets (often with small fruit delicacies inside), are the perfect gift to take back to Tokyo to impress anyone you might be meeting there.

Hiking is highly regarded in the area; take some serious time to go north and explore Kegon Falls, or go west and soak in some of Kinugawa's renowned hot springs. Often missed but well worth a visit are both the Italian and British embassy villas on the delightful shores of Lake Chūzenji. These modernist time capsules give you a valuable insight into Japanese and European relations in the twentieth century.

ABOVE: Tōshō-gū Shrine OPPOSITE PAGE: Lake Chūzenji at British embassy

UNESCO World Heritage Sites

The United Nations grants the UNESCO title to cultural, natural and historical sites to ensure they are preserved for future generations. Japan has just shy of fifty listings, with more in the approval process. We've listed some of our favourites below. If you're a fan of temples, Nara, Kyoto and Nikkō are must-visits, while architecture and town-planning fans should get to Shirakawa-go and Gokayama, and nature enthusiasts to Mount Fuji, the Kii Mountains and/or Yakushima Island. Iwami Ginzan Silver Mine is an incredible experience off the tourist path, and visiting Itsukushima-jinja in the waters of Miyajima at sunset with deer roaming around is one of our favourite Japan memories.

NATURE
· Kii Mountains and Sacred
  Sites Pilgrimage
  (Kansai), p. 230
  tb-kumano.jp/en/world-heritage

· Mount Fuji
  (Chūbu), p. 222
  fujisan-climb.jp

VILLAGES
· Shirakawa-go and Gokayama
  (Chūbu), p. 224
  shirakawa-go.org

TEMPLES, SHRINES & MONUMENTS
· Himeji Castle
  (Kansai), p. 345
  www.city.himeji.lg.jp

· Hiroshima Genbaku Dome
  (Atomic Bomb Dome;
  Chūgoku), p. 265
  www.city.hiroshima.lg.jp

· Itsukushima-jinja
  (Chūgoku), p. 273
  en.itsukushimajinja.jp/index.html

· Kyoto landmarks
  (Kansai), p. 234
  kyoto.travel

· Nara landmarks
  and Hōryū-ji area
  (Kansai), p. 250
  www.visitnara.jp
  horyuji.or.jp

· Nikkō landmarks
  (Kantō), p. 178
  nikko-travel.jp

ISLANDS
· Ogasawara Islands or
  Bonin Islands (Kantō)
  ogasawaramura.com

· Yakushima Island
  (Kyūshū), p. 325
  town.yakushima.kagoshima.jp

CRAFTS & INDUSTRY
· Iwami Ginzan Silver Mine
  (Chūgoku), p. 275
  kankou-shimane.com

· Tomioka Silk Mills
  (Kantō)
  tomioka-silk.jp

OPPOSITE PAGE: Tōshō-gū Shrine, Nikkō, Kantō

A country move

HIKI AND RYO KOMURA, UGUiSU STORE, MASHIKO, KANTŌ, UGUISUSTORE.COM

What is it about Mashiko that made you want to swap a city life in Tokyo for a country life?

A couple of years ago we started imagining a life in the country. We didn't really have an idea of where, but we started to visit different places to see if there was somewhere we'd like to move to. We were both born and grew up in Tokyo, and we basically only knew life in the metropolis. We never really imagined a life in any other places in Japan. We knew some artists in the Mashiko area and we started visiting there. We got to love the town more and more each time we visited. And then an opportunity came up for us to move there.

Mashiko is a famous pottery town, known for its special clay, but it's also known for indigo-dyeing. Does it feel like a creative collective? Can you describe its spirit?

Yes, there's a wonderful indigo-dyeing studio that has been in Mashiko for more than 200 years. Inside the thatched-roofed complex of Higeta Aizome Kobo (Higeta Indigo House), you can see the process of indigo-dyeing by ninth-generation artisans.

It probably hasn't changed much since the Edo period (p. 28), and you get a really special feeling when you step inside this incredible building, like it's almost sacred.

Tell us about Mashiko's famous pottery fair.

There are two pottery fairs each year in Mashiko, one in spring and another in autumn. There are more than 500 stalls run by individual makers gathered from all around Japan and lots of people come to visit. The whole town has a really festive atmosphere during the fair.

What are your favourite creative places to visit in the town?

Shōji Hamada Memorial Museum (Sankokan) is always a peaceful and beautiful place full of inspiration. It's where the master potter and 'Living National Treasure' Shōji Hamada lived and worked. He was a major figure in the Mingei folk-art movement in the twentieth century.

Tell us about your store. How does it fit in with the Mashiko environment?

We sell a curated collection of Japanese products through our UGUiSU online store, which we opened in 2009. We select products with cultural or traditional significance, special items that tell a story, hard-to-find objects and beautiful everyday items, including paper items, linens and textiles, tableware, accessories, jewellery and books. As it's not too far from Tokyo, many young artists have set up their studios in Mashiko, and it's known to be a creative town. We feel that it's a great place for UGUiSU to be based, and from there we dispatch Japanese craft and culture to the world through our offerings online.

Mashiko

TOCHIGI PREFECTURE

An historic pottery town with a new young craft collective forging a bright future, Mashiko's dedication to the slow arts floods its streets. Proudly dedicated to two crafts: pottery and, to a lesser extent, indigo textile-dyeing, the town is alive with creativity and charm. The utilitarian pottery style Mashiko ware (or *mashiko-yaki*) was a flourishing ceramic style at the end of the Edo period, however it wasn't until 1920 when Shōji Hamada (designated a Living National Treasure) moved to town that this everyday pottery was elevated to the revered status of Mingei (folk craft). Internationally, Hamada is one of Japan's best-known potters so making a trip to Mashiko to visit the Shōji Hamada Museum (Sankokan) and Shōji Hamada House at Ceramic Art Messe Mashiko is a pilgrimage for lovers of ceramics and glazes. The enormous Noborigama Kilns are a highlight – residents now use these collectively to fire their creations. The rustic kilns are lined up under the wooden canopy of the potter's museum. The streets are a wellspring of Mingei and handcrafted creativity. Visit Higeta Indigo Dyeing Studio or Nihei Furukagu-ten for beautiful vintage furniture. Don't miss Daiseigama on the main street for *mashiko-yaki* and Mingei crafts – it also has a gallery and the building alone is worth a visit. Head to Starnet for a delicious organic lunch or sweets (they also have a lovely range of ceramics) and Tsuzuri for the perfect vegan lunch and a small shop selling handmade items. Stay the night at the Forest Inn Furuki Guest House or Mashiko-Kan. Before you leave, wave goodbye to the town's giant ceramic *tanuki* (p. 298)!

TRANSPORT

From Tokyo: Shinkansen to Utsunomiya Station, about 50 minutes; then Kanto Jidosha Bus, about an hour

Or take the pottery bus (Kantō Yakimono Liner) direct from Tokyo's Akihabara Station, 2 hours 30 minutes

Hire a bike from Mashiko station to get around

CLOSE BY

Utsunomiya, Nikkō, Tochigi City

ATMOSPHERE

Country town, youthful, relaxed, creative, traditional craft

REGIONAL FOOD & DRINK

Tonoike sake, pickles, strawberries, forest restaurants

OMIYAGE

Mashiko-yaki pottery, ceramics, *shibori* resist-dyed textiles

SIGHTS

Tsukamoto Pottery Museum, Shoji Hamada Museum, Noborigama Kilns, Yoshimura Strawberry Park (strawberry picking), Tonoike Sake Brewery, Higeta Indigo Dyeing Studio, Saimyō-ji Temple, Utsunomiya han Shrine, Mashikoyaki Kyōhan Centre (pottery)

FESTIVALS

Spring Pottery Fair (late April to early May), Autumn Pottery Fair (early November), Flower Festival (lemon sunflowers and pink cosmos)

WEB

mashiko-kankou.org

LEFT: Indigo-dyeing, Mashiko

Hakone &
Lake Ashi

Hakone is within easy reach of Tokyo, and is brimming with reasons to visit, from hot springs to delicious food specialties. As soon as you arrive at Hakone-Yumoto Station, you'll get an instant holiday feel. Couples walk hand in hand off the Odakyu Romancecar or wait patiently for the ultra-cute Tozan Railway train to whisk them off into the mountains. Japan's oldest mountain railway, Tozan takes you through tunnels, over high bridges that traverse forested caverns and through thick vegetation and beautiful blooming hydrangeas (when in season). Charmingly, the train stops at several 'switchback' stations along the way to change direction. Alight at Chōkoku-no-Mori Station to explore the Hakone Open-Air Museum, a sculpture park with works by artists including Pablo Picasso and Henry Moore, set in a beautiful garden.

From here, weather and temperamental volcano permitting (always check ahead), you can head to beautiful Gora (where upmarket hotels and *ryokan* abound) before taking the Komagatake Ropeway from quaint Gora Station up the smoking, sulfurous mountainside until you reach Ōwakudani, a volcanic crater sculpted by nature when Mount Hakone erupted some 3000 years ago. This hike features steaming vents, bubbling pits and sulfur-boiled black eggs. The top of Ōwakudani is a pitstop of souvenir stalls, more black eggs and some eateries; and on very clear days, a view of Mount Fuji awaits. Take it all in before descending towards Lake Ashi.

If you just want to head to Lake Ashi and Hakone Jinja, take the Hakone Tozan bus from Hakone-Yumoto station (thirty-five minutes and covered on the Hakone Free Pass). Lake Ashi is a vast open body of water girded by small green promontories and verdant forests. The famous pirate ships that cross the lake are colourful and fun, and daggily retro. Hakone Jinja's magnificent *torii* water gate (p. 333) can be seen from the town, but you'll have to head over to the shrine to get those all-important pictures of you standing at the mouth of the gate with Lake Ashi behind you. The shrine itself is wonderful, dedicated to the Hakone Ōkami ('great spirits' or gods), Shinto *gongen*, or manifestations of the Buddha. Hidden within deep forest, it has beautiful walks and the stunning shrine building itself. The true drawcard here is the water gate though, so line up and to take your turn.

The town features several shops that sell the local *yosegi* marquetry, boxes. These *omiyage* (regional souvenirs; p. 109) are quite special and you can buy them at a range of price points. The puzzle boxes are fun and have a long history. The different shapes and angles of the wood make it hard to work out how to open the box, where the openings are and which direction to slide various lids in order to reveal the treasures within. Travellers in times past would use the boxes to protect their valuables.

Hakone-Yumoto Station shouldn't be ignored. More than a transport hub, it's charming in its own right, with souvenir shops and a winding old-school street with plenty of black eggs (we should mention that it's bad luck to eat more than two and a half eggs in a day), *manjū* bun and soba noodle vendors. Roaring Haya River charges past the imposing late-twentieth-century behemoth hotel Yumoto Fujiya. The trail up from here, out of the tourist glare of Gora, feels older and more authentic. The premium water in the area has given rise to some top-quality *onsen* (hot springs), including rustic Tenzan and stylish new addition, Yuryo.

TRANSPORT

Romancecar from Shinjuku Station to Hakone Yumoto Station, about 85 minutes. Or Tokyo Station Shinkansen to Odawara Station; then Odakyu Hakone Tozan Line to Hakone Yamato Station, under one hour

ATMOSPHERE

Relaxing city escape, couples' day out, busy and fun

REGIONAL FOOD & DRINK

Black *onsen* eggs (*kuro tamago*), *onsen manju* (sweets steamed in hot springs), Japanese sweets in general, Hakone and Gora craft beers and ciders, soba

OMIYAGE

Yosegi (marquetry boxes), packaged *wagashi* (traditional sweets), pickled plums, craft beer, black egg trinkets

SIGHTS

Komagatake Ropeway, Hakone Tozan Railway, Hakone Ropeway, Owakudani, Hakone Jinja, Chisuji Falls

GARDENS & PARKS

Sengokuhara Pampas Grass Field, Hakone Moss Garden at the Hakone Museum of Art, Botanical Garden, Fuji-Hakone-Izu National Park

ART

Hakone Open-Air Museum, Pola Museum, Okada Museum of Art, Studio Shima Photo Studio, Hakone Museum of Art, Narukawa Art Museum

VIEWS

Ōwakudani, Lake Ashi from Hakone Jinja, Chisuji Falls, Narukawa Art Museum, Hakone Pirate Ship, views of Mount Fuji

ONSEN

Hakone Yuryo Tenzan Onsen, Yunessun Spa Resort

FESTIVALS

Daimonji Yaki, Hakone Summer Festival Week, cherry-blossom viewing

WEB

hakone-japan.com

OPPOSITE PAGE: Hakone Jinja

Onsen
in Gunma

Gunma is a wonderfully mountainous region with myriad opportunities for hiking and exploring. Its main claim to fame, however, is that it offers some of Japan's most unforgettable *onsen* (hot springs) experiences. Many of them are in *ryokan* (traditional inns; p. 87), but can be enjoyed as a day visit with a special day rate for bathing if you're unable to stay the night.

Ōtaki No Yu, Kusatsu Onsen

HOSHI ONSEN CHŌJUKAN

A magical experience secreted in the majestic forested glades of the Jōshin'etsu-kōgen National Park, Hoshi is a 140-year-old *onsen* that shines in any season. The building is an atmospheric museum that displays the natural history of the surrounding region in various states (including some taxidermy) in glass cases set in low-ceilinged corridors with sleek wooden floors. The main *onsen* room has vaulted wooden ceilings and beams, and magical light diffuses through arched windows. The bath is one of the best in Japan – an authentic wooden *onsen* separated into six segments, where the water bubbles up from deep underground. It's a mixed-gender bath – although if you're staying the night there are women-only times. Two other baths flow with the immaculate *onsen* water. Make sure to have lunch while you're at the *onsen*, but we recommend staying overnight at Hoshi for the full Japanese hospitality experience – amazing baths, food, service, accommodation and surroundings.

IKAHO ONSEN

An iron-rich thermal-water hotspot replete with quality baths, Ikaho is a 'secret' destination. The Hara Contemporary Art Museum adds to the allure, an excellent contemporary gallery with a sense of fun – a giant Warhol Campbell's Soup can stands on the grounds. The quaint township plus stunning Mizusawa Temple add to the charms of this less-travelled destination.

KUSATSU ONSEN

The quaint country village of Kusatsu is dotted with public *onsen* of all sizes, from the rustic to some of the best in the country. They're all centred around one of Japan's marvels, the Yubatake, a mineral-stained wooden system of fuming, steaming channels that cool and funnel the region's sulfurous waters into the many *onsen* and *ryokan* around town. The water is even used to heat the local houses and businesses.

Kusatsu has two unique ways of bathing: Jikan-yu, a timed system of bathing in scorchingly hot water for exactly three minutes, used for centuries for its benefits to circulation; and Yumomi, an unmissable ceremony where large wooden panels are used to 'stir' and cool the boiling water down (to a still-scorching 48 degrees) so the bather can enter. Another interesting practice is Kaburiyu, where bathers pour many buckets of water over their heads – dilating the head's blood vessels. Spectacular Sainokawara Park features a large outdoor *onsen* (*rotenburo*) with mountain views next to a flowing river and watched over by a large patch of open sky. Central Goza-no-yu is a stylish new building with wooden baths and an upstairs relaxation room that overlooks the Yubatake – a great opportunity for pictures. The story goes that the beneficial waters can cure every illness except love sickness, but we would argue with that, as a soak in these wonderful hot springs will take your mind off any real-world stress.

MANZA ONSEN

Manza is a ski resort, so much of its activity centres around the winter snows, when skiers traverse the slopes before heading into *ryokan* for hot meals and comfort. For us, though, it's the *onsen* that stand out. They're perfect for skiers, but even better for the *onsen*-hopper, who can enjoy them during the off-season. Premium baths include Nisshinkan, the Manza Prince Hotel, Manza Kogen and Manzatei. The quality of a ski resort that is also a rated *onsen* cannot be underestimated, so make use of it in any season (although avoid ski season unless you love to ski!).

SHIMA ONSEN

Considered one of the oldest *onsen* in Japan, Shima Onsen is known as the 'forty thousand hot spring' (it was thought to cure that many ailments), and with a braggable forty hot-spring sources, it's easy to see why. The picturesque township remains relatively unspoilt. Fans of the Studio Ghibli film *Spirited Away* will recognise Shima Onsen's approach and vermilion bridge as one of the film's main inspirations. Ryokan Sekizenkan holds the distinction of having an original Taishō-era 'Roman-style' bath within its walls that's several centuries old.

TAKARAGAWA ONSEN OSENKAKU

A popular day-visit *onsen* for foreign travellers due to its tattoo-friendly policy, picture-perfect scenery and easy access from Tokyo, Takaragawa features multiple stunning *rotenburo* (outdoor baths) overlooking the cascading rapids of Takaragawa River. While there are same-sex baths here, it's all about the outdoor mixed-sex bathing. Both women and men have to wear a special modesty gown provided by the *onsen*. Wander the grounds in your *yukata* (casual summer kimono) and *geta* (wooden sandals), lunch in the communal hall, and if you're lucky enough to stay the night, you can experience a midnight dip and go to sleep to the sounds of the river.

BELOW: Kusatsu Onsen hot spring tour pass

BELOW: Takaragawa Onsen Osenkaku

Takasaki

Takasaki is a great hub for exploring Gunma prefecture's myriad wonders. Although many people don't use it as a destination in itself, it holds some real treasures. Takasaki produces eighty per cent of Japan's *daruma* (p. 339). You may recognise this character (one of Steve's favourites), a squat, red, grumpy-looking man (an early image of the Buddha's sage Bodhidharma) with blank white eyes. The eyes tell a tale – when you buy a blank-eyed *daruma*, the idea is to draw or paint in one eye and then make a wish. When the wish comes true you fill in the other eye. If you see *daruma* displayed in shops where only one eye has been filled in, you know that a wish has not yet been granted.

Takasaki Station is a joy, filled with *daruma* merchandise from Kit Kats to sake to *bentō* boxes shaped like *daruma* and countless other souvenirs. *Daruma* statues are everywhere at the station, making for a great photo opportunity. Your destination, however, is Shōrinzan Daruma-ji, the Daruma Temple, which holds a *daruma* market every 6–7 January . The temple itself, a beautiful wooden structure from 1697, features *daruma* that have been brought in by visitors over the years and piled up within the borders of the building. For vintage fans there are two unmissable sights: the tiny museum next to the temple full of amazing vintage *daruma*; and the street entry to the shrine, which features some amazing retro *daruma* signage, including a huge metal *daruma*.

You can't miss Takasaki Byakue Daikannon, the White-robed Buddha, a towering statue built in 1936 and standing nearly 42 metres high on the mountainous temple grounds of Jigen-in. The interior features twenty Buddha and high-priest statues, and 146 stairs that take about fifteen minutes to climb. The surrounding mountain boasts 3000 cherry trees.

As an added bonus, Takasaki is known as 'pasta town', and is certainly the place to go if you want a pasta fix in Japan, especially if you like it in epic proportions. Takasaki has taken to European food in general, and you can find many meat grills and even fish-and-chip restaurants in and around the station.

TRANSPORT

Tokyo Shinkansen to Takasaki Station, about 50 minutes

CLOSE BY

Nagano, Utsunomiya, Chichibu, Nikkō, Ikaho Onsen, Mount Myogisan

ATMOSPHERE

City with a country atmosphere, friendly, the land of *daruma*!

REGIONAL FOOD & DRINK

Pasta, udon, *okirikomi* (vegetable noodle soup), *yakimanjū* (fried sweet buns), Takasaki Sodachi (a brand selling premium fruit and vegetables grown with pure local water)

OMIYAGE

Daruma everything

SIGHTS

Shōrinzan Daruma-ji, Takasaki Byakue Daikannon (White-robed Buddha), Jigen-in

GARDENS & PARKS

Tokumei-en (especially in autumn)

VIEWS

Mount Haruna, Takasaki Byakue Daikannon

FESTIVALS

Daruma Festival

WEB

visitgunma.jp/en

TOP LEFT & RIGHT: Shōrinzan Daruma-ji BOTTOM LEFT & RIGHT: *Daruma* drinks and *bentō* at Takasaki Station OPPOSITE PAGE: *Daruma* and Hello Kitty *bentō*

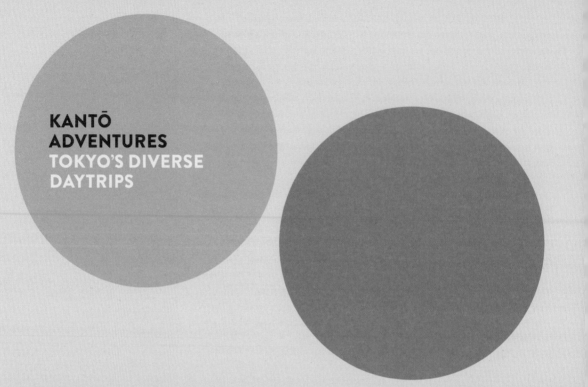

KANTŌ ADVENTURES
TOKYO'S DIVERSE DAYTRIPS

> Chinatown in Yokohama is legendary, as the first of its kind in the world. The Japanese connection with Chinese history cannot be underestimated.

NASU

Nuzzled within the beautiful mountainous region of Tochigi, Nasu is an easy jaunt from Tokyo (around seventy minutes on the Nasuno Shinkansen) and can be enjoyed as a daytrip or fully explored with a stopover. The highlight is undoubtedly the hot springs, especially rustic and sulfurous Shika no Yu (deer *onsen*), where a series of baths challenge you to get into hotter and hotter water. Other recommended spots to soak are Ōmaru Onsen and Oukoku Onsen; the latter has a view of capybara lazily soaking in their own hot springs. The region is part of the Nikkō National Park, and Mount Nasu (a still-active volcano) is a hiking spot famed for the Tsutsuji Suspension Bridge and spectacular azalea fields. The area's food specialties include dairy (milk and cheesecake especially) and apples.

UTSUNOMIYA

In Tochigi prefecture, near Nikkō and Mashiko, you'll find Utsunomiya. Besides being a hub to get to various spectacular locations, the area is renowned for *gyōza* eateries (p. 116) with specialty fillings and, subsequently, beer. It even has a *gyōza* statue. As the largest city in Tochigi, it naturally has a few more attractions. The Ōya Temple is a rustic spiritual enclave built into a stone cliff face. The nearby stone quarry has now become a memorable, cavernous museum.

YOKOHAMA

Yokohama can be reached in around fifty minutes on the Tōkyū Tōyoko line or even faster via the Shinkansen. Major sights are the 'International Passenger Terminal' (ferry boat terminal) – a contemporary architectural marvel, like a wooden waveform that echoes the movement of the water. Sakei-en, a garden opened in 1906, features a three-tiered pagoda (formerly Tōmoyō-ji temple), seasonal wild flowers (chrysanthemums, hydrangeas and azaleas), and three buildings: the Gekkaden (built by Tokugawa Ieyasu; p. 28), Jutō Ōi-dō (built by Toyotomi Hideyoshi; p. 22) and Chōshūkaku (attributed to Tokugawa Iemitsu) – making it the only garden in Japan that has buildings by all the major shoguns. The Cup Noodles Museum is a display of the brightly coloured packaging of the fast-food staple over the years, set in a beautifully designed space, a very popular attraction for kids and kidults. If you're off your noodle, also check out the Shin-Yokohama Ramen Museum – where you can walk through a detailed history of ramen and ramen eateries and styles through the ages.

Chinatown in Yokohama is legendary, as the first of its kind in the world. The Japanese connection with Chinese history cannot be underestimated; from food to religion and philosophy, China was a major source of inspiration for early Japanese culture. Yokohama's Chinatown features a museum dedicated to this history, aptly named the China Museum. Of course the main drawcard is food, and Yokohama's Chinatown is famous for many dishes of Chinese origin, including ramen (based on Chinese wheat noodles) and *manjū* (based on Chinese *mantou* steamed buns).

Fans of Japan's very special obsession with jazz can find many venues (like Jazz Live Adlib, Windjammer or Dorufi) in Yokohama, where jazz was first introduced by American soldiers after the Second World War.

OPPOSITE PAGE: Shika no Yu, Nasu Onsen, Kantō

TŌHOKU

TOKYO

SHINKANSEN
TO AOMORI

AOMORI

AOMORI
PREFECTURE

LAKE
TOWADA

AKITA
PREFECTURE

NYŪTŌ
ONSEN

LAKE
TAZAWA

AKITA CITY

MORIOKA

HANAMAKI

IWATE
PREFECTURE

SHINJŌ

ICHINOSEKI

YAMAGATA
PREFECTURE

NARUKO ONSEN

GINZAN ONSEN

YAMADERA

YAMAGATA

SENDAI

MIYAGI
PREFECTURE

ZAŌ ONSEN

MOUNT
BANDAI

FUKUSHIMA
PREFECTURE

LAKE INAWASHIRO

SHINKANSEN
TO TOKYO

東北

TŌHOKU

As you head further north on Honshū island, things become more lush, mountainous and rugged – hidden temples, secluded towns and less-visited cities make it an attractive prospect. Some of Japan's best *onsen* (hot springs), nature and spiritual sites seal the deal. The area is famous for hot springs, autumn foliage, winter snows, lakes, mountainous peaks and spectacular vistas. Tōhoku craft includes *kokeshi* dolls (p. 340), ironware, lacquerware, *agewappa* (curved wooden boxes), Nanbu *sakiori* (fabric woven from recycled kimonos), *akabeko* (nodding-head cows) and *imono* cast metal. Tōhoku food specialties range from high-quality rice and grilled beef tongue to interesting noodle dishes, *donburi* rice bowls, udon, Akita *mochi* and more.

Tōhoku is easy to reach from Tokyo Station. The region's biggest city, Sendai (p. 195), is only 100 minutes away by bullet train. The town furthest north, Aomori (p. 198), is just over three hours. Plan a trip and a few stopovers using the JR Pass and you'll experience some of the very best Japan has to offer.

TRANSPORT

Tokyo Shinkansen to Akita Station, about 4 hours. Or Tokyo Haneda to Akita Airport, about 1 hour, then 40 minute bus

CLOSE BY

Morioka, Hanamaki

ATMOSPHERE

City surrounded by nature, mountains, scenic, rustic, rural

REGIONAL FOOD & DRINK

Kiritanpo (grilled rice snack), Inaniwa udon (thin, dried udon), Jumonji ramen (fish and soy sauce), Yokote *yakisoba*, ham fry, Iwagaki oysters, miso, *nattō* (fermented soybeans), *kaiyaki* hotpot

OMIYAGE

Ginsenzaiku (silver-wire craft), Ideha paper, *mokume-gane* ('wood-grain metal'), *gakko* pickles, *mamegaki* rice crackers, *kinman* (white-bean sweets), sesame rice cakes, Namahage Tengu (local demon) souvenirs

SIGHTS

Senshū Park, Minzoku Geinou Densho-kan, Kubota Castle, Akita Minato Rest Area

GARDENS & PARKS

Senshū Park

MUSEUMS & GALLERIES

Akita Museum of Art

ARTS & CRAFTS

Akita dog everything, *mage-wappa* (bent-cedar woodcraft), cherry-bark craft

FESTIVALS

Kantō Lantern Festival, Akita Kantō Matsuri

WEB

visitakita.com

Akita City

AKITA PREFECTURE

Akita is famous for its dogs. Almost a national symbol, the cute Akita dog is one of the most popular breeds in Japan. The area is replete with heavenly hot springs and produces fine sake. It's also known for the Akita Museum of Art, designed by Tadao Ando (p. 353); Iwagaki oysters; Senshū Park (good for autumn leaves); and the Akita Moriama Zoo, whose highlights include raccoons, red pandas and capybaras.

The main festival is the Akita Kantō Matsuri, celebrating the harvest, but in wintertime Akita turns into a world of enchantment with the Yokote Kamakura Snow Festival, featuring famous glowing igloos. These *kamakura* (snow houses) are lit up inside to produce warm golden light, and when viewed en masse create one of the most picture-perfect fairyland moments. Visitors can enter the frozen pods to sit, drink warming sake and eat local delicacies – magical!

ABOVE: Yokote Kamakura Snow Festival
OPPOSITE PAGE: Zuihoden Mausoleum

Sendai

MIYAGI PREFECTURE

Sendai, the capital of Miyagi Prefecture, is a major junction for Shinkansen and the largest city in the Tōhoku region. Nicknamed the 'City of Trees', it has elms lining many of its main streets. Sendai is also home to Japan's largest Tanabata (Star) Festival, held on 7 July (p. 59). In December, the *Pageant of Starlight* fills the trees with lights. Sendai has its own *kokeshi* dolls (p. 340) in natural wood – a short and squat man and a woman with a happy or sad face.

Food specialties include *zunda mochi* (edamame rice cakes), *zunda ice cream*, *zunda shakes*, *walnut sweets*, *gyu-tan* (beef tongue), *sasa kamaboko* (a kind of salted seafood cake), *harakomeshi* (belly salmon and salmon roe on rice), Sendai *imoni* (a pot dish of vegetables, pork and extras, similar to a *nabe* and often enjoyed in the open air), and *datemaki*, a type of Baumkuchen cake filled with bean paste and cream and named after the city's founder, Date Masamune. If you're game to try the *gyu-tan*, you'll get the grilled beef tongue, some side dishes and an oxtail soup to complete the nose-to-tail profile. Head to highly regarded Aji Tasuke, Gyutan Sumiyaki Rikiu or Date No Gyutan Honpo.

You can find Date Masamune's ornate tomb, the Zuihoden Mausoleum (early 1600s), hiding among the secluded and beautiful mountains to the south-west of Sendai Station. Date was known as the 'one-eyed dragon', and you'll find this motif dotted around the grounds, along with several other smaller tombs and graves where other members of the Date clan are interred. There is also a small museum holding relics and information.

TRANSPORT

Tokyo Shinkansen to Sendai Station, about 90 minutes

CLOSE BY

Yamagata, Shiogama, Miyato Island

ATMOSPHERE

Tōhoku's biggest city, modern, station hub, nature, festivals, nearby beaches

REGIONAL FOOD & DRINK

Harakomeshi (belly salmon and salmon roe on rice), *sasa kamaboko* (fish cake), Sendai *imoni* (taro and meat soup), *zunda mochi* (edamame rice cakes), *zunda* shakes, *zunda* ice cream

OMIYAGE

Moon cake, *zunda mochi*, *zunda* roll cake, *gotto* cakes, *dorayaki* (pancake sandwich), *hasekurayaki* (walnut and white-bean sweet), frost pillar candy

SIGHTS

Zuihoden Mausoleum

GARDENS & PARKS

Izumi Botanical Garden, Tōhoku University Botanical Garden, Wild Plants Garden

MUSEUMS & GALLERIES

Serizawa Keisuke Art and Craft Museum, Akiu Craft Park, Sendai City Museum, Chiteinomori Museum, Sendai Kaleidoscope Museum, Museum of Kamei Collection

ARTS & CRAFTS

Ink stones, fishing poles, Sendai Ofude writing brushes, Yanagiu Washi (paper-making for 400 years), bogwood craft, Shiroishi washi (Date clan paper), *kokuji* ceramics (made for 200 years), Tsutsumi dolls, Sendaihira silk fabric, *shino* bamboo craft, papier-mâché, Sendai *tansu* (cabinetry), Tokiwakongata resist-dyeing, Sendai *tsuishu* (lacquerware), indigo-dyeing, picture banners

FESTIVALS

Sendai Tanabata (Star) Festival, Pageant of Starlight

WEB

www.city.sendai.jp

Nyūtō Onsen

Ensconced in the mountains of Towada-Hachimantai National Park, in the very heart of Japan's *onsen* (hot springs) territory, is Nyūtō Onsen. This mystical, magical destination overlooks Tazawako, the deepest caldera lake in Japan, and is somewhere you can soak your cares away, as people have been doing for some 300 years. In times past, travelling merchants would haul their goods along the sacred and beautiful trails of Japan until they found themselves in desperate need of food, rest and a bath. Nyūtō Onsen ('nipple *onsen*', named for the shape of a nearby mountain) was a premium stop then and it remains so today.

Tsurunoyu Onsen is quite simply one of Japan's most wonderful destinations. It's not five-star and has no mod cons. Rules are loose, food is rustic and the location remote. It's a traditional samurai or merchant roadside stop, complete with an *onsen* that celebrates the beneficial water sources of the area – sulfurous, milky and rich. Buildings are girded by rustic countryside. Corridors have sliding doors leading to rooms with either small hot-spring baths or tatami rooms where you will be served delicious meals. It's one of those life-changing experiences. Surrounding *onsen* are also impressive – Kuroyu and Taenoyu, where you can gaze onto a waterfall from the hot springs, in particular. Get the Yumeguri-cho pass for 1500 yen (it lasts for a year), which allows you to bathe once in each *onsen*.

TRANSPORT

Tokyo Shinkansen to Tazawako Station, about 3 hours; then Ugo Kotsu bus to Nyūtō Onsen, 50 minutes

CLOSE BY

Akita, Tazawako, Sendai, Morioka, Ginzan Onsen

ATMOSPHERE

Relaxed, secluded, rustic, historic *onsen* villages

REGIONAL FOOD & DRINK

Iwana (fresh-water char fish), *yama-no-imo nabe* (grated yam in a hotpot), *kiritanpo nabe* (grilled rice on a stick in a vegetable hotpot), *sansai* (wild mountain vegetables), new rice, seafood

OMIYAGE

Bath salts, hot-springs soda, hot-springs cider, samurai merchandise, sake and craft beer

SIGHTS

Tsurunoyu Onsen, Tsurunoyu Onsen, Yamanoyado Onsen, Kuroyu Onsen, Taenoyu Onsen, Ogama Onsen, Magoroku Onsen, Ganiba Onsen, Lake Tazawa

GARDENS & PARKS

Towada-Hachimantai National Park

ARTS & CRAFTS

Beechwood craft

WEB

www.tohokukanko.jp/en/attractions/detail_1651.html

THIS PAGE: Tsurunoyu Onsen
OPPOSITE PAGE: Taenoyu Onsen

Aomori

As Hakodate is the gatekeeper of the north, Aomori is the gatekeeper of the south, the point where you get the tunnel train under the water and across to Hokkaidō (Shin-Aomori to Shin-Hakodate is around one hour and forty minutes). As a city, Aomori is somewhat lost in time – that time being the 1980s. This means a few cool bits of signage, particularly with hairdressers and bars, that retro heads will be keen on. Apples are plentiful, and this region grows some of the biggest apples you'll ever see.

Aomori is best known for the Nebuta Matsuri (p. 59), a festival where large illuminated floats depicting samurai warriors roll through the streets. It's great fun for kids and adults alike, and one of Japan's most popular festivals (so book early if you want to go). If you can't make it for the festival, head to the Nebuta Museum Wa-Rasse (p. 361). The central part of the museum is a real treat, with many of the best floats arranged (and illuminated) in a large hall. There's also a display dedicated to the most respected float-makers.

The Sannai-Maruyama Historical Site offers a glimpse into the early inhabitants of the area (3900 BC early enough for you?). More than 500 'pit houses' have been unearthed on the site and there are other unique structures and reconstructed huts to explore.

It's definitely a food town – visit the A-Factory across from the Nebuta Museum Wa-Rasse, Furukawa Fish Market and Aomori Station for regional specialties and gifts. Surrounded by the sea, Aomori is known for seafood. Try *kaiyaki-miso* (seafood and miso grilled in a shell), apples, apple *gyōza*, miso curry, *senbei jiru* (rice cracker soup), miso–ginger *oden* (fish cakes) and miso milk curry ramen. If that doesn't get you up to Aomori then surely the strawberry sea urchin hotpot or the fried squid-meat patty will. Hang on, we might have gone a step too far there. Add a famous apple pie, vegetable potage and some excellent homegrown rice, and you have a food scene many cities would envy. There are a couple of galleries you won't want to miss: the Aomori Museum of Art (get shots of the huge Nara dog sculpture), and the wonderfully modernist Aomori Contemporary Art Centre.

The Aomori Tourist Information Centre is a thin, steep-side triangle perched on the waterfront. It cuts a fine figure against the sky and accommodates tourism information and restaurants, some of which boast fabulous sea views. Aomori also features the world's longest cherry-tree-lined road, with more than 6500 trees, spectacular when in bloom. *Onsen* (hot springs) lovers can use Aomori as a collection point for the shuttle to Sukayu Onsen. This striking, rustic, sulfurous *onsen* is a must-do for anyone into Japanese hot springs.

OPPOSITE PAGE: Nebuta Matsuri festival floats BELOW: Nebuta Museum Wa-Rasse

TRANSPORT

Tokyo Shinkansen to Shin-Aomori, about 3 hours 25 minutes

CLOSE BY

Sukayu Onsen, Hirosaki

ATMOSPHERE

Northern port city, relaxed, sleepy, festive, underground arts scene

REGIONAL FOOD & DRINK

Apples, apple cider, apple pie, fried squid patties, miso curry soup, dairy products, miso–ginger *oden*, vegetable potage, seafood and miso grilled in a shell, miso milk curry ramen, rice cracker soup, rice

OMIYAGE

Nebuta merchandise, Nanbu *senbei* (crackers baked over coals), *senbei jiru* (rice cracker soup), Fuji apples, apple rings, apple juice, apple pie (*kininaru ringo*), Momokawa Nigori Junmai Torouma (thick rice sake)

TEMPLES & SHRINES

Mount Osore, Seiryū-ji, Chōshō-ji, Zenringai, Saishō-in

SIGHTS

Cherry Tree Road, Sukayu Onsen, Sannai-Maruyama Historical Site, Furukawa Fish Market, Aomori Tourist Information Centre

GARDENS & PARKS

Ashino Park, Tsugaru Fujimi Lake Park, Gappo Park

MUSEUMS & GALLERIES

Aomori Contemporary Art Centre, Nebuta Museum Wa-Rasse, Aomori Museum of Art, Seikan Connection Memorial Ship *Hakkoda-Maru*, Aomori Prefectural Museum, Shiko Munakata Memorial Hall (woodblock print artist), Tsunedakenozono Atelier Museum

VIEWS

Aomori Tourist Information Centre, Mount Iwaki, Mount Osore

FESTIVALS

Nebuta Matsuri

WEB

en-aomori.com
www.pref.aomori.lg.jp

Morioka

IWATE PREFECTURE

Under the gaze of splendid Mount Iwate, Morioka is a city that can often be bypassed on the way north, but anyone seriously into craft will find many treasures here. A peaceful, somewhat gentle city, Morioka gives you a break from the madness of some of the major cities without giving up any of the benefits. In fact, Morioka has the double attack of traditional craft (wonderful Nambu Tekki ironware) and new craft (beer!), as well as some delightful indie record stores and bookshops, some great eateries and food specialties, and a couple of remarkable sights. Mount Iwate itself is a marvel. It might not be Fuji, but it puts in a pretty good showing. Snow-capped in winter, mystical in summer, the dormant volcano is often referred to as Nambu Katafuji (half-sided Fuji of the Nambu area) – its symmetrical form bears a strong resemblance to Japan's more famous mountain. Iwate was included in Kyūya Fukada's *100 Mountains of Japan*, where it is listed as one of Japan's 'ultras': mountains with spectacular peaks. →

THIS PAGE & OPPOSITE TOP: Meiji-era style at Nanshoso House OPPOSITE BOTTOM: Morioka packaging

TRANSPORT

Tokyo Shinkansen to Morioka Station, about 2 hours 15 minutes

CLOSE BY

Hanamaki, Tsunagi Hot Spring, Hiraizumi, Sanriku Coast, Kitakami, Michinoku Folklore Village

ATMOSPHERE

Relaxed, local, friendly, arts and crafts

REGIONAL FOOD & DRINK

Noodles (*jajamen*, *reimen*, *wanko soba*), *hitssumi jiru* (soy soup with flour dumpling), Nanbu *senbei* (crackers), Fukuda Pan sweet buns, Maezawa beef (wagyu), *sawauchi jinku* (tempura biscuit), kimchi and *nattō* (fermented soybean) ramen

OMIYAGE

Nambu Tekki ironware, lacquerware, Nanbu *senbei*, Nanbu Toji sake (Asabiraki, Hamachidori and Nanbu-Bijin), *kokeshi* dolls, folk toys made from brooms, woodwork

TEMPLES & SHRINES

Morioka Hachimangū, Hoon-ji Temple, Shojuzenji, Daihonzan Tozen, Chūson-ji, Mōtsū-ji Temple, Takoku-no-iwaya Temple

SIGHTS

Mount Iwate, Morioka Castle, Nanshoso House, Hanazawa Onsen, Tono Furusato Village, Handi-Works Square, Geibikei Gorge, Koiwai farm

GARDENS & PARKS

Iwayama Parkland, Takamatsu Park, Towada-Hachimantai National Park

MUSEUMS & GALLERIES

Iwate Museum of Art, Machiya Monogatarikan, Morioka Letter Museum, Takuboku and Kenji Museum

VIEWS

Mount Iwate, Morioka Castle Site Park, Kaiunbashi Bridge

FESTIVALS

Morioka Fall Festival, Chagu Chagu Umakko, Iwate Snow Festival

WEB

visitiwate.com

Visit super-cool Book Nerd for vintage and new art books, vinyl and exhibitions (say hi to owner Daisuke).

——— Morioka is best known for Nambu Tekki ironware. First created in the Edo period (1603–1868; p. 28), it's among the world's most rustic and exquisite cast-ironware. It's not just iconic for its looks, but is considered one of the best types of cookware due to its durability and heat distribution. The best places to see (and buy) the ironware are Iwachu Atelier, Suzuki Morihisa, Kunzan Kobo, Kozan Kobo and the wonderful Kamasada – worth the visit for its location in a traditional building alone. You can buy iron trivets, cooking pots, figurines, utensils and, of course, teapots, which come in various shapes and colours.

Fans of the Meiji era (p. 32) should visit Nanshoso House, a beautifully preserved relic built by copper magnate Yasugoro Sekawa. It has a wonderful winter garden and plenty of traditional features. Sip tea from the café as you gaze out onto the garden.

The dishes you must try are Morioka's Three Great Noodles – *wanko* soba, *jajamen* and *reimen*. *Wanko* soba is a lot of fun, and is basically all you can eat. Your server will slam soba into your bowl from a smaller bowl (you can add various accompaniments) – then you eat the soba as fast as you can before holding your bowl out for more. The server then sets the smaller bowl down and gives you another serve from the next small bowl, piling up the bowls as they go. See how many bowls you can stack up to the cries of '*Hai, jan jan*' (tada!) – and try to break the current record of 500 bowls! Head to charming Azumaya (1907), Hatsukoma Honten and Chokurian. *Jajamen*, a thick noodle served with meat, miso, cucumber, pickled vegetables and grated ginger, is the most popular of the three. *Reimen* is a cold noodle dish that features beef, kimchi, hard-boiled egg, vegetables and … fruit (watermelon, pear and apple). Locals and visitors love it, especially in summer. Recommended cafés include cute Café Rhino, Mi Café and Hataya. For craft beer try Aeron Standard or Sundance. Visit super-cool Book Nerd for vintage and new art books, vinyl and exhibitions (say hi to owner Daisuke) and check out Planet Morioka.

OPPOSITE PAGE TOP: Kamasada ironware BOTTOM: Azumaya

A crafty town

MAKIKO SUGITA,
MORIOKA LOCAL, TŌHOKU

Who are your favourite designers and makers?

SWISH! aka Hiroko Wayama, a knitting maker currently living in Tokyo. Homesickdesign, a design company based in Morioka.

What's your favourite festival?

Art Book Terminal Tōhoku, an art-book fair held every year at Cyg Art Gallery in Morioka.

A favourite place to eat or drink?

Karakoma, a vegan/macrobiotic restaurant. Tea house Liebe, a *kissaten*; the orange juice in iced tea called 'charming tea' is my favourite!

What's your favourite Morioka food or ingredient?

Morioka *jajamen*. My grandfather used to run a casual restaurant and I grew up eating his *jajamen*, which is similar to udon. We have it with meat, miso, chopped cucumbers and green onions, and we add grated ginger, garlic, chilli oil and vinegar.

Tell us your favourite bookshop.

Book Nerd (booknerd.jp). There's a gallery space in the shop and you never get bored. The owner Daisuke has fantastic taste and curation; he always helps you find the perfect book.

Naruko Onsen

Naruko Onsen, a small country town in the Miyagi prefecture about sixty kilometres to the north of Sendai, is distinguished by three things: it's a premium *onsen* (hot springs) town, it's obsessed with *kokeshi* dolls (p. 340), and the autumn colours in Naruko Gorge are among Japan's best. Recommended *onsen* within Naruko are the wonderfully rustic Takinoyu and Waseda Sajikiyu (built around a hot-spring source discovered by students from Tokyo's Waseda University). Higashi-Naruko Onsen, Kawatabi Onsen, Nakayamadaira Onsen and Onikobe Onsen are also nearby. Don't forget to order a bowl of soba noodle soup for lunch, the town speciality.

Naruko Gorge is just two kilometres away from the village of Naruko Onsen. Head to the gorge's Narukokyo Rest House in autumn; the observation deck has unmissable views of Ofukazawa Bridge (which crosses the gorge) surrounded by the ochre and burnt-umber hues of the autumn foliage on the surrounding mountains. The other famous sight, of trains emerging from a tunnel into the russet and yellow trees, can be snapped from the bridge itself. Hiking trails lead to other impressive scenic moments, mostly in autumn, but it's spectacular all year round. Try the Ofukazawa walking trail, which terminates at the Narukokyo Rest House.

Anyone who loves *kokeshi* will be enamoured with Naruko. The Japan Kokeshi Museum, a must for *kokeshi* fans, can be found at the east end of the gorge, the town's station is a shrine to *kokeshi*, and shops with long-time makers line the streets. Around the town you'll find *kokeshi* statues, mailboxes, phone booths and various wonderfully retro *kokeshi* signage. *Kawaii*.

TRANSPORT

Tokyo to Furukawa Station, about 2 hours; transfer to JR Rikuu-East Line to Naruko Onsen, 45 minutes

CLOSE BY

Yamagata, Sendai

ATMOSPHERE

Relaxed *onsen* towns, craft towns, train lines, rural

REGIONAL FOOD & DRINK

Soba noodle soup, *onsen* eggs

OMIYAGE

Kokeshi dolls, *koma* (spinning tops)

SIGHTS

Japan Kokeshi Museum, *onsen*, train station *kokeshi*

GARDENS & PARKS

Naruko Gorge, Oraga Naruko Tropical Botanical Garden, Naruko Tenjin-ja

ARTS & CRAFTS

Kokeshi dolls, *kokeshi no sugawaraya* (make your own *kokeshi*), wooden spinning tops

FESTIVALS

Kokeshi Festival (31 August), Yosakoi Naruko Odori

WEB

en.naruko.gr.jp

ALL IMAGES: A stroll around Naruko Onsen photographing *kokeshi* everything!

Yamadera

North-east of Yamagata City you'll find Yamadera, a small village hidden within mountain greenery. A quaint train station greets you on arrival, and the charming stores, eateries and bridges make for a pleasant destination. Yamadera is distinguished by Hojusanrishaku-ji (Mountain Temple; founded in 860 AD by Tendai monk Ennin), perched at the top of the mountain. Can you handle the 1000 (and fifteen, but who's counting) steps? If you're an avid hiker or don't mind a bit of a challenge, you'll be rewarded. Climb through an array of vegetation along a path lined with statues and stone lanterns to reach the temple, its buildings perched on the rocks. At the very top is a truly beautiful view of surrounding mountainous Yamadera. It is also said that with each step, the earthly desires that are stopping you from achieving enlightenment fall away. If the climb is a bit daunting or you're unable to attempt it, the temple grounds and gardens at the base of the mountain are spectacular.

TRANSPORT

Tokyo Shinkansen to Yamagata Station, about 2 hours 30 minutes; then Senzan Line to Yamadera, about 20 minutes

CLOSE BY

Yamagata, Ginzan Onsen, Naruko Onsen, Dewa Sanzan, Zaō Onsen, Kaminoyama Onsen, Sakata

ATMOSPHERE

Mountainous, scenic, rustic, rural

REGIONAL FOOD & DRINK

Cherries, soba, tempura, *imoni* (stewed potato), *chikara konnyaku* (potato dumplings), pumpkin *manjū* (sweet steamed buns)

OMIYAGE

Onegai Jizō (small protective Bodhisattva statues), Nadebotoke (good luck rubbing Buddha), temple dolls and toys

SIGHTS

Hojusanrishaku-ji, Konpon-chudo, Godai-dō, Semizuka, Kaisando Hall, Nokyodo, Konponchudo Hall, Mida Hora Rock, Godaido Hall, Niōmon Gate

GARDENS & PARKS

Fuga No Kuni (cherry-blossom hotspot), Konponchudo Hall Garden, Hojusanrishaku-ji Mountain

MUSEUMS & GALLERIES

Yamadera Bashō Memorial Museum, Museum of Western Art

LITERATURE

Bashō's famous haiku

ARTS & CRAFTS

Onegai Jizō statues

WEB

data.yamagatakanko.com/english/sightseeing

———— A walk around the town is also a great pleasure. Make sure you do some fossicking in the vintage stores, and in summer don't miss the soft-serve ice-cream flavours, especially the purple sweet potato, black sesame or edamame bean. One of Matsuo Bashō's (p. 29) most treasured haiku was composed here: *Shizukasa ya / iwa ni shimi iru / semi no koe* – deep silence / the shrill of cicadas / seeps into rocks, or stillness / seeps into the stones / the cry of the cicadas.

To reach Yamadera you'll pass through Yamagata City, which boasts some great *sakura* (cherry blossom) when in season, as well as Yamagata Castle. Apart from that, it's a great hub from which to explore Yamadera, Sendai, Fukushima, Osaki and Tendō.

THIS PAGE: Yamadera details
OPPOSITE PAGE: Steve at the highest viewing platform

TRANSPORT

Tokyo Shinkansen to Oishida Station, about 3 hours 20 minutes; then bus to Ginzan Onsen, 35 minutes

CLOSE BY

Choda Valley, Yamagata, Sendai, Osaki, Shirogane-yu, Shirogane Falls, Senshinkyo Valley, Bashō Seifu History Museum

ATMOSPHERE

Valley *onsen*, scenic, secluded, traditional, rural, picture-book

REGIONAL FOOD & DRINK

Curry bread, fresh tofu, local sake, Taishō *kaiseki*, soba water soft-serve ice cream (with crispy soba bits or soba water crackers)

OMIYAGE

Regional *kokeshi*, silver craft

SIGHTS

Nobezawa Silver Mine

WEB

ginzanso.jp

Ginzan Onsen

YAMAGATA PREFECTURE

Obanazawa holds one of Japan's most beautiful secrets: Ginzan Onsen (Silver Mountain Hot Spring – named after the nearby silver mine, which dates back some 500 years), a rare Taishō-era (p. 38) town in a valley that flows with some of Japan's most beneficial waters. A stay in Ginzan Onsen is spectacular – especially in winter when it's rugged, frozen and difficult. The Taishō-era wooden buildings are beautiful, and when icicles hang from the eaves and snow is heavy on the rooftops and thick alongside the river, Ginzan Onsen is a fairy wonderland.

Whatever the season though, Ginzan Onsen's *ryokan* (traditional inns; p. 87) are among the world's most picturesque sights, huddled together in a picture-book village and linked by old bridges that span the flowing river. The *onsen* are mostly inside *ryokan* and many can be accessed by day bathers. There are footbaths and public baths, including wonderfully contemporary Shirogane-yu, designed by superstar architect Kengo Kuma (p. 353), a modern, high-architecture addition to the Ginzan Onsen–scape.

You can explore a limited section of the nearby silver mine. Other highlights include exceptional hiking trails and the powerful Shirugane Falls.

RIGHT: Ginzan Onsen's main street in winter

Zaō Onsen

YAMAGATA PREFECTURE

A popular ski destination, Zaō Onsen is wonderful in any season. As an *onsen* town it's one of the best – many free, by donation or 100 yen baths can be found steaming and bubbling down lanes and around corners. Kawarayu is particularly special, as the hot-spring source bubbles up from directly underneath the bath. The town has a kind of sweet sulfur smell that's not overpowering, and the Tōhoku region's wonderful *kokeshi* dolls (p. 340) can be found gathered together in stores and eateries. There's one truly standout *onsen* in Zaō: Zaō Dai-Rotenburo (closed in winter! Sorry, skiers), a rustic outdoor *onsen* next to a flowing river. Zaō's wonderful acidic, sulfurous water flows from one pond to another, all under an open sky and surrounded by mountain vegetation.

During the winter months, Zaō's slopes are full of skiers and the snowfields play host to an army of invading 'snow monsters' – snow-covered pine trees and objects – that make for an eerie sci-fi landscape. In summer the mountains are great for hiking. Take the Zaō Ropeway from Zaō Sanroku Station to the top of Mount Zaō and trek to the still-active Okama Crater (*okama* means 'cooking pot', a reference to the shape of the crater) and its crater lake, which is known to change colour – depending on the daylight it can range from emerald to turquoise, earning it the name Lake of Five Colours. The town tends to close down at night, so stock up on food or make sure your *ryokan* or hotel has meals. There's also a nearby Fox Village (p. 78), where you can spend time with the cute little creatures.

TRANSPORT

Tokyo to Yamagata Station, about 2 hours 30 minutes; then bus to Zaō Onsen, about 40 minutes

CLOSE BY

Sendai, Yamagata, Fukushima, Mount Torikabuto

ATMOSPHERE

Skiing, hiking, *onsen*, relaxed country atmosphere

REGIONAL FOOD & DRINK

Onsen eggs, cheese, soba noodles, cherries

OMIYAGE

Snow monster souvenirs, *iga-mochi* (rice cakes), bath salts, *senbei* (rice crackers), *kokeshi* dolls

SIGHTS

Mount Zaō, Okama Crater, Zaō Dai-Rotenburo, Kawarayu, snow monsters, sulfur *onsen*

VIEWS

Mount Zaō, Okama Crater, Zaō Ropeway

FESTIVALS

Snow Monster Festival (1–3 February)

WEB

zao-spa.or.jp

ABOVE: One of the town's bathhouses

TŌHOKU
ADVENTURES
HOTSPOTS &
HIDDEN TREASURES

AKITA KANTŌ MATSURI

One of the three main festivals in Tōhoku, the Kantō Matsuri's main feature is mass lanterns on poles carried aloft on the foreheads of willing participants. Pretty impressive, and considering the procession runs for a kilometre along Chuo Dōri, it makes for a memorable festival.

LAKE TOWADA

The biggest crater lake on Honshū, Tawada is a stunning vibrant blue. A popular camping spot, Towada is still active as a volcano, although it hasn't erupted since 915 AD. One of the main features is the Otome-no-Zo ('Statue of Maidens'). Altogether, Towada is considered one of the 'Eight Scenic Views of Japan' (according to Japan's major newspapers, 1927).

TENDO NINGEN SHŌGI

This 'human chess' event is a major part of the local Sakura Festival. Chess fans need to see this – shōgi is a game similar to chess, and during the festival season real people dressed in traditional samurai garb take the place of the pieces on a giant board and enact the 'shōgi battle' controlled by two professional players.

SHINJŌ (MATSURI)

This 250-year-old festival, designated an Important Intangible Folk Cultural Property, is a festival in three parts: yoi matsuri (night festival), hon matsuri (main festival) and go matsuri (latter festival). The festival features elaborate floats and illuminations.

ICHINOSEKI

A midway point between Sendai and Morioka, Ichinoseki has standout attractions including the Gembi Valley, Geibikei (an impressive natural gorge and sheer rock face), Yugen Cave and Satetsu River.

HIROSAKI CASTLE

Tōhoku's best known sakura (cherry-blossom) hotspot, Hirosaki Castle and its surrounding park date back to 1611, when it was constructed by the Tsugaru clan. Apart from the wonderful park, its five-level castle keep, reconstructed in 1810 (the original burnt down in 1627), is one of the oldest reconstructions in Japan.

HANAMAKI

A short Shinkansen ride from Morioka (p. 200) and a perfect daytrip, Hanamaki is the birthplace of writer Kenji Miyazawa. It's also home to Miyazawa's 'Village of Fairy Tales' and the SL Ginga steam train (p. 107). From Shin-Hanamaki Station you can ride this story-book train, complete with on-board planetarium.

If you are an onsen (hot springs) fan like us, the Hanamaki onsen area is not to be missed. Bathe next to the river in the mixed bath at Oosawa Onsen for a life-changing experience. The winding corridors, rustic hidden baths and old-world atmosphere make for a memorable and intriguing overnight stay.

OPPOSITE PAGE & RIGHT: Oosawa Onsen ABOVE: Shin-Hanamaki Station

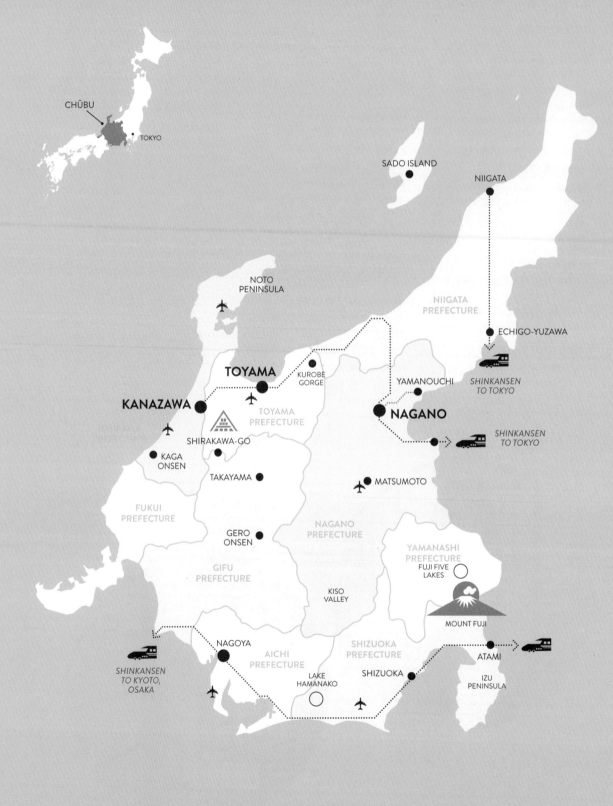

CHŪBU

TOKYO

SADO ISLAND

NIIGATA

NIIGATA PREFECTURE

ECHIGO-YUZAWA

NOTO PENINSULA

SHINKANSEN TO TOKYO

TOYAMA

KUROBE GORGE

YAMANOUCHI

KANAZAWA

TOYAMA PREFECTURE

NAGANO

SHIRAKAWA-GO

SHINKANSEN TO TOKYO

KAGA ONSEN

TAKAYAMA

MATSUMOTO

FUKUI PREFECTURE

NAGANO PREFECTURE

YAMANASHI PREFECTURE

GERO ONSEN

FUJI FIVE LAKES

GIFU PREFECTURE

KISO VALLEY

MOUNT FUJI

NAGOYA

SHIZUOKA PREFECTURE

SHINKANSEN TO KYOTO, OSAKA

AICHI PREFECTURE

ATAMI

LAKE HAMANAKO

SHIZUOKA

IZU PENINSULA

中部

CHŪBU

Taking up a significant chunk of central Honshū, Chūbu is a region to be reckoned with, a central point on the main island that takes in some of Japan's most noteworthy sights, cities and experiences. Mount Fuji (p. 222) looms large in the south-east, attended by five famous lakes (p. 221) and a host of spectacular mountains and forests. The southern beaches of Ito, Izu and Atami (p. 226) give way to inland castle towns like Matsumoto (p. 219), which in turn flow to premium northern city Kanazawa (p. 214) and the rugged coastlines of Noto Peninsula (p. 226).

Chūbu has some of Japan's best destinations – *onsen* (hot springs) towns, castles, stunning gardens and unique festivals, food specialties, traditional craft, contemporary art and many places of historical significance. The region is home to a host of experiences that are slightly off the grid and offer a true journey of discovery. It's the over-achieving middle child set between the might of Tokyo's Kantō region and the splendour of Kyoto and Osaka's Kansai.

JAPAN

日本

213

JAPAN BY REGION – CHŪBU

Kanazawa

Kanazawa's location in the north-west of Honshū makes this city, the capital of Ishikawa prefecture, a bit of a hidden jewel in Japan. It's a modern city with a deeply traditional past. Much of Higashi Chaya, the old part of town, survived Second World War bomb raids, making its old town district second only to Kyoto's – but with the added benefit of a relatively unspoilt samurai district, Ninjadera. Kenroku-en is one of the three best Japanese-style gardens in the country – beautiful in any season, but particularly vibrant in autumn. Nearby 21st Century Museum of Contemporary Art puts Kanazawa on the map as a progressive town when it comes to creativity. It famously features Leandro Erlich's *Swimming Pool*, an installation that you can appear to submerge yourself in – head downstairs to go under the pool and get someone upstairs to snap you as if you're underwater. It's eerie. →

Oriental Brewing, Kanazawa

TRANSPORT

Tokyo Shinkansen to Hokuriku Station, about 2 hours 30 minutes

CLOSE BY

Noto Peninsula, Kaga Onsen, Toyama

ATMOSPHERE

Northern city, historical, relaxed, seafood, mix of new and old, creative

REGIONAL FOOD & DRINK

Seafood, craft beer, sake, seaweed

OMIYAGE, ARTS & CRAFTS

Shikki lacquerware, gold leaf, Ohi ceramics, Kutani porcelain, Kaga dolls, Kaga *yūzen* (silk fabric-dyeing), *Kaga-nui* (detailed embroidery), Futamata paper, Kaga *mizuhiki* (paper string decoration), *wagasa* umbrellas, Kaga *zogan* metal inlay, *kirihibachi* (paulownia hand-and-room warmers)

TEMPLES & SHRINES

Ninjadera Temple, Oyama Jinja, Tentokuin, Daijō-ji

SIGHTS

Kenroku-en, Higashi Chaya, Omicho Market, Kanazawa Castle, Ninjadera, Seisonkaku Villa

GARDENS & PARKS

Kenroku-en, Gyokusen-en, Nishida Family Garden, Kanazawa Castle Park

MUSEUMS & GALLERIES

21st Century Museum of Contemporary Art, Ishikawa Prefectural Museum of Art, D.T. Suzuki Museum, Kanazawa Noh Museum, Ishikawa Prefectural Museum for Traditional Arts and Crafts, Kaga-Yuzen Kimono Center, Ishikawa Local Products Center

LITERATURE

Tokuda Shūsei (1871–1943), Murō Saisei (1889–1962), Izumi Kyōka (1873–1939)

FESTIVALS

Kagatobi Dezomeshiki, Hyakumangoku Matsuri, Kanazawa Jazz Street

WEB

visitkanazawa.jp

——— Kanazawa Castle is impressive, featuring extensive grounds and a huge building with plenty of open sky behind it. Although originally dating from 1583, most of the extant buildings were rebuilt in 1881. In *sakura* season, the pink cherry blossoms adorn the walkway. The Ishikawa-mon Gate, one of the original features, is echoed in Kanazawa Station's impressive Tsuzumi-mon (drum) Gate, designed by SANAA architects Kazuyo Sejima and Ryue Nishizawa (p. 355).

Kanazawa's Omicho Market (p. 154), devoted entirely to seafood, is one of the best in Japan, with a history stretching back nearly 300 years. It's so good it's often called the Kitchen of Kanazawa. Cheery vendors loudly hawk their merchandise. There are more than 200 stalls and shops, where you can sip beer or sake while eating oysters recently plucked from the ocean, order a seafood *donburi* (rice) bowl, and buy fresh fish, snow crab and prawns, or have them served to you. Naturally it follows that in Kanazawa, sushi and sashimi are of the highest quality and freshness.

THIS PAGE TOP: Kanazawa Castle grounds MIDDLE: Gold-leaf soft-serve ice cream
BOTTOM: Omicho Market breakfast OPPOSITE PAGE: Kanazawa Station

Nearby Noto Peninsula (p. 226) has magical waters (which you can buy in Kanazawa as 'Noto Water'), and this filters into Kanazawa's culinary delights (including craft sake and beer – Kanazawa's sake is considered some of the best in Japan). Head to Oriental Brewing to taste Kanazawa's finest craft beer and sake.

Koshihikari rice is one of Japan's most prized varieties of the staple grain, a perfect accompaniment to rice bowls, sushi and curry (made extra special by the secret ingredient; the waters of southern volcano Mount Haku). Fans of stew can't miss Kanazawa's Jibu-ni, a soy sauce base enriched with duck, mushrooms, parsley and bread. Noto-gyu beef, famed for its flavour and delicacy, pairs brilliantly with the quality local vegetables. The area's *wagashi* (traditional sweets) are also famous – used to accompany the local tea. Sweets will often be formed into shapes – such as leaves, fish or rabbits. The most touristy thing you can do, and of course one of the best, is indulge in Kanazawa's showiest dessert: gold-leaf soft-serve ice cream, served in a cone and completely covered in glinting gold leaf – photo opportunities galore! Rice dishes also include *kaburazushi* (featuring pickled turnips, salted yellowtail and *kōji*, fermented rice and soybeans).

Don't leave Kanazawa without immersing yourself in Zen philosophy at the wonderfully atmospheric and architecturally stunning D.T. Suzuki Museum (p. 361). Also worth visiting is Mount Hakusan, a sleeping volcano to the south that bubbles with exceptional mineral water.

Hidden gem

TAKA TSUBATA, GENERAL MANAGER OF WOW! KANAZAWA STAY, KANAZAWA, CHŪBU

Why visit Kanazawa?

The food, history and culture. After sightseeing around Ishikawa, prefecture many people want to eat delicious food and Kanazawa has some of the region's most amazing food.

What are the best daytrips and sightseeing spots?

Noto Peninsula, Wakura Onsen, Chirihama Beach, Mount Haku and surrounds, Kaga Onsen, Nomi and Terai (where they have *kutaniyaki* – famous local ceramics).

What are your favourite places to eat and drink in Kanazawa?

I'm looking for new places to suggest all the time because there are so many tourists now. I recommend Tsujike Teien and Gyokusen-tei.

What's so special about the waters of Ishikawa prefecture?

We have a lot of snow in winter ... the melted snow water is so pure and delicious! The spring water is full of minerals. The good water gives us rice, sake, soy sauce, vegetables, miso and more.

What's your favourite season in Ishikawa?

For me it's summer, but most people say winter is the 'real Kanazawa'.

Matsumoto

NAGANO PREFECTURE

Canal-side town Matsumoto is distinguished by the beautiful Matsumoto Castle (p. 345), one of Japan's few original castles, constructed in stages during the 1500s and 1600s. It's a prime cherry-blossom-viewing spot during *sakura* season and features hundreds of Japan's most popular variety of *sakura*, the Somei Yoshino. Shopping strip Nakamachi features some wonderful examples of the Japanese merchant warehouse architecture known as *kura* (p. 342) and, of course, plenty of souvenirs.

Of particular interest to art fans will be the Matsumoto City Museum of Art. Yayoi Kusama is Matsumoto born and bred, and the city celebrates this with a permanent exhibition. It's no token either; the works themselves are extensive and emotive – fans will be in heaven from the first step into the grounds. The Kusama monstrous flower is at the very least as photographable as those spotted pumpkins (p. 293), possibly more so. The spotty theme that runs through to the drink dispensers and seating is priceless, and there is plenty of Kusama merchandise to be had.

Another popular attraction is the Ukiyo-e Museum, a collection of woodblock prints that perfectly complements the town's creative aesthetic. The 300-year-old Sakai collection is one of the world's largest art collections with an estimated 100,000 pieces (although not all are available for viewing). The building was designed by Shinohara Kazuo. Japan's largest and oldest craft fair is held in Matsumoto each year in May.

OPPOSITE PAGE: Yayoi Kusama drink machines at Matsumoto City Museum of Art
ABOVE: Craft Fair Matsumoto

TRANSPORT

Tokyo JR 'Azusa' or 'Super Azusa' limited express from Shinjuku Station to Matsumoto Station, 2 hours 30 minutes

CLOSE BY

Takayama, Nagano, Gifu, Tateyama Kurobe Alpine Route, Kamikochi, Norikura, Gero, Chichibu

ATMOSPHERE

Peaceful, creative, historical, architectural

REGIONAL FOOD & DRINK

Sanzokuyaki (Matsumoto fried chicken), soba, miso paste, miso pizza, local sake

OMIYAGE

Lacquerware, ceramics, ironware, woodwork, Yayoi Kusama merchandise

TEMPLES & SHRINES

Matsumoto Shrine, Jorin-ji, Zenkyu-in

SIGHTS

Matsumoto Castle, Nakamachi (merchant warehouse district), Craft Market, Daio Wasabi Farm

GARDENS & PARKS

Matsumoto Castle Park, Matsumoto City Alps Park, Agata-no-mori Park

MUSEUMS & GALLERIES

Matsumoto City Museum of Art (Yayoi Kusama), Ukiyo-e Museum

VIEWS

Matsumoto Castle

ARTS & CRAFTS

Craft Fair Matsumoto (May), Craft Picnic in Agata-no-Mori Park

FESTIVALS

Asama Hot Springs Torch Festival, Matsumoto Ice Sculpture Festival, Shinshu Flower Festival

WEB

visitmatsumoto.com/en/event

Fuji Five Lakes

YAMANASHI PREFECTURE

The Fuji Five Lakes are spread around the north, north-western and eastern base of Mount Fuji (p. 222). Beautiful in their own right, their proximity to Fuji-san makes them even more popular, and people go to view the magnificent mountain from observation decks, restaurant windows, scenic trains and, above all, *ryokan* hot-spring baths. Of course views have to be paid for and, especially in high season, accommodation can be expensive – but for a view of Fuji from an *onsen* it will always be worth it.

Kawaguchiko is probably the best known of the lakes. Set in the middle of the five lakes, it has a quaint township, wonderful (especially in autumn) views from its northern shore, a famous 'reflection' of Fuji in the water girded by cherry blossoms in *sakura* season, a beautiful leaf corridor in autumn and one of Japan's best mini-museums – the Kubota Itchiku Art Museum, which celebrates the vibrant talents of one of Japan's great contemporary kimono artists. We say artist rather than maker because the kimono are for hanging on a wall – they're too precious to wear. The spectacular wooden vaulted ceiling adds to the impressive nature of the museum, and you can also stroll around the grounds of Kubota Itchiku's house where the museum is set.

Yamanakako is the largest lake of the five, and it's crowded with sailboards and yachts. Taking snaps of Fuji with 'people at play' in the foreground is one of Yamanakako's drawcards. The Fuji *marimo* can be found here, rare spherical algae that looks like balls of moss under the water's surface.

Saiko, also known as the 'Lake of the Maiden', is fringed by the beautiful Aokigahara Jukai Forest, giving a view of Fuji peeking up over both the forest and the lake, which is described as the colour of 'clear blue eyes'.

Although lesser known than Kawaguchiko, Motosuko has what is probably the closest view of Fuji, so good it was used on an early 5000 yen note. Shojiko is notable for its many Meiji-era hotels, which have stunning views of Fuji and a very authentic feel.

Oshino Hakkai – not a sixth lake but a cluster of ponds – is distinguished by incredible views of Fuji, a range of seasonal flowers including sunflowers and lupins (imagine them with a Fuji backdrop!), and a stunningly unspoilt snow vista. The melting snow also gives the region particularly pure water.

OPPOSITE PAGE: Kubota Itchiku Art Museum grounds

TRANSPORT

Tokyo JR Chuo Line from Shinjuku Station to Otsuki Station, about 70 minutes; Fujikyu Line to Kawaguchiko Station, about 50 minutes; then Omni buses from lake to lake

CLOSE BY

Mount Fuji, Chichibu Tama Kai National Park, Yamanashi, Gotemba, Odawara

ATMOSPHERE

Fun, holiday, picturesque, Fuji!

THE LAKES

Kawaguchiko, Saiko, Yamanakako, Motosuko, Shojiko

REGIONAL FOOD & DRINK

Venison curry, freshwater smelt, *Fujimabushi* (rice cooked with sock-eye salmon and rainbow trout from Saiko), *herabuna* carp, Oshino Hakkai water, soba noodles

OMIYAGE

Mount Fuji–shaped everything

TEMPLES & SHRINES

Kawaguchiko Asama Shrine, Arakura Sengen Shrine (featuring Chureito Pagoda), Fujiyoshida Sengen Shrine

SIGHTS

Fuji-san, the Five Lakes, Kubota Itchiku Art Museum, Shibazakura Festival

GARDENS & PARKS

Lake Yamanaka Flower Park, Hana-no-Miyako-Koen Flower Park, Yagasaki Park, Oishi Park

MUSEUMS & GALLERIES

Kawaguchiko Museum of Art, Kubota Itchiku Art Museum, Kawaguchiko Music Forest Museum

ARTS & CRAFTS

Oishi handwoven cloth, glass beads, gel candles, painted pottery

FESTIVALS

Fujikawaguchiko Autumn Leaves Festival, Winter Fireworks Festival, Saiko Ice Festival, Shibazakura Festival (pink moss phlox)

WEB

yamanashi-kankou.jp

Mount Fuji

Fuji-san is an enduring symbol of Japan and one of the world's most recognisable mountains. The *san* in Fuji-san is not a mark of respect; it simply means 'mountain' in this context, but it isn't a stretch to imagine the 3776-metre high, near-symmetrical mountain as a living being that presides benevolently over Honshū's south-east.

You'll often hear the mountain spoken of in these terms – Fuji is mysterious today, Fuji has been hiding all week, Fuji doesn't wish to be seen at the moment. Yes, quite often you'll travel to the Mount Fuji viewing hotspots only to be disappointed by Fuji's shyness when you go to snap some shots. On the other hand, if it's a cloudless day, you'll be rewarded with one of Japan's most exhilarating views.

FUJI STATS

Height: 3776 metres

Climbing stations: There are ten stations to Fuji's summit

Eruptions: Fuji is still an active volcano. The last eruption occurred in 1707 between the 5th and 8th station. Tremors in recent years have suggested a possible catastrophic eruption could be imminent

Most annual climbers: 430,000 in 2008

BEST SPOTS TO SEE FUJI

· Chūbu – Fuji Five Lakes (p. 221), Gotemba, Iyashi no Sato, Fuji Shibazakura Festival (Higashi Mokoto Shibazakura Park, Fujikawaguchiko; p. 221), West Izu (p. 226), Shizuoka (p. 227)

· Kantō – Hakone (p. 184), Kamakura (p. 177), Enoshima (p. 177)

KEY WORKS OF FUJI ART

· Katsushika Hokusai: Woodblock prints – *Thirty Six Views of Mount Fuji*

· T. Enami: *Mount Fuji and the Boaters*

· *The Man'yōshū*: Japan's oldest collection of poetry features works about Fuji, including Bashō's haiku *Over one ridge / do I see winter rain clouds? / snow for Mount Fuji*

· Utagawa Hiroshige: Woodblock prints – *One Hundred Famous Views of Edo*

CLIMBING FUJI

Fuji is a 'Power Spot' (p. 267) and one of the Japan's 'three holiest peaks'. Said to have been first traversed by a monk in the seventh century AD, Fuji is a spiritual pilgrimage for many and a spectacular hike for others. The mountain's female deity is Sengen-Sama. There are more than 13,000 shrines on the mountain, and the Japanese once believed it to be the centre of the universe. The mountain is fully open for hiking from 10 July to 10 September, when climbing conditions are the least treacherous. Some 250,000 people climb the peak during this time, so there are plenty of facilities and accommodation options along the way. Choose your route and difficulty setting – it goes from easy to hard to professional. The easiest is the Yoshida Trail, which takes around eight hours, beginning at impressive Fujiyoshida Sengen Shrine and culminating at Fuji's peak. To cut the hike in half, head to Fuji's fifth station, which can be accessed by shuttle bus on Sabaru Line toll road.

FUJI MAGIC

· Diamond Fuji – On a few rare occasions per year, the setting or rising sun lines up perfectly with Fuji's peak, creating a bright, glinting diamond

· Goraiko – The sunrise from Fuji's eighth station, the Goraikou-kan Hut

· Red Fuji – The sun rising or setting during a clear sky in autumn turns Fuji red

OPPOSITE: Tea fields and Mount Fuji

Takayama & Shirakawa-go

The Wide View Hida train (p. 105) whisks you to beautiful Takayama, its broad windows taking in sweeping views of the area – a stunning start to your adventure. Takayama is often called the Kyoto of the north, due to the many untouched Edo-period (p. 28) *machiya* (wooden townhouses) lining its streets. These rare examples of a long-ago era, unravaged by war or natural disaster, make Takayama a prime destination. Specialty food, fresh local produce, longstanding vendors and crafters, morning markets and quality water feeding nearby *onsen* (hot springs) and sake breweries add further magic to the area. Don't miss watching large *senbei* crackers being blistered and crisped over an open flame, or the town's delicious specialty – *hoba* miso, a meal of mountain vegetables and/or Hida beef grilled over a small open flame and served on a *hoba* leaf. Takayama excels in the crafts of yew woodcarving and *shunkei* (clear) lacquerware. If this wasn't already enough, Takayama is also known for its proximity to some of Japan's traditional wonders, Shirakawa-go, the Hida Folk Village and Gokayama.

From Takayama catch the bus to Shirakawa-go. This is the easiest way to access the town, where you can see the *Gasshō-zukuri* ('built like praying hands'), beautiful farmhouse cottages with steeply pitched roofs. Resplendent in any season, Shirakawa-go is especially magical in winter, when the snow hangs heavy on the roofs and dried persimmons dangle from the eaves, transforming the town into a fairytale, gingerbread wonderland. At more than 250 years old, the buildings are precious, and the area was declared a UNESCO World Heritage Site in 1995. Gokayama and the Hida Folk Village are smaller but no less picturesque examples of *Gasshō-zukuri* villages within easy access of the town of Takayama.

THIS PAGE TOP: Takayama store BOTTOM & OPPOSITE PAGE: Shirakawa-go

TRANSPORT

Tokyo to Takayama (4 hours 20 minutes); Takayama to Shirakawa-go, around 50 minutes by bus

CLOSE BY

Kanazawa, Toyama, Hida, Gifu, Gero, Matsumoto

ATMOSPHERE

Historical, traditional, relaxed

REGIONAL FOOD & DRINK

Hida beef and Hida soba, highland fruit and vegetables, *hoba* miso, local sake products, persimmons, *mitarashi dango* (sweet glazed rice balls), Takayama ramen

OMIYAGE

Sake, Hida laquerware, *Ichii-Ittobori* (yew woodcarving), pottery, pickled vegetables, Okuhida curry, Okuhida beef jerky, *senbei* (rice crackers)

TEMPLES & SHRINES

Higashiyama Hakusan Shrine, Takayama Jin'ya, Hokke-ji, Hida Kokubun-ji, Unryuji, Soyuji, Sogenji, Sakurayama Hachimangu Shrine, Hida Gokoku Shrine, Shoren-ji

SIGHTS

Shirakawa-go Historic Village, Gokayama, Hida Folk Village, Sanmachi-Suji, morning markets, Furui Machinami, Okuhida Hot Springs, Higashiyama hiking

GARDENS & PARKS

Shiroyama Park, Kitayama Park, Nakabashi Park, Takayama Sky Park, Miyagawa Ryokuchi Park, Garyu Park

MUSEUMS & GALLERIES

Takayama Museum of History and Art, Hida Takayama Museum of Art, Matsuri No Mori, Hirata Folk Art Museum, Fujii Folk Museum, Hida Folk Archaeological Museum

FESTIVALS

Takayama Matsuri, Hida Folk Village Winter Illuminations, Sanno Matsuri, Hachiman Matsuri, Hinamatsuri, Frozen Hirayu Grand Waterfall Festival

WEB

hida.jp

CHŪBU ADVENTURES
MAGIC IN THE MIDDLE

ATAMI

A seaside resort town close to Tokyo, Atami has long been considered *natsukashi*, a place of nostalgia for older Tokyoites who used to go there for summer holidays in the 1950s and 1960s. It's even featured as a holiday destination in Yasujirō Ozu's classic film *Tokyo Story* (1953). Retro charm still inhabits the area, from the signage, shops and crumbling hotels to a covered arcade that tendrils out from the station. There's plenty to love here: seaside views, seafood, quality sushi and spectacular fireworks displays. The area's *onsen* (hot springs) are also a drawcard, particularly in the *ryokan* (traditional inns; p. 87) that line the coast or lie secluded in the mountains.

NOTO PENINSULA

Northern Ishikawa prefecture's rugged Kongo coast – and its Noto Futami (Noto 'Wedded Rocks'; p. 335), rocky outcrops with gaping 'gate' holes linked together with ropes – are a sight to behold. Myōjō-ji and Sōji-ji temples are important spiritual destinations, while various secluded *onsen* make for an attractive getaway. Popular traditional *ryokan* Lamp no Yado can be found on the north-eastern tip.

IZU PENINSULA

Izu isn't too far from Tokyo and makes for a great stopover if you're interested in a beachside *onsen* town. Historic former *ryokan* Tokaikan (1928) can be explored; have tea in the wonderful tea room. The nearby Jogasaki Coast is a glorious bit of beachside Japan and great for hiking. Izu-Kōgen is the next stop, a villa district featuring stunning volcanic caldera Omuroyama. There's plenty to see here and some great views of Fuji from the west coast. Dogashima features some of Japan's most incredible volcanic coastal rock formations (a geological smorgasbord) and the cliffside *onsen* Sawada Koen Rotemburo is a hot-springs bath with amazing sea views.

NIIGATA PREFECTURE

Niigata is popular in the ski season, Yuzawa being one of Japan's best known ski towns. Just off the coast, Sado Island is also a popular destination, home to Earth Music Festival – a celebration of *taiko* drumming – and an island with a deep and fascinating history of political exiles. The old wooden *machiya* (townhouses) and interweaving canals are picturesque and atmospheric. Possibly Niigata's most intriguing feature is the Echigo Tsumari, a modern art festival in a rural setting. Contemporary art is spread throughout the region and visitors can walk, eat and even sleep among the artworks (p. 93).

TOYAMA

Toyama prefecture shines in every season. The Tateyama Kurobe Alpine Route connects Toyama with Nagano, a twenty-metre deep cavernous gorge of sheer white in winter and a sea of russet foliage in autumn. Cable cars, buses, ropeways and the scenic Toyama Chihō Railway, plus various hiking trails ranging from easy to treacherous, take in some of Japan's most spectacular scenery. Toyama is close to Shirakawa-go and Gokayama (also accessed from Takayama; p. 224), old villages removed from most mod cons and featuring the triangular farmhouses known as *Gasshō-zukuri* (p. 225). Toyama City itself is known for dark soy, which is used to flavour ramen and *karaage*. Don't miss stunning Ikeda Yasubei, a traditional Edo-period medicine shop that dates back to 1936.

ABOVE: Nihondaira Yume Terrace, Shizuoka

SHIZUOKA PREFECTURE

Already taking in picturesque beaches, *onsen* towns and Mount Fuji views, Shizuoka prefecture also lays claim to being the largest producer of tea in Japan (although not the oldest; p. 151). Tokugawa Ieyasu (p. 28) retired to Sumpu Castle, and Kunōzan Tōshōgū, an ornate mausoleum devoted to him, can be found on Mount Kunōzan. Miho Beach and Shimizu Port boast the best views of Fuji (p. 222). Don't miss Kengo Kuma's wonderful Nihondaira Yume Terrace, a lookout that mimics shapes from the Hōryū-ji temple in Nara (p. 353). Views of Fuji on a clear day are spectacular. Also make sure to check out Kenzō Tange's space-age Press and Broadcasting Centre (p. 353). A cool contemporary way to try tea in Shizuoka is at Maruzen Tea Roastery, where you can pour teas of different varieties and strengths over a picture-worthy *kakigōri* (shaved ice dessert).

KAGA ONSEN

Kaga's Yamashiro and Yamanaka Onsen hide a host of secrets. Yamanaka's main public bath is Kikunoyu, a piping-hot *onsen* in the town square. Lacquerware is a staple of the town and has a 400-year history. You can get some beautiful and authentic pieces here for less than you would pay in the big city. The town square features a tourist information centre with a serious secret – the Yamanaka-za, built in 2002, which has all the hallmarks of a classic and beautiful kabuki theatre. The women's bath nearby features some wonderfully crafted lacquerware doors. The secluded and stunning Kakusenkei Gorge is a short distance away, and features two wonderful bridges: Korogi-bashi Bridge (a lovely cypress bridge) and Kurotani-hashi Bridge. The Ayatori Hiroshi 'Cat's Cradle' bridge designed by Hiroshi Teshigahara is a must for engineers.

Edo-period poet Matsuo Bashō (p. 29) loved it here and penned several poems in ode to the area's beauty, one of which says it all: 'Who needs the dew of youth from the chrysanthemum when you have the restoring waters of Yamanaka?' Agreed. Bashō-do, a monument dedicated to him, now stands at the end of the Korogi Bridge. Don't miss the Bashō-no-Yakata Museum and 'secret' café Higashiyama Bonheur.

Yamashiro Onsen, another popular destination, features the famous Koso-yu Public Bath, a lantern-shaped gold-flecked building that hides a 'modern rustic' *onsen*. Nearby is Rosanjin's Hut Iroha, where the famous ceramicist produced most of his works. Admire the Kutani porcelain in the Kutinayaki Exhibition Hall, which features an impressive Edo-period (p. 28) kiln. The pottery tiles made there adorn the walls of Koso-yu. There are many *ryokan* in the area that make use of the hot-spring water. Be sure to visit the impressive Natadera Temple, with a *torii* gate (p. 333) and steps built into a stone cliff face.

YAMANOUCHI

From Nagano Station take the Snow Monkey Express to Yudanaka Station, the heart of Yamanouchi's *onsen* district. The station features a free outside footbath and a lovely attached *onsen*, Kaede-no-Yu, so make sure you have a soak before heading out into Yudanaka. The town itself is full of small local *onsen* that steam, bubble and spout along the main street. If you can stay at the *ryokan* Yoroduya, do so; if not, be sure to pop in for the *onsen* (it has a day rate) – it's excellent. From Yudanaka you can catch various shuttle buses to two other main destinations: Shibu Onsen and Jigokudani Monkey Park (p. 78). Shibu Onsen is a small *onsen* town where there is only one public bath. In other words, if you want to bathe there you need to stay at a *ryokan* and get the key to the

baths – a wooden one that allows you access to the town's splendours. It's worth it – *onsen*-hoppers can bathe to their hearts' content. The steaming, beautiful town is perfect for hot-spring fanatics and snow bunnies in winter.

From here it's not far to the entrance to Jigokudani, home of the snow monkey *onsen*, one of Japan's most popular attractions. It's worth mentioning that it's quite the hike to the monkey park, and in winter it can be treacherous, so wear appropriate attire and some boots with a good grip (chemists actually sell portable crampons). Jigokudani Monkey Park is set deep in the forest and features a paid area where you can observe the native macaques. Watching monkeys enjoying a hot-spring bath is endlessly cute, as they soak in the water and chatter and twitter to the crowd, heads bobbing above the water. Prepare for photo opportunities, squeals of '*Kawaii!*' and overall unbridled joy. The valley and smouldering Jigokudani *ryokan* surrounding the monkey *onsen* are truly spectacular, adding to the area's allure.

GIFU PREFECTURE

Gifu prefecture is famous for waterfalls – fanatics visit Osakacho, Hirayu, Yōrō-no-Taki and Amidaga. Gero Onsen makes up one of the 'three famous hot springs' alongside Arima (p. 260) and Kusatsu (p. 187). Gero Onsen Gasshō Village is a mini version of Shirakawa-go and Hida Folk Village that boasts some fabulous *Gasshō-zukuri* (p. 225), as well as the local craft beer Gero Gensen and some premium sake. The Mori Hachiman Shrine holds some of Japan's historical treasures: ten primitive Shinto statues that date back to the eleventh century AD. Zenshōji temple features a pretty stone bridge and an ancient cedar tree (estimated to be more than 1000 years old).

Sacred sites & pilgrimage trails

Walks and pilgrimages in Japan date back hundreds or even thousands of years. These walks were either set up as trade routes or by monks who used them to spread the word of Buddhism. Some were walked by the imperial family, many were popular with people from all social groups – and they remain so today.

LODGING

Ryokan (traditional inns; p. 87) have rooms with tatami floors and futon bedding. Many have shared bathrooms. Meals can be included and often also an *onsen* (natural hot-spring bath) or *sentō* (man-made bath). A *minshuku* is a small family-run lodging like a B&B. You may be the only guest/s or share the accommodation with the family and a few others. Rooms will be simple and modest, and again some will offer food, some won't. If food is offered it will be a hearty Japanese breakfast of miso, fish, pickles, rice and other small dishes like a soft-boiled egg. Dinners will comprise miso soup, fish or meat, and rice. Please note that there's little to no Western food served in this kind of accommodation. Many of these lodgings shut down over the New Year period.

HIKING GEAR YOU'LL NEED

- Backpack
- Band-Aids, blister patches and personal medicines
- Camera
- Chargers and batteries for phones and cameras
- Cold weather items – thermals, gloves and a warm jacket, fleece-style jacket/zip-up top, gloves, scarf, warm hat, warm hiking socks, rain gear
- Hiking boots/trekking shoes (already worn in)
- Hiking socks (good quality)
- Insect repellent (optional) – Japan makes excellent 'stickers' that keep bugs away
- Passport
- Pencil/pen and notebook
- Reusable chopsticks, fork and spoon
- Sleepwear – pants/leggings and top
- Small towel
- T-shirts/long-sleeved shirts
- Town clothes: pants, shirts, shoes, sandals, etc.
- Walking poles (collapsible)
- Warm weather items – sunscreen, sunglasses, hat, umbrella (optional, collapsible; purchase in a Japanese department or convenience store before you go), *tenugui* (Japanese cotton handtowel; buy on the trail)
- Water bottle (2 litre) or water flask that fits into your backpack
- Wind- and water-proof jacket
- Wind- and water-proof trousers (with zip-off/zip-on legs)
- Zip-up small waterproof bags (handy for passport, etc.)

SHIKOKU HENRO EIGHTY-EIGHT TEMPLE PILGRIMAGE TRAIL

1 Awakening
2 Ascetic training
3 Enlightenment
4 Nirvana

Where: Shikoku island

Access: The trail begins near Bandō Station. From Tokushima Airport, bus to Naruto, then train to Bandō Station. Or train from Kyoto to Okayama to Takamatsu to Itano to Bandō (about 4 hours).

Length: About 1100 kilometres

Time: 40 to 60 days depending on your pace

Sections: Four: 1 Awakening (temples 1–23), 2 Ascetic Training (temples 24–39), 3 Enlightenment (temples 40–65), 4 Nirvana (temples 66–88)

Best seasons: Autumn or spring. Summer and winter are for hikers of intermediate level and above. Cold weather, snow, humidity and the rainy season all make the hike more difficult.

Web: tourismshikoku.org

This 1200-year-old trek, known as the Eighty-eight Temple Pilgrimage, is not for the faint hearted. For the *henro* (pilgrim) this is a long hike, spanning the whole island of Shikoku, and requires commitment and stamina. You can dip in and out of this trail, completing a section at a time (even many years apart), a real option if you don't have one to two months' holidays owing.

Temples 40–65 ('Enlightenment') are in a manageable cluster if you want to sample a slice of this incredible trail. If you choose to just complete 'Nirvana', Temple 88 is close to Temple 4, so if you're feeling inspired you can easily travel to Temple 1 and start from the beginning.

There's a *henro* uniform of white *hakui* (jacket or top) and white pants or skirt, a purple cotton or silk *wagesa* (scarf), straw *sugegasa* (*henro* hat) and *kongotsue* (walking stick with bell). While it's not essential, it's an important way of being part of something ancient and spiritual – one of a collective with the same goals and determination. There are all sorts of wonderful spiritual meanings behind the outfit and various additions to it – a larger bell to ring (*jirei*), a stamp book (*nokyo-cho*), a bag (*zudabukuro/ sanyabukuro*), Buddhist prayer beads (*juzu*), name slips (*osamefuda*), shoe covers, special socks and straw sandals (*waraji*), prayer books and more.

If you don't want to dress in the traditional *Ō-henro* pilgrim attire, it's good manners and respectful to wear all white on your trek. It's also a sign to local people that you're making this pilgrimage and you have respect for the spiritual traditions. You'll also receive help and warm wishes from passers-by and local communities. →

KII MOUNTAIN RANGE (UNESCO WORLD HERITAGE SITE)

Nakahechi Route
Kiiji Route
Ohechi Route
Iseji Route
Kōyasan Choishimichi
Kohechi Route
Ōmine Okugakemichi

KANSAI

TOKYO

SHIGA PREFECTURE

MAIBARA
HIKONE
KYOTO PREFECTURE
LAKE BIWA
KYOTO
OTSU
HYŌGO PREFECTURE
UJI
HIMEJI
KOBE
NARA
OSAKA
MIE PREFECTURE
OSAKA PREFECTURE
ISE
WAKAYAMA
MOUNT KŌYA
YOSHINO
ISE JINGU
WAKAYAMA PREFECTURE
KUMANO HONGŪ TAISHA
NARA PREFECTURE
TANABE
SHINGU
KUMANO HAYATAMA TAISHA
KUMANO NACHI TAISHA

Where: Wakayama, Nara and Mie prefectures (Kansai), including the Kii Mountains

Access: Train from Kansai Airport to Hineno then Kii-Tanabe stations (about 2 hours). Or train from Kyoto or Osaka to Hineno then Kii-Tanabe (3–4 hours). Or train from Namba (Osaka) to Kōyasan.

Length: Routes from 68 to 170 kilometres

Web: shikoku-tourism.com

Three sacred sites – Yoshino and Ōmine, Kumano Sanzan, and Mount Kōya – are linked by pilgrimage routes to the ancient capital cities of Nara and Kyoto.

KUMANO KODŌ

Age: 1200 years old

Time: 2–10 days depending on the weather and/or which part of the hike you choose

Routes: Three: Kiiji, Kohechi and Iseji, which are three incredibly popular hikes based in and around the Kii Mountain Range. Kodō means 'old ways'.

KIIJI ROUTE

Forks into two routes, Nakahechi (imperial route) and Ohechi (coastal route).

NAKAHECHI

Where: Takijiri-oji to Kumano Nachi Taisha

Length: 68 kilometres

Time: 4–7 days

Known as the imperial route, this is the most popular of the Kumano Kodō trails. From the tenth century (Heian period, p. 17) the imperial family regularly walked its path from Takijiri-oji to Hongū, a thirty-kilometre two-day walk.

OHECHI

Where: Tanabe to Kumano Nachi Taisha Shrine

Length: 90 kilometres

Time: 4–5 days

Known as the coastal route, this path was big with many poets and artists in the Edo period (p. 28).

KOHECHI ROUTE

Where: Mount Kōya (Kōya-san) to Kumano Hongū Taisha Shrine

Length: 70 kilometres

Time: 4–5 days

The mountain route through the incredible Kōya-san area makes a glorious mountain trek for the experienced or well-prepared hiker. Visiting the Ise-Jingu shrine (p. 334) was popular in the Edo period.

ISEJI ROUTE

Where: Ise-Jingu Shrine to Kumano Hongū Taisha Shrine

Length: 170 kilometres

Time: 7–9 days

The eastern route, through forest, mountains and along beaches. Popular in the Edo period (p. 28)

NAKASENDŌ WAY (KISO KAIDŌ)

Where: Kyoto (Kansai) to Tokyo (Kantō) via the Kiso Valley

Access: Train to Nagai Station, then a short bus or taxi ride to Tsumago. Or train to Nakatsugawa Station, then a 30 minute bus ride to Magome. There is a bus connecting both towns, but it has a limited timetable.

Length: 7.8 kilometres from Magome to Tsumago (the whole distance from Kyoto to Tokyo is 534 kilometres)

Time: 3–4 hours from Magome to Tsumago (most tours are 3–4 days or about 7 days for the whole distance)

Best seasons: Autumn or spring

Resources:
kiso-hinoki.jp/en/03nakasendo.html

www.city.nakatsugawa.gifu.jp

jnto.org.au/nakasendo-trail-villages-of-old-japan

Stroll back in time on the merchants' trail from Kyoto to Edo (now known as Tokyo) through mountains and forests: ring bells to warn off bears, take in deep breaths of the hinoki cypress scent, gaze at the beauty of the trees and the architecture … this hike is one of the most accessible you can do, almost a primer to see if you might be interested in some of Japan's more challenging walks.

We walked the Magome to Tsumago section on a daytrip from Kyoto in late autumn. It took us about three and a half hours, strolling along stone pathways and steps (with a few gruelling bits), taking detours for photos and nature-spotting. If you're lucky enough to visit in late November, you'll see persimmons hanging and drying out the front of houses and businesses. There's even a 'forest therapy' park on the Nakasendō trail (closed in winter) in Agematsu called the Akasawa Forest Therapy Park (you can also get a bus there from Agematsu Station).

We spent quite a lot of time in Tsumago buying the perfect Kiso wooden rice-warming pot and lacquerware. We ate freshly made rice crackers (*senbei*) and grilled savoury rice cakes on sticks (*gohei mochi*), a lunch of handmade soba noodles with fresh mushrooms in broth and delicious mountain-vegetable steamed buns (*oyaki* – meat ones are available too, so do ask if you're a meat-eater). And we finished with chestnut ice cream. All this walking and mountain air makes you hungrier than usual.

If you're a city person and want a leisurely country stroll, this is the walk for you. If you want to do the whole walk, there are lots of tours to take, or make up your own itinerary. Staying in local *ryokan*, the walk, the people you'll meet on the way, the food, and the smell of the trees and country air are sure to make this a memorable experience.

The pilgrim

TRISHA GARNER, DESIGNER

The Nakasendō Way is a trail that follows the ancient route connecting Edo (Tokyo) to Kyoto, winding through mountains and forests, past ancient shrines and temples, and meandering through *juku* post-towns, traditional post stations where travellers could rest. Accommodation can be found in centuries-old inns (*ryokan*), where restorative family *onsen* (hot springs) await at the end of a day-long trek.

A bunch of Australian friends and I undertook a ten-day guided hike (organised through Walk Japan, with a Japanese-speaking guide) starting in Kyoto and finishing in Tokyo. *Yukata* (casual kimono) were provided, and worn for dinner and to sleep in. *Geta* (wooden sandals) were often available for communal use outside the *ryokan*. Dinners were delicious, homemade by the owners from local fare: river fish, forest vegetables including mushrooms and other fungi, eggs, rice, miso soup, insects and the occasional raw horsemeat (I abstained). We enjoyed fresh, juicy persimmon (*kaki*) on our hike.

As it was October, it was hot and sunny, with little shade while walking through some of the smaller towns. A sunhat is a must, and a small collapsible umbrella is handy for extra shade and unexpected showers. Buy a *tenugui*, a thin Japanese hand towel made from cotton and printed with an intricate pattern. Soak it in water and tie it around your neck to help keep you cool on the trail.

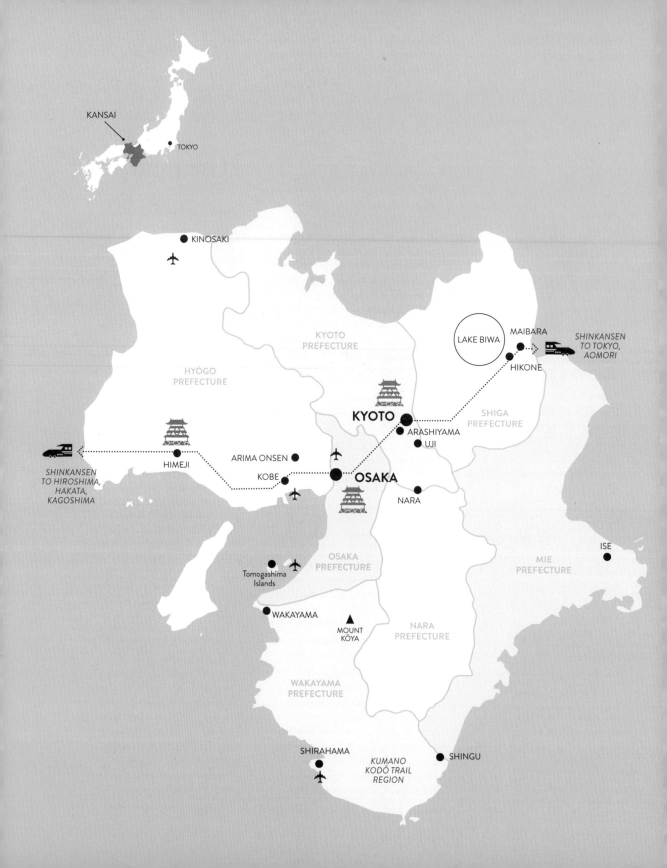

KANSAI

TOKYO

KINOSAKI

KYOTO
PREFECTURE

HYŌGO
PREFECTURE

LAKE BIWA

MAIBARA

*SHINKANSEN
TO TOKYO,
AOMORI*

HIKONE

KYOTO

SHIGA
PREFECTURE

ARASHIYAMA

UJI

*SHINKANSEN
TO HIROSHIMA,
HAKATA,
KAGOSHIMA*

HIMEJI

ARIMA ONSEN

KOBE

OSAKA

NARA

ISE

MIE
PREFECTURE

Tomogashima
Islands

OSAKA
PREFECTURE

WAKAYAMA

MOUNT
KŌYA

NARA
PREFECTURE

WAKAYAMA
PREFECTURE

SHIRAHAMA

*KUMANO
KODŌ TRAIL
REGION*

SHINGU

KANSAI

Kansai cuts a broad swathe across Honshū island, covering some of its most impressive and unforgettable sights and capturing the true essence of spiritual, traditional and inspirational Japan. From frenetic capital Osaka (p. 252) with all it has to offer and beautiful Kyoto (p. 234) and its immaculate surrounds, to stunning and historical Lake Biwa (p. 256), Wakayama (p. 261) and the holy mountain of Kōya (p. 258), you'll find the Japan most people search for – breathtaking temples and shrines, stunning mountains, local treasures and delicacies, as well as festivals, geisha, local crafts, food specialties and hidden secrets.

Destinations include some of Japan's most unmissable, historically important and outstanding locations, many of them only a very short daytrip away from the city centres. Some you can pop in to by just jumping off the train. Others may require a little more devotion, a local or shuttle bus, or a sleepover. As far as places to visit go, regional standout Kyoto has everything – a contemporary city, great shopping (for old wares and new), benevolent surrounding mountains, the highest concentration of World Heritage–listed shrines and structures in Japan, and a major train station that's nothing short of a structural marvel. The JR West Nara Line offers a myriad of experiences that won't easily be forgotten. Kansai is truly the epicentre of magical Japan.

Kyoto

Visitors flock to Kyoto to get in touch with old-world Japan and it's easy to see why. Ancient temples loom large among the abundantly forested mountains resplendent in seasonal beauty. Old *machiya*, Japanese townhouses, line quaint streets, with their dark wood facades and linen *noren* curtains floating in the breeze, evoking more tranquil times. Here, you can still catch a glimpse of *geiko* and *maiko* (geisha and their apprentices) slipping down alleys and lanes on the way to appointments where they will play games, pluck on instruments or dance. Traditional eateries, some centuries-old, perfect the recipes of their predecessors. Ancient streets frame views of the stunning surrounding mountains. All of this beauty cradles a contemporary city, which despite laying claim to some of the world's most ancient sites has one of the busiest and most hi-tech train stations you'll ever experience, a shrine in itself.

From lush hiking paths to looming temples with perfectly coiffured grounds, inspiring gardens, buildings of astounding architecture and deeply rooted culture, Kyoto is a beacon of sophistication and a haven for old-world crafts, for taking your time creating, for living the quiet life, for worshipping nature and everything it provides. In Kyoto, history is layered over history. The new collides with the old, or more relevantly, the new sits inside the old. Kyoto is a present-day city snuggled in the arms of an ancient world. →

A *geiko* (geisha) in the Gion district

TRANSPORT

Tokyo Shinagawa Station to Kyoto Station, about 2 hours 45 minutes. Or Tokyo airports to Osaka Kansai Airport, then limited-express Haruka to Kyoto Station, about 3 hours 30 minutes (via Shin-Osaka and Tennōji).

CLOSE BY

Arashiyama, Osaka, Nara

ATMOSPHERE

Zen (the town moves at what we call 'Kyoto pace'), temples, shrines, mountains, forests, geisha, deep history, contemporary attitude

WHAT TO EXPECT

Temples and shrines, old *machiya* (wooden townhouses), *geiko* (geisha), the Floating World (p. 29), beautiful mountains, ancient gates, long-established shops and eateries, *shibori* indigo-dyeing, pottery, *furoshiki* and *tenugui* cloths

A THOROUGHLY MODERN CITY

Kyoto Station, Teramachi, Shijō Dōri, Gojō Dōri, canal district

REGIONAL FOOD & DRINK

Soba, *kaiseki ryōri*, *shōjin ryōri*, mackerel sushi, *wagashi* (traditional sweets) sake, pickles, matcha, craft beer, udon, ramen, tofu, *yuba* (tofu skin), *konpeitō* (sugar candy), soft-serve ice cream, *mochi* (rice cakes)

OMIYAGE

Kyoto handcrafted dolls (Kyo-Ningyo), geisha hairpins and combs, Japanese knives, Furoshiki, oil-blotting sheets, camellia oil, *wagashi*, *yatuhashi*, *konpeitō*, matcha, pickles, umbrellas, kimono (and *yukata*), Seven Spice Mix

TEMPLES & SHRINES

Kiyomizu-dera, Kinkaku-ji (Golden Pavilion), Ginkaku-ji (Silver Pavilion), Fushimi Inari Shrine, Nanzen-ji, Sanjūsangen-dō, Hongan-ji, Daitoku-ji, Heian Shrine

SIGHTS

Gion, Imperial Palace, Nijō Castle, Ponto-chō, Philosopher's Path

GARDENS & PARKS

Ryōan-ji, Ginkaku-ji, Tōfuku-ji, Daitoku-ji (Kōtō-in), Heian Shrine, Taizō-in, Ōkōchi-Sansō Villa, Enkō-ji, Imperial Palace Gardens (Sentō Gosho), Kennin-ji, Kyoto Botanical Gardens, Shosei-en

MUSEUMS & GALLERIES

National Museum of Modern Art, Kyoto International Manga Museum, Kyoto Art Center, Imura Art Gallery, Kaho Gallery, Museum of Traditional Crafts

VIEWS

Kyoto Tower, Kyoto Station Skyway, Kiyomizu-dera, Amanohashidate (northern Kyoto), Ginkaku-ji, Enkō-ji, Nanzen-ji Sanmon Gate

LITERATURE

Shikibu Murasaki, *Genji Monogatari* (*The Tale of Genji*; c. 1008); Matsuo Bashō, 'Even in Kyoto' (c. 1689); Tanizaki Junichiro, *The Key* (1956); Yasumari Kawabata, *The Old Capital* (1962); Yukio Mishima, *The Temple of the Golden Pavilion* (1956); Komomo, *A Geisha's Journey* (2008); Ami Takusada, *The Yakuza Path* series (2016–2018)

ARTS & CRAFTS

Pottery, lacquerware, *furoshiki*, *tenugui* (cotton hand towels), *shibori* resist-dyed cloth, textiles, Kyo-ningyo dolls, folding fans, woodblock prints, origami

FESTIVALS

Gion Matsuri, Hatsumōde, Toka Ebisu, Jidai Matsuri, Arashiyama Hanatoro, Gion Odori Geisha Dance, Gojō-zaka Pottery Festival, Aoi Matsuri, Joya-no-kane (sacred bell-ringing), Setsubun, Gozan no Okuribi (Daimonji Fire Festival), Saiin Kasuga Shrine Festival, Higashiyama Hanatōro, Kurama Fire Festival, Autumn Moon Viewing, Jidai Matsuri, Higashiyama Temple Illuminations

WEB

kyototourism.org
kyoto.travel/en

KYOTO AREAS

KYOTO STATION & GOJŌ DŌRI

Arriving in Kyoto can be a bit of a surprise – you've expected a rustic city of *sakura* (cherry blossoms), mountains, temples and hiking paths, and here you are in a bustling train station with a soaring metal-lattice ceiling, endless shopping opportunities and an escalator that heads towards the heavens. Then you emerge in the 'town square' and see Kyoto Tower, an imposing 131-metre tower that stares down at you from a giddy height. This contemporary introduction to Kyoto is the perfect welcome – a late-twentieth/early twenty-first century shrine to a multilayered city.

Before you leave the station's main gate there are many opportunities to catch up on the *omiyage* (souvenirs; p. 109) of the region. Once you're out in the main atrium, marvel for a while at the cavernous structure of the main hall, snap some shots and ride the escalator to the top and take in some truly spectacular views from the Skywalk. There is a 'ramen street' on the tenth floor that brings in ramen masters from eight different Japanese regions.

Once outside the station, snap some shots of Kyoto Tower, a 1960s retro delight that still impresses today. Climb up for a striking view of the surrounding mountains – sometimes you can even see Osaka. Say 'See you soon' to the station – it will be your hub to unmissable destinations like Osaka, Nara, Arashiyama, Fushimi Inari, Tōfuku-ji and Uji – and head into Kyoto. South of the station you'll find beautiful Toji Temple, which features a five-tiered pagoda, the golden Kondō Hall and a flea market that takes place on the 21st of each month. This area is a more multicultural side of Kyoto, and has recently enjoyed a renaissance of sorts, with cafés and hotels like Anteroom, Lower East Nine and Hostel Ten popping up.

Not far north of Kyoto Station you'll discover Higashi Hongan-ji, often passed by because it is so near the station and so far away from the other temples, but its unmissable facade is the perfect introduction to your upcoming Kyoto experiences. A spectacular shrine on vast grounds greets you through an imposing gate. Stroll around the area and marvel at the wondrous ancient structures.

Further up, the extraordinarily expansive area around Gojō Dōri can be overwhelming, but it's worth braving the crowds. To the left are new design stores and old favourites tucked into corners, crevices, down alleyways and deep inside buildings, all circling Bukkō-ji, the Temple of Buddha's Light. Bukkō-ji is a wonderful temple – on its grounds are the D&Department design store, situated in a gorgeous small building, and the D&Department Shokudō Canteen, where you can get delicious food while gazing out onto the modest shrine in front of you. To the east are canal-side eateries and cafés where you can spend a few happy hours people-watching.

Walk the backstreets to discover some enchanting shopping opportunities. Mustard makes beautiful woollen products – they still knit using a hand-operated machine. The store itself is stunning, so head in and make that special investment purchase. Nearby Kitone has an impeccably selected range of homewares and a small, secluded café (check opening hours; they work to their own schedule here). Towards the canals stroll into cafés Kiln, Walden Woods, Kaikado and Murmur for a cup of green tea, matcha latte or coffee. →

ABOVE: Mustard BELOW: Gōjō Dōri sights
OPPOSITE PAGE: Kyoto Station

SHIJŌ DŌRI, GION & HANAMIKOJI

The mid-city section of Kyoto is like an oasis among the hills – the surrounding array of temples, old-world backstreets and mountain shrines is the destination, but the city is where you'll mostly lay your head. Shijō Dōri is the main thoroughfare leading up to Gion and Higashiyama. It's a shopping strip that reminds you that you're in a contemporary world, without taking you out of the magical. BAL is an upmarket department store, Fuji Daimaru features all the recommended youth fashion shops as well as % Arabica, a great stop for coffee. Tokyu Hands can sort you out for homewares and souvenirs. Elsewhere there are great gift shops, coffee houses, bookshops and eateries, and even the occasional shrine tucked away between stores. Nishiki Market (p. 154), the 'Kitchen of Kyoto', is just off Shijō Dōri and has an astounding array of delicacies – from seafood dishes to soft-serve ice cream (sometimes combined). The market is an estimated 400 years old, although the genesis of the space can be traced even further back than that. Anytime you visit is a vibrant experience; throngs of people cram the narrow thoroughfare, soaking up the atmosphere, shopping and laughing. You can buy many Kyoto specialties here: Japanese knives, *hōjicha* (roasted tea), pickles (there are barrels of fermented vegetables, many unrecognisable) and sweets.

Nishiki Market ends at Teramachi Dōri, a covered arcade you can always use to get your bearings. Towards Shijō Dōri, Shinkyogoku is a mess of t-shirt stores and name brands with the occasional gem – tea shop Horaido, where they invented *genmaicha* (p. 151) has a timeless charm. The further north you go on Teramachi, the more interesting it gets, taking in some remarkable and long-established stores – including the beautiful tea house Ippodo; calligraphy brushes at Saiundo; and old folk crafts, textiles and pottery at Gallery Kei – until you arrive at the southern edge of the Kyoto Imperial Palace Gardens.

GEISHA IN GION

Shijō Dōri is a conduit to Gion and Higashiyama (the East Mountains) beyond. Gion is the old Kyoto geisha district, well preserved with original *machiya* townhouses, tea houses and wonderful hidden shrines and galleries. Geisha in Kyoto are known as *geiko*, and you can certainly still spot a *geiko* or *maiko* (apprentice *geiko*); although their numbers have dwindled, they can often be seen tip-tapping along Hanamikoji Dōri, tiny *furoshiki*-wrapped parcels in hand, on the way to an appointment or errand. Just admire them for what they are – an otherworldly sophistication and beauty with a culture deeply steeped in the mists of time – and then move on. Snapping pictures aggressively sucks the magic and mystery out of it. We know most of you will act respectfully, because this area was built on respect and tradition, and if you want to experience that, you should also adhere to it. Strolling these streets and byways is such a beautiful and inspiring experience. Nearby temple Kennin-ji is a great introduction to some of the beauties of Higashiyama. Many artisans still work in shops in the area, creating bath bowls, geisha combs, camellia-nut hair oil and a range of other local specialties.

Return via Gion and you can slip down Ponto-chō at night, when it's at its most magical. The old geisha entertainment district has so many people wandering down the narrow alley in hope of getting a glimpse of ancient Kyoto and the *geiko* lifestyle that it has almost become a parody of itself – but the charm of the buildings and the feel of the cobblestoned streets will still enable you to extract some of that old Kyoto magic.

ABOVE: Capturing Yasaka Pagoda on the walk to Kiyomizu-dera

LEFT: Girls in *yukata* at Nanzen-ji ABOVE: Monk in Higashiyama BELOW: Little girl in *yukata* at a festival in Higashiyama

HIGASHIYAMA

The east mountains of Kyoto hold most of its ancient treasures. Shrines and temples are plentiful, and beautiful *ryokan* (traditional inns; p. 87) with intricate and delicate *kaiseki ryōri* (p. 127) lunches are strewn among the verdant hills. It's hard to imagine the magic of this area – you just have to go. A stroll along Sannenzaka and Ninenzaka to Kiyomizu-dera is a must-do experience. The winding streets are still flanked by old buildings hiding eateries and tiny enclaves with shrines, still lovingly tended by the same person who has looked after them their whole life.

Kiyomizu-dera is one of Kyoto's most spectacular sites. The temple, set on an elevated hill overlooking a vast swathe of greenery, is a joy to stroll through but is best viewed from the main path. From here you can see the temple in all its glory – an unmissable photo opportunity. You can arrive via Ninenzaka through the main entrance, or along Matsubara Dōri, which is fringed with souvenir shops, eateries and street-food stalls – a festive and colourful walk up to the temple.

The hills are alive with shrines and temples. From 1000-year-old Yasaka Shrine at the end of Gion, turn south for Ninenzaka or north to Chozen-ji, Heian Shrine (home to the famous stepping stones of *Lost in Translation*), and the nearby Philosopher's Path connecting Ginkaku-ji (the Silver Pavilion; p. 337) and Nanzen-ji (p. 337). There are so many extraordinary and ancient wonders to explore. →

THE BEAUTIFUL NORTH

If the throng of visitors ever becomes too much (Kyoto is very popular), why not take a trip up north – here you'll find quiet forest glades; hidden temples; old towns with a new attitude; trains that remind you of a time when stations were small, quiet spaces and station masters knew you by name; and the magic of old Kyoto. The enchanted north, the undiscovered territory in Kyoto, offers the greatest of escapes.

Perversely, the first stop is one of Kyoto's biggest tourist drawcards, Kinkaku-ji (the Golden Pavilion; p. 337), a resplendent gold-leaf-decorated temple sprouting from a lake accented by small islands with ancient, gnarled bonsai trees. The building was burnt down in 1950 by a monk suffering from mental illness, Hayashi Yoken, but rebuilt (actually for the second time; during the Ōnin War in the fifteenth century all of the buildings in the complex succumbed to fire). Yet despite the twentieth-century rebuild it's still a truly spectacular sight in any season. Go early or late to avoid the jostle. From here head to Kitano Tenmangu, a shrine that celebrates both plum blossoms and autumn foliage. A popular produce-and-antique market takes place here on the 25th of each month (yep, that means if you're looking for something to do on Christmas Day you've found the perfect spot; p. 373).

The 'suburbs' further north of here make up a network of streets, shops, lanes and temples that capture the truly magical essence of Kyoto, and for that matter Japan. Small shops and eateries with a modern twist are sprinkled around the streets. Charming old *sentō* (man-made hot-spring bath) Funaoka is just a short walk from old bathhouse-turned-café Sarasa Nishijin – have a soak and then head down for a beer and curry. The surrounding streets are full of reminders of old Kyoto.

The tip of the Kyoto Imperial Palace Gardens (p. 347) is another great starting point for a jaunt into the tranquil north. A gentle stroll away is the charming town of Demachiyanagi – head to Futaba to try *daifuku* (p. 140) in one of the oldest sweet shops in Japan. Demachiyanagi is perched on a delta – sip coffee at Bon Bon while gazing out onto the river and the famous 'turtle' stepping stones – and there are plenty of great cafés and eateries old and new dotting the area. Don't miss the often overlooked Shimogamo Shrine, a Shinto enclave secreted in a dense forest. →

DEMCHIYANAGI & BEYOND

Demchiyanagi Station marks the start of the Eizan Line (p. 105), an adorable old-school train line that chugs into the deep north, stopping along the way at tiny unmanned stations, dropping off students at various tertiary institutions. Don't be surprised if people speak excellent English; the Doshisha English University founded in 1875 is here. Essential stops along the Eizan Line are secluded towns Kurama and Kibune, with Shinto shrines, the mysterious Kurama-dera Buddhist temple, and Kurama hot springs. The other great attraction is *kawadoko* dining, a summer ritual where platforms are spread out across the river. Imagine eating lunch or dinner while perched over the ebbs and flows of the river – it's exhilarating.

Ichijōji is a stop with many attractions. It's a ramen and craft-beer hotspot and features a memorable indie bookshop, Keibunsha. Stop here for lunch and then head into the hills. Enkō-ji in particular is spectacular in autumn – a secluded and enchanting experience. If you have the energy, keep walking up to Tanukidanisan Fudo-in to uncover one of Kyoto's true secret gems.

THIS PAGE TOP: Enkō-ji, Ichijōji BOTTOM: Kitano Tenmangu OPPOSITE PAGE TOP: Enkō-ji, Ichijōji BOTTOM: Northern streets

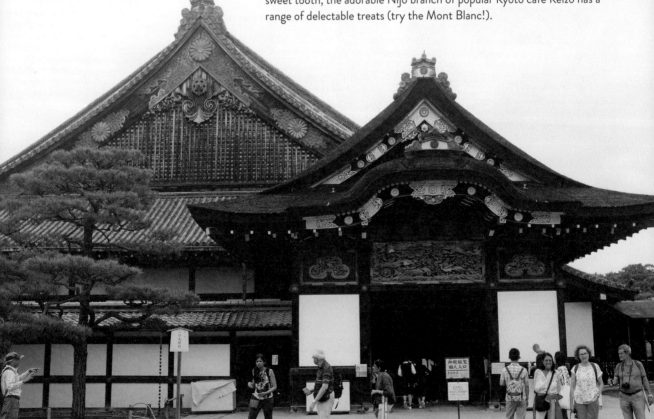

NIJŌ CASTLE AREA

Nijō is a vast area in Kyoto's west. To get your bearings, heading true west from the centre of Kyoto takes you through Nijō before arriving at beautiful Arashiyama (p. 245).

The first port of call in the area is Nijō Castle (p. 345), one of Japan's best. From most vantage points in Nijō you'll see its looming turrets and imposing tower walls – a massive central point surrounded by vast, open roads that give way to small hidden pockets, old established businesses and vibrant new craft-beer and coffee houses. The castle is a colourful, ornate structure with intricate carvings on the impressive gate that leads to the grounds, and on the entrance to the castle itself. It was the first residence of Tokugawa Ieyasu (p. 28), and you'll see thematic links between this and his splendid mausoleum in Nikkō (p. 178).

Constructed in 1603, the castle has seen its fair share of drama. Battles, ninja feuds, shogun rule, deposition – it all took place here in the early capital of Japan, until Ieyasu decided that Tokyo (Edo) was the place to be. He still visited often. He would have walked through decorative Karamon Gate before taking his rest at Ninomaru Palace, where he was protected by the 'nightingale floors', an early (and effective) form of enemy detection – these days referred to as squeaky floorboards. Explore the castle and its grounds; the ruins of the original walls of the keep are here, as well as beautiful pine trees girding traditional Ninomaru garden.

Make sure to refuel at Clamp Coffee Sarasa or Songbird, or indulge in an afternoon tea at Iyemon Salon. Feeling hungry? Head to Locale, Phalam or Curry and Bar 240. For homewares, don't miss Lader. If you have a sweet tooth, the adorable Nijō branch of popular Kyoto café Keizo has a range of delectable treats (try the Mont Blanc!).

BELOW: Nijō Castle ABOVE: Kyoto style

OTHER KYOTO EXPERIENCES

TŌFUKU-JI & FUSHIMI INARI

The Nara Line offers some of Kyoto's best temple and shrine experiences. Tōfuku-ji, founded in 1236, is one of the most important Zen temples of the Rinzai sect. The Fujiwara clan established their base here, and their Nara strongholds Tōdai-ji and Kōfuku-ji combine to form its name. Tōfuku-ji has three main drawcards. Its wooden bridges are spectacular, as is the autumn foliage that can be seen from them (especially Tsutenko Bridge). It also boasts two wonderful Zen gardens (the highly revered Hojo – priests' quarters – garden is designed to reflect the position of great Zen temples and islands around the world). Destroyed by fire and reconstructed in 1890, these gardens are among the finest examples of this style (p. 348). Spectacular twenty-two-metre tall Sanmon Gate (1425; p. 21) is the oldest Zen temple gate in Japan.

In recent years, Fushimi Inari (p. 334) has become incredibly popular, so expect absurd crowds, a plethora of souvenir stands and some great street food and coffee. Try the *dango* (dumplings on skewers) or the tofu soft-serve. Don't miss the area's namesake *inari*, sweet rice stuffed into *yuba* (tofu skin) pockets. The shrine is an impressive Shinto temple fringed with vermilion and gold. The grounds feature outer buildings and one or two special *kitsune* (fox; p. 339) shrines, but it's the vermilion *torii* gates (p. 333), donated by various businesses over the years, that make the real mark. Lining a path that leads up into the mountains, the gates form a seemingly endless tunnel. Go early or late; it's not just about avoiding the crowds – the atmosphere of early morning or slowly descending dusk adds a special magic to the walk. The path runs for around four kilometres and ends with a spectacular view of Kyoto.

TOP: Tofuku-ji BOTTOM: Fushimi Inari

Arashiyama

KYOTO PREFECTURE

Arashiyama is Kyoto on a condensed scale in the quaintest country setting, surrounded by verdant mountains and lying on the banks of the rolling Katsura River. Catch the cute purple tram that trundles through the city streets on the Randen Arashiyama Line from Shijo Omiya to Randen-Arashiyama Station (p. 100), a gentle country stop with easy access to Arashiyama's main street. The station features souvenir shops, its own footbath, the 'Atagoike Pond of Dragon' and the Kimono Forest – a cluster of poles adorned with kimono patterns that looks spectacular when lit up at night.

Arashiyama's treasures are many and diverse. The famous Arashiyama Bamboo Grove is an atmospheric glade of bamboo trees that provides great photo opportunities as you stroll through. Keep going to uncover beautiful Rakushisha (Fallen Persimmons Hut), the residence of Mukai Kyorai, one of Matsuo Bashō's (p. 29) students. Most temples and shrines are must-visits and feature some wonderful places for viewing autumn foliage, including Nison-in, Jōjakkō-ji and the Emperor's former residence, Daikaku-ji (p. 347). Tenryu-ji is probably the most prominent temple, counted as one of Kyoto's five best and most important Zen Buddhist temples. →

THIS PAGE: HOSHINOYA Kyoto, Arashiyama OPPOSITE: Arashiyama Bamboo Grove

TRANSPORT

From Kyoto Station, JR Sagano/San-in Line or City Bus #28, or Randen Tram Line from Shijo Omiya Station, between 15 minutes and 30 minutes

CLOSE BY

Kyoto, Nara, Osaka

ATMOSPHERE

Relaxed, walks, mountains, rivers, bridges, spiritual, temples and shrines

REGIONAL FOOD & DRINK

Zenzai (red-bean soup), matcha parfait, matcha *daifuku* (stuffed *mochi*), croquettes, *dango* (dumplings on skewers), *warabi mochi* (chewy jellies)

OMIYAGE

Bamboo products, music boxes, Wankodo Shiba Inu merchandise, Mamemasa sweets, *chirimen* (silk crepe)

TEMPLES & SHRINES

Tenryu-ji, Daikaku-ji, Saga Toriimoto, Jōjakkō-ji, Giō-ji, Otagi Nenbutsu-ji, Adashino Nenbutsu-ji

SIGHTS

Togetsu-kyō Bridge, Fufu-no-Yu Onsen, Arashiyama Monkey Park, Iwatayama

GARDENS & PARKS

Giō-ji, Koke-dera (Saihō-ji), Arashiyama Bamboo Grove, Rakushisha Residence, Ōkōchi-Sansō Villa

MUSEUMS & GALLERIES

Saga Arashiyama Museum of Arts and Culture, Fukuda Art Museum, Shigureden, Otaru Music Box Museum

VIEWS

Sagano Scenic Railway, Togetsu-kyō Bridge

ARTS & CRAFTS

Music boxes, bamboo craft, *chirimen* (silk crepe)

FESTIVALS

Kangetsu no Yūbe, Momiji (Maple) Festival, Hanatoro Illuminations

WEB

kyototourism.org

Arashiyama's treasures are many and diverse.

Stroll down the main street to Togetsu-kyō, the 150-metre-long, 400-year-old wooden 'moon-crossing bridge', where you can view an arsenal of colours throughout the seasons, from cherry-blossom pink to autumn reds and yellows flanking the eternal river wending its way through the lush Arashiyama mountains. On the northern side of Togetsu-kyō is Sagano, where you'll find fewer people and a more relaxed atmosphere, along with plenty of natural wonders and ancient sights. Cycle around the area or explore it on foot; you'll find many secrets and surprises along the way, such as small cafés and restaurants lining the river banks.

To the north-west you can stroll Saga Toriimoto, an early Arashiyama streetscape pickled in time (that time being the Meiji era of the late 1800s; p. 32). This atmospheric walk will deliver you to Adashino Nenbutsu-ji, a temple famed for its many small stone statues, which the monk Kōbō Daishi placed here to symbolise the souls of the dead. Nearby Otagi Nenbutsu-ji offers a similar experience, with some 1200 small, moss-greened *rakan* (statues of Buddhist disciples) forming a striking visual experience. Fans of deep-forest temples should venture to Giō-ji, which features an excellent moss garden (get the combined ticket with entrance to Daikaku-ji; p. 244). A more famous moss garden is at Saihō-ji, which takes a bit more effort to visit – you have to apply for entrance (p. 351). It's worth it; the garden is around one hectare of moss fringing a delightful lake. If you can't get in, don't despair. The side garden at Nanzen-ji (p. 239) in Kyoto is a similarly wonderful moss garden, with stepping stones and clutches of bamboo. Shhhh! A little secret.

Unlike Kyoto City, there is a well of mineral hot-spring water in Arashiyama, and this has given rise to two great *onsen*: Sagano Onsen Tenzan-no-yu; and Fufu-no-yu, which sits on the edge of the Katsura River.

BELOW: Katsura River OPPOSITE PAGE: % Arabica café

Uji

KYOTO PREFECTURE

Uji is on the Nara Line, a stopover often missed by tourists heading to Nara (p. 250) or the Fushimi Inari Shrine (p. 243). Along with Kagoshima (p. 320), Uji is Japan's oldest tea producer, and matcha (green tea) flavours the area. Many places along Byōdō-in Omotesandō Dōri serve green tea and green-tea-related products; Terashimaya Yahei Shotan features wonderful antique tea chests and lanterns. Try the green tea soft-serve in summer or hot, delicious matcha in winter. The matcha roll cake or matcha melon *pan* (bread) have to be tried, and make sure to buy boxes of matcha curry (yes, green tea curry!) to take home to friends.

At the end of the street you'll find Byōdō-in, one of Japan's early temples. It was built as a country residence for high-ranking politician Fujiwara no Michinaga but ended up as a primary temple for the major Buddhist sect 'Pure Land'. The temple is so popular that it features on the 10-yen coin, and the temple's symbol, the phoenix, appears on the 10,000-yen note. The grounds, treasure hall, temple and architect Akira Kuryu's stunning and atmospheric Hoshokan Museum make for one of Japan's less visited but most worthy attractions.

Uji is also famous for Japan's (and possibly the world's) first novel, Murasaki Shikibu's *Genji Monogatari* (*The Tale of Genji*; c. 1008; p. 17), and you'll find statues and references everywhere. Matcha dessert fanatics flock to Nakamura Tōkichi Uji Honten opposite Uji Station for tea and delicious matcha-sponge treats. The souvenir shop offers an impressive range of gifts, so expect a queue on the weekends. Nearby you can find another surprise – Genji-no-Yu, a contemporary *onsen* (hot spring) that's well worth the diversion if you're in need of a deep soak. You'll find it at Shinden Station, two stops from Uji, and from there it's a short walk to hot-spring heaven.

OPPOSITE PAGE: Uji River ABOVE LEFT: Green tea sweets ABOVE RIGHT: Byōdō-in

---

TRANSPORT

Kyoto JR Nara Line to Uni Station, about 20 minutes (make sure the train stops at Uji)

CLOSE BY

Kyoto, Tōfuku-ji, Fushimi Inari, Nara

ATMOSPHERE

Relaxed, historical, local, green-tea everything, hidden gem

REGIONAL FOOD & DRINK

Matcha (green tea), matcha soft-serve, matcha melon *pan* (bread), matcha curry, matcha soba

OMIYAGE

Matcha curry, matcha Baumkuchen (German tree cake), matcha Kit Kats, matcha-jelly crepe, matcha *dango* (dumplings on skewers), Jagadosue (matcha potato sticks)

SIGHTS

Byōdō-in, Byōdō-in Omotesandō Dōri, Murasaki Shikibu Statue, Uji River Floating Bridge (c. 646 AD), Terashimaya Yahei Shoten, Masuda Tea Store

GARDENS & PARKS

Uji City Botanical Park, Sanboin Garden

MUSEUMS & GALLERIES

Hoshokan Museum, Tale of Genji Museum, Uji City Historical Document Museum

VIEWS

Uji River

LITERATURE

Murasaki Shikibu, *Genji Monogatari* (*The Tale of Genji*; c. 1008); Yosano Akiko, *The Tale of Genji* poetic translation (1912)

ARTS & CRAFTS

Craft matcha, craft tea

FESTIVALS

Ujicha Ceremony, Firefly Viewing

WEB

www.city.uji.kyoto.jp

Nara

Nara was Japan's capital during the Nara period (710–794 AD; p. 15). Once a place of great discovery, knowledge, craft and invention, Nara still retains that spirit today, and you'll find many craft stores along Sanjō Dōri and dotting the surrounding streets. Nara Park, featuring the famous free-roaming deer (p. 78), is a short walk from Kintetsu-Nara Station. Buy some *shika senbei* (deer crackers) and you'll be the deers' best friend. The park holds some of Nara's (and Japan's) standout attractions. The powerful Fujiwara clan used to reside at Kōfuku-ji, a temple complex established in 730 AD. The five-tiered pagoda, Japan's second-tallest wooden structure, stands at an impressive fifty metres (p. 337). As with most things in Japan, it has been faithfully reconstructed, but we won't quibble with its 1426 reconstruction date. Various other buildings still exist on the grounds (expect to pay a fee to enter most major sites).

—— Further away from the station you'll come to the object of most travellers' interest: Tōdai-ji (p. 337). Kōfuku-ji Pagoda is impressive enough, but this wonder is the world's second-biggest wooden structure (recently losing out to the Metropol Parasol in Seville, Spain). Built in 784 AD, reconstructed in 1692, Tōdai-ji was the main Buddhist temple in Japan and remains one of the most important. Considering it was rebuilt at a mere two-thirds of its original size, the original must have been awe-inspiring. Towering timber roof aside, the central fifteen-metre-tall Buddha statue protected by two fearsome Bodhisattvas is an unforgettable experience. The Nandaimon entrance gate is a towering rustic marvel, through which the ubiquitous deer roam back and forth. The far eastern corner of the park will bring you to Kasuga Taisha, notable for its impressive vermilion facade and around 3000 ornate stone and bronze lanterns, some flanking the walkway to the temple and making for an impressive sight at dusk.

The shrine is an entrance of sorts to another impressive Nara experience: the Kasugayama Primeval Forest, the 'forest of the gods', comprising ancient woodlands (with over 175 kinds of tree), waterfalls, more than 60 species of bird and 1280 species of insect (repellent anyone?). The light filtering through the trees is mystical and enchanting, as is magical thatched tea house Mizuya Chaya hidden among them. The forest is a wonderful place for hiking.

If you're shopping for Nara trinkets, there are plenty of souvenir shops around both Higashimuki and Sanjō Dōri. Don't miss the charmingly dated Nara Prefectural Commerce and Tourism Museum, which has a shop selling some quality Nara specialties. Naramachi Street will take you right back to the Edo period (p. 28) and show you how merchants worked and lived. The street is lined with original Edo-period houses and shops.

A 'Calligraphy Cart' cycles around the Ogawacho area, so if you need some beautiful writing supplies flag it down. Coffee fiends should check out Bolik, Minami, Cauda, K Coffee and Cherry's Spoon. If you have a sweet tooth, be sure to drop in to Nakatanidou on Sanjō Dōri, and eel lovers should visit the highly rated Unagi no Kawahara. The area is full of specialty shops selling calligraphy brushes and ink slates, Nara wool, *shibori*-dyed cloth (p. 368), beautiful linen scarves and tea towels. For homewares check out Kuruminoki, and for ceramics head to Five.

BELOW: Steve deer-whispering OPPOSITE PAGE: Tōdai-ji

TRANSPORT

Kyoto Miyakoji Rapid on JR Nara Line to Nara Station, 45 minutes. Or private Kintetsu Line on same route

CLOSE BY

Uji, Osaka, Kyoto

ATMOSPHERE

Tranquil, ancient, spiritual, old crafts

REGIONAL FOOD & DRINK

Kuzumochi (jelly-like cakes made from kuzu strach), *narazuke* (sake pickles), Miwa somen, *chagayu* (tea-flavoured rice porridge), *kakinohazushi* (persimmon-leaf-wrapped fish), coffee

OMIYAGE, ARTS & CRAFTS

Tea whisks, 'deer poo' (chocolate-covered peanuts), *ararezake* (drinkable mirin), Buddha stamps, deer figurines textiles, weaving, calligraphy brushes, handmade washi paper, Nara *uchiwa* (fretwork fans), *fukin* (woven cotton)

TEMPLES & SHRINES

Tōdai-ji, Kōfuku-ji, Kasuga Taisha, Ōno-ji, Hase-dera

SIGHTS

Nandaimon Gate, Kasugayama Primeval Forest, Naramachi Street

GARDENS & PARKS

Nara Park, Yoshiki-en, Isui-en, Meisho Kyudaijoin Teien, Jiko-in

MUSEUMS & GALLERIES

Kōfuku-ji National Treasure Museum, Nara Craft Museum, Nara Prefecture Complex of Man'yo Culture, Takamatsuzuka Mural Hall

VIEWS

Mount Wakakusa, Mount Ikoma, Mount Takagi Observatory lookout

LITERATURE

Kojiki (Records of Ancient Matters; 712 AD), *Nihon Shoki* (The Chronicles of Japan; 720 AD)

FESTIVALS

Setsubun Mantoro, Kasuga Wakamiya On, Shika-no-Tsunokiri, Omizutori, Shigisan Tiger Festival

WEB

visitnara.jp

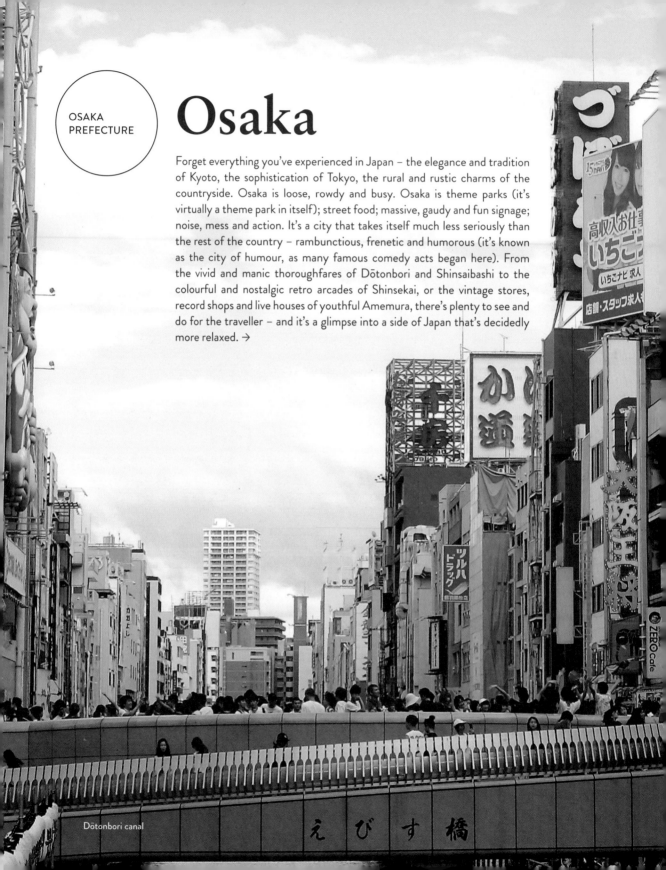

Osaka

Forget everything you've experienced in Japan – the elegance and tradition of Kyoto, the sophistication of Tokyo, the rural and rustic charms of the countryside. Osaka is loose, rowdy and busy. Osaka is theme parks (it's virtually a theme park in itself); street food; massive, gaudy and fun signage; noise, mess and action. It's a city that takes itself much less seriously than the rest of the country – rambunctious, frenetic and humorous (it's known as the city of humour, as many famous comedy acts began here). From the vivid and manic thoroughfares of Dōtonbori and Shinsaibashi to the colourful and nostalgic retro arcades of Shinsekai, or the vintage stores, record shops and live houses of youthful Amemura, there's plenty to see and do for the traveller – and it's a glimpse into a side of Japan that's decidedly more relaxed. →

Dōtonbori canal

TRANSPORT

Tokyo Shinkansen to Shin-Osaka Station, about 3 hours

CLOSE BY

Kyoto, Nara, Kobe, Wakayama, Mount Kōya, Himeji, Sakai

ATMOSPHERE

Busy, rowdy, fun, cheap eats, old and new Japan

REGIONAL FOOD & DRINK

Kushikatsu (deep-fried skewers), *takoyaki* (deep-fried octopus balls), *okonomiyaki* (savoury pancakes), yakitori (grilled skewers), *shumai* steamed buns, square sushi

OMIYAGE

Roll cake (Dojima roll and Hokusetsu), Baumkuchen (especially 'Madame Brulee'), *sampuru* (plastic food – you can make your own at Design Pocket), 551 Horai 'Nikuman' steamed buns, Calbee 'Jigariko' *takoyaki*-flavoured stick potato chips, Cui-daoré Taro Pudding, *gozasoro* (thicker *dorayaki* pancake sandwich), Osaka Petit Banana, meat miso, Bâton d'or (upmarket Glico version of Pocky sticks), Uncle Rikuro's cheesecake, *randoseru* (children's backpacks), *keshimochi* (chewy rice cake with poppy seeds), samurai weapons

TEMPLES & SHRINES

Shitennō-ji Temple, Osaka Tenmangū, Namba Shrine, Hōzen-ji

SIGHTS

Osaka Castle, Dōtonbori, the Glico Man, Shinsekai, Tsutenkaku Tower, Umeda Sky Building, Kuromon Market

GARDENS & PARKS

Nishinomaru Garden (Osaka Castle), Keitaku-en, Tennōji Park, Minami-Temma Park, Nakano Shima-koen, Sakuya Konohana Kan, Nagai Park, Osaka-Umeda Station Rooftop, World Expo Park

The *yokochō* underneath Osaka-Umeda Station is a retro slice of mid- to late-century Japan.

——— Shin-Osaka is a station hub that connects the west of Japan with the east and north. The area around the station is mostly broad streets, office blocks and empty calories. It's worth noting that the true Osaka begins at Osaka-Umeda Station and heads south through Shinsaibashi, Namba and Tennōji on the Midōsuji Line, with surrounding areas providing a wealth of sights and experiences.

The *yokochō* underneath Osaka-Umeda Station is a retro slice of mid- to late-twentieth-century Japan, one of the few old-school Japanese experiences you'll get in modern Osaka. The network of alleys under the station still operates as a 1960s-style late-night dining and drinking enclave – retro beer posters, small standing bars, old broken signs and dated tiling make for a nostalgic and charming wander. Newer bars and cafés have popped up along the way, but sharply styled craft-beer houses and barista show-offs won't be found here, just the faded glory of the haunts of office workers and vacationers past.

By contrast, inside the station you'll get a glimpse of the new Osaka. The gleaming Hankyu Department Store's wrought-iron-trellis windows and doors are striking. Inside, the atmosphere is upmarket, deliberately kicking against the Osaka reputation for being frayed around the edges, while also being a showcase for everything Osaka is known for. The food halls feature most of Osaka's street foods and *omiyage* (regional souvenirs; p. 109).

OSAKA AREAS

Osaka is a nonstop world of fun and frivolity that will confound and amaze you. The Wizarding World of Harry Potter at Universal Studios, the huge Ferris wheel, the world's largest aquarium, spa world ... anything big with a theme, you'll find it here. It's brash, bold and unrepentant. So get amongst it.

Nakazakichō is where you'll find Osaka's indie scene, a sidestep from the 'bigness' of Osaka into a quiet pocket of craft stores, small cafés and inspired young Osakans paving their own way. The area is populated by would-be artists and makers setting up shop in small alleys and tunnels under the rumble and clank of passing trains. 'Amerika Mura', or Amemura as the locals call it, is the more entrenched Osaka local cool, populated by vintage-clothing stores, cutting-edge record stores, corner spruikers, street-food vendors and loose night-time hangs. The vintage-clothing stores are everywhere – sift through the racks at Jam, Magnets, Sheep and Kinji.

Shinsekai and Dōtonbori are where you'll find Osaka's famous street food. In Shinsekai, sideshow and carnival games, retro arcade games and fast-food eateries sit alongside established *kissaten* (European-style coffee house; p. 152), old-timers playing board games and mom-and-pop shops that have been there since the glory days of the 1970 Expo, all powered by the local fast food staple *kushikatsu* (deep-fried skewers).

Dōtonbori (Dōton's Canal) is crammed with visitors at any time of the day or night. Brightly coloured, bloated street signs sway in the air – great photo opportunities, and lures to draw you into the various fast-food dens and dives that populate the strip. The nearby canal has walkways on either side, flanked by various shops. The standout feature is still the mighty Glico Man sign (near crowded Ebisu Bridge), bursting through the tape at the finish line, an enduring symbol of success. Osaka is lengthy, crowded covered arcades with endless shopping opportunities, quiet pockets with some of Japan's most ancient and oddball shrines, a street-food and souvenir mecca, and a modern, almost overwhelming metropolis. So if you want to see a rougher and readier side of Japan, Osaka has it covered.

FOOD IN OSAKA

Dōtonbori is one of Japan's most diverse food areas. In this 'city that loves to eat', you'll find restaurants and street food to cater for all tastes. Osaka's attitude to food is summed up in one of their most used expressions: '*Kuidaore*' or 'Eat till you drop'. Portions are larger than anywhere else in Japan, and we honestly think they would deep-fry anything in Osaka.

The best places to find street food are in Shinsekai, where *kushikatsu* and *takoyaki* (octopus dumplings) are offered by every second store, while Dōtonbori and Shinsaibashi are street-food meccas for *takoyaki*, *taiyaki* (fish-shaped hot pastries), *okonomiyaki* (savoury pancakes), *shabu-shabu* (hotpot), *fugu* (the famous poisonous puffer fish, one of Osaka's enduring symbols and famous dishes), crab, *yakisoba* (stir-fried wheat noodles), *kushikatsu*, ramen, yakitori (deep-fried skewers) and *yakiniku* (grilled meat). It's all cheap and very, very cheerful.

Add chocolate bananas on sticks, fairy floss and anything else you can hold in your hand and eat while walking, and you start to build an Osaka food profile.

VIEWS

Umeda Sky Building, Kuchu Teien Observatory lookout, Abeno Harukas 300, Tempozan Ferris wheel, Tsutenkaku Tower

ARTS & CRAFTS

Osaka pottery, Sakai cutlery (especially knives), Chibana-hanaori silk, Naniwa tinware, Hachio Island silk, Hakata brocade, Haebaru woven flowers, Awa-Shijira cotton cloth, *karaki* wood joinery, bamboo screens, paulownia-wood chests, food *sampuru* (plastic models), *taiko* drums, soba noodles, Sennichimae Doguyasuji Shotengai (for ceramics and lacquerware, knives and *takoyaki* pans, plus general food supplies)

KIDS' OSAKA

Osaka Kaiyukan Aquarium (the world's largest), The Wizarding World of Harry Potter, Maishima Sports Island, Kids' Plaza, Momofuku Ando Instant Ramen Museum, Tempozan Ferris wheel, Osaka Museum of Housing and Living

FESTIVALS

Aizen Matsuri, Tenjin Matsuri, Summer Sonic Music Festival, Himeji Yukata Matsuri, Kishiwada Danjiri Matsuri, Sumiyoshi Matsuri, Naniwa Yodogawa, Sakura No Torinuke, Toka Ebisu Festival, Osaka Festival of the Lights, Hikari Renaissance, Nipponbashi Street Festa, Setsubun Big Festival, Shinnosai Festival, Osaka Fireworks Festival

WEB

osaka-info.jp
shinsaibashi.or.jp

OPPOSITE PAGE: Shinsekai

Lake Biwa

The biggest of Japan's freshwater lakes (and considered one of the world's 'twenty ancient lakes'), Lake Biwa is a magical area that makes for the perfect Kansai daytrip.

Chikubu Island at the southern end of Lake Biwa is often referred to as the 'Island of the Gods'. Hōgon-ji on the island is considered one of the 'Three Great Shines of Benzaiten', goddess of the arts, which is impressive considering the other two are Miyajima (p. 272) and Enoshima (p. 177). The island is not populated, so make it a spiritual pilgrimage. It's not hard to reach from the ports of Nagahama, Imazu or Hikone – tourist boats run regularly. It's also one of Japan's 'Power Spots' (p. 267).

Hikone lies on the east bank of Biwa and features spectacular Hikone Castle, one of Japan's original castles – meaning it hasn't been rebuilt since it was constructed in 1622. It's a great example of Japan's Feudal Age, which ended in 1856. Climb the precipitous stairs of the castle keep to be rewarded with impressive views of Hikone's city. The wooden spiral ramp and bridge that lead into the keep were designed to be destroyed easily in the event of an invasion – so it's ironic that they are still standing in their original form to this day. Azuchi Castle was less fortunate. The once-enormous sixteenth-century stone castle is now just ruins, but still has a beautiful three-tiered pagoda. Visit Azuchi Tourist Information to see a detailed model of the castle as it would have been, which opens up to expose its inner workings.

———— The surrounding forests, canals and lakes make for a wonderful hike. Don't miss enchanting Kyorinbo Temple – especially in autumn, when the yellows and reds make it look like the setting for a fairy tale. The fairy tale continues at nearby Ōmihachiman, where destination confectioner La Collina is an ode to the Baumkuchen cake, in a quirky building complete with grass-thatched roof. The building, called 'Hill', was designed by architectural maverick Terunobu Fujimori, and features a chocolate-sprinkle-covered ceiling. Come for the building but stay for the cake.

Many interesting locations are situated on the lake's vast circumference, such as Kurokabe Square in Nagahama, famed for its glassware; the popular town of Maibara where you can glimpse Mount Ibuki and stroll around the Tawada Rose and Berry Gardens; or the old town of Samegaijyuku, which features a lovely canal and blooms of *baikamo*, a graceful Japanese water plant. Every year on 8 August, Lake Biwa hosts one of Japan's most popular fireworks displays.

South-east of the lake you'll find the spectacular Miho Museum (p. 299), created by Japan's wealthiest woman, Mihoko Koyama, and designed by legendary architect I.M. Pei (of the Louvre Pyramid fame). The collection, a mix of antiquities from ancient Japan, Egypt, Rome and China, is impressive enough, but is overshadowed by the building and its aspect. The cavernous tunnel from the car park to the museum literally goes through a mountain. It's atmospheric and exciting – the tensile rods that hold the tunnel in place and then welcome you at the museum's entrance are a magnificent flourish. The prism/web/kaleidoscope canopy in the front hall goes on the architectural tourist's must-do list.

Once inside the museum, all you can think about are the towering glass windows that take in panoramic views of the dense mountains. As a side note, in the distance you'll see the church that practises a religion set up by Koyama (I.M. Pei designed the church's bell tower). The religion, Shinjo Shūmeiki (Divine Love, Supreme Light), follows the teachings of Mokichi Okada, known as Johrei, which focus on directing spiritual light towards others. Shinjo Shūmeiki believes in building architectural masterpieces in remote locations to restore the balance of the earth. Looking at the Miho Museum you'll feel like there's a very real truth to that.

BELOW: Kyorinbo Temple OPPOSITE PAGE: La Collina

TRANSPORT

Kyoto Biwako Line to Otsu Station (south-west), 10 minutes, or Hikone Station (east), about 1 hour; or Kyoto Shinkansen Kodama to Maibara Station (north-east), about 20 minutes

CLOSE BY

Kyoto, Shigaraki, Mount Hiei, Uji, Mount Ibuki

ATMOSPHERE

Lakeside, hidden, creative, magical

REGIONAL FOOD & DRINK

Kamonabe (duck hotpot), castella cake, Ōmi beef (high-quality wagyu), Mandokoro tea, seafood, *funazushi* (fermented sushi), *ayomaki* (salmon in soy and kombu), *decchi-yōkan* (hard jelly sweets in bamboo), red konjac

OMIYAGE

Freshwater pearls, Tomita sake, castella cake, cheesecake, Yuzu Piriri chilli powder, Daika *shōyu* (soy sauce) Yamamoto tea, La Collina's Baumkuchen

TEMPLES & SHRINES

Hōgon-ji, Ōmi Shrine, Hiroshige Shrine, Kyorinbo Temple

SIGHTS

Hikone Castle, Azuchi Castle ruins, Chikubu Island, Hiyoshi Taisha, Ukimido, Mangetsu-ji

GARDENS & PARKS

Nagisa Park, Mizunomori Water Garden, Genkyu-en

MUSEUMS & GALLERIES

Miho Museum, Lake Biwa Museum, Sagawa Art Museum

VIEWS

Lake Biwa, Miho Museum

ARTS & CRAFTS

Buddhist shrines and beads, metal craft, glass art, ceramics

FESTIVALS

Lake Biwa Great Fireworks Festival, Hiyoshi Sanno Matsuri, Kimari Hajime

WEB

en.biwako-visitors.jp

Mount Kōya

WAKAYAMA PREFECTURE

Peaceful and spiritual Mount Kōya could not be more of a contrast to its closest city, modern and noisy Osaka. Kōyosan Shingon ('True Word') Buddhism, an important, esoteric and deeply spiritual sect, goes back as far as 805 AD. Based in Mount Kōya, its influence spread across the country through secluded forests, mountain ranges and ancient roads. Despite the huge popularity of the region with travellers, which has grown since the beginning of this century, Mount Kōya is no theme park. It's authentic and deeply moving. People go searching for peace, and it can be found in the temple stays, where you can enjoy the *shōjin ryōri* vegetarian banquets (p. 126), soak in hot springs and rise early with the monks to watch them at morning prayers. The incantations, wafting incense and tinkling of the chimes and bells make for a very special experience.

Okunoin Temple holds the mausoleum of Kōyasan founder Kōbō-Daishi. The atmospheric walk from the temple to the mausoleum begins at Ichinohashi Bridge – the path is lined with stone lanterns and replete with moss-covered tombs, statues and verdant nature. A major 'Power Spot' (p. 267), Okunoin is a holy and beautiful place, and hiking through the area will bring you that bit closer to enlightenment. Eventually you'll arrive at the stunning Gokusho Offering Hall, Gobyobashi Bridge and Miroku Stone (a bit of fun – the stone feels lighter to people who are good, so lift it with one hand from the bottom level and place it on the top level). Your ultimate destination is the Kōbō-Daishi Mausoleum. Danjō-garan, the main temple complex, is truly impressive. A history of the area, and many of its impressive treasures, are housed in the wonderful Reihōkan Museum.

Kongōbu-ji is the head monastery of the area, so make sure to look around its wonderful grounds. Don't miss the stunning painted sliding doors in the Ōhiroma (main room). The Banryutei Rock Garden is the largest Zen garden in Japan, and one of the most spectacular.

TRANSPORT

Osaka Nankai Kōya Line from Namba Station to Gokurakubashi Station, then cable car; about 1 hour 45 minutes

CLOSE BY

Osaka, Wakayama, Shirahama, Mie, Kumano Kodō Trail

ATMOSPHERE

Ancient, deeply spiritual, rustic, mountainous, hidden

REGIONAL FOOD & DRINK

Shōjin ryōri, *mochi* (rice cakes), *oyakodon* ('parent-and-child' rice bowls), *Kōya-dōfu* (local tofu)

OMIYAGE

Fresh *mochi*, monk and temple merchandise

TEMPLES & SHRINES

Danjō-garan, Okunoin, Kongōbu-ji

SIGHTS

Nanpodo sweet shop, Banryutei Rock Garden, Ichinohashi Bridge, Gokusho Offering Hall, Gobyobashi Bridge, Kōbō-Daishi Mausoleum

GARDENS & PARKS

Kongō Sanmai-in, Kongōbu-ji

MUSEUMS & GALLERIES

Reihōkan Museum

FESTIVALS

Goma Taki, Kyusho Mieku, Aoba Matsuri, Rosoku Matsuri, Dai Mandara Ku

WEB

koyasan.net

OPPOSITE PAGE: Kongōbu-ji ABOVE: Mount Kōya details

KANSAI
ADVENTURES
HISTORY
& HEART

ARIMA ONSEN

An easy daytrip from Kobe or Osaka, Arima Onsen is a small town said to be more than 1000 years old that lays claim to some premium hot-spring water. Arima has several public *onsen* and private *onsen ryokan* dotted about its quaint streets, and is famed for its 'gold' water, where iron reacts with the air to create a tarnished rose-gold colour. It's also known for several food specialties, including carbonated crackers, peppers simmered in soy sauce, Tanba black bean pie, Arima roll cake and Arima Cider. Kobe beef also features – try it in the local croquettes. Stroll the town and enjoy the steaming vents and hot-spring sources, and don't forget to take some Arima Onsen bath salts home with you.

HIMEJI

Easily reached from Kyoto or Osaka, Himeji is famous for its castle (p. 345), one of Japan's most spectacular examples of a feudal structure. The elegant 'white heron' castle is one of the country's twelve original castles, not having been destroyed by bombing, fire or natural disaster. Its grounds are extensive, and among its many great features is a view from the keep of the labyrinthine castle defences. Himeji is also a popular cherry-blossom spot. Engyō-ji, on nearby Mount Shosha, should not be missed. With a 1000-year history, the collection of strikingly beautiful old wooden temples and halls are often used in movies and television productions.

MIE PREFECTURE

Straddling both the Kansai and the Tōkai regions, the Mie prefecture has a major claim to fame apart from its striking scenery: it's home to one of Japan's most revered Shinto shrines, Ise-Shima. The inner shrine is Japan's most sacred, while the surrounding outer shrine and Oharaimachi, the preserved township on the approach to the shrines, are highly regarded. It's a major area for pearl-fishing, and the Mikimoto Pearl 'island' is here. Don't miss two wonderful photo opportunities: the Hinjitsukan, where the posh pilgrims stayed (the hikes can be pretty hard on soft city folk); and Meoto Iwa (p. 335), two sacred rocks in the sea that are bound together by rope.

KINOSAKI

Kinosaki is one of Japan's best *onsen* towns – certainly one of the most picturesque. A canal winds through the middle of Kinosaki, with several beautiful bridges linking the two sides of town together. Kinosaki is more than 1300 years old and features seven unique *onsen*. In summer, stroll around the town in *yukata* (casual summer kimono), *geta* sandals and *tabi* socks admiring the willows that line the canal. In winter, the snow on the bridges and buildings turn Kinosaki into a white wonderland. Buy a Yumepa Pass, which allows you access to all *onsen*. Among the best hot springs are Kouno-yu, the oldest of the *onsen*; Gosho-no-yu, with its beautiful frontage, *rotenburo* (outside bath) and vaulted ceilings; and Ichino-yu, set in a cavern carved into natural rock. Nearby Kinosaki Ropeway takes you high up on Mount Daishi, to a view that has actually been awarded a Michelin star.

KOBE

Kobe is one of Japan's biggest cities and a historical trading port, famed for beef and, sadly, earthquakes. It's a great stopover point or hub for your travels in Kansai. Its wagyu beef is world famous and considered one of the premium brands. You can find it in various dishes in eateries across the city, paired with the area's popular sake. The Earthquake Museum commemorates the tragic Hanshin-Awaji disaster in 1995 that killed 5000 people. There are very few signs that an earthquake ever took place now, due to extensive rebuilding and some impressive contemporary structures.

You can see both Kobe and Osaka from Mount Rokkō, a rare treat. For impressive Kobe views, take the Shin-Kobe Ropeway. Nearby, Tadao Ando's Hyōgo Prefectural Museum of Art is a must-stop for fans of art and architecture.

WAKAYAMA PREFECTURE

SEIGANTO-JI & THE KUMANO KODŌ TRAIL

A UNESCO World Heritage Site, Seiganto-ji in the south-east of Wakayama prefecture is a spectacular three-tiered pagoda (p. 337). The pagoda, situated in the Kumano Sanzan Shrine compound, is particularly famous for its striking aspect. Built next to stunning Nachi Falls, the pagoda and waterfall can be photographed together – a rare opportunity. It's one of the main sights along the Kumano Kodō Trail (p. 230), a World Heritage–listed, 1000-year-old pilgrimage trail around the verdant south of Wakayama prefecture. The trail, which also takes in Hongū Taisha, Hayatama Taisha, and the Oji Shrines, is a naturalist's dream of foliage, vegetation, geological wonders and rare species. If you like ocean scenery mixed with your forest views, hit the Ohechi Trail. The popular Iseji Route takes in the Ise Jingu Shrine (p. 334), plus a panorama of beaches, terraced fields and bamboo forests. The Nakehechi Trail is the most popular, set up as it is for long-term walks with rustic accommodation along the way.

SHIRAHAMA

The southern end of Wakayama prefecture is a beachside town with some amazing hot-spring experiences. Make sure to visit Japan's oldest *onsen*, Saki-no-Yu. This most rustic of *onsen* is literally part of the landscape, filling with warm seawater and volcanic spring water. Put your clothes in the wooden box (if you want to check in your valuables you have to do it in small lockers outside) and soak yourself as you gaze directly out to sea.

TOMOGASHIMA ISLANDS

A twenty-minute ferry from Nonaura Pier brings you to several islands that house fort ruins, lighthouses and rusted metal bunkers. If you're into creepy abandoned spaces, these islands have them in spades. Of particular creepy note is Awashima Shrine, which is full of hundreds of dolls that stare menacingly out at you. There are also many styles of *maneki neko* (lucky cat; p. 340) here to make things cuter, including some retro examples fans may not have seen before.

TAMADEN TRAIN

Head down to the very last, almost hidden track at Wakayama Station and you'll find the Tamaden (p. 104). *Kawaii* alert! It's a train with a cat face. Enjoy the train's super-cute interior on the thirty-minute ride to Tama Station, where you'll meet Station Master Tama (second generation by now), the cat who sleeps in the ticket booth. The station has cat ears and a small souvenir shop where you can buy some cute Tama merch.

WAKAYAMA RAMEN TAXIS

Ramen is a big deal in Wakayama. Two of Japan's highest-rated ramen eateries are here: Ide Shoten and Seino. If you find yourself staying in Wakayama City, the best way to seek out the ramen with your name on it is by hailing one of the ramen taxis. Head to Wakayamashi Station and look for the taxi with the small red sign (ラーメンタクシー). The driver will know exactly where to take you (after all, they've had to pass an exam covering the history and ramen of Wakayama). Spicy ramen? *Hai!* Light chicken ramen? *Hai!* Deep-fried ramen with lots of pork? *Hai!* Vegetarian ramen? *Hai!* Make use of some top local knowledge and have the ramen of your life.

OPPOSITE PAGE: Meoto Iwa, Mie Prefecture

CHŪGOKU

TOKYO

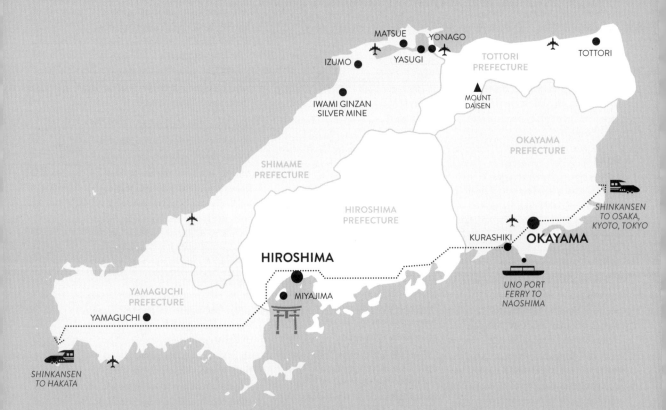

MATSUE

YONAGO

IZUMO

YASUGI

TOTTORI
PREFECTURE

TOTTORI

IWAMI GINZAN
SILVER MINE

MOUNT
DAISEN

OKAYAMA
PREFECTURE

SHIMAME
PREFECTURE

HIROSHIMA
PREFECTURE

SHINKANSEN
TO OSAKA,
KYOTO, TOKYO

KURASHIKI

OKAYAMA

HIROSHIMA

YAMAGUCHI
PREFECTURE

UNO PORT
FERRY TO
NAOSHIMA

MIYAJIMA

YAMAGUCHI

SHINKANSEN
TO HAKATA

CHŪGOKU

Chūgoku roughly translates as 'Central Country', a prosaic name for an area rich in culture and history, and an inaccurate name as it isn't central at all but the far west of Honshū island. Hiroshima (p. 264) will be the name most familiar to visitors; it's the region's major city hub and a place of highest cultural importance and historical significance.

The other areas are less well known but offer some rich rewards for the explorer. As well as being a destination in its own right, with one of Japan's loveliest gardens and a magnificent castle, Okayama (p. 268) is a gateway to Kurashiki (p. 269), which has a beautifully preserved Edo-period canal and warehouse district, and to Naoshima (p. 292) and the other art islands (p. 295). Tottori's sand dunes are legendary (pp. 275, 299), and Shimame (p. 271) is one of Japan's true undiscovered treasures, home to Japan's oldest shrine, one of its most spectacular gardens and some stunning architecture.

Areas to the north and far west are easy to miss, as pilgrims head to Hiroshima and then possibly on to Fukuoka (p. 308), but an exploration of Chūgoku is an absolute must if you want to unearth some of Japan's deeper magic.

Hiroshima

The name Hiroshima conjures up strong emotions. Visitors come for one reason and one reason alone: this is the city that was hit by an atomic bomb, the only one, apart from Nagasaki (p. 329), that has ever had to experience such horror. Many of Japan's citizens died, and many generations that remain are 'certified irradiated' and receive a small stipend from the government.

It's a wonderful city with an amazing transport system, a city that triumphantly defies its deeply sad history. It's a great place to stay, and the food (especially *okonomiyaki* and ramen) and shopping are fantastic. Microbreweries are on the rise, and as a hub leading to Fukuoka (p. 308), Onomichi, the Seto Inland Sea (p. 294) and Ōkunoshima (Rabbit Island; pp. 78, 296), it's the perfect place to make a temporary base camp.

——— For the visitor it might initially be a curiosity, a dip into a notorious piece of history – but from the first sight of the intact remains of the Atomic Bomb Dome, the weight of that history fills you. The Peace Memorial Park is the moving response to the dropping of the atomic bomb – a memorial where responding with anger gives way to responding with the only thing that can make sense of such a frightening episode: a desperate longing for peace. It's one of the most reverential places you'll ever visit. The 120,000-square-metre park, designed by Kenzō Tange (p. 353), is a contemplative, modernist space that includes the Memorial Cenotaph and the Peace Flame. The Atomic Bomb Dome is in the top right corner, probably the first thing you'll come across as you get off one of the city's excellent trams. The bombed-out husk of Jan Letzel's Chamber of Commerce building (constructed in the early 1900s), with its fragile spider-web dome, is the starkest possible reminder that you're not here for a tourist jaunt. It's a deeply emotive history lesson, one that will stay with you for a long time.

Various memorials dot the quasi-brutalist landscape. The other most moving moment comes in the form of the Children's Peace Monument, a glass box designed by Hiroshima locals Kazuo Kikuchi and Kiyoshi Ikebe and dedicated to Sadako Sasaki, who died of leukaemia in 1955 as a result of the bomb. Her story is deeply poignant: she resolved to fold 1000 paper cranes while she was sick in an attempt to be granted the wish of life. Many students took up her cause but despite their dedication she didn't survive. You can fold your own crane and add it to the glass cases – a simple gesture that makes for a powerful personal statement. A festival is held on Children's Day every year. The Peace Memorial Park also features the Peace Memorial Museum, where you can learn about the history of the bomb and view objects that tell its tale – like the watch that stopped at the exact time of the bomb's impact – and many photographs detailing life before and after the bomb. Make sure you ring the Peace Bell.

Shukku-en, an Edo-period (p. 28) garden dating back to 1620, offers a beautiful stroll with a dark history – after the attack it was a refuge for the immediate victims of the bomb. Schmoe House provides an interesting historical note – American Quaker Floyd Schmoe, horrified by his country dropping the atomic bomb, moved to Hiroshima and began the laborious process of reconstructing the Japanese houses that were destroyed. The museum celebrating his achievements is housed in his residence.

The Fukuromachi Elementary School Peace Museum tells another story – the students were spared due to a mass evacuation, but the teachers who remained behind were killed instantly. A grim memorial exhibits objects and moments from the time the bomb dropped, including heartbreaking inscriptions on the burned walls left by survivors. The school was both a refuge point after the bomb and a triumph of rebuilding – it reopened in 1945, and its history and many relevant artefacts are included in the museum. →

OPPOSITE PAGE: Peace Memorial Park

TRANSPORT

Tokyo JR Tōkaidō-Sanyo Shinkansen to Hiroshima Station, about 4 hours 30 minutes

Haneda Airport to Hiroshima Airport, about 90 minutes

CLOSE BY

Uno, Naoshima, Miyajima, Hakata (Fukuoka, Kyūshū), Okayama, Ōkunoshima (Rabbit Island), Onomichi, Seto Inland Sea, Imabari (Shikoku), Fukuyama

ATMOSPHERE

Contemplative, reverent, relaxed

REGIONAL FOOD & DRINK

Okonomiyaki, tsukemen (cold noodles with very spicy chillies), oysters, chicken-and-dried-sardine ramen, Onomichi ramen (fresh fish ramen), *anago* (saltwater eel), soft-water sake, *monaka* (sweet bean pastry)

OMIYAGE

Momiji (maple-leaf sweet steamed bun), *shakushi senbei* (ladle-shaped savoury crackers with messages of good fortune, safety and happiness), *shakushi* (rice scoops), Hiroshima Carps (local baseball team) merchandise, oyster soy sauce, seaweed salt, Onomichi instant ramen, oyster crackers, pickled vegetables, treated packaged oysters (pickled, steamed, in oil etc.), Kumano and Chikohudo make-up brushes, *okonomiyaki* crackers, *okonomiyaki* mix, sweet rice cakes, *hassaku* orange jelly

TEMPLES & SHRINES

Senkō-ji, Toshogu Shrine, Gokoku-ji, Mitaki-dera, Jingū-ji, Buttsū-ji, Itsukushima-jinja, Tennei-ji, Kōsan-ji, Tahoto Pagoda

SIGHTS

Peace Memorial Park, Atomic Bomb Dome, Peace Memorial Museum, Children's Peace Monument, Hiroshima MOCA (Museum of Contemporary Art), Hiroshima Museum of Art, Hiroshima Castle, Momijidani Park, Hijiyama Park, Kokoku Shrine, Onomichi

GARDENS & PARKS

Hiroshima Peace Memorial Park, Hijiyama Park, Hiroshima Botanical Garden, Shukkei-en

MUSEUMS & GALLERIES

Peace Memorial Museum, Hiroshima Museum of Art, National Peace Memorial Hall for the Atomic Bomb Victims, Hiroshima MOCA, Children's Museum, Schmoe House, Fukuromachi Elementary School Peace Museum, Honkawa Elementary School Peace Museum

VIEWS

Hiroshima Castle, World Peace Memorial Cathedral

FESTIVALS

Hiroshima Tōrō Nagashi, Ebisuko Festival, Peace Memorial Day (6 August), Hiroshima Flower Festival, Takehara Candle Festival, Hiroshima Toukasan Matsuri

WEB

visithiroshima.net

ABOVE: *Okonomiyaki* at Nagataya
RIGHT: The Atomic Bomb Dome

Hiroshima has many other places worth investigating, including Hijiyama Park, a hotspot for *sakura* (cherry blossoms) and outdoor sculptures; and Senkō-ji, an important temple with a similar structure to the famous Kiyomizu-dera in Kyoto, a temple perched on a detailed web of scaffolding with a spectacular view. Don't miss Hiroshima Toshogu Shrine, an intricately decorated shrine not far from the peace park, and Hiroshima MOCA (Museum of Contemporary Art), designed by legendary Metabolist architect Kishō Kurokawa (p. 354). It's an amazing addendum to the Peace Memorial Park, featuring many works that show artists' reaction to the bomb, including Henry Moore's wonderful sculpture *Atom Piece*, a great complement to his 1960s work *Nuclear Energy*.

Hiroshima Castle was built by Mōri Terumoto in 1589. Known affectionately as 'Carp Castle' due to both the plethora of carp in its moat and the name of the castle – 'Rijo' (*ri* means 'carp' in Japanese) – it was of strategic and economic importance. The current version dates from 1958, a faithful rebuild of the original that was destroyed by the bomb.

Locals will tell you Japan's best *okonomiyaki* is made here. This Japanese street-food staple consists of a savoury pancake or omelette with noodles, cabbage, oodles of spring onion, spices and sauce, plus whatever regional specialty is going. Osaka and Hiroshima have been in a stand-off for years, each making its own version and claiming it's the best. Basically, Hiroshima 'layers' the ingredients and Osaka mixes them up. Recommended *okonomiyaki* joints can be found very close to Hiroshima Peace Memorial Park in charming and frenetic Nagataya. Other favourite venues include Hassei, Hassho, Hazeya and Reichan.

Another specialty of the area you might not have tried is chicken-and-dried-sardine ramen, so hunt out places that specialise in the dish. Eel, shrimp and bean paste are also premium Hiroshima ingredients.

Power spots

Like Pokémon Go, a new craze has emerged where people visit as many of Japan's 'Power Spots' as possible. Put simply, Power Spots are the places considered to be the most spiritual in the world – think Stonehenge. A Power Spot should have quite a bit of spiritual weight and history behind it – such as Machu Picchu or the pyramids of Giza. If you're a Power Spot collector here's a list of all of the places you'll have to visit.

CHŪBU
· Atsuta Jingu (Nagoya)
· Mount Fuji (p. 222)
· Mount Tate/Tateyama
· Suwa Taisha (Nagano)
· Togakushi Shrine (Okaya)

CHŪGOKU
· Akiyoshido Cave (Yamaguchi)
· Izumo Taisha (Izumo; pp. 271, 335)

HOKKAIDŌ
· Lake Akan (p. 288)
· Mount Asahi-dake (Higashikawa)

KANSAI
· Ise-Shima Shrine (Ise; p. 260)
· Kumano Nachi Taisha (Nachikatsuura; p. 230)
· Kurama-dera (Kurama; p. 240)
· Lake Biwa (p. 256)
· Okunoin Temple (Mount Kōya; p. 259)

KANTŌ
· Meiji Jingumae Shrine (Tokyo; p. 165)
· Tōshō-gū Shrine (Nikkō; p. 178)

KYŪSHŪ
· Amanoiwato Shrine (Miyazaki)
· Kirishima Shrine (Kirishima; p. 324)
· Mount Aso (Aso)
· Takachiho Gorge (Takachiho)
· Yakushima (p. 325)

SHIKOKU
· Mount Ishizuchi

TŌHOKU
· Dewa Sanzan (Tsuruoka)
· Mount Osore (Mutsu)

TOP: Meiji Jingumae, Tokyo, Kantō
MIDDLE: Izumo Taisha, Izumo, Chūgoku
BOTTOM: Mount Fuji, Chūbu

TRANSPORT

Shinkansen Hikari from Kyoto to Okayama, around 90 minutes

CLOSE BY

Kurashiki, Naoshima, Teshima, Shōdoshima, Kobe, Kyoto, Takamatsu, Himeji, Onomichi

ATMOSPHERE

Transport hub, full of temple and garden tourists

REGIONAL FOOD & DRINK

Oyster *okonomiyaki*, steamed octopus and rice, pork cutlet with demi-glace sauce, Spanish mackerel, scattered sashimi over rice, herring sushi, stir-fried udon and offal

OMIYAGE

Walnut *mochi* (rice cakes), peach pudding, peach *dango* (dumplings on skewers), ponzu rice crackers, peach rice crackers, grape *dango*, lotus flower honey, white peach juice, *amazake* (fermented rice) *dango*

TEMPLES & SHRINES

Saijo Inari, Kibitsu Shrine

SIGHTS

Okayama Castle, Inujima island

GARDENS & PARKS

Okayama Kōraku-en

MUSEUMS & GALLERIES

Inujima Seirensho Art Museum, Yumeji Art Museum

FESTIVALS

Hadaka Matsuri, Kōraku-en Sakura, Kibi Daijin Shrine New Year Festival, Matsuyama Odori, Dogeza Matsuri

WEB

okayama-japan.jp

Okayama

OKAYAMA PREFECTURE

Although Okayama serves as a great starting point for several of Japan's best adventures – Kurashiki (p. 269), Takamatsu (p. 301) and the art islands (p. 295) to name a few – it has two spectacular sights of its own. Kōraku-en is one of the three best landscaped gardens in Japan (along with Mito's Kairaku-en with its 3000 plum trees and Kanazawa's Kenroku-en ... or Ritsurin Kōen in Takamatsu, depending on who you ask). Kōraku-en's standout features are vast open spaces, a large pond brimming with koi (p. 340) and featuring three islands to replicate Lake Biwa (p. 256); beautiful Enyo-tei tea house (with its circular window looking out onto the garden) and the 'borrowed scenery' of Okayama Castle. The castle, reconstructed in 1966 (but featuring an original 1620 moon-viewing turret), was given the nickname 'Crow Castle' due to its dark walls. The riverside view of the castle from the banks outside Kōraku-en or from the adjacent bridge is marvellous.

ABOVE: Kōraku-en OPPOSITE PAGE: Kurashiki canal, Bikan Historical Quarter

Kurashiki

OKAYAMA PREFECTURE

A short train ride from Okayama takes you out of the city and into the Bikan Historical Quarter, a rustic canal-side district with elements of the Edo period and Meiji and Taishō eras (pp. 28, 32, 38) dotting the streets and lanes. Once an important area for merchants, particularly those importing and storing rice (Kurashiki means 'Storehouse Town'), it still has many Meiji-era rice warehouses. These are notable for their striking architectural style of white latticed-wood *namako* walls, and tremendously thick windows with a detailed step-like structure that, when closed, interlocks tightly with the walls and protects the rice from the elements. Honmachi and Higashimachi streets exhibit many historical artisan quarters, merchant warehouses and eateries, while the Kurabo Memorial Museum, Kurashiki Monogatari-kan and Kusudo House are excellent examples of the area's architecture. Ohashi House, a preserved dwelling, is a good chance to see how a merchant actually lived, and the Ohara Museum of Art holds the distinction of being the oldest Western-art museum in Japan.

Up on the hill you'll find tranquil Achi Shrine, where you can get a great view of the surrounding town. Fans of old Japanese toys will find many delights at the Japanese Folk Toys Museum (there's also a piggy-bank museum in Ivy Square). The area is famous for Japanese denim, and around thirty shops line Kurashiki Denim Street. People travel from all over Japan to shop for denim in Kurashiki, making it a great place to buy a pair of jeans.

TRANSPORT

Okayama Station Rapid Train to Kurashiki Station, 15 minutes

CLOSE BY

Okayama, Naoshima, Teshima, Shōdoshima, Takamatsu, Himeji, Onomichi

ATMOSPHERE

Relaxed, historic, canal-side, strollable

REGIONAL FOOD & DRINK

Rice, croquettes, Kurashiki sushi, *bukkake* (chilled) udon noodles, *murasuzume* (sweet bean-paste cakes), Kurashiki sake, muscat grapes, muscat wine, peaches

OMIYAGE

Denim, folk toys, textiles, *bichu* washi (handmade rice paper), handwoven mats, woven rush-grass merchandise, *daruma* (p. 339)

TEMPLES & SHRINES

Achi Shrine

SIGHTS

Honmachi, Higashimachi, Kusudo House, Kurashiki Denim Street

GARDENS & PARKS

Shinkei-en, Tsurugatayama Park

MUSEUMS & GALLERIES

Japanese Folk Toys Museum, Ohara Museum of Art, Kurabo Memorial Museum, Ohashi House

VIEWS

Achi Shrine

ARTS & CRAFTS

Folk crafts, folk toys, textile-dyeing, cotton, pottery

FESTIVALS

Tenryo Taiko, Kurashiki Tenryu Summer Festival, Tamashima Festival Fireworks, Byobu Festival, Hina Meguri, Su-Inkyo

WEB

kurashiki-tabi.jp

Izumo

SHIMAME PREFECTURE

A beautiful piece of hidden Honshū, Izumo has a big claim: the Izumo Taisha (p. 335) and *torii* gate (p. 333) leading to it are likely the oldest in Japan. The shrine is described as the largest wooden structure in Japan in both the *Kojiki* (*Records of Ancient Matters*; 712 AD) and the *Nihon Shoki* (*The Chronicles of Japan*; 720 AD), Japan's oldest and second-oldest book respectively, meaning it dates back to at least 700 AD. Its significance was reaffirmed in 2018, when the imperial family chose it to confirm Akihito's abdication. You can sense the age of the shrine. The trees exude a deep woody aroma and a quiet spiritual calm. The buildings are dark, mysterious and suffused with an older magic.

The Haiden (Worship Hall), front and centre on the grounds of the shrine, features a spectacular *shimenawa* (enclosing rope) hanging from the eaves. The Honden (Main Hall) is the tallest shrine in Japan at around twenty-four metres. The grounds' many wonders include the Treasure Hall, which exhibits important artefacts and drawings from Izumo Taisha's history.

Izumo Taisha has many festivals, but Kami-ari-zuki is one of Japan's best. In a month of celebrations, every single deity in Japan meets at Inasanohama beach (which features Bentenjima, a large rock that's home to a small *torii* shrine) before congregating at Izumo Taisha to make decisions upon the individual destinies of the people. This gives visitors an unprecedented chance to pray to all deities at once.

Not far down the road from Izumo Taisha you'll find the old Izumo Taisha-mae train station, opened in 1912 and used until 1990. The main building was constructed in 1924, an example of the Taishō era's (p. 38) 'Imperial Crown' architectural style. The beautiful frontage and interior, along with the ticket booth, tollgates, steam train and various other elements, make it well worth a visit and a must for trainspotters.

TRANSPORT

Tokyo Shinkansen to Izumoshi Station, 7 hours; Tokyo Sunrise Izumo (the last overnight sleeper train in Japan) to Okayama Station, about 8 hours 30 minutes; then train to Izumoshi Station, about 1 hour. Or plane from Tokyo airports to Izumo Airport, about 1 hour 30 minutes

CLOSE BY

Matsue, Yasugi, Yonago

ATMOSPHERE

Historic, spiritual, tranquil, ancient

REGIONAL FOOD & DRINK

Warigo soba (served in three-tiered lacquer *bentō*), Shimane wine, *zenzai* (boiled sweet adzuki beans), freshwater clams, dried persimmon, red-meat sushi

OMIYAGE

Prayer beads, good luck beads, agate, handmade paper, Shinto straw rope

TEMPLES & SHRINES

Izumo Taisha

SIGHTS

Izumo Taisha-mae historic train station, Inasanohama Beach

GARDENS & PARKS

Hikawa Park, Hamayama Park

MUSEUMS & GALLERIES

Shimane Museum of Ancient Izumo, Izumo Quilt Museum, Tezen Art Museum

FESTIVALS

Kami-ari-zuki, Kitcho-san, Fukujin-sai, Rei-tai-sai, Koden Shinjō-sai

WEB

kankou-shimane.com

OPPOSITE PAGE: Izumo Taisha

Miyajima

The island of the gods, the home of the floating shrine, the jewel of the
Seto Inland Sea. Describe it as you will, Miyajima – or to give it its real
name, Itsukushi ('Shrine Island') – is tranquil, historic and teeming with
free-roaming deer. Visiting for the day is one thing, but staying in a *ryokan*
(traditional inn; p. 87) is truly special, because at dusk or dawn the world-
famous O-torii gate (p. 333) is at its most beautiful and the deer their
most nuzzly. The island itself is a deity, so tread lightly.

TRANSPORT

▶ Hiroshima Station JR Sanyo Line to Miyajimaguchi Station, 26 minutes; then ferry to Itsukushima, 10 minutes

CLOSE BY

▶ Hiroshima

ATMOSPHERE

▶ Spiritual, walks, nature, deer

ONSEN

▶ Kinsuikan, Morinoyado

REGIONAL FOOD & DRINK

▶ *Momiji manjū* (maple-leaf-shaped steamed buns), 'sea milk' oysters, conger eel, *hijiki* seaweed salad

OMIYAGE, ARTS & CRAFTS

▶ *Shakushi* (rice scoops), clay bells, engraved trays, engraved tea utensils, papier mâché

TEMPLES & SHRINES

▶ Itsukushima-jinja, Daishō-in, Daigan-ji, Omoto Shrine, Tahoto Pagoda

SIGHTS

▶ Free-roaming deer, Mount Misen, Senjōkaku Pavilion, Miyajima Aquarium, O-torii gate

GARDENS & PARKS

▶ Momijidani Park, Miyajima Natural Botanical Garden, walking trails

MUSEUMS & GALLERIES

▶ Miyajima History and Folk Museum, Itsukushima-jinja Treasure Hall, Miyajima Traditional Craft Center

VIEWS

▶ Miyajima Ropeway, Mount Misen, Hiroshima to Miyajima ferry

FESTIVALS

▶ Shin Noh In Toka-sai Festival, Goshin-i Kenjo Shiki Ceremony, Futsuka-sai, Genshi-sai, Chikyu-sai, Momote-sai

WEB

▶ *visit-miyajima-japan.com*

——— Itsukushima-jinja (p. 334), a Shinto shrine masterpiece built in the Heian period (p. 17) almost 900 years ago, gives the island its name. The UNESCO World Heritage–listed shrine (ranked as one of the 'three views of Japan' since 1643) is stunning when illuminated at night. Staying on the island gives you a chance to experience the O-torii gate at both high tide, when it 'floats' in the water, and low tide, when you can walk out onto the mudflats for close-up pictures. Itsukushima-jinja has its own *Noh* theatre (p. 363), across the water from the audience. In April a festival is held where plays are performed in this magical setting.

Holy Mount Misen is a spectacular hiking spot, and the island's free-roaming deer can be found on trails along the way and around the *torii* gate (no doubt looking for titbits from the tourists). The streets back to the ferry terminal are lined with enchanting old-world souvenir and food stands.

OPPOSITE PAGE & LEFT: O-torii gate, Itsukushima-jinja ABOVE: *Iwaso ryokan*

YONAGO

Yonago is an easy train ride from Yasugi (opposite). From the station catch a taxi to the Shoji Ueda Museum of Photography. Ueda took some of twentieth-century Japan's best images, including world-famous shots of figures on the nearby Tottori sand dunes (opposite). His love of perspective, Salvador Dalí and Charlie Chaplin combine to make his work truly eclectic and unique in Japanese photography (it was very popular in France, where it was called Ueda-Cho). He took many shots of nearby brooding Mount Daisen. The museum, set in an open space with a view of the mountain, is a feature out of time and place, a brutal concrete bunker designed by Shin Takamatsu that imposes itself on the lush landscape. Several vistas of the mountain are highlighted by large windows and waterways in the building, which frames Mount Daisen as if taking a permanent photograph, a paradox given the live image is always changing subtly, always waiting for Ueda's camera to steal that next picture. Ueda's love of Chaplin comes charmingly to the fore with his 'bowler hat window', which cheers up grumpy Mount Daisen by perching a bowler hat on its head. The visitor can pose before the mountain, lining the hat up on themselves or the mountain while they hold a pink balloon or walking cane. Ueda's haunting and bleak portraits on the Tottori sand dunes are standouts of the exhibition – de Chirico–like figures cast shadows over Tottori's unforgiving dunes melting into the sand, accenting each figure's loneliness.

IWAMI GINZAN SILVER MINE

The area around Ōda features an unusual UNESCO World Heritage listing: the Iwami Ginzan Silver Mine (p. 181). For once gold takes a back seat to silver in this hidden area, where the mine's impressive 600 tunnels dot the landscape like the burrows and dwellings of some large, frightening beast. The Ryugenji-mabu mine shaft is open to the public and you can walk 273 metres into the mine (it's 600-metres long). The mine can be reached from the Omori bus stop.

MATSUE

The capital of Shimane prefecture, Matsue is the home of one of Japan's original castles (p. 345). The main keep has survived the ravages of time, fire, flood, earthquake and bombing (and even the demolitions that were the result of anti-feudal sentiment in the Meiji era; p. 32). The exterior is black and white (with a heavy emphasis on black), which has earned the fortress its nickname, the Black Castle. A boat trip around the moat gives you a wonderful view of the castle and grounds.

YAMAGUCHI

The Ōuchi family founded Yamaguchi in the fourteenth century. The town is often called the 'Kyoto of the West' because of its cultural properties and mountainous nature. The main feature is Rurikō-ji and its spectacular five-tiered pagoda, which is ranked among Japan's three greatest (in company with Kyoto's Daigo-ji and Nara's Hōryū-ji). The Uguisubari Stone Pavement leading to the grave of the powerful Mori clan produces an 'echoed sound' when you clap your hands and stamp your feet that is said to mimic the song of the *uguisu* (Japanese bush warbler).

TOTTORI

Tottori is famous for one thing: sand dunes. You might not think sand dunes are such a big deal, especially if you grew up in a beach area, but Tottori's dunes are like the Sahara Desert. Part of the Sanin Kaigan National Park, the dunes formed over 1000 years. They run for around sixteen kilometres along the coast of the Sea of Japan and are up to two kilometres deep in places. Many reach a height of fifty metres. Tottori's dunes are huge, rolling, desolate waves of sand that featured in Shōji Ueda's famous photographs and in one of Japan's best known films, the creepy and suffocating metaphorical masterpiece *Suna no Onna (Woman in the Dunes)*, directed by Hiroshi Teshigahara in 1964. All of the menace is still there, as well as some photo opportunities for those of us who like stark, shadowy figures placed in alien landscapes.

OPPOSITE: Michelle at Shoji Ueda Museum
ABOVE: Tottori sand dunes

YASUGI

Yasugi Station is quite a find, with its impressive vaulted wooden ceiling and a wonderful souvenir shop selling the local specialties. Japan is hiding a couple of its best secrets not far from here. Zuikoyama Kiyomizu-dera bears the name of one of Kyoto's most famous shrines for a reason – it's the sister shrine and was established just one day after Kyoto's. It too is a standout – a five-tiered pagoda is perched on the mountain and rises above the lush foliage, overlooking the magnificent wooden structure of the temple. Nearby you'll find mountain walks, *torii* gates (p. 333), hidden ponds, and the gloriously rustic *ryokan* Koyokan. Staying here means you can visit the shrine at sunrise – a truly magical experience.

A little further west is the Adachi Museum of Art, showing an amazing selection of Japanese art from over the eras. Of particular interest is the second-floor Glamorous Women of Japan, a great collection of portraits of geisha and Japanese women that highlights changes in style, fashion and status. None of this can compete with the real star of the show – the Adachi Museum Garden. It's regarded as the best 'Japanese' garden, so you're not allowed to put your destructive feet anywhere near it but must view it from behind large glass windows or bamboo barriers. The 'living scroll' windows are a treat, rectangular shapes that mimic scrolls overlooking some of the garden's best vistas. It's a compact, perfectly coiffured space with every element precisely placed, from waterfalls, bridges and clipped gardens to Zen gardens (p. 348), moss and lakes with stepping stones, all set against a backdrop of Yasugi's beautiful mountains.

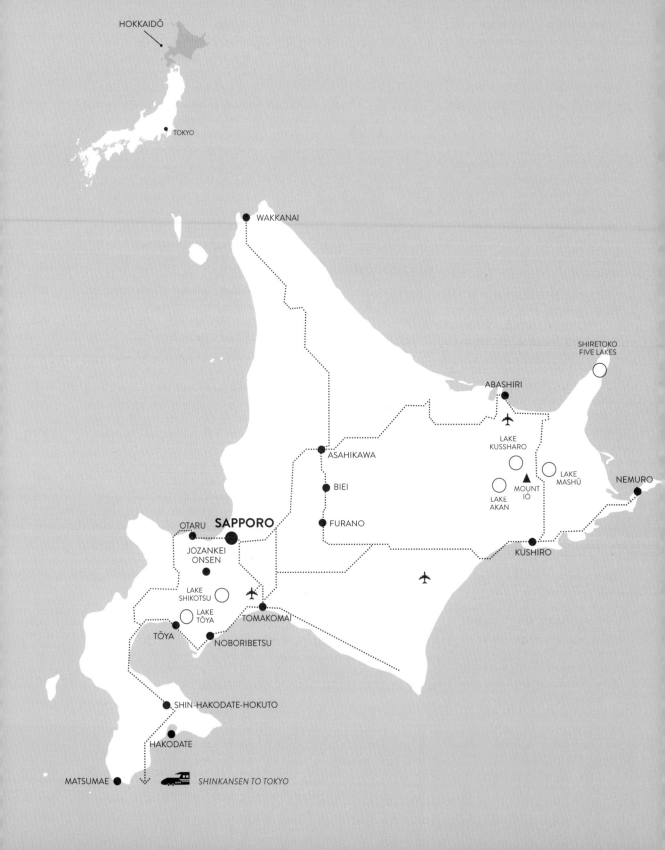

HOKKAIDŌ

TOKYO

WAKKANAI

SHIRETOKO
FIVE LAKES

ABASHIRI

LAKE
KUSSHARO

ASAHIKAWA

LAKE
MASHŪ

NEMURO

BIEI

MOUNT
IŌ

LAKE
AKAN

FURANO

OTARU

SAPPORO

KUSHIRO

JOZANKEI
ONSEN

LAKE
SHIKOTSU

LAKE
TŌYA

TOMAKOMAI

TŌYA

NOBORIBETSU

SHIN-HAKODATE-HOKUTO

HAKODATE

MATSUMAE

SHINKANSEN TO TOKYO

HOKKAIDŌ

北海道

To get in touch with the true essence of Hokkaidō you'll have to traverse rugged coastlines, haul yourself over frosty mountains, venture deep into hidden country and go further north in Japan than you've gone before. Hokkaidō is Japan's frozen north, the second-biggest island, and there you will find a journey of discovery, an ancient history and a vast terrain that takes its time revealing itself.

It's an older Japan in the north, with the history of the island's first people, the Ainu, looming large over regional culture. Here, you'll feel truly remote – the Shinkansen stops at Hakodate (p. 278), and there are no bullet trains further north, not even to Sapporo (p. 281) – though a Shinkansen link is due for completion there in 2030. Most of the action is around the south-western corner, which is where you'll find the capital, Sapporo, as well as Hakodate, Lake Tōya (p. 279) and Noboribetsu (p. 280). Sapporo is the closest you'll get to a Japanese city with all the mod cons, but the atmosphere is a mix city and country, and this welcomes you with open arms as soon as you arrive at Sapporo Station.

Hokkaidō has winter in the soul – Hokkaidō hotpot, Hokkaidō hot pockets, soup curry, warming miso ramen, creamy milk, fortifying cheese, it is truly an island set up to deal with the cold but one that certainly flourishes in other seasons. Across Hokkaidō you'll discover vast blue lakes, fields of brightly coloured flowers, views stretching out to rough rolling seas crashing against jagged rocks and tiny islands, small peaceful towns with long histories of fishing and seafaring, hidden snow-covered pagodas in forests and of course, in the extreme north, the drift ice in the Sea of Okhotsk, one of Japan's most extreme and impressive pilgrimages.

TRANSPORT

Tokyo Shinkansen to Shin-Hakodate-Hokuto, about 4 hours; then Hakodate Liner to Hakodate Station, about 20 minutes

CLOSE BY

Aomori, Lake Tōya, Matsumae, Ōnuma Park

ATMOSPHERE

Railway terminus, mountain terrain with stunning city views, impressive, bustling market town

REGIONAL FOOD & DRINK

Snow crab *bentō*, seafood *donburi* (rice bowl), sushi rice bowl, *uni* (sea urchin), sushi, seafood ramen, oysters

OMIYAGE

'Kita Usagi' merchandise by local designer Suiko Narita, dried squid, squid merchandise, sweet wine, kelp, Ozio bags, textiles and leather bags

TEMPLES & SHRINES

Hakodate Hachiman-gu, Ōtani Hongan-ji Hakodate Betsu-in, Yukura Shrine

SIGHTS

Mount Hakodate, Hakodate Asaichi (Morning Market), Yunokawa Hot Springs, Goryōkaku (old fort) star-shaped park, Motomachi

GARDENS & PARKS

Hakodate Tropical Botanical Garden, Hakodate Park, Miharashi Park, Goryōkaku Park

VIEWS

Top of Mount Hakodate (reachable by cable car)

FESTIVALS

Kaminokuni Iozan Festival, Hakodate Port Fireworks, Hakodate Goryōkaku Festival, Esan Azalea Festival, Russian Festival, Burning Rock Festival

WEB

www.hakodate.travel

Hakodate

OSHIMA SUBPREFECTURE

To reach Hakodate from Honshū, trains travel through the Seikan Tunnel, the longest underground, underwater tunnel in the world. Your destination is Shin-Hakodate-Hokuto station, mostly used as a stop on the way to Sapporo, but with one of the best *ekiben* in the country – the red snow crab *bentō* (p. 99) – so make sure you get one for the train ride to the north. For a special diversion, catch the Hakodate Liner (20 minutes) to Hakodate, a port town at the very base of Hokkaidō.

Seafood in Hakodate is a big deal and you'll discover some amazing dishes that use local sea urchin, bluefin tuna, shrimps, prawns, abalone, sea squirts (yep), sea cucumber and all manner of under-the-sea curiosities. Crab is king here, and yes, that includes king crab. It also means snow crab and horsehair crab. Hakodate Asaichi (Morning Market; p. 154) is a good place to explore the range of edibles from the ocean depths. Don't miss the '1 coin donburi', a rice bowl topped with a selection of freshest morning catch, all for one coin (500 yen to be exact). Hakodate also features memorable ramen, including the Hakodate specialty, *shio* (salt) ramen.

Catch a tram east to Yunokawa Onsen. Set along the coastline, the area boasts some premium hotels that have impressive hot-spring baths with views. Along the tram route you'll find footbaths filled with the quality local *onsen* water. One of the main drawcards in this area is the *onsen* park for bathing macaque monkeys in the botanical gardens. This rustic hot-spring serves a bunch of chattering, over-enthusiastic monkeys, heating them in winter and giving them somewhere to play in summer. Enjoy it while you can – the plan is to make this the Hokkaidō Shinkansen Station when the bullet train comes to Sapporo, scheduled to open in 2030.

Lake Tōya

IBURI SUBPREFECTURE

Tōyako, or Lake Tōya, is a popular spot with summer holiday-makers, who love to paddle across the lake to the small islands on swan boats or snap pictures lakeside while eating ice cream. In winter it's a snow-covered, steamy, *onsen*-rich winter wonderland. The lake is actually a (still-active) volcano, and the water-filled caldera has small hump-like islands that look like a sleeping dragon's back; the warmth from below the water stops the lake from freezing over when winter arrives. A host of *ryokan* (traditional inns; p. 87) and hotels run along the lake, most with their own *onsen* and many that open for day bathers. Soaking in an *onsen* with a view of the sparkling lake is a must. Dotted around the streets are footbaths and handbaths that are free for everyone to use. The area is also very popular for hiking trails and the major tourist hotspot Shikotsu-Tōya National Park.

Food specialties are plentiful, but top of the list is the Michelin-starred *ramen-ya* Ippontei, famous for its unmissable 'Tōya Black' ramen. *Yakiniku* (grilled meat), curry and coffee from here are also highly regarded. The *wakasaimo* (sweet steamed buns) are so starchy and juicy they give the impression of being sweet potato (but are in fact made from the beans of the local area). Sweets in general are a drawcard – cheesecake and the soft-serve ice cream in particular. Make sure you leave with a bagful of treats from Wakasaimo Honpo, Lake Hill Farm or Pâtisserie Violette. Tōyako Echigoya also has a great range of local sweets, as well as another Tōyako take-home: intricate wood carvings, particularly carved wooden swords.

TRANSPORT

Tokyo Shinkansen to Shin-Hakodate-Hokuto, about 4 hours; then limited express to JR Tōya Station, about 2 hours; then bus to Lake Tōya, about 15 minutes

CLOSE BY

Noboribetsu, Hakodate, Sapporo

ATMOSPHERE

Relaxed, secluded, lakeside hot-springs town, stunning views

ONSEN

Kanko Hotel, Kohantei Ryokan Abuta, Manseikaku Hotel Lakeside Terrace, Lake View Tōya Nonokaze Resort

REGIONAL FOOD & DRINK

Ramen, *yakiniku* (grilled meat), soba, sweets (especially *wakasaimo* – sweet *konbu* and bean steamed buns), soft-serve ice cream

OMIYAGE

Wakasaimo, cheesecake, sweets, engraved wooden swords, carved wooden items (especially fish and owls)

TEMPLES & SHRINES

Abuta Shrine

SIGHTS

Lake Tōya, Mount Usu

VIEWS

Silo Observatory Viewing Platform, Mount Usu Trail

FESTIVALS

Tōyako Onsen Summer Festival, Tōyako Onsen Winter Festival

WEB

laketoya.com

OPPOSITE PAGE: Crab *bentō* and Nebuta sake ABOVE: Lake Tōya

TRANSPORT

Tokyo Shinkansen to Shin-Hakodate-Hokuto Station, about 4 hours; limited express to Noboribetsu Station, about 2 hours 30 minutes

CLOSE BY

Sapporo, Lake Tōya, Lake Shikotsu

ATMOSPHERE

Relaxed, popular, volcanic, steaming, bubbling, sulfurous, hot-spring baths

REGIONAL FOOD & DRINK

Onsen-steamed food, soba, *yakisoba* (buckwheat noodle stir-fry)

OMIYAGE

Bath salts, demon statues, demon cookies, demon chocolate

TEMPLES & SHRINES

Enmado Temple

SIGHTS

Noboribetsu Hot Springs, Noboribetsu Bear Park, Jigokudani (Hell Valley), Noboribetsu Ropeway

VIEWS

Jigokudani Walkway

FESTIVALS

Noboribetsu Jigoku Matsuri, Noboribetsu Hot Springs Festival

WEB

noboribetsu-spa.jp

Noboribetsu

IBURI SUBPREFECTURE

Noboribetsu's twin drawcards are two stunning geological marvels: Jigokudani, or Hell Valley, and a concentrated hub of hot-spring baths, most of which are part of a hotel complex. Jigokudani is a gurgling plain of scorched earth, bubbling mud pits, steaming vents, misty pools and lurking demons (local favourite Yukujin is actually a demon of good luck – which makes him slightly less scary). The dry valley has an eerie, desolate charm and the feeling of danger is ever present, along with the scent of sulfur. Various paths and cordoned-off walkways make the whole experience easy and fun. At night illuminations give Jigokudani the look of being the very plain of hell itself, with the illusion of white-hot lava pits and eternal burning damnation. The Oyunumagawa river flows menacingly out of wooded glades and into Jigokudani, steaming and fuming all the while. Follow it long enough and it cools its boots just enough for you to soak your tired feet.

Autumn is the best time to view the striking foliage of the surrounding mountains. The Noboribetsu hot-springs resort area is Hokkaidō's best known and one of Japan's most popular. Great bathing experiences are to be had at Sekisuitei, Hotel Yumoto and the Noboribetsu Grand, but for a first-class contemporary bathing experience don't miss the plethora of baths fed by seven different hot springs at Dai-ichi Takimotokan. With more than eleven baths and many hotels open to the hordes of day visitors, it's no wonder soaking at Noboribetsu is a favourite pastime. The Noboribetsu Bear Park brings you up close and personal with the region's brown bears – and you can watch them soaking in their own *onsen*.

RIGHT: Jigokudani OPPOSITE PAGE: Miso ramen at Ramen Republic, Sapporo Station

Sapporo

ISHIKARI SUBPREFECTURE

Sapporo is surrounded by mountains, forests and vast open spaces. As the capital of Hokkaidō and the only real city on the northern island, it has the largest population. Known for its snow festival and famous ice sculptures (p. 74), it's a winter city that feels remote from the main centres of Japan and boasts its own particular atmosphere and flavour. Sapporo is known all over Japan for its food, in particular seafood, dairy, miso ramen, soup curry and, of course, Sapporo beer.

From a small base of people in 1857 (seven people to be exact), Sapporo quickly grew, becoming known throughout the world when it hosted the Winter Olympic Games in 1972. Surrounding areas are usually associated with skiing and, in summer, hiking. Some of the most notable areas in Hokkaidō are a short distance from Sapporo itself. →

TRANSPORT

Tokyo by train to Sapporo, 8 hours. Or Tokyo Haneda to New Chitose Airport, 1 hour 35 minutes, then 40 minute train

CLOSE BY

Otaru, Jozankei Onsen, Noboribetsu, Nopporo Forest Park

ATMOSPHERE

Relaxed, country feel in a city setting

REGIONAL FOOD & DRINK

Cheesecake, miso ramen, beer, fresh seafood, milk caramels, soup curry, squid jerky, barbecued mutton

OMIYAGE

Cheesecake, Hokkaidō Milk Cookie, hand-blown glass, chocolate potato chips, *sanporoku* (slat cake), Hokkaidō corn snacks, cheese, White Black Thunder (a chocolate rice crisp bar)

TEMPLES & SHRINES

Hokkaidō Shrine, Hokkaidō Shrine Tongu, Sapporo Fushimi Inari Shrine, Shinei-ji, Hokkaidō Shrine Mikado, Oyachi Shrine

SIGHTS

Susukino, Historical Village of Hokkaidō, Hokkaidō Museum of Modern Art, Sapporo Beer Museum, Nijo Market, Curb Market, Teine Ski Resort

GARDENS & PARKS

Sapporo Art Park, Moerenuma Park, Maruyama Park, Odori park, Kobito Park

VIEWS

Mount Maruyama, Sapporo TV Tower, Asahiyama Memorial Park, JR Tower Observation Deck T38, Mount Moiwa

ARTS & CRAFTS

Glass blowing, wind chimes, craft beer, Ainu weaving and embroidery

FESTIVALS

Sapporo Snow Festival, Sapporo White Illumination, Sapporo Lilac Festival

WEB

sapporo.travel
www.city.sapporo.jp/city/english
uu-hokkaido.com/corporate

Susukino is the city's main centre, and holds the distinction of being the biggest entertainment district in Japan north of Toyko – no small deal, as there are many cities to Tokyo's north. Susukino is like the Shibuya Crossing (p. 165) of Sapporo, a central city point packed with karaoke bars, shopping, pachinko and even a red-light district (people in Sapporo have to do something to keep warm after all). The main drawcard is one of Sapporo's big ramen meccas, Ramen Yokochō, a narrow alley filled with specialty ramen shops that is always crowded and regularly featured on cooking shows around the world. Pop in for a Sapporo-style miso ramen (p. 122). At Sapporo Station is Ramen Republic, styled to look like a ramen *yokochō* (alleyway) and with a pop-culture charm of its own. Situated on the eighth floor of the Esta Building, Ramen Republic boasts a collection of the top Hokkaidō ramen specialties in the one spot – including miso ramen, Otaru-style soy sauce ramen and Hakodate's *shio* (salt) ramen. There's a recommended vegetarian ramen here as well, while pescetarians should try the clam broth ramen. Queue up with the hordes at Ramen Shingen, and don't forget to include a side order of *gyōza* (p. 116). Maruyama Zoo does a take-away pre-packaged Sapporo ramen (check out its other products – just look for the super-cute polar bear face on the packets or tins).

Sapporo is also known for soup curry, an unctuous mix of soup and curry with tender chicken and a variety of vegetables. Sample it with shrimp-based soup and chunky veg at renowned soup curry joint Okushiba, set inside a beautiful *machiya* (wooden townhouse). Sapporo is also known for *kissaten* (European-style coffee houses; p. 152) and jazz, and you'll find the two blended perfectly (along with an impressive record collection) at Bossa. Morihico serves coffee and cake, and there are few better ways to while away the afternoon than in this seventy-year-old townhouse. As far as *kissaten* chains go, Sapporo's Miyakoshi-Ya, which started in 1985, is one of the coolest.

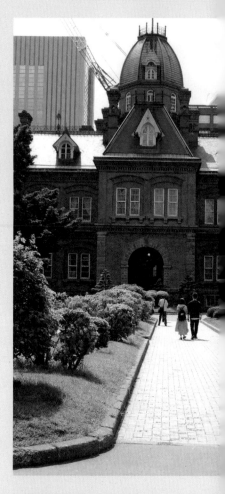

A NOTE ON THE AINU PEOPLE

The Ainu are the indigenous people of northern Japan, many of whom still live in the north today. The Ainu have a long and rich culture of hunting, building, crafting, collecting and creating. The national costume of furs, leathers and intricate embroidery are similar to Native American or Inuit dress. Museums and exhibitions dedicated to Ainu culture are dotted all over Hokkaidō, and there are statues and tableaux celebrating Ainu culture at Sapporo Station.

LEFT: Milk coffee at Nijo Market ABOVE: Sapporo City Hall TOP & BOTTOM RIGHT: Seafood at Nijo Market

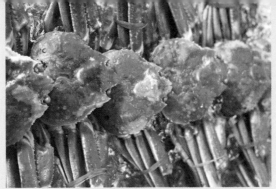

Sapporo is also known for seafood, especially crab, salmon roe, sea urchin and the famous *uni ikura donburi* – sea urchin and salmon roe on rice – which is a great way to start the day. Head to Nijo Market (p. 154) to experience these legendary northern specialties. Hokkaidō also makes more than forty per cent of Japan's buckwheat. You can even see the buckwheat in bloom during autumn. There's a buckwheat shrine and museum a little further out in Horokanai for the enthusiast, but if you don't want to make the trek, try some noodles in Sapporo for the freshest soba you're likely to eat.

Obviously beer is a big deal. One of the world's most famous beers was once made in the city, and still bears the city's name – Sapporo. Although it's now brewed elsewhere, Sapporo Beer was established here in 1876, making it Japan's oldest. You can explore all that history at the Sapporo Beer Museum, a kind of beer theme park established in 1987. It's an odd mix of European beer hall and English-ivy-clad pub/factory, various uncertainly themed beer gardens and large banquet halls. Sapporo Five Star (which ironically gets two and a half stars online) can only be bought at the Hokkaidō Beer Garden. Sapporo Beer can't have all the fun though, despite being the city's namesake. Craft beer haunts have sprung up over the last ten years to challenge the monolithic brew. Hunt out Cool Beer Craft, Moon and Sun Brewing and Beer Bar North Island.

Sapporo Station is a great spot to find Sapporo *omiyage*, gifts to take back to friends (p. 109). Hokkaidō's food specialties are well represented here. Don't miss the cheesecake – dairy is big in Sapporo and this treat is delicious in any form. Make sure you try the famous Snaffle's brand, and Kinotoya Bake makes a cheesecake tart you'll be dreaming of long after you've left. Due to the quality of the milk, ice cream is also a must-try in Sapporo. Definitely grab a Hokkaidō Milk Cookie and try the 'Times Square', a sponge cake filled with soft cream. Of course you can't miss the chocolate-coated potato chips – chocolate and salt go well together, of course, but chocolate and potato? One for the curiosities cabinet. Add to that the chocolate corn – Ganso Tokibi Choco is a corn bar coated in white chocolate. Corn is a big deal, and the corn and *mochi* rice *yakitokibi* snack Okaki Oh! is a must to stock up on for the train or plane journey back south. The Daiheigen is one for madeleine lovers – the sponge is drenched in rich Hokkaidō butter. Milk caramels, strawberries coated in chocolate, 'double fromage' cheese, White Black Thunder (a white-chocolate version of the famous Black Thunder treat), a Milk Castella and a Baumkuchen cake renowned as the softest and sweetest in Japan – well, you're starting to build the unique northern flavour profile. →

TOP: Isamu Noguchi sculpture MIDDLE: Sapporo *omiyage* snacks BOTTOM: Sapporo dessert

Anyone travelling for design or architecture will discover that Sapporo is one of Japan's best cities for municipal art and design. You can't miss Moerenuma Park, created by famed Japanese designer Isamu Noguchi. A passionate believer in public art, Noguchi put his beliefs into practice in this park. While work on the park started in 1988, it only opened in 2005, winning a slew of design awards in the process. Noguchi considered the park to be 'one complete sculpture', and to walk it now you definitely feel the curves and flow of Noguchi's vision. Sadly, Noguchi died of heart failure before he could see this public space begin to take shape, but what remains is a living testament to his vision and a rare city spot that can be enjoyed by everyone. The park (*moerenuma* is an Ainu term for 'slowly flowing river') takes in various Noguchi sculptures you can interact with like the *Tetra Mound*, a stainless steel triangle, the glass *Hidamari (Sunny Spot) Pyramid*, the *Aqua Plaza* fountain, plus there's a 150-foot canal and 3000 cherry trees. You'll find more public art in the underground art walk, which runs through the train station for 500 metres under Sapporo Odori park. The Ishiyama Green Space is also a must for art lovers, a quarry transformed into an abstract sculpture park by art collective Cinq.

The Hokkaidō Shrine, considered one of northern Japan's most important, is a hotspot during plum-blossom season. Around five kilometres into the suburbs of Sapporo you'll find the Historical Village of Hokkaidō, which gathers examples of Hokkaidō building styles from the mid-1800s to the early 1920s (a period of great expansion for Hokkaidō) all in the one place. More than sixty structures are exhibited in four styles of village: town, fishing, farm and mountain.

Northern exposure

SARAH RICHMOND, UNIVERSITY LECTURER, BOOKWORM AND SAPPORO RESIDENT

Are you more a summer or winter person?

I don't think you can survive in Hokkaidō if you're not a winter person. The winters last almost half the year. Sapporo is the second snowiest city in the world, with snow piling up to shoulder height. The blizzards and ice storms and howling winds ... if you don't find it romantic, then maybe living in Sapporo might not be the best idea.

What's your favourite festival?

For food and atmosphere-based festivals, I enjoy the German Christmas Market and the annual Autumn Fest (p. 67). The Yosakoi Festival that happens every June is a vibrant celebration of the traditional Yosakoi dance and makes me fall in love with Japan every time I watch it. I've never left the festival without feeling almost high off the energy and the sheer amount of glitter.

Which is your favourite season?

Definitely autumn. The Sapporo summer isn't too long, but it's just humid enough to make the transition to autumn feel like a blissful escape. The Hokkaidō hills are set aflame with Japanese maple foliage, the pumpkin and chestnut cakes could launch a thousand ships, the slow preparation for the winter hibernation, it's all a lesson in slow beauty.

And your favourite café or lunch spot?

Right now I tend to go to one of the Morihico cafés – there are about six dotted around the city, each with a unique menu and vibe. Shiawase no Pancake (A Happy Pancake) is my favourite pancake place right now (but ask me again in a week), and for a good strong brew with a nice view of Nakajima Park, Smooch Coffee Stand is always a good bet.

What food should we try in Sapporo?

Sapporo sushi is amazing, and much fresher and cheaper than anything you'd get in Tokyo. I'd recommend any seafood here, but the crab seems to hold the top spot for gourmet tourism. To be honest, you can even just grab a sushi *bentō* from the local supermarket and it would be top-notch.

Are you a soup curry or ramen person – or both? Explain the passion for hot soup in Hokkaidō.

I'm fine with eating one bowl of ramen a year – and that's usually a bowl of Hokkaidō corn butter miso ramen at Ramen Yokochō (p. 282) – but I need a soup curry fix once a week or I would die. The soup curry topped with garlic-fried broccoli at Samurai is a religious experience, and the coconut-based curry at Sama warms the cockles of my frost-bitten February heart.

What is your favourite Hokkaidō nature day out or mini break?

Oh man, Hokkaidō nature is a stunner. Daisetsuzan (p. 287) is Hokkaidō's largest national park and is gorgeous in all seasons. Sōunkyō, a collection of gorges within Daisetsuzan, has knockout waterfalls and cliffs. It also has an annual Ice Fall Festival in winter where fireworks are set off over the frozen waterfalls.

HOKKAIDŌ ADVENTURES

THE BOUNTIFUL NORTH

NEAR SAPPORO

ASAHIKAWA

Hokkaidō's second-largest city gives you a number of reasons to visit, including being one of the main areas for the Winter Festival (p. 74) and a primary exhibitor of ice sculptures. Premium spots for skiing and snowboarding are also a drawcard. The area is known for a fortifying *shōyu* (soy sauce) and lard-based ramen (featuring the area's highly regarded noodles). In fact, Asahikawa has a ramen village, where they offer small-bowl versions of their local ramen specialties for anyone who wants to try a few different kinds.

Asahikawa is home to Japan's northernmost and second-most visited zoo, Asahiyama. Expect penguins, seals and foxes, but the polar bears are the principal attraction and can be observed swimming in underground water tunnels.

Fans of anything wintry can't miss the Snow Crystal Museum, which features a room with a snowflake wall and a slow and cold descent into a corridor of ice stalactites. Otokoyama is a sake that uses the area's pristine ice meltwater as its base – the Otokoyama Sake Brewery Museum features a history of its production, which predates the Edo period (p. 28). There are tastings aplenty and you can purchase seasonal products at the gift shop. Anyone visiting the area to feel the power of the flowers has to visit Ueno Farm. The colourful displays here change with the seasons, so you can visit anytime.

BIEI

Between Furano and Asahikawa, Biei has a major drawcard of its own: the Shirogane Blue Pond. On the banks of the Biei River, the radiant blue lake is the stunning midpoint of several hiking trails that take in the impressive Sounkyo Gorge of the Daisetsuzan National Park. It's the largest national park in Japan – larger than the whole prefecture of Kanagawa. Spectacular Sounkyo Gorge burns red and gold in autumn. Other highlights include the Ishikawa River Canyon and breathtaking Ginga Waterfall. Biei also takes in another fine flower park (featuring some lavender), Shikisai Hill. Takushinkan is a museum that exhibits the landscape photography of Maeda and Akira Shinzo.

FURANO

To the east of Sapporo, Furano is known for three things: lavender fields, the Furano Ski Resort and the popular television show *Kita No Kuni Kara (From a North Country),* which was filmed there. This 1980s drama depicted the plight of the people in rural northern Japan, an important record of their fading lifestyle. Lavender has been a main crop in Hokkaidō since the 1960s, and the sight of vibrant purple fields stretching to the horizon is unforgettable. Farm Tomita (p. 349) is home to the main lavender fields, peaking in summer (around mid-July to early August). They offer lavender cutting and pressing and tractor rides through the fields. The Furano Biei Norokko train takes you on a journey through the lavender fields, stopping at the Lavender-Batake Station, some five minutes from Farm Tomita. Furano stargazing is a popular pastime from 1 March, when the vast open northern skies are at their most accessible.

JOZANKEI ONSEN

Noboribetsu (p. 280) might lay claim to being Hokkaidō's most popular *onsen* but Jozankei, nestled between the looming cliffs that gird the Toyohira River, has many special charms of its own, including fiery red and yellow autumnal foliage. It's around an hour from Sapporo, making it the perfect side trip for those wanting to take advantage of the healing waters. There are many hotels with *onsen* and views dotted about the area. Iwato Kannon-do is an unusual temple taking in a cave with more than thirty statues of Kannon (the Buddha of compassion) erected as a memorial to construction workers who lost their lives building the Otaru–Jozankei road, the second toll road to be built in Japan. They also hold the annual Iwato Kannon-do Festival here.

The area's mascot is Kappa, the green water monster of Tokyo's Kappabashi Dōri (p. 172) fame, a cheery fellow who makes a regular appearance at festivals and shopping centres. Catch the free shuttle bus to Hōheikyō to experience some of the area's main features: Hōheikyō Dam, Shiraito no Taki Waterfall and Jozankei Gensen Park. Stop for a soak in Hōheikyō Onsen.

OTARU

Otaru is a pleasant daytrip from Sapporo on the JR Hakodate Main Line Rapid Train (30 minutes). The architecture has a distinct European feel mixed with Japanese *machiya* (wooden townhouses), making for a unique style of town. Visions of tweed suits and whisky barrels fill the streets. A 'steam clock' (a gift from Vancouver) whistles every fifteen minutes, adding a nautical flavour. The north-west port city slumbers lazily alongside Ishikari Bay. Picturesque Otaru Canal is lined with warehouses that have been converted into cafés and shops. It's a major fishing port, so you can't escape without seeing something fish-related. The Herring Mansion is a highly decorated house with exhibits that will clue you in to the extent of fishing in the area. If whisky is your thing, head to the Nikka Yoichi Whisky Distillery in neighbouring Yoichi (twenty kilometres west) for a tour and tasting. →

OPPOSITE PAGE: Flower park in Biei

FURTHER AFIELD

ABASHIRI

In the far north-east of Hokkaidō, Abashiri pulls in travellers from afar for one reason: the ice on the Sea of Okhotsk breaks up during winter, forming an alien world of floating white blocks that cover the sea like clouds. The *Garinko-go II* ferries passengers across the drift ice from 20 January to 31 March, giving them a rare photo opportunity. Seals often lie lazily on the thicker and larger clumps of ice. Impressively, in places where the ice gets too thick, the *Garinko* uses a large and powerful drill to break it up. Abashiri is also known for a less salubrious reason: it's the site of the original Abashiri Prison, a foggy, frozen, harsh facility for political prisoners set up in 1890 that now serves as a somewhat sobering museum where you can see just how unforgiving life was on the wrong side of the law in late-nineteenth-century Japan – except for the fact they had their own *onsen*. The impressive wooden structure was built by the prisoners, many of whom became skilled woodworkers. Along with the *onsen*, the prisoners also made *nipopo kokeshi*, a unique form of the handcarved *kokeshi* doll (p. 340). Abashiri Prison notably became self-sufficient, and its farming practices were adopted across most prisons in Japan (although sadly more than 200 prisoners lost their lives to the cold in the process). Abashiri is also famous for 'bilk', a mixture of beer and milk – essentially Japan's first foray into the making of stout. Kangoku No Kuro (Black Prison Stout) is now popular all over Japan.

OPPOSITE PAGE TOP: Snowy drink machines BOTTOM: Shirogane Blue Pond, Biei

NEMURO

On Hokkaidō's eastern tip (Cape Nosappu is Japan's easternmost point), Nemuro is made up of striking rocky outcrops and ruggedly picturesque coastlines. The Shunkunitai Primeval Wild Bird Sanctuary allows you to see local cranes and swans in a splendid, untouched natural habitat. Local deer and foxes roam the area freely, and at several points on the coastline you can spot neighbouring islands through binoculars. Nemuro is also famous for seafood, especially sushi, which is considered among the freshest in the country.

WAKKANAI

Anyone feeling intrepid and with a staunch resistance to cold should head up to the official northernmost point of Hokkaidō for a glimpse of extreme rural Japan – and on a clear day, a sight of Russian-owned island Sakhalin. Yes, you are *that* far north here – and it's exhilarating. The sleepy town features two mysterious locations, the Path of White Shells (just as it sounds) and the Gate of Ice and Snow. True standouts, however, are nearby Rishiri and Rebun islands. Catch a ferry twenty kilometres out and explore these natural marvels. Rishiri is an extinct volcano famous for sea urchin and dried kombu and a vast national park. American Ranald MacDonald landed here in 1848 before becoming the first native English-speaking teacher in Japan. Rishiri Island staged a failed takeover of nearby Sakhalin Island in 1807–1808.

The winters are extreme, but during warmer months the island is noted for its alpine flowers. Nearby Rebun Island is also famous for alpine blooms, many of which can't be seen anywhere else in the world (including the ultra-rare Japanese edelweiss), making this stop a must

for the professional (or budding) botanist. The island is replete with beautiful natural sights, including beaches and mountains (Peach Rock is popular and a top spot for hiking). The spectacular terrain also affords great views of Rishiri Island. It's worth noting that you can catch the ferry all the way to Otaru (p. 287), not far from Hokkaidō's capital Sapporo.

KUSHIRO

Often called the 'City of Mist', Kushiro is a mystical place where a vast marsh plays host to the rare red-crowned crane and, in winter, the ultra-rare wild whooper swan. Often enshrouded in dense fog (hence the name), Kushiro is a kind of condensed Hokkaidō, featuring rainbow flower fields, fresh seafood (the area's *katte don* is a raw seafood rice bowl worth travelling for), hiking, rugged terrain and skiing all in the one area. Winters are more mellow in Kushiro, and the fishing industry is one of Japan's most important. Lake Akan is known for its *marimo* 'moss balls', round spheres of green that form in huddles under the water.

Lake Mashū, often regarded as the clearest lake in the world, is renowned for its reflections of the blue sky. One of the great things about this spot is that combined, the clear lake, the green mountains and dense forest make for one of Japan's most beautiful sights ... if it's not covered in thick fog, which it is in a frequency described as 'most of the time'.

If you're interested in exploring the indigenous culture of the Ainu, the small village of Ainu Kotan is a historic landmark, a thriving original Ainu village where you can experience many facets of this ancient culture.

MATSUMAE

To the south of Hokkaidō you'll find Matsumae, a 'former' castle town that features the ruins of Fukushima Castle, the seat of the only northern fiefdom of the Edo period (p. 28). The tunnel linking Aomori to Hakodate runs right past Matsumae. The castle is nothing more than a 1960s structure built to house a historical museum (not so great for fans of historical Japanese castles, quite good for fans of mid-century modernism), but the grounds have been turned into a spectacular garden that flourishes in cherry-blossom season, featuring some 10,000 (and 250 varieties) of ornamental cherry trees. The park features the Kechimyaku Sakura, or 'bloodline cherry', from which most of the trees are said to have been grafted.

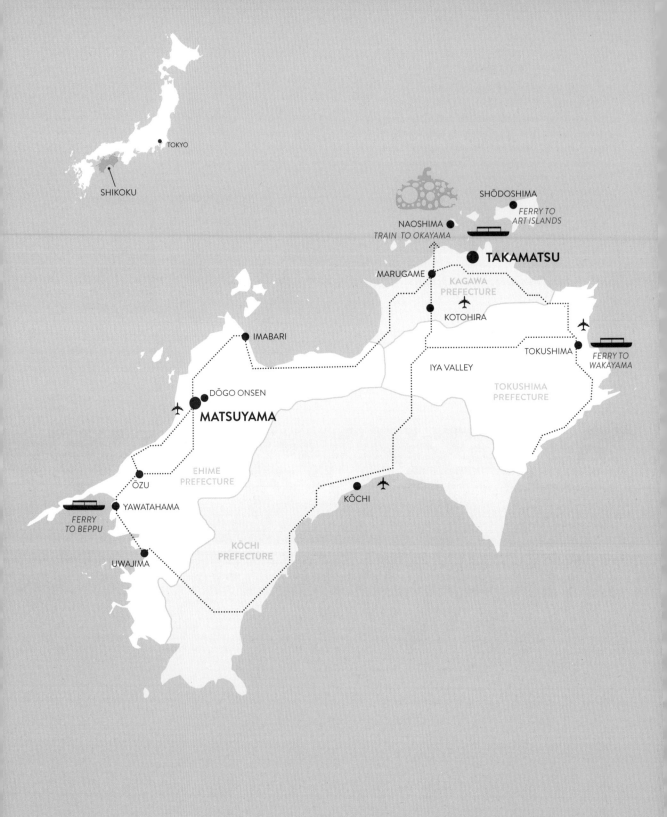

TOKYO

SHIKOKU

SHŌDOSHIMA
*FERRY TO
ART ISLANDS*

NAOSHIMA
TRAIN TO OKAYAMA

TAKAMATSU

MARUGAME

KAGAWA
PREFECTURE

KOTOHIRA

IMABARI

IYA VALLEY

TOKUSHIMA

*FERRY TO
WAKAYAMA*

DŌGO ONSEN

MATSUYAMA

TOKUSHIMA
PREFECTURE

EHIME
PREFECTURE

ŌZU

KŌCHI

YAWATAHAMA

*FERRY
TO BEPPU*

KŌCHI
PREFECTURE

UWAJIMA

SHIKOKU

It might be the second smallest of Japan's main islands (after Okinawa), but despite its small frame, Shikoku manages to make a big impression. The name simply means 'Four Countries', indicating the four original areas that made up the island. The island is now divided into four prefectures, each with its own unique feel: Kagawa, Ehime, Tokushima and Kōchi. Kagawa is best known, laying claim to famed art islands Naoshima (p. 292) and Teshima (p. 295), with their unforgettable art museums, architecture and installations; and olive-rich Shōdoshima (p. 297). Ehime prefecture has one of Japan's most famous hot-spring areas, which features old and picturesque Dōgo Onsen (p. 302). It also takes in Matsuyama, with its Edo-period castle (p. 302), and the cotton-producing region of Imabari, whose quality towels are considered Japan's finest.

Japan has long sung the praises of the island's beautiful Iya Valley and Tokushima prefecture has a few secrets of its own – a famous dance festival and one of Japan's oddities, the thunderous Naruto whirlpools (p. 297). Hikers can't miss one of Japan's best walking experiences, the Eighty-eight Temple Pilgrimage Trail (p. 229). Take the time to go 'off Honshū' and explore an exciting and less-travelled part of Japan.

291

Naoshima

The Seto Inland Sea holds many treasures, the most famous of which is the island of Naoshima. One of several 'art islands', rustic and rural Naoshima has various outdoor and indoor artworks spread over many locations, all overseen by the Benesse Group. A number of buildings on the island were designed by Tadao Ando (p. 353), making it a great spot for architecture lovers as well as contemporary art fans. Access to the island is by ferry – times are limited and once on the island transport is sparse (there's only one taxi, which holds nine people) – so this is one trip where you should become intimate with timetables and plan to the nth degree ... and, of course, try to catch the Yayoi Kusama (p. 375) spotted bus!

The ferry from Uno arrives at Miyanoura Port, home to a beautiful minimalist ferry terminal designed by SANAA architects (p. 355). The other main island port is Honmura, also worth investigating for its architecture – again by SANAA – a bubble- or cloud-like structure that's the complete opposite of the brutalist Miyanoura terminal and an artwork in itself. Electric bikes are a great way to get around – hire them from cafés like Little Plum.

The Chichu Art Museum (reserve beforehand; p. 375) is Ando's ode to the surrounding environs. Set deep in the ground, it involves rather than defies nature, allowing diffused natural light to enhance the works within (look from above to see 'windows' of various shapes cut into the landscape). Using Monet's breathtaking *Water Lilies* as a starting point, the museum allows the viewer to further commune with art and nature through a series of works by American artists James Turrell (make sure you see the sunset viewing of *Open Sky* if you can) and Walter De Maria. Ando's most recent project on Naoshima is the Valley Gallery, a brutalist metal bunker softened by the surrounding forest.

The Art House Project converts a whole portside town of derelict storehouses into installations and small galleries (some require bookings). Narrow streets hold many hidden pleasures, as well as the ultra-cute Konnichiwa cosy café adjacent to the SANAA bubble/cloud terminal. Benesse House is both hotel and gallery; the advantage of staying here is that you can visit the gallery at *any* time – it's twenty-four hours of art. This is where you can find Yayoi Kusama's *Yellow Pumpkin* (1994; in the era of the 'look at me' photo, this has become one of the world's top opportunities. The sculpture has now been recovered, refurbished and is back in place after being washed out to sea during a typhoon in 2021). Apart from its obvious pop charm, its setting on a pier with the ocean for a gallery space is perfect. Kusama's pumpkins are her own pop art moment, her Campbell's Soup cans, if you will – she was a major inspiration for both Warhol and Yoko Ono. Kusama's *Red Pumpkin* (2006) can be found at Miyanoura port – it's there to greet you as you disembark the ferry from Takamatsu (p. 301). Many other wonderful 'outside' artworks are dotted around.

Consider taking the slow ferry from Naoshima across to Takamatsu (around one hour) for some beautiful views and a magical sunset. From Takamatsu you can head to another main art island, Teshima (p. 295). Many people choose to spend the night on Takamatsu and do both islands (or three including Inujima; p. 295) in a couple of days. The Setouchi Triennale is a major event with three seasonal sessions.

Food opportunities are varied on Naoshima. Miyanoura and Honmura have the highest concentration of eateries. Vegans should try Iwao's Café or Café Ippo. Noodle-lovers head for Kinosaki Udon, and for a *shokudō* (casual home-style eatery) lunch try New Olympia. Ramen Tsumu will provide your ramen fix.

TRANSPORT

Okayama Ryobi Express bus to Uno Port, about 40 minutes; then ferry to Miyanoura Port or Honmura Port, both about 20 minutes. Remember, Naoshima has one taxi!

CLOSE BY

Seto Inland Sea, Teshima, Inujima, Shōdoshima, Okayama, Takamatsu

ATMOSPHERE

Inspiring, relaxed, artistic, contemplative

REGIONAL FOOD & DRINK

Sawachi ryōri (seafood platters), *katsuo no tataki* (grilled bonito fish), Sanuki (square) udon, mandarins, oysters

OMIYAGE

Yayoi Kusama *Pumpkin* keyrings, *furoshiki* scarves

TEMPLES & SHRINES

Gokuraku-ji, Minamidera, Go'o shrine

SIGHTS

Yayoi Kusama's pumpkins, Art House Project, Shinro Ohtake's *I Love Yu Bath House* (2009), Shinro Ohtake's *Shipyard Works – Stern with Hole* (1990)

GARDENS & PARKS

Chichu Garden

MUSEUMS & GALLERIES

Chichu Art Museum, Benesse House, Lee Ufan Museum, Valley Gallery

FESTIVALS

Setouchi Triennale

WEB

naoshima.net

LEFT: Yayoi Kusama ferry

ISLAND-HOPPING ON THE SETO INLAND SEA

The Seto Inland Sea is home to a cluster of islands (a gasp-making 3000 of them, many uninhabited) set between Honshū, Shikoku and Kyūshū. A mostly warm climate, the ferries shuttling between islands and the blissful setting invites comparisons with the Greek or Italian island clusters in the Mediterranean or with the Caribbean (albeit with a very Japanese twist).

THE ART ISLANDS

Once you take the ferry from Uno Port to Naoshima (p. 292), a whole network of ferries opens up to you, allowing access to islands across the Seto Inland Sea. Many of these lay claim to a variety of art, food specialties and experiences with great charm. Teshima is an easy ferry ride from Takamatsu (p. 301), taking around thirty-five minutes. Naoshima's Honmaru Port links to Teshima's Leura Port and takes twenty minutes. Consult timetables carefully to find the best connections.

Teshima also takes part in the Setouchi Triennale and has some standout art of its own, most notably the Teshima Art Museum, a concrete structure in the middle of rice paddies with a famous bubble dome and circular sky porthole – an amazing work designed by architect Ryue Nishizawa from the mystical musings of artist Rei Naito. Also of note is Christian Boltanski's Les Archives du Coeur, where you can record your heartbeat and listen to those of others, a simultaneously moving and unnerving experience.

North of Teshima you'll find tiny Inujima, the third piece of the main Setouchi Triennale puzzle. Of particular note are the ruins of the industrial refinery, a functional item in the past, now considered an artwork in its own right. The Inujima Art House Project mimics Naoshima's, a smaller, more rustic version in a town occupied by a mere 100 people. A satellite of the Triennale is Shōdoshima (p. 297), the inland sea's largest island. Forty artworks are spread about the island. Megijima and Ogijima also feature a small number of artworks and are part of the Triennale if you want to complete the set.

Make sure to pick up both ferry and bus timetables, and stick to your schedule. →

THIS PAGE & OPPOSITE: Ferry ride from Naoshima to Takamatsu

CATS & RABBITS

Cats outnumber humans at a ratio of about six to one on Aoshima (Cat Island). More than 100 cats prowl the island, particularly around the harbour, where they mob arriving visitors in the hope of a morsel or two of fish. There are designated feeding areas but the cats are opportunistic and will get food when they can. The island residents share the space with them – sometimes begrudgingly, sometimes with great affection. Crazy cat people will be in heaven.

If you prefer bunnies, Ōkunoshima (Rabbit Island) might be more your thing. On this island, which has plenty of hiking trails and campsites, it's the feral (but tame) rabbits that end up stealing the show. If you like floppy ears, head there on the ferry from Tadanoumi or Ōmishima. The island also features the Poison Gas Museum, a bleak reminder of its creepy history as home to the Imperial Army's mustard- and tear-gas factory for both world wars in the early twentieth century.

SHIMANAMI KAIDŌ

Starting in Onomichi City, the spectacular Shimanami Kaidō Bridge spans six different islands – Mukaishima, Innoshima, Ikuchijima, Ōmishima, Hakatajima and Oshima – depositing you on Shikoku at Imabari. Free of cars, the highway can only be crossed by foot or bicycle. Along the way you can enjoy the beauty of the islands, the Hirayama Ikuo Museum of Art celebrating *Nihonga* (traditional Japanese painting) artist Hirayama Ikuo, and colourful 1936 Kōsan-ji temple where you'll find an extensive cave with paintings and sculptures of Buddhist hell.

FOOD

As well as being one of the art islands, Shōdoshima is known as one of Japan's primary producers of *shōyu* (soy sauce), with a history going back more than 400 years. There are around twelve factories on the island, including the Marukin Soy Sauce Factory. Not surprisingly, the island also makes *tsukudani*, seafood and meat preserves in soy. As an added challenge you can try the *moromi* (mash) soft-serve, an ice cream flavoured with the soybean pulp left over from the soy-sauce-making process (spoiler alert: it's good/interesting).

Shōdoshima also has one of Japan's most revered gorges, Kankakei, well known for its olive trees. It's a great spot for hiking.

ONSEN

Naoshima has its own *sentō* (man-made bathhouse), the artsy I Love Yu, but if you need to relax after all that island-hopping, Setouchi Onsen Tamanoyu is a super *sentō* near Uno. Actually, it's more accurate to call it a super *onsen* – a natural hot-water spring with plenty of baths and a *ganban-yoku* (bedrock sauna) among other comforts. The perfect way to relax.

NATURAL OCCURRENCES

The channel between Naruto and Awaji Island features a popular natural phenomenon – the Naruto whirlpools, powerful eddies that rank among the largest in the world and can be viewed from tour boats and the Naruto Bridge. Utagawa Hiroshige captured the whirlpools in a wood-block print made around 1853.

THIS PAGE: Michelle and Yayoi Kusama's *Red Pumpkin* at Miyanoura Port OPPOSITE PAGE TOP: SANAA ferry terminal at Honmura Port, Naoshima BOTTOM: The ferry at Miyanoura Port, Naoshima

Unique places

We've already covered one of our favourite out-of-the-way experiences at length – the *onsen* (hot springs) in Gunma prefecture (p. 186). Some of our other favourites are listed below.

FLOWERS IN FURANO & BIEI (FURANO, HOKKAIDŌ)

If you ever dream of being in a field surrounded by flowers, the flower farms of Furano and Biei (both p. 287) will make all your dreams come true.
furanotourism.com/en/bigkey/course,
farm-tomita.co.jp/en

KUROKAWA ONSEN (KUROKAWA, KYŪSHŪ)

Tucked deep in the mountains in the Kumamoto prefecture, this rustic *onsen* town (p. 313) is perfect if you're seeking stillness, quiet contemplation and nature. It offers some of the most beautiful *onsen* bathing and Japanese architecture you'll ever see. We love to visit in wintertime.
kurokawaonsen.or.jp/eng_new

MASHIKO POTTERY TOWN (MASHIKO, KANTŌ)

A craft town (p. 183) dedicated to the slow arts of pottery and indigo-dyeing. Hire a bike and visit the museums and stores selling work by local makers. It's an easy daytrip from Tokyo.
mashiko-kankou.org

MATSUMOTO CRAFT FAIR (MATSUMOTO, CHŪBU)

Craft lovers will be in heaven at this fair held in a beautiful rural setting (p. 219). Hundreds of makers set up shop to sell exquisite handmade pottery, textiles, ironware and more. Held over a weekend in late May.
http://matsumoto-crafts.com/craftsfair

MIHO MUSEUM (SHIGA, KANSAI)

A train from Kyoto followed by a long and winding bus ride deposits you near one of the world's finest pieces of architecture and one of its best museums (p. 257). From there, take a walk or small buggy ride through a mountain tunnel to I. M. Pei's gallery masterpiece set against a mountain backdrop.
miho.or.jp

NARUKO ONSEN (NARUKO, TŌHOKU)

A town of master *kokeshi*-makers, with the added bonus of amazing *onsen* water and public baths (p. 204). Plan your trip for autumn, as Naruko Gorge has some of the best autumn colours in the country.
en.naruko.gr.jp

TOTTORI SAND DUNES (TOTTORI, CHŪGOKU)

Tottori (p. 275) has been on our radar ever since we became fascinated with the 1964 black-and-white film *Suna no Onna* (*Woman in the Dunes*). The otherworldly experience of walking on giant sand dunes in a country like Japan – not known for either sea or sand – makes for a really unique experience.
city.tottori.lg.jp/geopark/en/index.html

YAKUSHIMA ISLAND (KAGOSHIMA, KYŪSHŪ)

The combination of remote location, forest, nature and atmosphere make Yakushima Island (p. 325) truly magical.
www.town.yakushima.kagoshima.jp/en

YAMADERA (YAMAGATA, TŌHOKU)

A mountain hike – up stone steps, over moss and brambles, and among temples, complete withfrog-spotting and bird-watching – to the top of Yamadera (p. 206), is one of our favourite Japan experiences. The temple Hojusanrishaku-ji, built in 806 AD, has extraordinary views over the local towns.
data.yamagatakanko.com/english/
sightseeing/yamadera.html

OPPOSITE PAGE TOP: Miho Museum, Shiga, Kansai BOTTOM: *Kokeshi* master Yasuo Okazaki at Naruko Onsen, Tōhoku

ALL IMAGES: Ritsurin Koen

Takamatsu

KAGAWA PREFECTURE

Kagawa is Japan's smallest prefecture and Takamatsu is its capital, a castle town that is home to one of Japan's 'big three' landscaped gardens (the others are in Kanazawa, Mito and Okayama – yes, we know, that's four; there's some debate). Ritsurin Kōen (Chestnut Grove Garden) was created by feudal lord Takamatsu in 1625. Standout points include Kikugetsu-tei ('Moon-scooping Pavilion'), a sublime tea house that dates back to 1640; two delightful lakes, Sai-ko and Nan-ko; the Hakomatsu, shaped black pines; and the Sanuki Folk Craft Museum. Shikoku Mura is a delightful 'village' of buildings, storehouses, farmhouses and workshops making soy sauce and olive oil that date from the Edo period (p. 28) and Meiji era (p. 32). A traditional vine suspension bridge is a main feature.

Design fans should head to the Isamu Noguchi Garden Museum, where the American sculptor lived and worked when he was in Japan. His workshop and tools, plus more than 150 sculptures, are spread about the property. Nearby is a Noguchi-restored warehouse, which features other works, including one of his famous Energy Void series of sculptures from the early 1970s, a huge triangular black-granite loop. Takamatsu's Marugamemachi covered shopping arcade is potentially Japan's longest at 2.7 kilometres (ten centimetres longer than Osaka's Tenjinbashisuji), and some sections are more than 400 years old.

Takamatsu is the perfect spot to set up camp if you're planning to explore the art islands (p. 295). It's a forty-minute ferry ride to Ogijima and Megijima (Ogre Island), both of which can easily be done in a day. Don't forget to try the area's famous dish, Sanuki udon – a premium udon noodle made in the prefecture and famous all over Japan (p. 124). A well-known canteen, Meriken, right outside Takamatsu train station, serves a delicious *bukkake* (chilled) udon. Kokoro Udon is run by a sprightly grandmother and is like an open kitchen with a sitting area, while Yamada Udon makes the region's delicious udon in a traditional house with a beautiful garden.

TRANSPORT

Okayama Marine Liner train to Takamatsu Station, about 50 minutes. Or Uno Port ferry to Takamatsu, about 50 minutes

CLOSE BY

Okayama, the art islands, Ehime, Iya Valley

ATMOSPHERE

Calm, natural, historical, beautiful

REGIONAL FOOD & DRINK

Sanuki udon, *wasanbon* (refined-sugar sweets), *age pippi* (fried udon), grilled chicken thigh, Seto seafood, Sanuki beef, Sanuki no Mezame asparagus, Seto no Haru field mustard, barbecue

OMIYAGE

Packaged Sanuki udon, olive oil, soy sauce, *temari* balls (made of thread), Sanuki *chochin* lanterns, *daruma* lanterns, Aji granite products, Kagawa lacquerware, wooden *wagashi* (sweets) moulds, Takamatsu *wagasa* (umbrellas)

TEMPLES & SHRINES

Yashima-ji, Takamatsu-shi

SIGHTS

Ritsurin Kōen, Noguchi Museum, Ogijima, Megijima, Shikoku Mura, Takamatsu Castle

GARDENS & PARKS

Ritsurin Koen, Shikoku Mura, Tamamo Park

MUSEUMS & GALLERIES

Takamatsu City Museum of Art, Sanuki Folkcraft Museum, Kagawa Museum

VIEWS

Yashima-ji, Ogijima, Megijima, Takamatsu Symbol Tower

ARTS & CRAFTS

Stone sculpture, bonsai, George Nakashima wooden furniture

FESTIVALS

Sanuki Takamatsu Festival, Shishimai, Shionoe Firefly Festival, Winter Festival

WEB

art-takamatsu.com

Matsuyama & Dōgo Onsen

The capital of Ehime prefecture, Matsuyama is home to one of Japan's original castles and one of the country's most famous and picturesque bathhouses and hot-springs towns, Dōgo Onsen. Matsuyama Castle can be reached by cable car or chairlift from Chojaganaru Station. The castle gates are designated important national cultural properties, mighty structures that show how well the castle was protected. The castle itself is admired for its ten-foot-high stone walls, elegantly curved and said to be reminiscent of a folding fan. The surrounding Ninomaru Historical Garden is beautiful in cherry-blossom season and in autumn, and has been structured to mimic the layout of the castle's original buildings. The amorous in nature will be happy to know that the garden is referred to as the 'Lover's Sanctuary'.

Dōgo Onsen can be conveniently reached by cable car. It's a delight from start to finish. Stroll around in a *yukata* (casual kimono) and enjoy the baths. One of the main inspirations for Studio Ghibli's *Spirited Away*, Dōgo Onsen Honkan in the middle of the city square has a striking wooden facade and a tall bell tower. Its features include the Shinrokaku (White Heron Watchtower); the Yushinden, a bathroom built for use by visiting Emperors (with the 'Camellia Room' where Prince Shōtoku stayed when he visited); and the two atmospheric public baths Tama-no-yu and Kami-no-yu. Ceramic tiles from nearby Tobe adorn the walls of the annex on the first floor. Some 3000 years have passed since Dōgo Onsen Honkan was first constructed, making it Japan's oldest *onsen*.

The area has many other attractions, including popular bath Dōgo Onsen Tsubaki-no-yu, nostalgic Dōgo Onsen Station, the Botchan Karakuri Clock (a large clock with a heron instead of a cuckoo) and the Botchan steam trains made famous by Natsuma Sōseki's novel *Botchan* (1906). Dōgo's new annex building (2017) is a gorgeous addition to the Dōgo story. Local modern novelists and poets Shiki Masaoka, Shiba Ryōtarō and Natsume Sōseki are often thought of as Japan's 'Bloomsbury Set'.

Haiku is the birthplace of famed haiku poet Shiki Masaoka. There's a museum dedicated to him and the town has many stone monuments inscribed with haiku. A very poetic place, it's also home to haiku poet Chodō Kurita's thatched cabin, and 'free verse' haiku poet Santōka Tenada's retirement hut. Fans of architecture should visit the Toyo Ito Museum in Imabari (pp. 305, 354), and for a luxe experience think about staying at Setouchi Retreat Aonagi (p. 305), housed in an ex-museum designed by Tadao Ando, complete with views of the Seto Inland Sea, incredible cuisine and striking architecture.

Matsuyama has eight temples placed around the city that form the basis of the eighty-eight-temple Shikoku Pilgrimage Trail (p. 229). Visit them all to become an *O-henro* (spiritual pilgrim). The sites are Hanta-ji, Jōdo-ji, Enmyō-ji, Jōruri-ji, Sairin-ji, Yasaka-ji, and of particular note Taisan-ji and Ishite-ji. You'll find special spiritual 'hiking gear' in the stores, and many people make the trek with the traditional white outfit, straw hat and walking cane. It lends the area a calm and contemplative atmosphere.

Don't forget to try the area's specialties. *Mikan* (mandarin) is big here, as are other citrus fruits, so make sure you try some fresh and as a flavouring for sweets and other products. *Matsuyamazushi* and five-coloured noodles is a famous local dish made during festival days – rice topped with Setouchi seafood and featuring noodles in yellow egg, brown buckwheat, green matcha, red plum (and *shiso*) and plain white. Matsuyama is also renown for having the best *unagi* (eel) dishes in the country.

TRANSPORT

Hiroshima Super Jet ferry to Matsuyama, about 70 minutes. Or Okayama Station to Matsuyama Station, about 2 hours 30 minutes

CLOSE BY

Hiroshima, Okayama, Miyajima, Ōzu

ATMOSPHERE

Relaxed, *onsen* resort, historical

ONSEN

Dōgo Onsen Honkan, Dōgo Onsen Tsubaki-no-yu

REGIONAL FOOD & DRINK

Mikan (mandarin), *unagi* (eel), Dōgo beer, sea bream rice, Taruto and Botchan *dango*, *matsuyamazushi* and five-coloured noodles, *mitsuhamayaki*

OMIYAGE, ARTS & CRAFTS

Bamboo craft, Iyo Kasuri fabric, *himedaruma* dolls, Imabari towels, *mikan* (mandarin) products, fabric products, traditional pilgrim hiking gear

SIGHTS

Matsuyama Castle, Dōgo Onsen Honkan, Shimanami Kaidō, Botchan steam trains, Kurushima Strait tidal currents

TEMPLES & SHRINES

Hanta-ji, Jōdo-ji, Enmyō-ji, Jōruri-ji, Sairin-ji, Yasaka-ji

GARDENS & PARKS

Ninomaru Historical Garden, Kōshin-an

MUSEUMS & GALLERIES

Ehime Prefectural Museum of Art, Toyo Ito Museum, Shiki Memorial Museum, Shikido, Saka no Ue no Kumo Museum, Itami Juzo Museum

VIEWS

Matsuyama Castle

FESTIVALS

Dōgo Onsen Festival, Haru Matsuri, Hojo Aki Matsuri, Natsu Matsuri

WEB

en.matsuyama-sightseeing.com

OPPOSITE PAGE LEFT: Inside Dōgo Onsen Honkan OPPOSITE PAGE RIGHT: Little boy in traditional wear at Dōgo Onsen

IMABARI

The town of Imabari has access to high-quality water, which results in a high-grade cotton used to make some of the world's finest towels, flannels and tea towels. The products can be bought all over Japan and are found in many stores in the Shikoku region. You can even visit the Towel Museum in Imabari, which has artworks based on towels and spots where you can see the towels being made. Side note: Imabari also has a castle – a reconstruction, albeit a good one – where sea water flows into the moat. It's a spectacular sight lit up at night.

ABOVE: Infinity pool at Setouchi Retreat Aonagi OPPOSITE PAGE: Toyo Ito Museum of Architecture

IYA VALLEY

Cutting a swathe through north-eastern Shikoku, just south of Takamatsu (p. 301), you'll find one of Japan's premium trails, which goes through the Iya Valley. Hidden and mountainous, it's accented by deep gorges with sheer rock faces and vine bridges. The Iya Kazurabashi and the Oku-Iya Kazurabashi collection of vine bridges are regularly maintained and are popular icons of the valley.

After the Genpei War (1180–1185) the Heike clan used the area as their refuge, leading to a long and interesting history that also takes in the charms of Shirakawa-go (p. 224) and the Noto Peninsula (p. 226). The Iya Valley is Japanese nature at its most charming and treacherous. Along the way there are many standout sights, making it in many ways one of Japan's unsung treasures.

ONSEN

There are many spectacular hot-spring baths dotting the landscape in Shikoku. For a secluded mountain hot-spring retreat, try Okudogo Onsen. Konpira Onsenkyo in Kotohira Town features a shrine with more than 1000 steps, surrounded by an *onsen* town with uniquely silky, transparent water. Shionoe Onsenkyo is more than 1300 years old and features a beautiful wooden bridge overlooking a river that sparkles with fireflies at night. Nibukawa Onsen, set in the stunning Nibukawa Gorge, features many hot-spring baths and *ryokan* with wonderful forest and mountain views. If you're looking for a sea view, however, head to Ashizuri Onsenkyo, where many *onsen* look over the Pacific Ocean – stretch out in the hot water and gaze at the deep blue sea!

SETOUCHI RETREAT AONAGI

Not far from Matsuyama (p. 302), in an out-of-the-way area, you'll find an impressive Tadao Ando (p. 353) building that was once a gallery and is now a 'wellness retreat'. The architecture of Setouchi Retreat Aonagi is striking against the verdant backdrop, and an infinity pool looks out over the Seto Inland Sea (p. 294). If that's not enough reason to stay, there's the food, based on seasonal, local produce – it's outstanding. There are only seven rooms, so you'll feel like you have a piece of Ando architecture to yourself. It's an interesting duality: a 'minimal luxury' where pretence and affluence are stripped away and yet you'll feel like you're somewhere spiritually rich.

TOYO ITO MUSEUM OF ARCHITECTURE

Toyo Ito (p. 354) is one of Japan's most influential architects, and his many-sided pod-like structure on Ōmishima is a museum, a school and a sci-fi blip on the landscape. Opened in 2011, it has become a pilgrimage site for many architecture students and design fans. Made up of two buildings, one of which, the 'steel hut', is quite the eye-opener – a contemporary black-metal pavilion made up of many arches and spread over two floors. Ito's famous works are presented in miniature on the museum grounds, including the Mikimoto 'paper cut-out' department store tower in Ginza, Tokyo, and the Tama Art University Library.

UCHIKO-ZA & YOKAICHI OLD TOWN

Uchiko-za Kabuki Theatre rivals Dōgo Onsen Honkan for gasp-inducing architecture. Built in 1916, Uchiko-za still hosts kabuki (and *bunraku* puppet theatre) today. As an added bonus, you can tour the building and see how it all works: the trapdoor, devices, designs and mechanims that allow the magic to happen.

Yokaichi Old Town is a preserved district in Uchiko of old houses and shops, many more than 100 years old. Important residences and merchant houses can be found in the area, including the Honhaga Residence, the Omura Residence, the Kamihaga Residence, the Machiya Museum and Kosho-ji temple.

KYŪSHŪ

TOKYO

SHINKANSEN
TO HIROSHIMA,
KYOTO, OSAKA,
TOKYO

FUKUOKA
& HAKATA

FUKUOKA
PREFECTURE

MOUNT
FUTAGO ▲

IMARI

SAGA
PREFECTURE

ARITA

SAGA

ONTAYAKI POTTERY
VILLAGE

YUFUIN

BEPPU

ŌITA
CITY

FERRY TO
YAWATAHAMA
(SHIKOKU)

KUROKAWA

KUJŪ
MOUNTAINS

ŌITA
PREFECTURE

ASO

NAGASAKI
PREFECTURE

NAGASAKI

KUMAMOTO

MOUNT
ASO ▲

MOUNT
UNZEN ▲

MIYAZAKI
PREFECTURE

KUMAMOTO
PREFECTURE

KAGOSHIMA
PREFECTURE

MOUNT
KIRISHIMA ▲

MIYAZAKI

KAGOSHIMA

SAKURAJIMA ▲

FERRY TO
IBUSUKI

IBUSUKI

FERRY TO
YAKUSHIMA

YAKUSHIMA

OKINAWA
↓

九州

KYŪSHŪ

Japan's south-west island region of Kyūshū has that perfect 'undiscovered' feel, a sense that in a world where every corner has been mapped, there's still somewhere to escape from it all. As Japan's deep south, it has a warmer climate, a friendlier disposition and an abundance of local food specialties. The volcanic soil means that local crops grow at an absurdly prodigious rate. The region is often called Kyūshū/Okinawa due to Okinawa's unique culture and atmosphere.

Since its bombing in the Second World War, Nagasaki (p. 329) has reinvented itself (although many scars remain) and is now a fascinating port town with lookouts, mountains, islands (James Bond's *Skyfall* made Gunkajima, or Battleship Island, famous) and the freshest of seafood. The Portuguese and Dutch trading history in Nagasaki led to an influx of people from the surrounding islands, other Asian countries (South Korea's Busan is closer to Kyūshū than Tokyo), and elsewhere in Japan looking for work. This has led to a wealth of quality cheap eats and street food throughout the island. Hakata and Fukuoka (p. 308), for example, boast deep, rich ramen and canal-side open-air dining.

Volcanic waters mean hot springs. Kumamoto City (p. 329) offers a springboard to Kurokawa (p. 312), Mount Aso, Beppu (p. 316) and Yufuin (p. 311), some of Japan's most impressive *onsen* bathing and hiking areas. Arita and Imari (p. 310) on Kyūshū's western mountain cluster are renowned for exceptional and unique pottery.

A city on the southern tip, Kagoshima (p. 320) currently holds the Guinness World Record for the world's heaviest radish, weighing in at over thirty-one kilograms. Fruit is also enormous, and extremely tasty. All the while, jaw-dropping Sakurajima looks proudly on, a mammoth volcanic mountain smoking moodily just a short ferry ride from the edge of Kagoshima. Nearby Ibusuki (p. 329) is known for sand-bathing, while a boat ride south will take you to Yakushima (p. 325), an island of tangled forests and rugged coastline – unspoiled Japan, and heaven for hikers.

Much further south, across the sea, you'll find Okinawa Prefecture (p. 326), made up of 160 islands and often thought of as Japan's Hawaii – subtropical, friendly and with an abundance of unique flora and fauna and World Heritage sites. Okinawa is also imbued with *yuimaru*, the spirit of helping others. Whatever situation arises, Okinawans band together to sort it out. This extends to visitors.

Fukuoka & Hakata

Known as the 'front gate' of Kyūshū, Fukuoka (and its main station and area Hakata) is literally the first port of call when entering Kyūshū's volcanic south. Workers and immigrants come across from Nagasaki (p. 329) and the surrounding islands (and even South Korea) and Hakata is set up to cater for them, especially when it comes to cheap but exceptional food. Of course, as a visitor, you can capitalise on this.

Hakata is fractured by several canals that play host to a fringe of eateries known as *yatai*. The canals themselves are a major focal point and as a result the main shopping district is Canal City, an over-the-top mix of dancing lightshows, fountains, mock Viennese tableaux, and the haunted halls of 1980s remnant stores, contemporary refits and the requisite brands.

THIS PAGE: Yatai street-food stalls **OPPOSITE PAGE:** *Tonkotsu* ramen

Head to Hakata Old Town to get a sense of how the city worked as an important trading port for hundreds of years. The Traditional Craft and Design Museum showcases two of Hakata's famous icons: Hakata dolls, small colourful statuettes of well-known poets and figures from up to 1000 years ago; and *Hakata-ori* fabric used to make kimono and obi sashes all over the country.

The Kushida Shrine, founded in 757 AD, hosts Fukuoka's biggest festival, Gion Yamakasa Matsuri, in July. The shrine features a 1000-year-old ginkgo tree, various *tengu* masks (p. 341) and some large round stones said to be anchors from Mongolian ships. Tōchō-ji, founded in 806 AD, has a magnificent five-tiered pagoda. Uminonakamichi Seaside Park is a famous spot for viewing tulips in autumn and cherry blossoms in spring.

Fukuoka Tower stands at the sea's edge just fifteen minutes from Nishijin Subway Station. Known as the tallest 'beach' tower in Japan at 234 metres, it includes a striking 8000 mirrors. Views are mesmerising, especially at night, and illuminations are displayed for Valentine's Day, Christmas and the Star Festival in early July.

Yanagibashi Fish Market is a great way to enjoy the port city's finest seafood, including sashimi, amberjack, tuna, cod roe and squid. A hearty seafood stew, a traditional food for fishermen, is a fortifying delight.

Hakata is famous for its ramen (p. 123). *Tonkotsu* ramen alone is worth the trip, a creamy broth, indulgent but simple, with perfect noodles in a piquant and pungent mix. The *karaage* (fried chicken; p. 118) offers a chunkier experience, with hunks of chicken smothered in a glorious wheat-flour batter.

The *yatai* food stalls serve up the area's specialties: *tonkotsu* ramen, *gyōza* and *tonkatsu* (crumbed pork cutlet; p. 136). The city is also known for *mentaiko* (spiced and salted cod roe), which is added to rice balls or, most famously, pasta. *Motsunabe* is the gourmet adventurer's choice, a *nabe* hotpot with tripe, cabbage, garlic and chives in a soy or miso broth (p. 119).

Gyokuro tea, the finest grade of green tea in all of Japan, is produced in the Yame area south of Fukuoka. Asahi beer has a major factory in Hakata, and the area is also known for sake (visit the Meiji-era Ishikura Brewery Hakata Hyakunengura to find out why).

TRANSPORT

Tokyo Shinkansen to Hakata Station, about 5 hours. Or Tokyo airports to Fukuoka Airport, about 2 hours. Or Busan, South Korea, Camellia Line Kyūshū Beetle hydrofoil to Hakata, about 3 hour 30 minutes

CLOSE BY

Arita, Imari, Nagasaki

ATMOSPHERE

Loose, historical port city, shopping and food, canal district

REGIONAL FOOD & DRINK

Tonkotsu ramen, *karaage* (fried chicken), sake, *gyōza*

OMIYAGE

Anything with *mentaiko* (cod roe), Menbei crackers (squid/octopus and *mentaiko*), packaged ramen, Hakata Kajuen Ichigo Ichigo (strawberry and white-chocolate cookies), Tirolian (wafers filled with cream in matcha, strawberry, coffee and vanilla flavours)

TEMPLES & SHRINES

Kashii-gū, Tōchō-ji, Atago Shrine, Shōfuku-ji, Kushida Shrine

SIGHTS

Hakata Old Town, Canal City

GARDENS & PARKS

Chikuzen Sumioshi, Ohori Park, Maizuru Park

MUSEUMS & GALLERIES

Fukuoka Asian Art Museum, Fukuoka Art Museum, Fukuoka City Museum

VIEWS

Fukuoka Tower, Hakata Port Tower, Atago Shrine, Katae Observatory

ARTS & CRAFTS

Hakata dolls, *Hakata-ori* fabric

FESTIVALS

Dontaku Port Festival, Hakata Gion Yamakasa, Hojoya, Ebisu Festival, Tamaseseri Festival

WEB

yokanavi.com

TRANSPORT

Tokyo Shinkansen to Fukuoka (Hakata Station), then limited express to Arita, about 7 hours. Or Tokyo Haneda Airport to Fukuoka Airport; then limited express to Arita, about 1 hour 30 minutes

CLOSE BY

Fukuoka/Hakata, Nagasaki

ATMOSPHERE

Crafty, historical, village, tranquil

ONSEN

Imari Onsen Hakujinoyu

REGIONAL FOOD & DRINK

Imari beef curry, Saga beef, squid, *zarudōfu* (tofu made in a basket), miso soup with dumplings, *kakinohazushi* (persimmon-leaf-wrapped sushi)

OMIYAGE

Arita-yaki pottery, *Nabeshima-yaki* pottery, ceramics, porcelain

TEMPLES & SHRINES

Tōzan Shrine

SIGHTS

Okawachiyama Village, Arita Porcelain Park, Nabeshima Clan Kiln Bridge

GARDENS & PARKS

Nabeshima Hanyo Park

MUSEUMS & GALLERIES

Kyūshū Ceramic Museum, Nabeshima Ware Exhibition Hall, Imari-Arita Ware Traditional Crafts Center

ARTS & CRAFTS

Pottery, ceramics, porcelain

FESTIVALS

Ceramics Fair, Sarayama Festival

WEB

aritaporcelainlab.com

Arita & Imari

SAGA PREFECTURE

Arita and Imari are amongst Japan's most famous towns for pottery, porcelain and ceramics. Their history goes back more than 400 years, giving them a legitimate claim to being Japan's first area to produce porcelain (the discovery of kaolin mineral deposits led to porcelain becoming the main product of this region). Craft and pottery fanatics make the pilgrimage to the area to experience the centuries of mastery that continue to produce beautiful bowls, cups and plates. Arita was the centre of production, Imari the port where the wares would be taken out into the big wide world.

Okawachiyama Village (or 'Village of the Secret Kilns') is a quaint town inland from Imari where you can still experience old-world porcelain production. Around thirty porcelain stores line the main street, and many of them still have their famous tall kiln chimneys. The gentle town features the Nabeshima Clan Kiln Bridge, the Imari-Arita Ware Traditional Crafts Center and the Nabeshima Ware Exhibition Hall.

If you want to worship pottery and porcelain, head to Tōzan Shrine, which features an actual *torii* gate (p. 333) made from *Arita-yaki*, the name for local pottery. Many examples of the craft can also be found at the shrine. Other pottery-based sites in the region include the Kyūshū Ceramic Museum, which has an extensive selection of porcelain for the enthusiast. There is even a pottery 'theme park', Arita Porcelain Park, a re-creation of an eighteenth-century German-style village with ceramic wares on sale.

ABOVE: Arita Ceramics Fair

Yufuin

ŌITA PREFECTURE

Yufuin is often referred to as the 'back of Beppu', the back garden as it were, where people stroll, soak in hot springs and eat local food. The atmosphere is relaxed, the pace is deliberately slow (although less so on weekends and holidays when daytrippers swarm up Yunotsubo Kaido, the main street).

From the enchanting old station, head in the direction of Mount Yufuin's two peaks. The central street is lined with souvenir shops and cafés. Swiss roll is the most popular cake (the P-roll is made from the finest Yufuin water). Croquettes, matcha soft-serve ice cream, semi-baked cheesecake, cheese and fruit are also high on the agenda. The *purin dora* is famous all over Japan, a *dorayaki* (pancake sandwich) with crème-caramel-like egg-custard pudding inside. Shops and small galleries with craft of varying quality might have some premium carved wooden toys and porcelain cups. Yufuin Floral Village is great for kids, an *Alice in Wonderland*–themed enclave with oodles of cute.

Don't miss the grounds of Onsen Musouen, where the restaurant serves up *onsen*-steamed foods. The 1970s café Ban Ban is another highlight, a wooden Shōwa-era (p. 42) building with stunning views and must-try crème caramels.

Serious gallery-hoppers will want to check out the Kengo Kuma–designed Comico Art Museum (p. 353), which features works by Takashi Murakami (p. 375) and Hiroshi Sugimoto and has a strong leaning towards contemporary art, manga, books and cinema. Kuso no Mori Artegio is a unique gallery in that all of its art is based around music, while charming Watakushi highlights famous Kyūshū artists.

TRANSPORT

Beppu Kyūshū Odan Kumamoto bus to Yufuin, about 1 hour. Or Beppu Kamenoi Bus to Yufuin, about 50 minutes

CLOSE BY

Beppu, Kurokawa, Mount Yufu, Ōita City

ATMOSPHERE

Tranquil, peaceful, relaxed, pastoral

ONSEN

Musouen, Baien, Tsuka no Ma, Sansuikan, Shitan-yu Public Bath

REGIONAL FOOD & DRINK

Swiss roll, *purin dora* (*dorayaki* with egg pudding), *kinsho* (beef and potato croquettes), soft-serve ice cream, dairy, sweets

OMIYAGE

Local craft, porcelain, wooden toys

TEMPLES & SHRINES

Bussan-ji, Tenso Shrine, Oogosha, Unagihime Shrine

SIGHTS

Rotenburo (outdoor hot springs), Mount Yufu-dake, Yunotsubo Kaido, Lake Kinrin

MUSEUMS & GALLERIES

Comico Art Museum, Kuso no Mori Artegio, Watakushi Museum

KIDS' YUFUIN

Yufuin Floral Village, Snoopy Café, Donguri no Mori (Ghibli Store)

FESTIVALS

Yufuin Film Festival

WEB

yufuin.or.jp

ABOVE: Crème caramel at Ban Ban

THIS PAGE: Kurokawa town centre OPPOSITE PAGE: Bijin no Yu

Kurokawa

KUMAMOTO PREFECTURE

Kurokawa is a 300-year-old *onsen* (hot springs) town reclining in the hills between Mount Aso, Beppu (p. 316) and Yufuin (p. 311). The area offers mountain hikes and plenty of verdant nature, but the main draw here is the extensive range of small and beautiful *onsen*, ensconced in the mountains some 700 metres above sea level.

Kurokawa has twenty-four different *ryokan* (traditional inns; p. 87) that line the river, a waterway fringed by abundant vegetation. Many of the *ryokan* have day-bathing options, so visitors who aren't staying can still make the most of the hot springs. Having said that, make sure to stay in Kurokawa if you can. It offers a good concentration of outdoor baths (some of the best in Japan), baths that overlook tumbling waterfalls, grotto baths, footbaths, baths that run through the middle of *ryokan* fed by rolling rapids, baths that gush water from steaming pipes, baths with eggs boiling in stone or wooden receptacles nearby, and baths that look lovingly out over the rushing Tanohara and Chikugo rivers. The best spots include atmospheric Ryokan Sanga, Yamamizuki, Yamabiko, Nanjyoen, Wakaba, Satonoyu Waraku, Takefue and Bijin no Yu (the women's beauty bath), but you really can't go wrong.

Igoita Zizo Hot Spring is a natural kitchen where people gather to cook food in the boiling waters. Food is provided or you can join the locals and bring your own. You can even drink the hot-spring water. It's all cash-based, with no ATMs, so make sure you're prepared.

TRANSPORT
Bus from Beppu to Kurokawa, about 2 hours 30 minutes

CLOSE BY
Kumamoto, Mount Aso, Nakadake Crater, Yufuin, Beppu, Ōita City

ATMOSPHERE
Mysterious, secluded, magical

ONSEN
Ryokan Sanga, Yamamizuki, Yamabiko, Nanjyoen, Wakaba, Satonoyu Waraku, Takefue and Bijin no Yu

REGIONAL FOOD & DRINK
Onsen eggs, *basashi* (horse meat), Aso beef, *shōchū* (sweet potato spirit), Yaki Mochi rice crackers, sake

OMIYAGE
Bath salts, Kumamon (town mascot) cider and *shōchū*, Kiyomasa Seika's ginkgo-leaf *senbei* (rice crackers), *onsen* towels

TEMPLES & SHRINES
Mangan-ji, Gentoku-ji, Yoko-ji

SIGHTS
Kurokawa Onsen Kawabata Night Market

GARDENS & PARKS
Mount Aso, Nakadake Crater, Kurokawa forest

MUSEUMS & GALLERIES
Kitazato Shibasaburo Museum (Aso)

VIEWS
Forest views from most outdoor baths

ARTS & CRAFTS
Pottery, patterned *furoshiki* (wrapping cloths)

FESTIVALS
Onsen Festival, Asa Picnic

WEB
kurokawaonsen.or.jp
kumamoto.guide/en

Cycling adventures

Japan is perfect for bike rides, whether you're in the city or the country. It's a way to get off the beaten track, discover local shops, shrines and eateries and get a little bit of exercise at the same time. You can rent a bike in Japan reasonably cheaply in four-hour increments. It's almost impossible to select just a few bike paths in this amazing country, as most cities in Japan are fantastic to get around on wheels. Here are a few of our favourites.

ASAHIKAWA ●
BIEI ●
FURANO
SAPPORO ●

NASU
NIKKŌ &
LAKE CHŪZENJI
KANAZAWA ●
TOKYO
KYOTO ●
OSAKA ● ● NARA
HIROSHIMA ●
MIHO BEACH
FUKUOKA ●

YAKUSHIMA

OKINAWA
↓

ARCHITECTURE, ONSEN, WATERFALLS & A LAKE

Where: Lake Chūzenji (Kantō; p. 178)

Access: The lake is 45 minutes by bus from Nikkō Station

Length: 25 kilometres around the lake (not including detours)

Time: Take a full day

Price: Daily fee (buy tickets at Nikkō Natural Science Museum)

Lake Chūzenji is one of our favourite places to visit in Japan. The Italian and British embassies were built here in 1928 and 1896 respectively, and both buildings are magnificent examples of East meets West. Cycle past Ryūzu Falls, Futarasan-jinja shrine, Kegon Falls and Chūzen-ji temple. Stop for a bath in Chūzenji Onsen at Nikkō Sansui, Oku Nikkō Hotel Shikisai, Chūzenji Kanaya Hotel or Nikkō Astraea Hotel, all of which have day rates. This is one of Japan's most beautiful spots in autumn, so if you're travelling at this time try an early morning or dusk ride to avoid the crowds.

A LEISURELY RIDE PAST TEA FIELDS & SHRINES

Where: Arashiyama, Kyoto, to Kizu, Nara (Kansai; pp. 245, 250)

Access: From Togetsukyo Bridge, Arashiyama

Length: 47 kilometres

Time: 4 hours (another hour or less to Nara)
Web: kyotoarashiyama.jp/about
www.sagano-kanko.co.jp/en/saga.php

History-rich Kyoto and Nara can keep your itinerary full for weeks if not months, but if you'd like to spend a quieter, more introspective day, this flat ride along a dedicated bike path, past machiya (traditional wooden townhouses, p. 342), tea fields and shrines, is a lovely way to do so. If you start this ride in Nara and end up in Arashiyama, visit the footbath at Randen-Arashiyama Station or Fufu-no-yu Onsen for a bit of R and R.

FOXES, FLOWERS, THE BLUE POND & HOT SPRINGS

Where: Round trip from Asahikawa Airport through Biei and Furano (Hokkaidō; p. 287)

Length: 155 kilometres

Time: 10–11 hours; allow 2 days

Types: Regular or electric bike

Web: hokkaido-cycling.en.visit-hokkaido.jp/course/normal.html

This is a two-day bike ride though some of Japan's prettiest countryside. Late spring, summer and early autumn are the best times to make this journey, as Hokkaidō is, of course, very cold in winter. If you only have a day, Biei has lots of bike rentals, and the ride from Biei to the Shirogane Blue Pond and Shirogane Onsen is just under twenty kilometres. Set aside a good amount of time for an onsen before jumping on your bike and heading back to Biei. As the whole course is for experienced bike riders, an electric bike could be a great solution if you're more in the beginner category.

· Incredible day-rate onsen in Biei: Taisetsuzan Shirogane Kanko Hotel, Yumoto Shirogane Onsen Hotel, Yamabe-no-Kazoku, Kokumin Hoyo Center, Morino Ryotei Biei, Shirogane Park Hills
Web: biei-hokkaido.jp/en/shirogane

TOKYO ON TWO WHEELS

· A ride around Yanaka (p. 172) – Tokyobike rentals
tokyobikerentals.com

· A ride around Meguro and Gakugei-Daigaku (p. 174) – Tokyobike rentals
claska.com/en/news/2012/11/claskabike-rental-by-tokyobike.html

· A ride around the Imperial Palace Gardens – Free Sunday rentals. Rent your bike from Exit 2 of Nijūbashimae Station

· A ride near Ginza (p. 166) – Tokyobike rentals
muji.com/jp/shop/service/bicycle_rental

OTHER AMAZING PLACES FOR A BIKE RIDE

· Miho Beach (Chūbu; p. 227)
· Nasu (Kantō; p. 191)
. Yanbaru (Okinawa; p. 326)
. Yakushima Island (Kyūshū; p. 325)

Beppu

Beppu, on the east coast of Kyūshū, is thermal and relaxed, a resort destination with *sentō* (man-made) and *onsen* (natural) hot-spring baths numbering in the hundreds. It's the 'flower' city – and this symbol is emblazoned on the colourful drain covers. It's also a port and beach town where you can catch a ferry across to Shikoku (p. 291), or just take the Yufuin no Mori train (p. 105) into the countryside – the best of both worlds. Beppu is one of Japan's less visited but must-do cities, offering incredible natural beauty, unique and delicious local food specialties and a user-friendly city centre.

Part of Beppu's charm is the pleasure of being able to waft from one small bath to the next to relax; another is Ritsumeikan Asia Pacific University bringing in a diverse range of national and international students. Its location also attracts workers from islands further afield, creating one of the most interesting population mixes in Japan.

Beppu is actually the second most volcanic place in the world (after Yellowstone in the US), and the Jigoku Beppu Hells are one of the area's main attractions. These eight hot-spring pools well up from the ground in a large geothermal park, a mix of boiling mud pits, geysers and coloured ponds that are amazing to look at but much too hot for bathing. Our favourite, Umi 'Sea Pond Hell', is a wonderful sky blue – it smokes and steams like an angry dragon and spews water into the air like a geyser. There's also a great gift shop, so stock up on bath salts. Other ponds include Chinoike, the 'Blood Pond Hell'; and Kamado, 'Cooking Pot Hell', and various other ponds have different hues due to the mineral content of the water. Elsewhere crocodiles lounge in their own hot-spring mud – seemingly immune to the extreme heat. You can walk all of the hells in forty minutes, or catch the local buses.

Beppu is also known for its art projects (p. 319), which periodically take over the town. Bamboo craft is big, especially intricate woven baskets, the area's specialty. Prices can be high – this is a very ancient and involved process – but a Beppu bamboo basket makes the perfect gift. The special thermal mud means that local pottery looks that extra bit earthier, rustic and unique.

The station has a pop-up produce market for local fruit and veg. The revered *kabosu* fruit, a type of lime that's sweeter than sharp, is used to flavour many things, including sake and *shōchū*, the distilled Japanese spirit akin to vodka. Steamed food is also a big deal here, and you haven't lived until you've eaten a meat bun steamed in volcanic waters or an egg (*onsen tamago*) cooked in the depths of a Beppu Hell. Sake, bath salts, *senbei* (crackers) and *wagashi* (traditional sweets steamed in the hot waters) are all unmissable. Tempura rarely uses meat, but Beppu has a tender and tasty specialty – the chicken tempura (p. 132). Plump and delicious, it makes an interesting counterpoint to *karaage* (fried chicken). →

OPPOSITE PAGE: Umi Jigoku (Sea Pond Hell) **ABOVE:** Steamed food at Jigoku Beppu Hells

TRANSPORT

Tokyo Shinkansen to Hakata Station; then Sonic train to Beppu Station, about 6 hours. Tokyo airports to Ōita Airport, about 90 minutes. Osaka ferry to Beppu, about 12 hours

CLOSE BY

Ōita City, Yufuin, Usuki

ATMOSPHERE

Relaxed, summery, holiday town

ONSEN

Takegawara, Hyōtan, Beppu Beach Sand Bath, Kannawa Mushiyu, Myoban

REGIONAL FOOD & DRINK

Kabosu (citrus), tempura chicken, onsen-steamed food, Iichiko *shōchū* (barley spirit made with *koji* fungi)

OMIYAGE

Takezaiku bamboo-weaving, bath salts, *Kabosu* products, *Onta-yaki* pottery

TEMPLES & SHRINES

Hachiman Asami Shrine, Usuki Stone Buddhas

SIGHTS

Jigoku Beppu Hells, Otobaru-no-Taki Falls, Mount Tsurumi (Beppu Ropeway)

GARDENS & PARKS

Minamitateishi Ryokuka Botanical Gardens

MUSEUMS & GALLERIES

The Beppu Project (p. 319)

VIEWS

Yukemuri Observatory lookout

ARTS & CRAFTS

Bamboo, pottery

KIDS' BEPPU

Rakutenchi Amusement Park (1929), Takasakiyama Monkey Park

FESTIVALS

Beppu Sea of Fire Festival, Beppu Hatto Hot Spring Festival, Usuki Bamboo Lantern Festival

WEB

enjoyonsen.city.beppu.oita.jp

BEPPU ONSEN

Beppu is dotted with adorable small hot-spring baths – an estimated 144 all up, both *onsen* (natural) and *sentō* (man-made) – each hot-spring source with its own unique water. The main areas have their own defined sources: Kamegawa Onsen, Beppu Onsen, Shibaseki Onsen, Kannawa Mushiyu Onsen, Myoban Yunosato Onsen, Horita Onsen, Kankaiji Onsen and Hamawaki Onsen. A true *onsen* fan would spend a few days visiting the springs in each area to enjoy their different water and atmosphere.

Onsen Takegawara ('Bamboo Tile') is an unmissable sight. The stunning early Meiji-era (p. 32) frontage makes for a perfect snapshot and the interior with its small baths will give you a very real taste of what a local *onsen* experience is like. The original building was constructed in 1879. Old-fashioned and local, it's an unmissable *onsen* experience. Have a sand bath (p. 329) – you're buried in volcanic sand up to your neck while wearing a kimono – for a deeply relaxing experience. They say it's brilliant for your skin.

Hyōtan is a bigger, popular place that does great food, where you can also try a sand bath. They have a *rotenburo* (outdoor bath) and an impressive waterfall *onsen* that acts as a water massage. Locals and visitors alike go here. The Suginoi Hotel is a sprawling monster that caters for tourists, a kind of abstract world where you can get lost in endless halls, play in various game zones, do karaoke or stroll the expansive grounds. Of course, don't forget to bathe in the spectacular 'infinity' hot spring perched on a rooftop, where you can soak away your cares while watching the steam waft over the distant city lights. There are myriad other baths throughout the hotel as well.

Hotel Shiragiku is the hotel time forgot, all 1970s decor and attentive service. The *onsen* are great as well, especially the outdoor bath, a vast hot spring under an open sky. The hotel also does a delectable *onsen*-steamed sesame or caramel pudding for afternoon tea.

In some places you also can drink the mineral waters, which are considered healing and restorative, as is breathing in the hot-spring steam from narrow pipes – especially good for a sore throat.

KANNAWA

Head further afield to delightful Kannawa. Stroll the old backstreets – then go higher up through the layers of hills if you want a view of the town steaming and smouldering from myriad pipes and wells that funnel the power of the volcanic waters into the various *onsen*. Fujiya Gallery Ryokan Hanayamomo is a beautiful Meiji-era *ryokan* (inn; p. 87) from 1899 repurposed into a café and craft shop, with exquisite bamboo and ceramic items. Don't miss the striking dark-wood roof beams, set beautifully against the white walls.

The surrounding area offers a wonderful walk brimming with Shōwa-era (p. 42) finds. Nearby Kokochi Café Musubino is an enchanting eatery beside a free *onsen*. Various *onsen* and *sentō* dot the streets, many with open windows – filling the area with laughter. Make a night of it and stay at the beautiful Yanagiya Guest House, or just float by for a piece of their famed chiffon cake.

LEFT: Steve entering Hell
ABOVE: *Onsen egg*

The Beppu art scene

RYOKO TASHIMA, CURATOR OF THE BEPPU PROJECT, BEPPU, KYŪSHŪ

Tell us a bit about the art scene in Beppu and what makes it unique.

There are many local art projects in Japan. The Beppu Project is a non-profit art organisation based in Beppu city. Beppu is known as one of the world's greatest hot-spring areas. We hope to develop local potential through art, and make more regional places attractive for the world.

What events do you put on?

Contemporary art festivals and art exhibitions in unique venues, such as:

· artworks on the wall of the public bath
· a performance event in a shopping arcade in Beppu City
· an exhibition in an underground arcade that was closed more than fifty years ago.

Other activities:

· organising apartments for the artists-in-residence program
· an exhibition and art-making workshop at a facility for the elderly and disabled
· using design and art ideas for branding Ōita souvenirs
· supporting local companies with marketing and raising their value.

How important is it for Ōita prefecture to support local artists?

I think it's important to provide an opportunity to appreciate artists at the same time as supporting them. Art stimulates our creativity. It's also useful for living daily life from a different perspective. We think art is a medium that promotes new ideas and new systems. We believe we can realise a prosperous society by providing art to the community through artist support, provision of art appreciation and large-scale exhibitions in public spaces (such as parks, department stores and train stations).

Tell us about some of your artists.

· Masamitsu Katsu is an artist who creates pencil drawings. He's been living in a Kiyoshima artist's apartment for ten years. His artworks are drawings based on his memories.
· Tomohiko Yukihashi is a fashion designer. Tomohiko is researching hot-spring dyeing, in which the color of the yarn changes depending on the mineral make-up of the hot spring.
· Ine Izumi is a painter whose artworks are based on experiences that involve space and the body, sessions with dancers and workshops.

Tell us about your store, Select Beppu?

Select Beppu is a curated shop opened in a renovated 100-year-old *nagaya* (row house). Downstairs there's a range of original products as well as works created by artists and artisans with connections to Beppu. Upstairs features a *fusuma* (room screen) painting by artist Michael Lin, allowing visitors to come into contact with art in the everyday.

ABOVE: Select Beppu *fusuma* (room screen) painting by Michael Lin

Kagoshima

Kagoshima City is overlooked by an astounding (and active) volcano, Sakurajima, which erupts 1000 times a year – although most eruptions can be graded from a puff of smoke to a semi-interested squirt of lava. In 2014, however, Sakurajima decided to make a personal statement, and the resulting lava flow actually attached the island volcano to the central land mass. You can now walk across the water from Kagoshima to the smouldering mountain, and then enjoy many of the steamed treats that are cooked under Sakurajima's imposing shadow. Chinese *shūmai* steamed buns are local delicacies that should not be missed.

Sakurajima at sunrise from Shiroyama Hotel Kagoshima

Many people don't venture this far south or can't handle the seven-hour-plus train journey from Tokyo, but it's about being prepared – grab a *bentō* and some booze, kick back and relax. Kagoshima has many treats, but the sight of the sun glinting on the horizon over Sakurajima's awe-inspiring peak is something you'll never forget. If you stay at a local hotel like Shiroyama Hotel Kagoshima, you can even bathe in hot springs while watching the sun come up behind Sakurajima. Shiroyama Observatory offers a premium Sakurajima view, while on Sakurajima Island you can 'dig your own *onsen*'. You can also soak your tired feet in the dockside Dolphin Port Footbath. →

TRANSPORT

Tokyo Shinkansen to Fukuoka (Hakata Station), then limited express to Kagoshima Chuo Station, about 8 hours. Or Tokyo airports to Kagoshima airport, about 2 hours

CLOSE BY

Yakushima, Ibusuki, Kirishima

ATMOSPHERE

Relaxed, tropical, volcanic

REGIONAL FOOD & DRINK

Satsuma *age* (dried fish cakes), *kurobuta* (black pork), matcha, *tsukemen* ramen, *onsen*-steamed food, *tobiuo* (flying fish), pomelos, *kame no te* ('turtle hand' barnacles), Satsuma *imo* (sweet potato), Kagoshima *shōyu* (sweeter than usual soy sauce), massive turnips

OMIYAGE

Satsuma *kiriko* glassware, Black Satsuma earthenware, Ōshima *tsumugi* textiles, *karukan manju* (sweet steamed buns), *shincha* and Sunrouge green tea, Meijigura *shōchū*, Kintsuba *wagashi*

TEMPLES & SHRINES

Terukuni Shrine

SIGHTS

Sakurajima Island and volcano, Sengan-en, Hirakawa Zoological Park (capybaras in their own *onsen*), Kagoshima Fish Market, Kagoshima Morning Market (farmers' market), Dolphin Port Footbath, dig your own *onsen* on Sakurajima Island

GARDENS & PARKS

Sengan-en, Shiroyama Park

MUSEUMS & GALLERIES

Museum of the Meiji Restoration, Kagoshima Culture Craft Village

VIEWS

Shiroyama Observatory lookout

FESTIVALS

Ohara Matsuri, Kagoshima Kinko Bay Fireworks

WEB

www.kagoshima-yokanavi.jp

> Kagoshima
> is the
> birthplace
> of tea
> production
> in Japan
> (along with
> Uji near Nara),
> and Kagoshima
> tea is truly
> top quality.

Don't miss the Satsuma pottery and Satsuma kiriko cut glass, both decorative and highly detailed, a tradition that stretches back more than 100 years. In a city with many standouts, the crowning jewel is Sengan-en (Isotei-en; pp. 349, 351), a garden and household built by the Shimazu clan in 1658. The grounds are extensive and replete with waterfalls, grottos, ponds, tropical gardens, and impressive flower and fruit plantings. The house is open to the public and affords a wonderful chance to see how the clan lived (the old bathroom is a gem). The portrait gallery of visiting dignitaries gives you a rare glimpse into Japanese international ties through the years.

Kagoshima's food palette is extensive. The Kagoshima Fish Market and Kagoshima Morning Market will introduce you to the wonderful seafood and produce of the area. Famed local dishes include Satsuma *age* (dried fish cakes), which can be plain, dipped in sauce or added to an udon soup. Meat-lovers should try the black pork (*kurobuta*), one of Japan's premium dishes, which is usually stewed or braised until tender and melt-in-the-mouth.

Fruit is also big in Kagoshima, and we don't just mean popular – the pomelos and mandarins (*mikan*) are larger and juicier than most (the impressive pomelo hang on the tree like yellow balloons) and add a deep and sweet flavour to drinks and sweets. Kagoshima is the birthplace of tea production in Japan (along with Uji near Nara; p. 151), and Kagoshima tea is truly top quality. Other local dishes include tempura *gane* (sweet potato) and chicken sashimi (*torisashi*), which is not dissimilar to carpaccio. *Kibinago* is silver-stripe herring unique to this region.

Kagoshima's flavourful ramen, the *tsukemen*, is a thicker, creamier soup that originated here. It's perfect accompanied by a *kobosu* (sweet lime) juice with a sly addition of *shōchū* (sweet potato vodka).

薩摩きんつば

薩摩きんつば

OPPOSITE PAGE: Sengan-en **THIS PAGE CLOCKWISE FROM TOP:** Giant fruit and vegetables on display; Double-decker Shinkansen *bentō*; Kintsuba *wagashi* at Sengan-en; Satsuma *age* (dried fish cakes) and *kurobuta* (black pork)

TRANSPORT

Bus from Kagoshima, about 1 hour; or bus from Kagoshima Airport, about 40 minutes

CLOSE BY

Kagoshima, Ibusuki

ATMOSPHERE

Spiritual, tranquil, volcanic

ONSEN

Kirishima Hotel, Shinyu, Sakura Sakura, Kirishima Yunotani Sanso, Myoken Onsen, Tajima Honkan, Kiraku Onsen

REGIONAL FOOD & DRINK

Shōchū (sweet potato spirit), soba, black pork, Sekihira mineral water

OMIYAGE

Morihata tea, Sakamoto no Kurozu *aman* (black rice vinegar)

TEMPLES & SHRINES

Kirishima Shrine

SIGHTS

Mount Karakuni, Hundred Year Sulfur Valley, Maruo-no-Taki Falls, Kareigawa Station

GARDENS & PARKS

Yaku National Park, Kirishima Shinwanosato Park, Shiohitashi Onsen Ryoma Park

MUSEUMS & GALLERIES

Uenohara Jōmon no Mori Exhibit Building

VIEWS

Mount Karakuni

FESTIVALS

Tenson Korin Kirishima Festival, Hatsu-Uma Festival

WEB

kirishimakankou.com/charms_en

Kirishima

KAGOSHIMA PREFECTURE

Japan's first Geopark, Kirishima is an exhilarating mix of rugged nature, cloudy light-blue sulfuric *onsen* (hot springs) and a stunning temple. A haven for *shinrin yoku* (forest bathing; taking a walk in the forest for its restorative benefits), Kirishima is the kind of Japan that seeps into your being, the ethereal world you dream about long after your visit is over. Hike in the mountains or walk in the countryside – there are plenty of standout sights.

Some of the best are the views of Sakurajima volcano (p. 320) from fields of azaleas blooming joyously in the warm climate. Steam billows from various vents in the charming township, where you can enjoy a soak in the many *onsen*, including some spectacular *rotenburo* (outdoor baths). The 'Hundred Year Sulfur Valley' has rich soil, which has led to the growth of some truly majestic cedars.

Steeped in history and mythology and flanked by spectacular Mount Takachiho-no Mine, Kirishima Shrine has been destroyed, moved and rebuilt – the latest incarnation is more than 300 years old. According to legend, the god Ninigi-no-Mikoto married a human and began the line of the Japanese royal family. Don't forget to pick up some of the local souvenirs, such as Morihata tea (premium and organic) and the famed *aman* or black rice vinegar. Culinary obsessives shouldn't miss the Tshubobatake, or 'field of vinegar jars' (literally a vast field of vinegar jars), before picking up some bottles of this dark, milder vinegar.

ABOVE: Kirishima *onsen* steam

Yakushima

KAGOSHIMA PREFECTURE

Used as a setting for Studio Ghibli's film *Princess Mononoke* (head to Shiratani Unsui Gorge for the exact locations), Yakushima has become something of a pilgrimage for intrepid nature-lovers as well as animation fans. The island is archetypical unspoilt Japan, a remote destination that can be reached only by ferry or hydrofoil, a lush, tangled forest of gnarled ancient tree roots, moss-covered stones and brightly coloured fungus sprouting from the damp bark on fallen logs. Some of the *Yakusugi* (Yakushima *sugi*, or cedar trees) are more than 1000 years old, making them shrines in their own right. There's a rumour that one tree is more than 7000 years old (Jōmon Sugi, estimated age between 2000 and 7000 years) – suffice it to say that you'll be hiking through ancient cedar trees in a World Heritage–protected forest. Locals charmingly say that it rains thirty-five days a month, so pack your gumboots.

The bountiful island also features tea fields, *onsen* (hot springs), waterfalls and abundant wildlife. Roaming deer, monkeys, butterflies and birds – including the rare whistling greenpigeon and the ruddy kingfisher – make for the perfect nature escape. Most people choose to circumvent the island's perimeter, a three-hour drive of approximately 135 kilometres, taking in sights as they go. Yakushima is also famous for its loggerhead turtles, who emerge to lay their eggs between the months of May and August. You can see the turtles by booking special guided tours in the summer months.

TRANSPORT

Kagoshima Toppy or Rocket hydrofoil to Yakushima, 2–3 hours

CLOSE BY

Kagoshima, Tanegashima

ATMOSPHERE

Remote, secret, forested, magical

ONSEN

Hirauchi Kaichu Natural Onsen, Yudomari Hot Spring

REGIONAL FOOD & DRINK

Ponkan and *tankan* (citrus fruits and juices), flying fish, sweet potato, *shōchū* (sweet potato spirit)

OMIYAGE

Koidamari ceramics and candles, ginger syrup, turmeric products, *tankan mochi*, *Yakusugi* (cedar) oil, Asence Wood Craft products, sea salt

TEMPLES & SHRINES

Yaku-jinja

SIGHTS

Onoaida Hot Spring, Hirauchi Kaichu Natural Onsen, *shinrin-yoku* (forest bathing) with macaques and deer, butterfly- and bird-watching, nighttime turtle-viewing

NATURE

Shiratani Unsui Gorge, Jōmonsugi World Heritage Site, Mount Miyanoura, Ohko Waterfall

FESTIVALS

Yakushima Goshinzan Festival

WEB

yesyakushima.com

ABOVE: Yakushima forest fairyland

Okinawa

Made up of 160 islands, it's astounding how far Okinawa is from central Japan – in fact it's as close to China as it is to Kagoshima City (p. 320). Okinawa has been shaped by its interesting history, most famously that it was the main location for the US Armed Forces, who occupied the island after the Second World War and remain stationed there – despite Okinawa not being under American rule since 1972. The climate is warm, the people are friendly and the cuisine is markedly different from that of the rest of Japan. The geography is volcanic, with bubbling hot springs and steaming geysers. The subtropical climate makes for warm beaches and abundant marine life. It's also the birthplace of karate, so make sure you catch a traditional karate demonstration.

Okinawa's capital, Naha, is on its largest island – Okinawa Island. Naha is home to Shurijo Castle, destroyed during the Second World War, rebuilt in the 1980s and still packing a punch. Okinawa Island also features Japan's best aquarium, Churaumi, which has one of the world's largest tanks, the Kuroshio Tank, used to house huge whale sharks and manta rays. The Peace Memorial Park commemorates the 1945 Battle of Okinawa, a long battle between the Allied forces and Japanese army in the Second World War in which both sides experienced horrific casualties.

The Yaeyama Islands (all twenty-three of them), known for their beautiful beaches and clear water, hold the distinction of being the remotest islands from Japan's mainland and both the most southern and most western inhabited islands in Japan. Taketomi Island is renowned for its preserved Ryūkyū Village, whose culture extends back to the fifteenth century. Iriomote Island, Yaeyama's largest, is covered in picturesque jungle, waterways and mangrove forests. Keep an eye out for the Iriomote *yamaneko*, an ultra-rare wild cat found only on the island. Ishigaki Island acts as a jumping-off point for many of the islands and as a result has more amenities. It also features many pristine beaches, but watch out for the deadly *habu* box jellyfish.

If you're looking for spectacular beaches, head to Miyako Island, where you'll find some of Japan's best – as well as aquatic activites such as snorkelling. The Kerama Islands are known for their white sand beaches, while Kume Island features the well-known Hatenohama Beach, a seven-kilometre-long white sandbar surrounded by blue water.

One of Okinawa's best-known foods is taco rice – not rice made from tacos but essentially taco-flavoured rice (p. 138). Whatever goes into a taco – minced beef, beans, cheese, lettuce – flavours the rice. The original was made in the 1960s by a chef wanting to recreate the favourite flavours of the US soldiers stationed at Okinawa. *Chikiagi*, very similar to the dried fish cakes of Kagoshima, is also popular in Okinawa. Okinawa soba (soba in more of a ramen soup) is popular served with the local Orion beer.

ABOVE LEFT & OPPOSITE PAGE: Naha RIGHT: Regional food at HOSHINOYA Okinawa

TRANSPORT

Tokyo Shinkansen to Kagoshima Chuo Station (change at Shin-Osaka or Hakata/Fukuoka), about 7 hours; then ferry from Kagoshima to Naha, about 25 hours. Or Tokyo airports (and other major airports) to Naha Airport, about 2 hours 30 minutes

CLOSE BY

Okinawan Islands

ATMOSPHERE

Tropical, warm, friendly, pristine beaches, volcanic

ISLANDS

Yaeyama Islands, Okinawa Island, Miyako Island, Kerama Islands, Kume Island

REGIONAL FOOD & DRINK

Taco rice, Orion beer, Blue Seal ice cream, *mimigā* (pig's ear), *umibudo* (seaweed), *gōya chanpurū* (tofu stir-fry), Okinawa soba, *tofuyo* (fermented tofu), *chikiagi* (dried fish cakes), Spam, *hirayachi* (Okinawan pancake), *jushi* (rice soup), *rafute* (shōyu and pork), salted ice cream, *awamori* (long-grain rice alcohol), *chinsuko* (lard biscuits), pineapples, brown sugar, goat sashimi

OMIYAGE

Shisa statues and sheet masks, Orion beer, Hi-Chew candy, *chinsuko* biscuits, Benimo Tart, Okinawa dried soba, *sata andagi* (deep-fried buns)

FESTIVALS

Hari Festival, Eisa Dance Festival (p. 59), Miyakojima Panto Festival, Shuri Castle Festival, The Great Tug of War, Naha Hari Boat Race, Mushaama Harvest Festival

STAY

HOSHINOYA Okinawa channels the area's *gusuku*, ancient stone castles, whose walls surround the complex. Local culture is brought to life through decorative *bingata* wallpaper and with local produce served on the area's famous lacquerware.

WEB

visitokinawa.jp

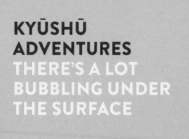

KYŪSHŪ ADVENTURES
THERE'S A LOT BUBBLING UNDER THE SURFACE

KONAGAI

These fruit-motif bus shelters in Nagasaki prefecture really have 'a peel' ... the sixteen shelters line a sixteen-kilometre strip along the Ariake Sea coast. Originally made for the 1990 Osaka World Expo Park, the pieces were considered too unique to scrap and were shipped across to the west coast, where you can wait patiently for your bus in a watermelon, strawberry, tomato, orange or that other one, possibly a honeydew melon. Waiting for a bus in these colourful, whimsical, humorous, picture-worthy shelters will be a ripe and juicy experience.

SASAGURI KYUDAI FOREST

Just north-east of Fukuoka you'll find Sasaguri 'Forest of Kyūshū' University, a location that epitomises the experience of forest bathing (*shinrin-yoku*; taking a walk in the forest for its restorative benefits). The forest circles Rakuusho Pond – its famous for the bald cypress trees (called *rakuusho*), which seem to walk on the water, their thick wooden skirts tickling the surface. The rare metasequoia redwood is also a standout feature.

FUTAGO-JI

Mount Futago hosts this Tendai Buddhist temple, established in 718 AD and secreted in lush forests. Treasures include a wooden statue of Amida, the celestial Buddha, that dates as far back as the late Kamakura period (p. 20), a *raigō* painting of the Amida Buddha on a floating cloud, and several stone masks, one dating back to 1618. Apparently, if you traverse the bridge of stone as a heretic, you will become an instant believer.

NAGASAKI

A foreign-trade port, Nagasaki is of major historical importance and this is reflected in its port towns and fishing villages (like Jumbo) to this day. Of course it's also the city on which the Americans dropped the second atomic bomb, and this looms large over the culture of the

area. A permanent memorial is set up at the Nagasaki Peace Park, a companion to the Hiroshima Peace Memorial Park (p. 265), another contemplative space that features a museum and the one remaining pillar of the original Urakami Cathedral. The Memorial Hall is a masterclass in brutalist architecture that promotes peace through a wonderful interplay of light and water.

People also visit Nagasaki to take the guided tour of Gunkanjima (formerly Hashima) Island, or 'Battleship Island', a ghost island that was once home to 5000 people. This eerie, crumbling space famously featured in the James Bond film *Skyfall*. You can take boat tours, immerse yourself in the creepiness, and view the top of the infamous 'stairway to hell' down to the undersea coalmines.

ONTAYAKI POTTERY VILLAGE

A true slice of old Japan, Onta has been a destination for pottery enthusiasts since the eighteenth century. Despite being one of the main hubs for the Japanese Mingei (folk arts) movement, one of its most famous potters was an Englishman, Bernard Howell Leach. Stroll around town and visit charming water channels, rows of old kilns (still family-run and -owned), and potters working away at the wheel, intricately glazing and firing the ceramics.

ŌITA CITY

Born as recently as 2005, this love child of two smaller towns, Saganoseki and Notsuhara, is the perfect jumping-off point for most of Kyūshū's pearls: Beppu, Yufuin, Ibusuki, Kirishima, Kagoshima and the Seto Inland Sea. It's surprisingly large and infused with the warmth of the south. Renowned for its wheat *shōchū*, a vodka-like spirit (p. 147), Ōita has many craft *shōchū* distillers. The regional Bungo-gyu beef has plenty of fat and a soft texture.

Ōita City is home to the stunning Ōita Prefectural Art Museum (OPAM), which highlights local artists.

IBUSUKI

Sometimes called the Satsuma Peninsula, Ibusuki is a hot-spring bathing resort south of Kagoshima (p. 320). There are many good *onsen* here, including 'Healthy Land', which has stunning views from large outdoor baths. Ibusuki's main drawcard is the sand-bathing, and the Saraku Sand Bath Hall is Japan's largest and best known sand-bathing facility. Put on a *yukata* (casual summer kimono), then be buried lengthwise in volcanic sand, with just your head peeking from the earth. The hot steam from the volcanic underground warms your body like a sauna. Its benefits are said to be more potent than the hot springs.

The history of the area around Kagoshima dates back to the early Meiji era in the late 1800s (p. 32), when it was known as Satsuma. The Satsuma Denshokan Museum showcases one of the area's other famous exports, Satsuma pottery.

KUMAMOTO

A city in Kyūshū's west, Kumamoto is distinguished by a huge fortress. The grounds are vast and the buildings date back to 1607, although many of them are now reconstructions, due to battle, fire and earthquake. Despite this, Kumamoto Castle has all of the major buildings, extensive grounds and gardens, and 800 cherry trees to be enjoyed during Hanami (p. 80).

The opulent Honmaru Goten Palace is a must-visit that offers, thanks to a very faithful reconstruction, a rare chance to see how ornate a castle interior would have been at the time. Kumamoto also boasts the delightful Suizen-ji Jōju-en garden (p. 329) and the Hosokawa Residence, once the home of the legendary Hosokawa samurai clan. The city's location makes it a pivotal town from which to 'bus-hop' for a bit of hiking on Mount Aso, or to visit Kurokawa (p. 313) for a soak before heading to Yufuin (p. 311) and Beppu (p. 316).

OPPOSITE: Konagai bus shelter, Nagasaki

文化

CULTURE

BELIEFS & RELIGION

——— Shinto and Buddhism have a peaceful relationship, and many Japanese people worship elements of both religions and schools of thought. Shinto, the first and central set of beliefs in Japan, is more than 2000 years old, followed by Buddhism (and its different schools of thought), which was introduced from Korea and China in the mid-sixth century AD.

Shinto (*Kami-no-Michi*) – often called a way of life, not a religion – is practised by more than eighty per cent of Japanese people. Without a founder, ancient texts or scrolls, its beliefs focus on purity, harmony, a person's place in society, respect, fertility, wellness and nature. Deities (*kami*) inhabit each Shinto shrine, and are visited and worshipped for specific purposes and reasons. *Kami* are deeply connected to nature and often inhabit incredible natural treasures, such as Mount Fuji (p. 222), Meoto Iwa (the Wedded Rocks in Ise; pp. 260, 335), animals, trees and waterfalls.

BELOW: Detail from Mount Kōya, Kansai OPPOSITE PAGE TOP: Kami at Izumo Taisha, Izumo, Chūgoku BOTTOM: Detail from Shimogamo Shrine, Kyoto, Kansai

SHINTO

HOW TO PRAY AT A SHINTO SHRINE

1. PURIFICATION FOUNTAIN
Purify your hands and mouth at the fountain near the shrine's entrance. With the ladle, fill your cupped hands with water and rinse. Then fill your hands with water and rinse out your mouth, discarding the water next to the fountain. Don't drink directly from the fountain. This symbolic getsure is part of a cleansing ritual called *okiyome*.

2. OFFERING HALL
Put a coin in the box then ring the bell to let the *kami* know you're visiting. Bow twice then clap your hands twice. Say a prayer, then bow again.

3. ON THE WAY OUT
Buy a small wooden plaque (*ema*) and write your prayer on it, hang it with the others so the *kami* can read it. Pick up a charm (*omamori*) when leaving to take your good luck home with you.

INTERESTING FACTS

· Spirits, good and evil, and ghosts are all part of Shinto beliefs.

· The Emperor is believed to be a descendant of the Shinto sun goddess, Amaterasu.

· The imperial family perform their own set of Shinto rites.

· Shinto priests may purify a new building or business to rid it of evil spirits.

· *Noh* theatre (p. 363) has its origins in Shinto beliefs.

· Small Shinto shrines are part of many homes. Foods, including rice and fruit, and drinks such as sake are offered to the *kami* (deities).

· Every child born in Japan is added to a list at the local Shinto shrine.

· Shinto festivals include Hatsumōde (the first shrine visit of the Japanese New Year; p. 75), Obon Matsuri (the festival to honour ancestors; p. 61) and Setsubun (the celebration before the first day of spring; p. 74).

TORII GATES
Marking the threshold from the ordinary to the sacred, these can appear as a single gate or there can be dozens or even thousands. Many are painted orange, but they can be black or white, or the colour of their natural materials, such as stone or wood.

RITUALS AT A SHINTO SHRINE
Visiting a Shinto shrine if you're unwell is a sign of impurity. Dress respectfully and keep your voice low. People will be praying for all sorts of reasons, so be respectful and help to maintain a peaceful shrine atmosphere.

OUR FAVOURITE SHINTO SHRINES

FUSHIMI INARI SHRINE, 711 AD (KYOTO, KANSAI; P. 243)

KAMI: INARI ŌKAMI

Hundreds of orange *torii* gates (p. 333) winding their way around the landscape of Fushimi Inari are what make this shrine one of Japan's most visited. Visit at dusk or dawn – the crowds in the middle of the day can become too intense. There are many Inari shrines around Japan, identifiable by *kitsune* (fox; p. 339) statues wearing red bibs. The fox is the carrier of rice, and legend has it that foxes love to eat fried tofu, so around these shrines you'll find many a store selling *inari* sushi (a pocket of fried tofu stuffed with rice) or *kitsune* (fox) udon (noodles in broth topped with fried tofu).

inari.jp

THIS PAGE: Izumo Taisha, Izumo, Chūgoku
OPPOSITE: Hakone Jinja, Hakone, Kantō

FUTENMA SHRINE, 1450 (FUTENMA, OKINAWA; P. 326)

KAMI: MEGAMI AND KUMANO

This is the only cave shrine we know of in Japan, and it really is something to behold. You can enter the caves for thirty minutes or join a guided tour.

okinawatravelinfo.com

HAKONE JINJA, 757 AD, RELOCATED 1667 (HAKONE, KANTŌ; P. 184)

KAMI: NINIGI-NO-MIKOTO, KONOHANASAKUYA-HIME, HŌRI-NO-MIKOTO

Sitting proudly on the shores of Lake Ashi, at the base of Mount Hakone – with Mount Fuji (p. 222) mysteriously appearing (if you're lucky) in the background – this forest shrine makes a perfect daytrip from Tokyo (p. 162). Line up to get your photo taken overlooking the sea.

www.hakonenavi.jp

ISE JINGŪ, 4 BC (UJI-TACHI, KANSAI; P. 261)

KAMI: AMATERASU

It's a toss up as to whether Ise Jingū or Izumo Taisha (opposite) is Japan's first shrine, but let's not get hung up on the details – they're both incredible and well worth visiting.

isejingu.or.jp

ITSUKUSHIMA-JINJA, 593 AD (MIYAJIMA, CHŪGOKU; P. 272)

KAMI: SANJOSHIN OR 'THREE FEMALE DEITIES'

This UNESCO World Heritage–listed site is one of the most impressive shrines you'll see in Japan. Set in the waters just off the island of Miyajima, the large orange *torii* gate (p. 333) is washed by the tides, while deer roam the shores.

en.itsukushimajinja.jp

IZUMO TAISHA, 700s AD (IZUMO, CHŪGOKU; P. 271)

KAMI: ŌKUNINUSHI NO OKAMI

Sometimes called the oldest shrine in Japan, Izumo Taisha, fittingly, has the founder of Japan as its *kami*. Visited regularly by the imperial family and many devoted Japanese people, this shrine is not only important but also incredibly beautiful. Its impressively large straw rope (*shimenawa*) and picturesque grounds make for a special day out.

www.kankou-shimane.com

MEOTO IWA (WEDDED ROCKS), 1910 (ISE, KANSAI; P. 260)

SYMBOLIC REPRESENTATIONS: IZANAGI AND IZANAMI

Two 'married' rocks. They are connected by a straw rope (*shimenawa*), which is replaced three times per year, and visited by thousands of people, including many couples who believe the rocks will bring good fortune to their relationship. Beautiful at dusk.

NIKKŌ TŌSHŌ-GŪ, 1617 (TOCHIGI, KANTŌ; P. 178)

KAMI: TŌSHŌ DAIGONGEN

Dedicated to the powerful shogun Tokugawa Ieyasu, this highly decorative and masterfully crafted shrine makes for a great daytrip from Tokyo (p. 162) or a nearby *ryokan* (traditional inn; p. 87) with an *onsen* (hot spring). Nikkō's shrines and temples are categorised as a UNESCO World Heritage Site (p. 181).

toshogu.jp/english

SUWA SHRINE, 1500s, REBUILT 1648 (NAGASAKI, KYŪSHŪ; P. 329)

KAMI: SUWA-NO-KAMI

This beautiful wooden shrine is home to the Nagasaki Kunchi festival, one of the three biggest festivals in Japan, held every autumn.

osuwasan.jp

BUDDHISM

INTERESTING FACTS

· There are 1600 Buddhist temples in Kyoto (p. 234).

· There are many different Buddhist sects, the four most popular in Japan being Pure Land (Jōdo) , Nichiren, Shingon and Zen.

· Sixty per cent of Japanese homes have a small Buddhist shrine.

· The Meiji government (p. 32) sought to eliminate Buddhism in favour of Shintoism (p. 333).

· Many amazing examples of Buddhist temples can be seen at Nara (p. 250), Kyoto (p. 234) and Mount Kōya (p. 259).

· The tea ceremony and meditation have their roots in Zen Buddhism.

· The Obon (p. 61) or Bon festival is an important Buddhist festival for remembering the dead.

GARDENS

Zen gardens (p. 348) are some of the most beautiful gardens in the world. These dry gardens of raked stones, perfectly placed rocks, beauty and minimalism are designed to be viewed from a fixed point for meditation. They are a completely different way of seeing a garden space, as both religious and natural.

SHODŌ

Shodō – 'the way of writing' – is Japanese calligraphy, a practice that turns pictorial characters into art. Like ikebana (flower-arranging; p. 350) and the Japanese tea ceremony (p. 151), shodō is deeply connected to Buddhism, and is still practised by Buddhist monks.

You can take calligraphy classes all over Japan. Our favourites are at Saihō-ji, Koke-dera (Kyoto, Kansai; p. 337) and the temples in Mount Kōya (Kansai; p. 259). Check online for temples offering calligraphy classes. eng.shukubo.net/experiences.html

TIERED PAGODAS (TŌ OR BUTTŌ)

A tall tower used to house or enshrine sacred texts, relics and the remains of important people, pagodas can have a variety of different tiers. A five-tiered pagoda has a floor for each of the elements: earth, fire, water, wind and heaven (or sky). Tiered pagodas do not appear at Pure Land or Zen temples. Odd numbers of tiers (three, five and seven) are popular.

WHERE TO SEE THEM

MOUNT KŌYA, KANSAI
Kongōsanmai-in Pagoda, 1223

Tōtō, East Pagoda, and Saitō, West Pagoda, 1127

NACHI-KATSUURA, KANSAI
Seiganto-ji (p. 261)
Stunning three-tiered pagoda with a waterfall backdrop on the UNESCO World Heritage List found on the Kumano Kodō Pilgrimage Route (p. 230).
nachikan.jp

KYOTO, KANSAI
Koyasu Pagoda, Kiyomizu-dera, 1633 (Higashiyama; p. 239)

Tō-ji Pagoda, 826 AD (Kyoto Station area; p. 236)

Yasaka Pagoda, Hōkan-ji, 592 AD (Higashiyama; p. 239)

NARA, KANSAI
Kōfuku-ji Pagoda, 700s AD (p. 250)

Murō-ji Pagoda, late ninth century AD (Uda)

ZEN MEDITATION (ZAZEN)

Meditation is a core belief in Zen Buddhism, used for mindfulness and wellness, and as a path to enlightenment. This practice has been adopted in the West as a way to de-stress and put life in perspective.

WHERE TO EXPERIENCE IT

RINNŌ-JI (SENDAI, TŌHOKU; P. 195)
Free lessons on Saturdays.
hisgo.com/us/destination-japan/miyagi/rinnoji_temple.html

SHUNKOIN TEMPLE (ŌITA, KYŪSHŪ; P. 329)
Rinzai sect meditation retreat.
shunkoinzentemple.blogspot.com

SHUNKOIN (KYOTO, KANSAI; P. 234)
Lessons daily and you can stay overnight.
shunkoin.com

TOKYO (KANTŌ; P. 162)
tokyomeditation.com

BUDDHIST TEMPLES

HŌRYŪ-JI, 607 AD (NARA, KANSAI)
UNESCO World Heritage Site (p. 181) housing the remains of the oldest wooden structure in the world.
horyuji.or.jp

KINKAKU-JI, 1397, AND GINKAKU-JI, 1460 (KYOTO, KANSAI; P. 234)
The Gold and Silver Pavilions.
www.shokoku-ji.jp

NANZEN-JI, 1291 (KYOTO, KANSAI)
Complete with a tea room, aqueduct and two gardens at one end of the Philosopher's Path (p. 239).
nanzen.net

SAIHŌ-JI, KOKE-DERA, 729–749 AD (KYOTO, KANSAI)
The moss temple (p. 246).
Reservation by mail is mandatory.
saihoji-kokedera.com

TŌDAI-JI, 728 AD (NARA, KANSAI)
One of the oldest Buddhist temples in Japan (p. 251).
todaiji.or.jp

GIANT BUDDHAS (DAIBUTSU)

FUKUOKA BUDDHA (SHAKA NEHAN), NANZO-IN, 1899 (SASAGURI, KYŪSHŪ; P. 307)

DEITY: BIRUSHA
SECT: SEVEN GODS OF FORTUNE

At this UNESCO World Heritage Site, there's a reclining Buddha, originally located at Mount Kōya. It is the largest bronze statue in the world.
nanzoin.net

KAMAKURA DAIBUTSU, KŌTOKU-IN, 1252 (KAMAKURA, KANTŌ; P. 177)

DEITY: AMIDA NYORAI
Sect: Pure Land (Jōdo) Buddhism
An easy daytrip from Tokyo.
kotoku-in.jp

NARA DAIBUTSU, TŌDAI-JI, 1252 (NARA, KANSAI)

DEITY: BIRUSHANA-BUTSU, VAIROCANA BUDDHA
Sect: Kegon (Huayan)
Located in the Great Buddha Hall (Daibutsuden; p. 251).
todaiji.or.jp

SHŌWA DAIBUTSU, SEIRYŪ-JI, 1984 (AOMORI, TŌHOKU; P. 198)

DEITY: VAIROCANA BUDDHA
SECT: SHINGON
Japan's tallest seated bronze Buddha.
en-aomori.com/culture-049.html

OPPOSITE PAGE: Monks at Kiyomizu-dera, Kyoto, Kansai

CULTURAL
ICONS

DARUMA

The *daruma* doll is based on the Bodhidharma, the Buddhist monk who founded Zen Buddhism. This rotund, decorated, slightly angry-looking doll can be found in most souvenir shops in Japan, and in abundance around Takasaki Station and at the Shōrinzan Daruma-ji shrine in Takasaki (p. 188).

A symbol of good luck and perseverance, the doll you see today is likely based on the 1887 woodblock by Tsukioka Yoshitoshi. Primarily red, *daruma* dolls can come in pink, and the stripes can be yellow rather than gold. The eyebrows are often in the shape of a crane, with cheeks like the shell of a tortoise – both animals being symbols of longevity in Eastern culture. Female *daruma* are Princess Daruma and Lady Daruma.

Daruma otoshi is a well-known game where a hammer is used to hit blocks out from a stack under a *daruma* head without toppling the doll from its perch. *Daruma* dolls are so popular that Japanese children make snow *daruma* instead of snowmen.

The Russian matryoshka doll was inspired by the *daruma* – the original version being based on the Japanese 'Seven Lucky Gods' stacking doll, a variant of the *daruma*.

WHERE TO SEE DARUMA
· Takasaki, Kantō (p. 188)

JIZŌ (OJIZŌ-SAMA)

Representing a 'Bodhisattva' (Buddhist pilgrim who is yet to attain enlightenment), the Jizō are tiny clustered statues you'll see when temple-hopping in Japan. They frequently wear a small red apron or bib and their primary purpose is the protection of children – they are the guardians of children and the gods of deceased children. Jizō are based on Kşitigarbha, a Buddhist monk whose name translates to anything from 'Earth Treasury' to 'Earth Womb'. Delving more deeply, they represent a deity who vowed never to achieve enlightenment until all the seven hells were emptied. They have a lot of work to do.

Jizō depict a shaven-headed Buddhist monk with a staff, usually with a jewel to cast a heavenly light into the dark pits of hell once its gates are prised open. The mini Jizō come in various forms. The Brahmin Maiden, the main manifestation of this deity, will appear with a scarf wrapped around her head. A defender of a kind of children's purgatory, she'll fend off demons carrying iron clubs and keep children safe while they make their way from this world to the next.

WHERE TO SEE JIZŌ
· Arashiyama (p. 245) and Eifukuchō (Kyoto, Kansai)

KITSUNE

This is the Japanese word for 'fox', and you'll find *kitsune* figures dotted all around Japan. There are more than 1000 shrines dedicated to the fox (visit them all!), ranging from small shrines to bigger complexes like the famous Fushimi Inari Shrine in Kyoto (p. 243), where you'll come across various shrines to the fox as you walk along the corridors of *torii* gates. The shapeshifting beings can be seen as tricksters (*yako*) or benevolent creatures (*zenko*). They also love a bit of tofu – deep-fried, in fact – so shrines often have offerings of tofu and prayer plaques. *Kitsune* is also the Shinto god of rice, so the *inarizushi* is the perfect blend of fried tofu and sweetened rice (*oishii!*). *Kitsune* are also the spirits of tea and sake, so they're pretty important (and pretty busy). →

WHERE TO SEE KITSUNE
· Fushimi Inari Shrine, Kyoto, Kansai (p. 243)
· Hase-dera, Kamakura, Kantō (p. 177)
· Makekirai-Inari, Ojiyama, Sasayama, Kantō

KOKESHI

A children's toy, crafted for more than 150 years, the *kokeshi* has long been one of the most recognisable icons in Japan. Originally made in the Edo period (p. 28), the *kokeshi* were souvenirs for people visiting the various *onsen* (hot springs) around the country, originating in the *onsen* of Tōhoku (p. 193). Their connection with *onsen* seems to stem from the fact that they were initially made by potters who used the fine water of the area to finesse their products. The dolls were possibly used as massage tools too.

Naruko Onsen (p. 204) has some claim to *kokeshi* fame. The Kokeshi Exhibition held there in 1939 helped cement the doll as an iconic figure in the public consciousness. The Naruko *kokeshi* is the best known of the *kokeshi* shapes – a geisha-like head perched atop the most basic of wooden bodies. The name itself comes from *ko*, most likely meaning 'small', or perhaps 'wood', and *keshi*, meaning 'doll'.

WHERE TO SEE KOKESHI

· Akita, Aomori, Fukushima, Iwate, Miyagi and Yamagata (Tōhoku region)
· Naruko Onsen (Tōhoku region; p. 204). The *kokeshi* doll is the symbol of the town. You'll find small makers, train-station displays, stalls and even *kokeshi* telephone and postboxes.

KOI

This spectacular member of the carp family and close relative of the goldfish can be spotted in ponds and ornamental gardens all over Japan. You will find them decorating the water features in restaurants as well, and even in many shopping centres. Now and then you'll find them 'in the wild' – easily the best way to see them. Koi is literally Japanese for carp, so if you say 'koi carp' you're saying 'carp carp'. *Nishikigoi*, or brocaded carp, are banded, brightly coloured ornamental gems, prehistoric-looking creatures gliding along a watery runway.

Ultimately what will astound you is their size: some of them are like tiny sharks but without the menace. The Japanese revere them, and keeping and breeding koi is a favourite hobby in Japan. Over the years they have become an indispensable part of the Japanese iconographic landscape, coming to symbolise luck, good fortune and prosperity. The origins of this are thought to go back to the 1820s in the Niigata prefecture (p. 226). The koi is a popular choice for a tattoo, as it also represents perseverance and strength (the koi swim against the current, showing resistance to social norms).

WHERE TO SEE KOI

· Most Japanese ornamental gardens and various restaurant grounds

MANEKI NEKO

The *maneki neko*, or 'lucky cat', is a potent symbol of luck in Japan. It is a talisman often used in shop windows, and you'll also find the cat adorning the counters of most lottery-ticket sellers and in many restaurants and bars (Jazz Bar Samurai in Shinjuku, Tokyo, has hundreds of them).

INTERESTING FACTS

· The right hand is usually up but this can vary.
· They can come in red, white, gold and sometimes blue.
· Pokémon Meowth is based on the *maneki neko*.
· They can be made out of many materials and into all sorts of trinkets, such as keyrings and money boxes.
· Its origins might lie in the cat-like supernatural creatures Bakeneko and Nekomata.
· There's a saying: *Neko ni koban*, meaning 'Gold coins before cats' (i.e. 'Pearls before swine').

WHERE TO SEE MANEKI NEKO

· Gōtoku-ji (Cat Temple), Tokyo, Kantō)
· Konoshima-jinja, Kyoto, Kansai
· Neko-no-Miya Shrine (Takahata, Tōhoku)
· Tashirojima (Cat Island), Nekojinja, Tōhoku – don't miss the cat shrine!

TANUKI

This extraordinary (and extra-cute) creature is known as the raccoon dog – because of its appearance as a cross between the two, although in truth it's a type of fox. The mythical version of this animal can be seen everywhere in Japan. If you spot a statue of a raccoon-shaped fellow holding a pitcher or flagon of booze, you'll know you're with the *tanuki*. He'll have a big hat, a big belly, a staff and yes, he has a large scrotum for all to see. He also carries a flask of sake and a 'promissory note'. Be careful (not just of the giant scrotum) – he's known to be a bit of a trickster. Perhaps this is why he's placed out the front of many bars and eateries across Japan, the message being 'Come inside and spend your money'. He's known as a monster or spirit, but when he shapeshifts into a humanoid character, he's more of a jolly fellow who will entice you into a good time.

WHERE TO SEE TANUKI
· A gigantic *tanuki* welcomes visitors to Mashiko, Kantō (p. 183)
· Out the front of *izakaya* (pubs; p. 117)
· See real *tanuki* in forests and some suburban streets (Steve saw one in Gakugeidaigaku, Tokyo!)
· Shigaraki Tanuki Village, Shigariki, Kansai
· Tanukidani-san Fudō-in Temple and Pontocho Tanuki Shrine, Kyoto, Kansai
· Yashima-ji, Takamatsu, Shikoku

TENGU

These severe-looking fellows with red faces and long noses are regarded as Shinto *kami* (deities) or as *yōkai* (supernatural beings). Early versions depict a kite-like being (kite as in bird of prey) while more recent ones have *tengu* as a crow. The beak becomes a long nose in human-like depictions.

Careful with these creatures. If you have committed the sin of arrogance or have damaged the forest (especially around Takao and Kurama mountains) you could find yourself with a longer (or even shorter) nose or dropped naked onto the nearby streets of the big city. Yes, *tengu* deal in odd punishments.

Appearing on Japanese scrolls as early as 1291 and mentioned in the *Nihon Shoki* chronicles of the eighth century, *tengu* became a potent symbol of their favourite mountain hideaways and will appear on all manner of *senbei* (rice crackers), local confectionery and souvenirs.

WHERE TO SEE TENGU
· Beppu (Kyūshū; p. 316) – A shrine can be found in the Yayoi part of town.
· Kurama (northern Kyoto, Kansai; p. 240) – The big *tengu* statue is hard to miss as you exit the station!
· Mount Takao (Kantō; p. 176) – The crow *tengu* is a symbol of this mountain.
· Mount Tengu (Hokkaidō) – This skiing destination is named after the mythical being.

OTHER LEGENDARY CREATURES

· *Ryuu* – The classic Japanese dragon.
· *Kappa* – A lecherous, vampiric, mischievous green water spirit. Thought to have taught humans the skill of setting bones. Loves sumo wrestling and cucumbers. Has a dish of water on its head.
· *Tsukumogami* – Animated tools or inanimate objects brought to life, such as the *Zorigami*, a living clock.
· *Yōkai* – A general term for ghosts, spirits and supernatural beings. Also known as *Akashi* or *Mononoke*. *Yūrei* are the more 'Western' style of ghost.
· *Oni* – The classic type of Japanese demon: red face, big fangs, clawed feet and very tall. They carry large clubs and appear often in theatre and fairy tales as the evil character.
· *Okuri-inu* – Ghostly dog that follows you. Don't trip! It will attack.
· *Ōnyūdō* – A giant.
· *Tennin* – Heavenly angel-like spirits.
· *Yōsei* – Creatures similar to fairies.

AND THERE ARE SOME QUITE, ERM, SPECIFIC ONES TOO:
· *Shirime* – A man-shaped spirit with an eye where his anus should be.
· *Uma-no-ashi* – A horse leg that hangs from a tree, kicking passers-by.
· *Ushi-onna* – A cow-headed woman in a kimono.

HISTORICAL BUILDING STYLES

KURA WAREHOUSES WITH NAMAKO WALLS

EDO PERIOD (P. 28)

WHY ARE THEY SPECIAL?

Wooden and earthen-plastered buildings in pale grey with tiles or latticed wood near the ground. The incredible layered windows (p. 224) are the thing that makes them so special. When we first saw one in Morioka (p. 200) we couldn't believe we'd found a style of building we'd never seen before. The buildings are fireproof and were used as warehouses for important or expensive things, so they are very secure.

WHAT TO LOOK FOR

· White and grey buildings with crisscrossed 'lattice' tiles at the bottom
· Rounded joints (*umanori* joints) resembling a sea cucumber (*namako*); the straighter ones are called *shihan* joints
· Shutter-style windows with 'stepped' edges that slot into a stepped outer frame

WHERE TO SEE THEM

· Chūbu – Nawate Dōri (Nagano); Matsumoto; Matsuzaki
· Chūgoku – Kurashiki; San'yō region (Okayama, Hiroshima and Yamaguchi)
· Kantō – Kawagoe; Setagaya Daikan Yashiki (Tokyo)

RECONSTRUCTED YAYOI-PERIOD HOUSES

JŌMON AND YAYOI PERIODS (P. 14)

WHY ARE THEY SPECIAL?

Sannai-Maruyama and the Yoshinogari Historical Park are built on the archaeological sites where all the historical evidence of life in the Jōmon and Yayoi periods was found. Both are a wonderful look at early Japan, and even more fascinating if you're a student of history.

WHAT TO LOOK FOR

· Thatched roofs
· Long, low housing
· Earthy and rustic materials
· Some houses are on stilts
· Teepee-like huts made with natural materials

WHERE TO SEE THEM

· Sannai-Maruyama (Aomori, Tōhoku; p. 198) *sannaimaruyama.pref.aomori.jp*
· Yoshinogari Historical Park (Yoshinogari, Kyūshū) Heian and Edo periods *yoshinogari.jp*

MACHIYA HOUSES

EDO PERIOD (P. 28)

WHY ARE THEY SPECIAL?

This is the Japanese architecture you see in pictures and movies. *Machiya* translates as 'townhouse' or 'town shop'. These wooden beauties have been renovated and restored as shops, hotels, Airbnbs, galleries and museums.

WHAT TO LOOK FOR

· Blackened or dark wood exterior walls on the ground floor
· An upper storey, if there is one, made of earth
· Large front door and small side door
· Long buildings with latticework at the front
· One, two or three storeys

WHERE TO SEE THEM

· Most cities unaffected by the Second World War or major natural disasters
· Yanaka, Nezu and Sumida areas in Tokyo (Kantō)

ABOVE: *Kura* warehouse with *namako* walls in Matsumoto, Chūbu

GASSHŌ-STYLE MINKA FARM HOUSES

EDO PERIOD (P. 28)

WHY ARE THEY SPECIAL?
Fairytale-like in appearance, these gorgeous *minka* (which means 'for the people' in Japanese) normally appear in clusters. Some of these villages are UNESCO World Heritage Sites and seen as treasures in Japanese society.

WHAT TO LOOK FOR
· Triangular (A-framed) houses with thatched gabled roofs almost to the ground
· An interior with a built-in hearth, a cooking area with tea pot hanging above

WHERE TO SEE THEM
· Shirakawa-go
(Shirakawa, Chūbu; p. 224)
UNESCO World Heritage–listed
ml.shirakawa-go.org/en
· Gokayama (Toyama, Chūbu; p. 226)
UNESCO World Heritage–listed
gokayama-info.jp
· Gero Onsen Gasshō Village
(Gero, Chūbu)
gero-gassho.jp
· Hida Folk Village
(Takayama, Chūbu; p. 224)
hida.jp

KAMAKURA (SNOW IGLOOS)

EDO PERIOD (P. 28)

WHY ARE THEY SPECIAL?
Candle-lit cute-as-a-button Japanese igloos.

WHAT TO LOOK FOR
· Distinctive shape and igloos en masse, glowing at night from candle-lit yellow lantern light
· A *kamakura* festival with street food and drinks to keep you warm

WHERE TO SEE THEM

TŌHOKU REGION
· Yokote Kamakura Festival (Yokote, Tōhoku) – mid-February (p. 75)
· Yunishigawa Onsen Kamakura Festival (Nikkō, Kantō) – late January to early March
travel.tochigiji.or.jp

HISTORICAL BUILDING EXPERIENCES

· Kura Warehouse Museum, Chiisana Kura no Shiryokan (Hinode, Tokyo, Kantō)
· Edo-Tokyo Museum (Tokyo, Kantō)
· Hakata Machiya Folk Museum (Fukuoka, Kyūshū)
· Japan Folk Crafts Museum, Mingeikan (Tokyo, Kantō)
· Gassho-zukuri Minkaen (Shirakawa, Chūbu; p. 224)
· Osaka Museum of Housing and Living (Osaka, Kansai)

ONSEN
· Funaoka Onsen (Kyoto, Kansai; p. 240)
· Takegawara (Beppu, Kyūshū; p. 318)
· Dōgo Onsen (Ehime, Shikoku; p. 302)

HOTELS & HOME STAYS
· Shirakawa-go farm house stays
japaneseguesthouses.com

· *Machiya* stays
machiya-hotel-kyoto.com

ABOVE LEFT: Gasshō-style *minka* farmhouse, Shirakawa-go, Chūbu

ABOVE RIGHT: Japan Folk Crafts Museum, Mingeikan, Tokyo, Kantō

お城

CASTLES

—— Thanks to samurai rule, feuding prefectures and the country's island geography, Japan has some of the world's most impressive castles. While there are ruins and writings about early castles from the 1100s, instability meant more and more structures were built from the 1600s onwards. Often sited on top of a hill, next to a river or looming large over their very own town, the castles were home to samurai politics, battle strategies and intrigues. After the Meiji Restoration in 1868 (p. 32), many were besieged and destroyed, and more were lost in the Second World War or in natural disasters. This means only twelve complete original examples are left standing in Japan today. Luckily, there are many great reconstructions and rustic ruins to visit if you're on a castle tour of Japan.

OUR FIVE FAVOURITE 'INTACT' CASTLES IN JAPAN

HIMEJI CASTLE

HAKURO-JŌ OR SHIRASAGI-JŌ,
1333–1618 (HIMEJI, KANSAI; P. 260)

Without a doubt, Himeji is Japan's best-loved, most-celebrated and most-visited castle. This extraordinary piece of history makes an easy daytrip from Kyoto, Osaka, Kobe or Okayama, and you won't be disappointed. Its chic white-plaster walls and position over the city have given it the nickname White Heron or White Egret Castle, as it's said to mimic a white bird taking flight.
city.himeji.lg.jp

INUYAMA CASTLE

INUYAMA-JŌ, 1440
(INUYAMA, CHŪBU)

This incredible wooden structure is perched high on a hill overlooking the Kiso River. Scaling the four flights of stairs to the castle is mandatory, as the views over the river and castle grounds are breathtaking. The grounds have more than 400 cherry-blossom trees that burst into glorious shades of pink each springtime. An easy daytrip from Nagoya or Gifu.
inuyama-castle.jp

MARUOKA CASTLE

KASUMI-GA-JŌ, 1576
(SAKAI, CHŪBU)

Legends have named Maruoka the Castle of Mist, as apparently upon attack it hid itself in a shroud of mist. The wooden architecture, stone steps and impressive cherry blossom trees in spring add to its allure.
www.maruoka-kanko.org

MATSUE CASTLE

CHIDORI-JŌ, 1611
(MATSUE, CHŪGOKU; P. 275)

This lakeside castle, complete with moat and blossom trees, is also called the Plover Castle, as it has been likened to a black seabird taking off over the water. Nearby you'll find Izumo Taisha (p. 270), Shoji Ueda Museum of Photography (p. 274) and the city of Tottori. (p. 275). This is a gorgeous lesser-known part of Japan.
www.matsue-castle.jp

MATSUMOTO CASTLE

KARASU-JŌ, 1594
(MATSUMOTO CITY, CHŪBU; P. 219)

Also called Crow Castle for its incredible black structure, this castle is built on a flat plane with the Japanese Alps as backdrop. It's a brilliant daytrip from Tokyo.
matsumoto-castle.jp

FAVOURITE RUINS & RECONSTRUCTIONS

- Kanazawa Castle, 1583 (Kanazawa, Chūbu; p. 214)
  www.pref.ishikawa.jp
- Kumamoto Castle, 1467 (Kumamoto, Kyūshū; p. 329) Don't discount the ruins!
  kumamoto-guide.jp
- Nijō Castle, 1603 (Kyoto, Kansai; p. 242)
  nijo-jocastle.city.kyoto.lg.jp
- Oka Castle, 1185 (Taketa, Kyūshū)
  welcomekyushu.com
- Takeda Castle ruins, 1441 (Asago City, Kansai)
  visitkinosaki.com

GARDEN
STYLES

TEA GARDEN (CHANIWA)

AZUCHI-MOMOYAMA PERIOD (P. 22)

WHAT IS IT?

The popularity and perfection of the tea house inside a garden came into its own in the late 1500s. A stone path, often lantern-lit with simple planting, weaves its way to a humble abode, a modest shrine to tea. Tea houses were designed to be rustic and unpretentious so that all could meet inside as equals. Small doors meant the samurai left his sword outside and the wealthy man's attire needed to be simple enough to fit into the room and be comfortable. The garden design focuses on the pathway made of stepping stones, so the tea drinkers can contemplate the ritual as they negotiate the steps.

WHY IS IT SPECIAL?

This was the start of wabi sabi, the perfect imperfect. Finery and perfection have no place in the design of the garden or the interior of the tea house.

WHAT TO LOOK FOR

The wavy or wonky path leading to the tea-house door.

BEAUTIFUL EXAMPLES

- Iho-an Tea House, Kōdai-ji (Kyoto, Kansai)
  www.kodaiji.com

- Jo-an Tea House, Urakuen Garden (Inuyama, Chūbu),
  m-inuyama-h.co.jp/urakuen

- Yūgao-tei, Kenroku-en (Kanazawa, Chūbu; p. 214),
  kanazawastation.com/ kenrokuen-garden

→

SHINDEN GARDEN

HEIAN PERIOD (P. 17)

WHAT IS IT?

Written about in *Genji Monogatari* (*The Tale of Genji; c. 1008; p. 17*), these gardens were made up of large ponds for boating, waterways with bridges, large gravel areas and beautiful plantings. As this garden style is so old, none remain intact, but you can visit the examples below for a little insight.

WHY IS IT SPECIAL?

It's the birth of the modern Japanese garden, a fusion of Chinese and local philosophy.

WHAT TO LOOK FOR

The vast pond, bridges and waterways.

BEAUTIFUL EXAMPLES WITH SOME ORIGINAL ELEMENTS

- Kyoto Imperial Palace Gardens (Kyoto, Kansai) – Built in the Edo period in the Shinden style
  www.env.go.jp/garden/kyotogyoen

- Osawa-ike pond, Daikaku-ji (Arashiyama, Kansai; p. 245)
  daikakuji.or.jp

PARADISE GARDEN (PURE LAND BUDDHIST GARDEN)

LATE HEIAN PERIOD (P. 17)

WHAT IS IT?

The Pure Land–style Buddhist garden aims to create a paradise on earth. These gardens all feature a large pond full of lotus, with a small island in the middle connected by a bridge. It was thought that Buddha could sit on the island, gaze out onto the beautiful lotus and meditate.

WHY IS IT SPECIAL?

Combining religion with nature, this garden concept from the twelfth century still looks contemporary.

WHAT TO LOOK FOR

Lotus, island/s and bridges.

BEAUTIFUL EXAMPLES WITH SOME ORIGINAL ELEMENTS

- Byōdō-in (Uji, Kansai; p. 249)
  byodoin.or.jp

- Mōtsū-ji Temple (Hiraizumi, Tōhoku)
  motsuji.or.jp

OPPOSITE: Kōraku-en, Okayama, Chūgoku ABOVE: Yugao-tei, Kenroku-en, Kanazawa, Chūbu

ZEN GARDEN (KARESANSUI OR DRY LANDSCAPE GARDEN)
KAMAKURA AND MUROMACHI PERIODS (PP. 20, 22)

WHAT IS IT?

Originating in China, Zen Buddhism was introduced to Japan in the twelfth century and flourished in the Kamakura period (p. 20). Zen temples were designed with small contemplative gardens, often surrounded by walls, and were thought to be best admired from a fixed viewpoint while sitting. The monks sought to translate nature's beauty and essence into dry gardens through abstraction and simplicity. These thoughtful spartan landscapes, consisting of rocks, pebbles and sometimes a small amount of moss or greenery, were the perfect environment for Zen meditation and general contemplation.

WHY IS IT SPECIAL?

The sand or small pebbles are raked to look like water, streams, rivers or ponds; large rocks can be arranged to look like islands or mountains; and sand can be perfectly moulded into shapes, such as the moon-viewing platform at Ginkaku-ji (Silver Pavilion, Kyoto; p. 239). Through the ages, Zen gardens have changed and evolved; two of the most beautiful examples are Tōfuku-ji's Zen garden (Kyoto; p. 243), designed in 1880, and the garden of the Adachi Museum (Yasugi, Chūgoku; p. 275), designed in 1980.

WHAT TO LOOK FOR

Take off your shoes and walk onto the porch-like structure (*hōjō*). Contemplate the way the rocks are placed, the waves in the stones, the patterns of leaves or flowers that fall on the dry garden. Try shutting your eyes and taking a few deep breaths to meditate on being in the here and now, then sit in a few different places to really take in the atmosphere.

BEAUTIFUL EXAMPLES

Nanzen-ji, Ryōan-ji, Tenryū-ji, Daisen-in, Kinkaku-ji and Ginkaku-ji (all Kyoto, Kansai; p. 234)

MODERN ZEN GARDENS

- Adachi Museum, 1980 (Yasugi, Chūgoku; p. 275)
- Canadian Embassy Garden, 1991 (Tokyo, Kantō)
- Tōfuku-ji (Kyoto, Kansai; p. 243) A new garden design after a fire in the 1930s

THIS PAGE: Adachi Museum, Yasugi, Chūgoku OPPOSITE PAGE: Kiyosumi Teien, Tokyo, Kantō

STROLLING GARDEN (DAIMYŌ GARDEN)
EDO PERIOD (P. 28)

WHAT IS IT?
When the samurai ruled Japan they created large gardens to strut and stroll around in. These were meticulously designed spaces with a path working its way around the garden in a clockwise direction. Each corner you turn a new delight or view awaits you. Ponds, small hills that replicate Mount Fuji, tea houses, streams full of koi, and bridges are all arranged in such a way as to keep you captivated for hours. Sensitive planting ensures each season's heroes have been considered.

WHY IS IT SPECIAL?
You can spend hours in these elaborate and incredibly detailed gardens simply whiling away the day. And please don't forget to visit the tea house.

WHAT TO LOOK FOR
Ask one of the many volunteers to explain the garden to you. A volunteer in Ritsurin Kōen showed us a rock formation that represented Mount Fuji!

BEAUTIFUL EXAMPLES
· Kenroku-en (Kanazawa, Chūbu; p. 214)
· Koishikawa-Kōrakuen, Rikugi-en and Kiyosumi Teien (Tokyo, Kantō)
· Kōraku-en (Okayama, Chūgoku; p. 268)
· Ritsurin Kōen (Takamatsu, Shikoku; p. 301)
· Sengan-en (Kagoshima, Kyūshū; p. 322)
· Shugakuin Imperial Villa, Sanzen-in and Ninna-ji (Kyoto, Kansai)
· Suizen-ji Jōju-en (Kumamoto, Kyūshū; p. 329)

FIELDS (& A TUNNEL) OF FLOWERS

If you're in Japan in the right season you'll be floating along perfumed paths or gazing over colourful fields.

BEAUTIFUL EXAMPLES
· Hitachi Seaside Park (Ibaraki, Kantō)
  Nemophila mid-April to early May; kochia turns red July to October.
  hitachikaihin.jp
· Shibazakura Park (Fuji Five Lakes, Kantō; p. 221)
  Moss phlox mid-April to late May.
  www.shibazakura.jp
· Furano Flower Fields (Furano/Kamifurano, Hokkaidō; p. 287)
· Farm Tomita (Furano, Hokkaidō; p. 287)
  Irodori blooms mid- to late July; lavender early to mid-July.
  farm-tomita.co.jp
· Flowerland (Kamifurano, Hokkaidō)
  A range of flowers can be seen from April to November.
· Kawachi Wisteria Garden (Kitakyūshū, Kyūshū)
  Twenty-two varieties of purple wisteria form a beautiful tunnel.
  kawachi-fujien.com
  →

FALLING LEAVES

Trees with branches overlapping, pathways blazing with autumn colour, leaves floating down and carpeting the floor, crisp air – it's something out of a Matsuo Bashō (p. 29) poem.

BEAUTIFUL EXAMPLES

· Bishamon-dō temple, (Kyoto, Kansai) November (check dates online) *bishamon.or.jp*

· Maple Corridor (Fujikawaguchiko, Chūbu; p. 221) Momiji Festival, early to mid-November *en.kawaguchiko.net/event-en/ fujikawaguchiko-momiji-festival*

· Meiji Jingū Gaien (Ginkgo Avenue, Tokyo, Kantō) November (check dates online) *www.meijijingugaien.jp*

OTHER PLANT-BASED BEAUTY

BONSAI

The cultivation of plants as miniature fully grown trees in small trays or shallow planters has been practised in Japan since the late 1100s. The art of tiny trees, perfectly shaped branches and mini-scapes was created for contemplation and meditation. The daily ritual of care and preservation blended perfectly with Japanese religious practices. By the 1800s, the art of bonsai had moved into the mainstream and become a hobby. The Omiya Bonsai Museum (Saitama, (Kantō, *bonsai-art-museum.jp*); Happo-en (Tokyo, Kantō, *www.happo-en.com*) and Kinashi Bonsai Village (Takamatsu, Shikoku, *kinashi-bonsai.com*) all have incredible examples.

DRIED PERSIMMON & CORN

The blackened exteriors of *machiya* townhouses (p. 342) come alive with the drying of both persimmon and corn in the late autumn and winter. It's a beautiful sight to behold, especially the deep orange hues of the persimmons, their plump shapes changing, darkening and dropping, waiting to be eaten. Our favourite place to see persimmons is Tsumago (Kiso Valley, Chūbu, *tumago.jp*).

GREENHOUSES

Most people don't associate Japan with tropical plants, but if the tropics are on your radar you must visit one of the many greenhouses across the country. In Kannawa Onsen's (p. 318) Umi Jigoku in Beppu, Kyūshū (*www.umijigoku.co.jp*), there's an incredible greenhouse where plants are grown with *onsen* (hot springs) water. The pond has some of the biggest lily pads and flowers we've ever seen. In Yunokawa Onsen, Hakodate, Hokkaidō (p. 278), you can bask in the glory of tropical plants when it's minus fifteen degrees Celsius outside (*hako-eco.com*); you'll also have the added bonus of seeing monkeys bathing in a giant hot tub full of *onsen* water!

IKEBANA

One of the most beautiful plant-art philosophies in the world, ikebana (p. 369) has been admired, copied and influenced by the West since Japan opened itself up to the world in 1853. The exact art of placing branches and flowers in the right vessel, with the best heights and colourways, is something to be studied and learned, not just picked up from one viewing or an online search. Try lessons at Ikenobō (Kyoto, Kansai, *www.ikenobo.jp*), Sōgetsu (*sogetsu.or.jp*) or Ohara (*ohararyu.or.jp*).

KOKEDAMA

Koke means moss in Japanese and *dama* means ball or jewel. These small, round, mossy creations can be seen outside *machiya* houses on plates or hanging off buildings in Kyoto (Kansai; p. 234), Takayama (Chūbu; p. 224) and all over rural Japan. Ferns may be popping out of the top of them or they may just be a thick fuzzy ball tied up with string. We look for them wherever we go; to us they symbolise the everyday beauty of Japan.

MOSS

After the rainy season, Japan will have beautiful pockets of mossy areas. These may be on the side of a road or path, inside a formal garden or in a courtyard. So look down, wherever you are, and do some moss-spotting. If the weather is dry, take your shoes off and walk on the soft pillowy carpet – there's nothing nicer. If you love moss you'll need to book ahead and visit Saihō-ji in Kyoto (Kansai, *saihoji-kokedera.com*; p. 246), for a life-changing experience.

TSUBONIWA

These small courtyard gardens are seen in *machiya* (townhouses; p. 342), *ryokan* (traditional inns; p. 87) and other small buildings. These tiny spaces mix rocks and greenery and add a small slice of nature and beauty to everyday life. Japanese gardens in Western houses are often modelled on these compact arrangements.

YORISHIRO

In the Shinto religion (p. 333), a sacred tree or other object (*yorishiro*) thought to be inhabited by a spirit has a rope-like structure with hanging paper elements called a *shimenawa* wrapped around it to contain the spirit for ceremonies.

YUKIZURI ROPES

In any important garden you'll see trees supported by ropes, in an almost teepee-like construction. The purpose of these ropes is to secure and protect the trees from heavy snow or difficult weather conditions. Of course, as we're talking about Japan here, something so practical takes on a beautiful artistic form. Amazing examples are at Yoyogi Park (Tokyo, Kantō, *www.tokyo-park.or.jp*) and Kenroku-en (Kanazawa, Chūbu, *www.pref.ishikawa.jp/siro-niwa/ kenrokuen/e/index.html*; p. 214).

FAVOURITE GREEN SPACES

· Adachi Museum
(Yasugi, Chūgoku; p. 275)
www.adachi-museum.or.jp/en/garden
· Higashimokoto Shibazakura Park
(Ozora, Hokkaidō)
shibazakura.net
· International House Garden
(Kyoto, Kansai)
i-house.or.jp
· Nanzen-in, Nanzen-ji
(Kyoto, Kansai; p. 234)
nanzen.net
· Ritsurin Kōen
(Takamatsu, Shikoku; p. 301)
my-kagawa.jp/en/ritsurin

· Saihō-ji, Koke-dera
(Kyoto, Kansai; p. 246)
saihoji-kokedera.com
· Sengan-en
(Kagoshima, Kyūshū; p. 322)
senganen.jp
· Shiratani Unsuikyō
(Yakushima Island, Kyūshū; p. 325)
y-rekumori.com
· Taizō-in
(Kyoto, Kansai)
taizoin.com
· Tōfuku-ji
(Kyoto, Kansai; p. 243)
tofukuji.jp

BELOW: Dried corn in Yanaka, Kantō; Persimmons in Tsumago, Kantō

CONTEMPORARY
ARCHITECTS

TADAO ANDO

A self-taught genius, always looking at the relationship between his structures and nature. His sweeping concrete masterpieces, almost de Chirico-esque from afar, may look daunting, but up close they are user-friendly, even warm and inviting. Angles seemingly jut from nowhere, while the alcoves and staircases are unlike anything you've ever seen before. It's a style so distinct you can spot it straight away. A master of the flat house, concrete, glass and steel, a lover of simplicity, his almost alien structures seem more at home with nature than most other buildings.

TOKYO (KANTŌ)
- 21_21 Design Sight (2007)
- Omotesandō Hills (2005)
- Tokyo Skytree (2012)

OUTSIDE TOKYO
- Akita Museum of Art (p. 194) (Akita, Tōhoku; 2012) *www.akita-museum-of-art.jp*
- Benesse House (1992), Lee Ufan Museum (2010), Chichu Art Museum (2004) and Valley Gallery (2022) (all Naoshima, Shikoku; p. 292) *benesse-artsite.jp*
- Forest of Tombs Museum (Kumamoto, Kyūshū; 1992)
- Garden of Fine Arts (Kyoto, Kansai; 1994) *kansaiartbeat.com*
- Hill of the Buddha (Sapporo, Hokkaidō; 2015) *takinoreien.com*
- Honpukuji Water Temple (Awaji Island, Kansai; 2000) *awajishimablog.wordpress.com/ water-temple*
- Hyōgo Prefectural Museum of Art (p. 261) (Kobe, Kansai; 2002)
- Museum of Literature (Himeji, Kansai; 1991)
- Setouchi Retreat Aonagi (Matsuyama, Shikoku; 1998), p. 305 *setouchi-aonagi.com*
- Shiba Ryōtarō Memorial Museum (Osaka, Kansai; 2001) *shibazaidan.or.jp*

KENGO KUMA

Superstar architect, weaver of wooden structures and professor at Tokyo University, Kengo Kuma is ahead of his time – a futurist, intellectual and international creative who brings a Japanese aesthetic to the world. A passion for traditional Japanese craft techniques can be seen in his masterful use of wood in buildings that almost look like woven baskets or wooden toys – rethought and remodelled into contemporary buildings that look utterly unique. Combining his respect for the past with utter joy for the future, his constant quest is to bring beauty to public spaces for all to enjoy. His strong interest in town planning and his ability to transform a whole town (Yusuhara, for example), reveal why he is so loved in Japan and abroad.

TOKYO (KANTŌ)
- Asakusa Culture Tourist Information Center (2012) *www.city.taito.lg.jp*
- Kabuki-za Towers (2013)
- Meiji Jingu Museum (2019), p. 165 *meijijingu.or.jp/en*
- New National Stadium (2019) For the 2020 Tokyo Olympics *www.gotokyo.org*
- Nezu Museum (2009) *nezu-muse.or.jp*
- SunnyHills (2013) *www.sunnyhills.com.tw/index/ja-jp/*

OUTSIDE TOKYO
- Kadokawa Culture Museum (Saitama, Kantō; 2020) *kadcul.com/en*
- Nagasaki Prefectural Art Museum (Nagasaki, Kyūshū; 2005) *www.nagasaki-museum.jp*
- Nihondaira Yume Terrace (Nihondaira, Chūbu; 2018), p. 227 *nihondaira-yume-terrace.jp*
- Renovation of Fujiya Hotel Ryokan (Ginzan Onsen, Tōhoku; 2006), p. 208 *fujiya-ginzan.com*
- 'Yunoeki Oyu' Community Center (Kazuno, Tōhoku; 2018)
- Yusuhara town projects (Yusuhara, Shikoku; 2006–2010), *www.town.yusuhara.kochi.jp*

KENZŌ TANGE

The grandfather of modernism in Japan and member of the Metabolism movement, Tange sought to invent the future of modern architecture. His National Stadium design for the 1964 Olympics showed the new face of Japan to the world. Visiting his buildings is a must if you're a student of history or pop culture. It's impossible to stand before one without feeling a sense of time and place.

TOKYO (KANTŌ)
- Shizuoka Press and Broadcasting Centre (1967)
- St Mary's Cathedral (Tokyo Cathedral; 1964)
- Tokyo Metropolitan Government Building (1991)
- Yoyogi National Gymnasium (1964)

OUTSIDE TOKYO
- Osaka Exposition (Osaka, Kansai; 1970) The Expo '70 site is now Expo Commemoration Park. Part of the roof of Tange's Festival Plaza remains.
- Peace Memorial Park (p. 265) (Hiroshima, Chūgoku; 1955)
- Yamanashi Broadcasting and Press Centre (Kōfu, Chūbu; 1966) →

OPPOSITE PAGE: St Mary's Cathedral, Tokyo, Kantō

KISHŌ KUROKAWA

An agitator, intellectual and founding member of the Metabolism movement, Kurokawa was a master of detail, exposing the normally hidden and using materials in their raw state. He took on a philosophy of impermanence, contending that Japanese cities had been destroyed in warring states, the Second World War and many natural disasters. His structures, especially in the early Metabolism days, are founded on the idea of being temporary, changeable and in harmony with nature.

His project list shows his passion for designing spaces for the people – stadiums, museums, galleries and some politically charged community projects including youth and cancer centres. He even ran for governor of Tokyo in 2007.

Kurokawa designed the Melbourne Central building in Australia. Michelle designed the award-winning logo for this building (just one clue as to how her passion for Japanese design and culture developed such deep roots).

TOKYO (KANTŌ)
· The National Art Center
  (2005; p. 167)

OUTSIDE TOKYO
· Hiroshima City Museum
  of Contemporary Art
  (Hiroshima, Chūgoku; 1989)
  hiroshima-moca.jp
· Ōita Stadium
  (Ōita, Kyūshū; 2002)
  For the 2002 FIFA World Cup
· Osaka International Convention
  Center (Osaka, Kansai; 2000)
· Toyota Stadium
  (Toyota, Chūbu; 2001)

TOYO ITO

Ito was born during the Second World War and learned his craft in a Japan decimated by bombing and natural disasters. His studio, Urban Robot, sought to invent the future, most notably through tall buildings where light shone through geometric cracks and holes. He hit his stride in the 2000s with some of Japan's most breathtaking buildings: the Tama Art University Library (p. 358); his reinvention of Mikimoto; and his very own museum, the Toyo Ito Museum of Architecture (p. 305), jutting out over the Seto Inland Sea in Imabari.

TOKYO (KANTŌ)
· Mikimoto Building (2003)
· Tama Art University Library (2007)
· Tod's Omotesandō Building (2004)
· Za-Koenji Public Theatre (2009)

OUTSIDE TOKYO
· Toyo Ito Museum of Architecture
  (Imabari, Shikoku; 2011)

HIROSHI NAKAMURA & NAP

We had been admirers of the Ribbon Chapel for a few years and then the Sayama Forest Chapel – realising only at this point that the same brilliance was behind both places of worship. Protégés of Kengo Kuma (p. 353), Hiroshi Nakamura & NAP are *the* new talent in contemporary intellectual architecture. We can't wait to see what they do next.

OUTSIDE TOKYO
· Ribbon Chapel
  (Onomichi, Chūgoku; 2014)
  bella-vista.jp
· Roku Museum
  (Tochigi, Kantō; 2010)
  roku-museum.com
· Sayama Forest Chapel
  (Saitama, Kantō; 2014)
  boenf.org

ABOVE: Ribbon Chapel, Onomichi, Chūgoku

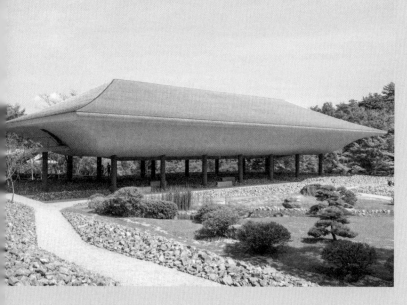

OTHERS OF NOTE

TOKYO (KANTŌ)
· Paul Noritaka Tange's Mode Gakuen Cocoon Tower, Shinjuku (2008)
  mode.ac.jp
· Philippe Starck's Asahi Beer Hall, the Asahi Flame (Flamme d'Or), Asakusa (1989)
  starck.com
· Shusaku Arakawa and Madeline Gins' Reversible Destiny Lofts, Mitaka (2005; p. 92)
  reversibledestiny.org

TOKYO DAYTRIP
· aat+Makoto Yokomizo Architects, Inc's Tomihiro Art Museum (Midori City, Kantō; 2005)
  www.city.midori.gunma.jp/tomihiro
· Nikken Sekkei's Hōki Museum (Chiba, Kantō; 2010)
  hoki-museum.jp

FURTHER AFIELD
· Emilio Ambasz's Acros Building (Fukuoka, Kyūshū; 1995)
  acros.or.jp
· I.M. Pei's Miho Museum (near Shigaraki, Kansai; 1997), p. 257
  miho.or.jp
· Kohei Nawa and SANDWICH's (Yoshitaka Lee, Yuichi Kodai) KOHTEI art pavilion (Fukuyama, Chūgoku; 2016)
  szmg.jp
· Molo's Nebuta Museum Wa-Rasse (Aomori, Tōhoku; 2011), p. 198
  www.nebuta.jp
· Ryuzo Shiroe's Tsuzumi-mon Gate, Kanazawa Station (Kanazawa, Chūbu; 2005), p. 216
  kanazawastation.com
· Shin Takamatsu's Shoji Ueda Museum of Photography (Tottori, Chūgoku; 1995), p. 274
  www.houki-town.jp/ueda
· Takasaki Masaharu's Nanohana-Kan Communication and Recreation Plaza (Ibusuki, Kyūshū; 1998)
· Terunobu Fujimori's La Collina (Ōmihachiman, Lake Biwa, Kansai; 2015), p. 257

ARATA ISOZAKI

Buildings designed by 2019 Pritzker Architecture Prize winner Isozaki can be seen all over the world. An intellectual from Kyūshū, he has an indefinable architectural style. His brilliance lies in his ability to reinvent himself for each project, deeply committing himself to each individual building's needs and thus creating new styles and ways of thinking.

OUTSIDE TOKYO
· Museum of Modern Art (Takasaki, Kantō; 1974)
· Art Tower Mito (Ibaraki, Kantō; 1990)
· Ceramic Park Mino (Tajimi, Chūbu; 2002)
· Nagi Museum of Contemporary Art (Okayama, Chūgoku; 1994)
· Ōita Prefectural Library (Ōita, Kyūshū; 1966)

SANAA – RYUE NISHIZAWA & KAZUYO SEJIMA

Anyone visiting Naoshima will see the cloud-like terminal building (p. 296) designed by SANAA. The way it floats on the art island and blends in with the other sculptures are classic traits of SANAA, who produce a curious mix of sculpture and practicality. The same can be said of their 2019 retro-futurist space-bubble commuter train from Tokyo to Saitama.

TOKYO (KANTŌ)
· Christian Dior Building (2003)
· Laview train to Saitama (Ikebukuru to Chichibu stations; 2019)

OUTSIDE TOKYO
· 21st Century Museum of Contemporary Art (p. 214) (Kanazawa, Chūbu; 2004)
  kanazawa21.jp
· Naoshima Ferry Terminal (Naoshima, Shikoku; 2006)
· Teshima Art Museum (p. 295) (Teshima, Shikoku; 2010)

ABOVE: KOHTEI, Fukuyama, Chūgoku

Manhole art & station stamps

One of the most important things to bring on your Japan trip is a small notebook so you can fill it with the ink impressions of regional rubber stamps available at every station around the country. Each stamp shows a specialty of the region – think *kokeshi* for Naruko Onsen (p. 204) or temari balls for Matsumoto (p. 219).

Japanese enthusiasts collect the set (a daunting task), but for us it's a great way to have a pictorial souvenir of the areas we've visited. Stamps and ink pads are normally positioned just before you enter the ticket gate – ask the station attendant at the entrance for guidance. Michelle carries a small ink pad with her in case the station pad is too dry, but we do understand that this is extreme stamping behaviour!

Out on the street, look down to admire the manhole art showcasing the icons and specialties of each region. The decorative manhole covers for the sewer system began in the late 1970s – by the mid-1980s looking down at them became a great way to discover a city's places of interest. If you love illustration, logo design and intricate graphic representation, this is a fun thing to do on your trip. It's also a great game for kids to spot the manholes or collect the stamp set – unique, free and a pictorial learning adventure.

Growing up in 1980s Japan

FLORA WAYCOTT, ILLUSTRATOR, PERTH BY WAY OF THE UK AND JAPAN, FLORAWAYCOTT.COM

Your mother is Japanese and your father is British. At what age did you live in Japan and how did it feel moving there from Britain?

I was six when we moved as a family to Japan. I don't remember much about leaving England, but I have very strong memories of arriving in Japan. At that age everything felt like an adventure. Within a few weeks we had enrolled at the local Japanese primary school and were exploring our neighbourhood and settling in to our new life. We travelled to the countryside in Niigata to meet our grandparents, aunts, uncles and cousins, which was wonderful. Moving to Japan wasn't a difficult transition for me; I felt very comfortable being there and immersed myself in the culture.

Did your mother teach you Japanese at home or did you learn at school, or both?

We did learn some Japanese from our mother, but most of it came from being at school and speaking the language every day. It only took my sister and me around six months to become fluent, and from then on we always spoke Japanese when it was just the two of us. At home we spoke English, but I found it difficult to juggle both languages when I was that age!

What was it like being at school in Japan?

We attended a local primary school in Yokohama. Back in 1988, my sister and I were the only foreign children at the school and no one spoke any English, so this helped us pick up the language very quickly. One thing I remember vividly was that so many children loved stationery, drawing, origami and other crafts. There was a lot of creativity there. When we left Japan, my teacher and classmates had a party for me and wrote me essays and poems to say goodbye. I have some really fond memories of my time at school in Japan.

Did you do many creative things in or outside of school?

Soon after we arrived in Japan, my parents enrolled me in after-school art classes. Every Wednesday, I'd cycle to a small Japanese house where my art teacher lived, and, along with around ten other children, spend the afternoon making art. Those years were the start of my creative journey.

Tell us a little about going back to Japan to study in Kyoto.

I studied at Kawashima Textile School in Kyoto for a term in 2003 as part of my textiles degree in England. I learned many new skills, such as indigo-dyeing, weaving a kimono length and spinning wool. I'd always wanted to spend a length of time in Kyoto, so to be able to study there was truly a dream.

What draws you back to Japan?

Japan feels like a second home and the memories of my time there as a child are incredibly vivid. I'm drawn to the culture as so much of it is embedded within me. Wherever I am in the world I know that Japan will always pull me back, reminding me of our life there all those years ago.

LIBRARIES

——— Are you, like us, a book nerd, obsessed with vintage books, modern designs, the smell of a library, the quiet and still atmosphere? If your answer is yes, then at least one of the libraries listed below should be on your schedule.

Some libraries need an application to visit (Tama and Musashino, for example), so check ahead on their websites for their hours and to apply. Many of these libraries are designed by famous architects (Toyo Ito and Tadao Ando to name but two).

AMAZING EXAMPLES

· International Library of Children's Literature, National Diet Library (Tokyo, Kantō)
www.kodomo.go.jp

· Kadokawa Culture Museum (Saitama, Kantō)
kadcul.com/en

· Kyoto Botanical Gardens 'Mushroom Library' (Kyoto, Kansai)
pref.kyoto.jp/plant

· Musashino Art University Library (Tokyo, Kantō)
mauml.musabi.ac.jp

· Nakajima Library, Akita University (Akita, Tōhoku)
web.aiu.ac.jp

· Nakanoshima Children's Book Forest (Osaka, Kansai)
kodomohonnomori.osaka

· Shiba Ryōtarō Library (Osaka, Kansai)
shibazaidan.or.jp

· Takao Shiotsuka Atelier (Ōita, Kyūshū)
shio-atl.com

· Takeo City Library (Takeo, Kyūshū)
epochal.city.takeo.lg.jp

· Tama Art University Library (Tokyo, Kantō)
libopac.tamabi.ac.jp

· Yusuhara Kumo no Ue Community Library (Yusuhara, Shikoku)
kumonoue-lib.jp

美術館

MUSEUMS

————— Japan has a multitude of
impressive and unusual museums.
Below are some of our favourites,
but also check the architecture
(p. 352), craft (p. 366) and art
(p. 374) sections for more museum
beauty. Our regional guides
(pp. 157–329) have keys listing
local museums of note. →

OPPOSITE PAGE: Tama Art University Library, Tokyo, Kantō **THIS PAGE TOP**: Teshima Art Museum, Kagawa, Shikoku **THIS PAGE**
BOTTOM: D.T. Suzuki Museum, Kanazawa, Chūbu

ITAMI JUZO MUSEUM (MATSUYAMA, SHIKOKU)

Tampopo (1985) is one of our favourite movies and this dedicated museum tracks its maker's career as a designer, actor, editor and television presenter.
itami-kinenkan.jp

KAWAGUCHIKO MUSIC FOREST (KAWAGUCHIKO, CHŪBU)

This unusual museum has views of Mount Fuji and was built with a European Alps atmosphere in mind. It showcases automatic musical instruments.
fuji.kawaguchikomusicforest.jp

KYOTO INTERNATIONAL MANGA MUSEUM (KYOTO, KANSAI)

Manga fans will love both the permanent and changing exhibitions here. Check online for workshops and demonstration times.
kyotomm.jp

MIRAIKAN (TOKYO, KANTŌ)

If you're looking for robots and modern-day Japanese tech wizardry, look no further than the National Museum of Emerging Science and innovation.
www.miraikan.jst.go.jp

NEBUTA MUSEUM WA-RASSE (AOMORI, TŌHOKU)

Equal parts colourful and wonderful, this museum showcases legendary local *nebuta* (floats; p. 198) in an equally impressive building by Molo Design.
www.nebuta.jp/warasse

TESHIMA ART MUSEUM (TESHIMA, SHIKOKU)

Contemplative and immersive (p. 295). benesse-artsite.jp/en/art/teshima-artmuseum.html

TOTO MUSEUM (TOKYO, KANTŌ)

Cool modern architecture that matches Japan's most intuitive toilet.
jp.toto.com/museum

CUP NOODLES MUSEUM (YOKOHAMA, KANTŌ)

For an only-in-Japan moment, journey through this museum (p. 191) marvelling at the displays, making your own noodles and trying different varieties. Fun for the whole family.
cupnoodles-museum.jp

D.T. SUZUKI MUSEUM (KANAZAWA, CHŪBU)

Beautiful museum showcasing the works and ideas of Buddhist philosopher Daitsetsu Suzuki.
kanazawa-museum.jp/daisetz

FUKUI PREFECTURAL DINOSAUR MUSEUM (KATSUYAMA CITY, CHŪBU)

The perfect place for dinosaur-obsessed kids and adults alike.
www.dinosaur.pref.fukui.jp

GHIBLI MUSEUM (TOKYO, KANTŌ)

One of Japan's most charming museums (p. 175). Fans of Totoro and other Ghibli animated characters can wander, play, watch – and jump on the soft Cat Bus (kids only!).
ghibli-museum.jp

HIROSHIMA PEACE MEMORIAL MUSEUM (HIROSHIMA, CHŪGOKU)

A museum with an important message and collection housed in Kenzō Tange's masterful building (p. 265).
hpmmuseum.jp

ISHIKAWA INSECT MUSEUM (HAKUSAN, CHŪBU)

Come for the giant silver beetle sculpture, stay for the butterfly garden. A great Kanazawa daytrip.
furekon.jp

OPPOSITE: Cranes at Hiroshima Peace Memorial Museum, Hiroshima, Chūgoku

ABOVE: Nebuta Museum Wa-Rasse, Aomori, Tōhoku

Japanese arts

KABUKI THEATRE

These historical plays were once performed by women, but now only by men (the Tokugawa shogunate banned female performers in the 1600s), so many male kabuki performers specialise in playing women. Kabuki is filled with stories of intrigue, family feuds and romantic trysts. Actors wear intricate costumes and their make-up is very dramatic. Sets are complex, often involving moving scenery, trapdoors, shifting walls and revolving stages. A standout feature is the *hanamachi*, a footbridge through the audience, allowing actors to make over-the-top entrances. Often a kabuki show is only one part of a longer tale – the part with the best bits – so knowing all the spoilers is an advantage. Because of this you can choose to see only one act (which can still take over two hours).

BEST PLACES TO SEE KABUKI

· Hakata-za (Fukuoka, Kyūshū)
  hakataza.co.jp
· Kabuki-za (Tokyo, Kantō; p. 166)
  kabukiweb.net/theatres/kabukiza
· Minami-za (Kyoto, Kansai)
  shochiku.co.jp
· Misono-za (Nagoya, Chūbu)
  www.misonoza.co.jp
· Shochiku-za (Osaka, Kansai)
  shochiku.co.jp

NOH THEATRE

Decidedly more mysterious than kabuki, *Noh* actors wear masks in place of make-up and act out historical themes with deliberate pacing, rhythmic movements and ethereal gestures in highly elaborate costumes. The set is basic, the roof with four pillars and a backdrop of a pine forest, recreating the original *Noh* theatres, which were outdoors.

BEST PLACES TO SEE NOH

· Cerulean Tower Noh Theatre
  (Tokyo, Kantō)
  www.ceruleantower-noh.com
· Fushimi Inari Shrine
  (Kyoto, Kansai; p. 243)
· Kanze Noh Theatre
  (Tokyo, Kantō)
  kanze.net
· Miyajima Shin-noh, Toka-sai
  Festival (Hatsukaichi, Chūgoku)
  miyajima.or.jp/english/event/event_tokashinnou.html
· Nagoya Noh Theatre,
  Nagoya Castle (Nagoya, Chūbu)
  nagoya-info.jp/en/see/facilities/nagoya_noh_theater.html
· National Noh Theatre
  (Tokyo, Kantō)
  www.ntj.jac.go.jp
· Ohtsuki Noh Theatre
  (Osaka, Kansai)
  noh-kyogen.com

SUMO

Sumo is Japan's main sport and tournaments are held regularly, capturing the attention of the nation. However, it is also a highly regarded art, a deeply spiritual and ceremonial event with many rituals – for example, the sumo throw salt before each clinch in a nod to the Shinto salt purification ceremony. The tasselled roof that hangs over the ring and the diet and lifestyle also include elements of the Shinto religion (p. 333). Three out of the six yearly tournaments are held in Tokyo (p. 162), the others in Osaka (p. 252). At first sumo can seem like a few minutes of nothing happening, but after a while, the deep anticipation, ceremony, tactics and subtle moves make most other sports seem simplistic.

BEST PLACE TO SEE SUMO

· Edion Arena Osaka (Osaka, Kansai)
  Tournament held in March
· Ryōgoku Kokugikan sumo stadium
  and sumo museum (Tokyo, Kantō)
  The Hatsu Basho tournament is held
  in January, Natsu Basho in May and
  Aki Basho in September
· Sumo shrines Ekō-in and Tomioka
  Hachiman-gū (Tokyo, Kantō)

OPPOSITE PAGE: Sumo spotting at Kichijōji Station, Tokyo, Kantō

The beauty of simplicity

BETH KEMPTON, AUTHOR OF *WABI SABI: JAPANESE WISDOM FOR A PERFECTLY IMPERFECT LIFE*,
UNITED KINGDOM @BETHKEMPTON, BETHKEMPTON.COM

What made you fall in love with Japan?

I chose to study Japanese simply because I wanted to go on an adventure. I'd never been and didn't know much about Japan at all, but I started to fall for it as soon as I began to learn kanji, and find out about the culture and history. Even so, it was still quite the shock when I arrived at Kansai Airport at the tender age of nineteen to find everyone actually speaking Japanese. I spent that year living with a homestay family who spoke no English, in a beautiful part of western Kyoto by a lake, surrounded by bamboo forests and paddy fields. After that I was smitten.

How do you bring Japanese culture into your everyday life?

I'll often be going about my daily life and suddenly feel an unexplainable pang, like a deep homesickness. When that happens I take myself into the garden with a cup of *hōjicha* and a good Japanese book, or start planning my next trip. My husband has also spent time in Japan so he gets it, which helps. In our home we remove shoes at the door and wear slippers, we often cook Japanese food and we sleep on a futon on tatami. We live in an old thatched cottage, which in many ways reminds me of Japanese country houses. I grow *shiso* by the front door and daikon in my garden.

What is it about the philosophy of *wabi sabi* that strikes a chord in so many cultures?

There's an underlying discontent in modern society. We have too much choice, too much stimulus and too many demands on our precious time. I think many of us are looking for permission to slow down, and for ideas about how to live well. Wabi sabi turns the tide on the race for perfection by reminding us that we're works in progress, and we're not supposed to be perfect. That's a revelation.

What are some of your favourite small moments in Japanese culture?

I love finding pockets of calm in the midst of city life, be that in a garden or a tea house or in a quiet café. I love coming across unexpected moments of beauty – the way someone has taken care to leave a single flower in a vase by a window, or the way an architect has designed a room so the shadows fall like a painting. And I love moments of connection with Japanese people going about their day – the old woman calling good morning from the rice fields as you cycle past, the man pausing on his way to work to help you figure out where you're trying to get to, the pickle seller enthusing about the way her wares are made by hand at the temple around the corner. My heart is torn between Kyoto and the Japanese countryside, where people have more time, where the hot springs ease your weary bones and the local organic food is like nothing you've ever tasted.

What can we learn from Japanese wellness techniques?

They're ultimately about simplicity, gentleness and 'enoughness': stopping eating when you're eighty per cent full, spending time in nature, taking care of your mind–body connection, curating beauty in your everyday life.

TRADITIONAL ART & CRAFT

———— Traditional Japanese handicrafts are among the world's most refined and beautiful. The Japanese have a deep affinity for creating things without the use of complex machinery – something that may seem at odds with the country's position at the forefront of technology. But the past sits comfortably beside the present (and the future) in Japan, and traditional arts and crafts like ikebana (flower-arranging; pp. 350, 369), *shibori* (indigo-dyeing; p. 368) and *shodō* (calligraphy; p. 336) are still practised and perfected today. For an immersive introduction to Japan's traditional arts and crafts, try visiting a tea house in a temple or garden. Artful ikebana displays may adorn the space where you take the tea ceremony, and you might be seated on a chair covered in *shibori* textile.

Tea made from hand-ground matcha (green tea; p. 151) powder will be mixed in front of you and delicately served up in a vintage ceramic cup by your host, whose kimono will likely be handmade and hand-dyed.

You can find unique markets in most cities with handmade wooden items and vintage textiles for sale (see our favourites on p. 373). If you'd like to travel for crafts, Mashiko (p. 183) is known for both indigo-dyeing and pottery, Imari and Arita (p. 310) have some of the finest ceramicists in the country, Echizen Washi Village is a town dedicated to making paper, and basket-weaving is taken to masterful heights in Ōita (p. 329) and Beppu (p. 316). Tokyo's

Mingeikan and Kanazawa's National Crafts Museum are must-visits for the craft obsessed. Make sure to turn off your phone and wander through the streets as if you were living in a less cluttered, less digital time, finding your own treasures and experiences.

MOTTAINAI (ADJ.) 'TOO GOOD TO WASTE'

In an imperfect world, the techniques of *shibori*, *boro* and *kintsugi* provide the opportunity for both artistic expression and the contemplation of beauty, one's place in the world and the nature of what it is to be remade and reborn. To the Japanese, 'old, broken and used' are just jumping-off points for a new life, a new history and new memories.

ABOVE: Brushes from Kirishiki, Chūgoku
OPPOSITE PAGE: Boro fabric from Oedo Antique Market, Tokyo, Kantō

BORO

Boro means 'rag', and in the context of Japanese handicrafts is the technique of stitching small pieces of fabric together to form one large piece – a striking take on patchwork that arose from the poverty of the Edo-period (p. 28)working class. Hemp and *shibori* (p. 368) fabrics that were once part of household furnishings or clothing were masterfully stitched together, updated, re-dyed and reshaped throughout a working-class person's lifetime.

Boro makes an art of creating new from old, and many fine examples are highly detailed, with great care taken in the placement of patches and decorative flourishes added with *sashiko* stitching, which also serves to reinforce the piece.

A recent resurgence in both *shibori* and *boro* has meant fashion labels, especially ones that use denim, have started incorporating yesterday's lessons into the clothes of today.

Although *boro* tends to be associated with a dreamy, romantic feeling these days, with vintage *boro* only affordable and appealing to some, the roots of this craft are purely working class. *Boro* is an object lesson in preservation, building on tradition, reducing waste, and the willingness to change and update something already owned. Perhaps the next time you find a hole in your best shirt, or a moth eats through your favourite jumper, you too might consider repairing it rather than throwing it away – mending it so that the patch shows, and telling your own special *boro* story. →

WHERE TO FIND IT

· Kobo-ichi Market, Toji Temple (Kyoto, Kansai), pp. 236, 373
  kyotostation.com/toji-temple-kobo-ichi-market

· Oedo Antique Market (Tokyo, Kantō), p. 373
  antique-market.jp

SHIBORI

When we think of *shibori*, we imagine working-class people of the Edo period (p. 28) dyeing and hanging large sheets of patterned indigo fabric in and around classic Japanese buildings, with hinoki cypress and cherry trees swaying in the breeze, the smell of miso and incense in the air. We are transported back to a society where everyday people wore outfits made of one-off, artisan-crafted cloth; an age of creativity and invention, of making the most of what you had and elevating everyday chores to fine arts and crafts. *Shibori* is a textile art that involves binding, twisting or folding cloth before dyeing it with indigo, giving each piece of fabric its own unique design.

It was first practised in the Nara period (710–794 AD; p. 15), and became popular in the Edo period, when the technique was used by the working class to dye inexpensive hemp, as silk and cotton were unaffordable. Natural dyes made from readily available sources like madder root and beetroot were used to obtain the rich purple-blue colour. When clothes wore out, they were mended (see *boro*; p. 367) and re-dyed to appear new again. In essence, *shibori* was a method of reusing and recycling, only with added artisan qualities: born out of necessity, but made to be beautiful as well as practical.

Delve deep into the history of *shibori* and you'll find microcosms where unique styles and trends have developed, keeping this ancient art alive through the ages. There are six major techniques in *shibori*: *arashi*, where fabric is wrapped around, bound to and scrunched on a pole; *itajime*, where cloth is sandwiched between wooden shapes to prevent the dye from penetrating; *kanoko*, which we know in the West as tie-dye; *kumo*, which involves pleating and binding the fabric before dyeing; *miura*, where thread is wrapped around small sections of cloth; and *nui*, where the fabric has been gathered using a running stitch. Fabric choice determines which technique is used, and each one results in different patterns and shapes. By selecting one technique over another, indigo-dyers can create complex beauty or timeless simplicity.

WHERE TO FIND IT

· Arimatsu Narumi Tie-Dyeing Museum (Nagoya, Chūbu) The town of Arimatsu, in the suburbs of Nagoya, is famous for its indigo-dyeing. *aichi-now.jp*
· Shibori Museum (Kyoto), p. 372 *kyotoshibori.com*
· Vintage *shibori* at flea markets (p. 373). On your strolls around Nara (p. 250) and Kyoto (p. 234) you'll see many examples of *shibori noren* curtains and cushion fabric.

WHERE TO LEARN IT

· Amano Kouya (Yasugi, Chūgoku). *Shibori* workshop (in Japanese, teaching through demonstrations). *www.kankou-shimane.com*

KINTSUGI

Kintsugi ('golden joinery') or *kintsukuroi* ('golden repair') is the repairing of glass, porcelain, earthenware and other forms of pottery with *urushi* lacquer mixed with precious metals. Its origin is thought to lie as far back as the fifteenth century: a famous story tells of the eighth shogun of the Ashikaga shogunate, Yoshimasa (ruled 1449–1473), who sent his favourite tea bowl to be repaired by Japanese craftsmen. As the bowl could not be properly put back together (at the time ugly metal staples were used, a technique that has since become one of the arts of *kintsugi*), they decided instead to transform the bowl using gold powder and lacquer. Yoshimasa loved it, and the art of *kintsugi* was born.

With *kintsugi*, if a plate or cup breaks into large pieces, it can be put back together in a way that allows it to exhibit its breaks proudly, showing its history and emerging even more beautiful and unique than it once was. If the piece suffers a chip, the hole can be filled, sanded and painted, transformed into something better than new – something that has a story to tell.

Kintsugi's value as a metaphor for overcoming the hardships in our lives is hard to ignore. The band Death Cab for Cutie released an album called *Kintsugi*, which dealt with the issues of being broken and remade, of being more beautiful because of our fractures and cracks. Like healing ourselves in real life, *kintsugi* can take a long time. Days or even weeks are needed for planning, filling, drying and curing. A piece can take up to a month to be transformed into something wonderful and unique. But the beauty in the end is worth the wait, like witnessing a caterpillar emerge from a chrysalis as a butterfly.

WHERE TO FIND IT

A *kintsugi* cup or item will pop up on your travels in the most likely or unlikely of spots. A ceramics town or museum may have some fine examples, vintage tea houses may serve your tea in a cup with golden mending, or you may get lucky with a vintage-market find.

WHERE TO LEARN IT

Classes with *kintsugi* master Showzi Tsukamoto *kintsugitsukamoto.wixsite.com/kintsugi*

OPPOSITE PAGE: Display at a Kyoto restaurant, Kyoto, Kansai

IKEBANA

This form of flower-arranging brings nature indoors, giving it a place of importance in the home. In ikebana, practitioners bend and twist flowers and foliage as nature intended; favouring one way or another depending on the season and position in relation to the sun. Unlike Western flower-arranging, ikebana is often minimal and sparse, and makes twigs, bracken, seed pods and fronds important components. Seasonal foliage, stem height, vessel choice, balance and harmony are all taken into consideration. White flowers are popular; red flowers less so, as they are traditionally used for funerary arrangements. Ikebana can be used for celebrations, ceremonies and condolences. You'll often see white orchids arranged beautifully outside a shop; this signifies that the shop has just opened.

The beauty of ikebana is grounded in the Japanese love of the seasons (p. 52) and the way they affect the appearance of flora. For instance, in March, when it's windy, arrangements are often curved or bent as if in a strong wind. There is a practical use for ikebana as well. The preparation, methods and style of the arrangements often prolong the life of the cut flowers.

Ikebana is an ancient art, with its origins in the late eighth century, but it was not until the eighteenth century that it reached peak popularity. There are different philosophies and more than 1000 schools of ikebana, but its roots lie in Buddhist theory, and in fact flower-arranging was first brought to Japan from China at the same time as Buddhism. Interestingly, many military leaders (including Toyotomi Hideyoshi and Yoshimasa Ashikaga) were versed in the art of ikebana. It was said to help calm their minds when strategising. →

WHERE TO FIND IT

· Ikenobo (Kyoto, Kansai) *ikenobo.jp*
· *Kaiseki ryōri* (p. 127) restaurants
· Public spaces and perhaps also your room in a *ryokan* (traditional inn; p. 87)
· Tea ceremonies (p. 151) and vintage tea stores

WHERE TO LEARN IT

· Ami Kyoto (Kyoto, Kansai) *whattodoinkyoto.com/ikebana*
· Kikunoya (Kanazawa, Chūbu) Ikebana, tea ceremony and calligraphy, *kanazawa-experience.com*
· Ohara School (Tokyo, Kantō) *ohararyu.or.jp*
· Sogetsu Ikebana StudioF (Tokyo, Kantō) *www.flower-studiof.com*

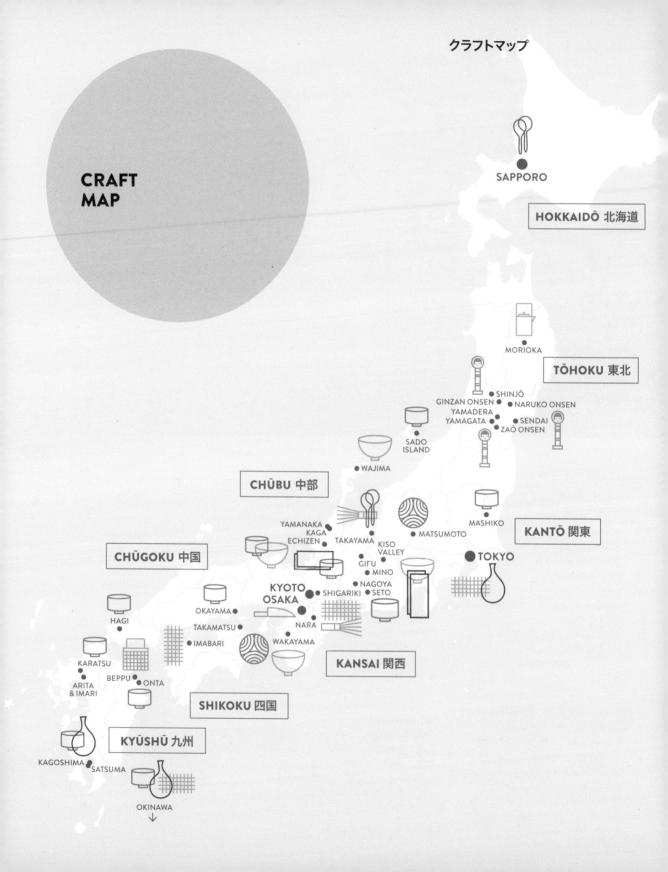

クラフトマップ

CRAFT
MAP

SAPPORO

HOKKAIDŌ 北海道

MORIOKA

TŌHOKU 東北

SHINJŌ
GINZAN ONSEN   NARUKO ONSEN
YAMADERA
YAMAGATA   SENDAI
ZAŌ ONSEN

SADO
ISLAND

CHŪBU 中部

WAJIMA

MASHIKO

YAMANAKA
KAGA   MATSUMOTO
ECHIZEN   TAKAYAMA
KISO
VALLEY

KANTŌ 関東

CHŪGOKU 中国

GIFU
MINO

TOKYO

KYOTO
OSAKA   SHIGARIKI   NAGOYA
SETO

OKAYAMA

HAGI

TAKAMATSU   NARA

KARATSU

IMABARI   WAKAYAMA

KANSAI 関西

ARITA
& IMARI   BEPPU   ONTA

SHIKOKU 四国

KAGOSHIMA   KYŪSHŪ 九州

SATSUMA

OKINAWA
↓

JAPANESE
CRAFT TOWNS

———— Most towns in Japan are known for something special, and many are famous for crafts that have been bought as *omiyage* (regional souvenirs; p. 109) for years or even centuries. Here is a small list of some of our favourite places, but remember that you'll find unexpected treasures up small alleys and around most corners wherever you are in Japan.

BAMBOO WEAVING
Beppu

CERAMICS
Arita, Bizen, Gifu, Hagi, Hasami, Imari, Kaga, Karatsu, Kasama, Mashiko, Mino, Naha, Okayama, Onta, Sado Island, Satsuma, Seto, Shigaraki, Tokoname

FABRIC
Shibori (Arimatsu, Nagoya; Sumida, Tokyo); silk (Nishijin, Kyoto); fabric-buying (Nippori, Tokyo); Saori weaving (Osaka); Yaeyama *minsa* (Ishigaki City, Okinawa); cotton towels (Imabari, Shikoku)

GLASS
Kiriko glass (Tokyo), Satsuma *kiriko* glass (Kagoshima), *ryukyu* glass (Okinawa)

KITCHEN KNIVES
Sakai

KOKESHI DOLLS (P. 340)
Tōhoku region: Naruko Onsen, Sendai, Shinjō, Tsuchiyu Onsen, Tsugaru, Yajiro Kokeshi Village, Yamagata, Zaō Onsen; two giant *kokeshi* at Misawa Airport (Aomori)

LACQUERWARE
Kiso Valley, Takaoka, Wajima, Wakayama, Yamanaka

NAMBU TEKKI IRONWARE
Morioka

TEA WHISKS
Nara, Takayama

TEMARI BALLS
Matsumoto, Wakayama

WASHI PAPER
Gifu, Mino, Echizen

WOODCARVING
Hokkaidō, Takayama, Kiso Valley

CRAFT FAIRS

· Arita Ceramics Fair (Arita, Kyūshū), Golden Week
kyushu-japan-holidays.com/ kyushu-guide/events/87-arita-ceramics-fair.html

· Craft Fair (Matsumoto, Chūbu), late May
visitmatsumoto.com/en/event/ craftfair

· Kiyomizu Pottery Festival (Kyoto, Kansai), mid- to late October
kyoto.travel/en/planyourvisit/events/ schedule/17

· Mashiko Pottery Fair (Mashiko, Kantō), Golden Week and early November
mashiko-kankou.org/english/mta1/ mashikoyaki/toukiiti/tokiichi.htm

· Pottery Momiji Festival (Kyoto, Kansai), mid- to late November
en.seiyoukai.com

· Tokyo Traditional Crafts Fair (Tokyo, Kantō), mid- to late January
www.sangyo-rodo.metro.tokyo.jp/ shoko/dentokogei/english/hinmoku/ index.html

WHERE TO BUY CRAFT

GENERAL

CHŪBU
· Analogue Life (Nagoya)
analoguelife.com

HOKKAIDŌ
· D&Department (Sapporo)
d-department.com
· Nakasatsunai Art Village
rokkatei.co.jp/facilities

KANSAI
· Kiso Artec (Kyoto)
kiso-artech.co.jp
· Tango Tanimura (tea whisks; Nara)
tango-tanimura.com
· Teramachi Dōri (Kyoto)

KANTŌ
· 2k540 Aki Oka Artisan (Tokyo)
jrtk.jp
· Bingoya, Shinjuku (Tokyo)
bingoya.tokyo
· Japan Traditional Crafts Aoyama
Square (Tokyo)
kougeihin.jp
· Kiya (knives; Tokyo)
kiya-hamono.co.jp
· Lucite Gallery (antique craft; Tokyo)
lucite-gallery.com

KYŪSHŪ
· Beppu Traditional Bamboo
Crafts Center (Beppu)
*discover-oita.com/en/japan-
attractions/beppu-traditonal-
bamboo-crafts-center*
· Ōita Made (Ōita)
oitamade.jp
· Select Beppu (including
bamboo; Beppu), p. 319
beppuproject.com

TŌHOKU
· Craft Hall Shop 'Vest Pocket' (Sendai)
artpark.or.jp/en/vest-pocket
· Kamasada (ironware; Morioka)
· Kogensha (Sendai)
kogensya.sakura.ne.jp
· Kogensya (Morioka)
morioka-kogensya.sakura.ne.jp

POTTERY
· Asahido Honten (Kyoto, Kansai)
asahido.co.jp
· Kitone (Kyoto, Kansai)
kitone.jp
· Utsuwa Kaede (Tokyo, Kantō)
utsuwa-kaede.com
· Utsuwa Monotsuki (Kyoto, Kansai)
www.monotsuki.com

KIMONO
· Itchiku Kubota Museum
(Fuji Kawaguchiko, Chūbu)
itchiku-museum.com
· Kioi Art Gallery Edo Ise-Katagami
Kimono Museum (Tokyo, Kantō)
kioi.jp
· Kimono National Museum
(Fuji Kawaguchiko, Chūbu)
www.kyohaku.go.jp
· Ome Kimono Museum
(Tokyo, Kantō)
omekimono.jp/english
· Tōkamachi (Chūbu)
Known as a 'kimono town'; don't
miss Aoyagi and Kinusho
tokamachi-tourism.jp/experience

FABRIC
· Bunka Gakuen Shop (Tokyo, Kantō)
bunka-koubai.com
· Kyoto Shibori Museum
(Kyoto, Kansai)
kyotoshibori.com
· Materialli (Tokyo, Kantō),
also in Daikanyama Tokyo
mina-perhonen.jp
· Momenya Makino (Tokyo, Kantō)
momenyamakino.com
· Nippori (Tokyo, Kantō)
Known as a 'Fabric Street'; grab
a fabric map and don't miss Tomato
nippori-senigai.com
· Nishijin Textile Center
(Kyoto, Kansai)
nishijin.or.jp
· Orinasukan (Kyoto, Kansai)
orinasukan.com

WASHI PAPER
· Fukunishi Washi Honpo (Nara, Kansai)
fukunishiwashihonpo.com
· Haibara (Tokyo, Kantō)
haibara.co.jp
· Isetatsu (Tokyo, Kantō)
isetatsu.com
· Kamiji Kakimoto (Kyoto, Kansai)
kamiji-kakimoto.jp
· Kamisoe (Kyoto, Kansai)
kamisoe.com
· Morita Washi (Kyoto, Kansai)
www.wagami.jp
· Pigment (Tokyo, Kantō)
pigment.tokyo

PLACES TO EXPERIENCE CRAFT
· Akui Craft Park (Sendai, Tōhoku)
· Edo Taito Traditional Crafts
Center (Tokyo, Kantō)
craft.city.taito.lg.jp
· Evam Eva (Yamanashi, Chūbu)
evameva-yamanashi.com
· Kyoto Museum of Traditional
Crafts (Kyoto, Kansai)
kmtc.jp
· Matsumoto Folk Craft Museum
(Matsumoto, Chūbu)
visitmatsumoto.com
· Mingeikan (Tokyo, Kantō)
mingeikan.or.jp
· MOMAT Craft Gallery (Tokyo, Kantō)
momat.go.jp
· Morioka Handi-Works Square
(Morioka, Tōhoku)
visitiwate.com
· Omiya Bonsai Village (Saitama, Kantō)
www.city.saitama.jp
· Ozu Washi Paper Museum
(Tokyo, Kantō)
ozuwashi.net
· Shimadzu Satsuma Kiriko
Glassworks (Kagoshima, Kyūshū)
senganen.jp/en/experience
· Sumida Edo Kiriko Museum
(Tokyo, Kantō)
edokiriko.net
· Takumi No Sato Craft Village
(Minakami, Kantō)
visitgunma.jp

ANTIQUE & FLEA MARKETS

——— Antique and flea markets have fixed days and weekend opening times, so plan ahead if you're looking to visit one of those listed. Cultural events and New Year celebrations can also affect their schedules, so always check online. Big cities have multiple markets, so ask your hotel and/or host for advice when you arrive. We love markets in shrines (see the two Kyoto markets) for food, culture and old wares. Expect vintage kimono, photographs, ceramics, ironware, children's toys, ephemera, an abundance of street food, and colourful characters. If it's raining, most markets will not open.

- Arai Yakushi Flea Market
  (Nakano, Kantō)
  First Sunday of the month
  araiyakushi.or.jp

- Kobo-ichi Market,
  Toji Temple (Kyoto, Kansai)
  21st of each month
  kyotostation.com/toji-temple-kobo-ichi-market

ABOVE: Vintage finds at Oedo Antique Market, Tokyo, Kantō

- Nogi Shrine Antique Market
  (Tokyo, Kantō)
  Fourth Sunday of the month
  www.nogikotto.com

- Oedo Antique Market
  (Tokyo, Kantō)
  First and third Sunday of each month *antique-market.jp*

- Senda Wasshoi Matsuri
  Flea Market
  (Hiroshima, Chūgoku)
  Check schedule for dates
  gethiroshima.com

- Shitennō-ji Flea Market
  (Osaka, Kansai)
  21st–22nd of every month
  shitennoji.or.jp

- Tenjin-san Flea Market, Kitano Tenmangu (Kyoto, Kansai) ·
  25th of each month
  kitanotenmangu.or.jp

- Yamaguchi Flea Market
  (Yamaguchi, Chūgoku)
  First Sunday of each month
  www.pref.yamaguchi.lg.jp/cms/a12900/access/0704_feature2.html

現代美術

CONTEMPORARY ART & ARTISTS

—— All of our trips to Japan over the years have included one art trek – either into a secluded part of a big city or a seriously planned three-hour daytrip exhibition pilgrimage. Travelling for art can be as much about the building as the works themselves. Here are some of our favourites, but there is so much incredible art in Japan that we almost need a separate book to talk about it.

BELOW: Michelle at Hara Museum ARC, Ikaho Onsen, Gunma, Kantō

CHŪBU

- 21st Century Museum of Contemporary Art (Kanazawa; p. 214), kanazawa21.jp
- Echigo-Tsumari Art Field (Niigata; p. 226), echigo-tsumari.jp
- Gifu Media Cosmos (Gifu), g-mediacosmos.jp
- Kanazawa Library (Kanazawa), www.lib.kanazawa.ishikawa.jp
- Matsumoto City Museum of Art (Matsumoto; p. 219), matsumoto-artmuse.jp

CHŪGOKU

- Hiroshima MOCA (Hiroshima; p. 266), hiroshima-moca.jp
- Shoji Ueda Museum of Photography (Yonago; p. 274), www.houki-town.jp
- Adachi Museum of Art (Yasugi; p. 275), www.adachi-museum.or.jp

HOKKAIDŌ

- Hokkaidō Museum of Modern Art (Sapporo), dokyoi.pref.hokkaido. lg/hk/knb
- Sapporo Art Park (Sapporo), artpark.or.jp

KANSAI

- Miho Museum (near Shigaraki; pp. 257, 299), miho.or.jp
- Osaka Contemporary Art Center, (Osaka)

KANTŌ

- Hara Museum ARC (Ikaho Onsen), haramuseum.or.jp
- Tomihiro Art Museum (Midori City), www.city.midori.gunma.jp

KYŪSHŪ

- Ōita Prefectural Art Museum (Ōita), opam.jp

SHIKOKU/THE SETO INLAND SEA

- Chichu Art Museum (Naoshima; p. 293), benesse-artsite.jp
- Inujima Seirensho Art Museum (Inujima), benesse-artsite.jp
- Isamu Noguchi Garden Museum (Takamatsu; p. 301), isamunoguchi.or.jp
- Lee Ufan Museum (Naoshima), benesse-artsite.jp
- Teshima Art Museum (Teshima; p. 295), benesse-artsite.jp

TŌHOKU

- Akita Museum of Art (Akita; p. 194), www.akita-museum-of-art.jp
- Aomori Museum of Art (Aomori; p. 199), aomori-museum.jp
- Reborn-Art Festival (Miyagi), reborn-art-fes.jp

TOKYO & SURROUNDS

- 21_21 Design Sight (p. 167), 2121designsight.jp
- Mori Art Museum (p. 167), mori.art.museum
- MOT, mot-art-museum.jp/en
- Roppongi Art Night – late May, www.roppongiartnight.com
- teamLab Borderless (p. 171), borderless.teamlab.art
- Teien Art Museum, www.teien-art-museum.ne.jp
- Yayoi Kusama Museum, yayoikusamamuseum.jp

NEAR TOKYO

- Hakone Open-Air Museum (Hakone; p. 185), hakone-oam.or.jp
- Homma Museum of Art (Yamagata), homma-museum.or.jp
- Yokohama Museum of Art (Yokohama), yokohama.art.museum

KEY ARTISTS

YAYOI KUSAMA

Japanese pop artist Yayoi Kusama, now in her nineties, is a living treasure. She is best known for her sculptures and installations, but over the years she has painted, written novels, directed a film, had a fashion collection in Bloomingdales New York, and worked as an art dealer. Her work with spots are her most famous, enveloping us inside installations or forcing us to see pumpkins in a different way.

SEE HER WORK AT:
Yayoi Kusama Gallery (Tokyo, Kantō), National Museum of Modern Art (Tokyo, Kantō), Matsumoto City Museum of Art (Matsumoto, Chūbu; p. 219), Miyanoura Port (Naoshima, Shikoku; p. 293), Benesse House (Naoshima, Shikoku; p. 293)

TAKASHI MURAKAMI

Murakami's colourful psychedelic flowers, mushrooms and characters are loved around the world. A fan of pop culture and inventor of the Superflat style, his quirky sense of humour and plays on everyday objects, nature and Buddhist iconography have seen him collaborate with Louis Vuitton, Issey Miyake, Kanye West and Kid Cudi.

BUY HIS WORK AT:
Roppongi Hills Design and Art Store

YOSHIMOTO NARA

Nara's naive paintings and sculptures of childlike characters smoking cigarettes or looking at you in an unnerving way have made their way into galleries all over the world and have been popularised on postcards, T-shirts and in books. His gallery, N's Yard, is situated in the middle of a quiet forest in Nasushiobara (Kantō).

SEE HIS WORK AT:
Aomori Prefectural Museum of Art (Aomori, Tōhoku), Hara Museum of Art (Tokyo, Kantō), A-Z Café (Tokyo, Kantō)

KOHEI NAWA

Nawa's taxidermy deer sculptures covered with glass balls are globally revered. A darling of the Japanese art scene, he funnels his creativity into sculptural projects and collaborations in his Uji-based factory workroom SANDWICH. He is a lecturer at Kyoto University of Art and Design.

SEE HIS WORK AT:
Hara Museum Tokyo (Kantō), Tokyo Midtown (Kantō; p. 167), MOT (Tokyo, Kantō), Mori Art Museum (Tokyo, Kantō; p. 167), Takamatsu City Museum of Art (Shikoku)

PROJECTS:
KOHTEI Art Pavilion, Shinshoji Zen Museum and Gardens (Hiroshima, Chūgoku; p. 355); Vessel, ROHM Theatre (Kyoto, Kansai) and Creative Center (Osaka, Kansai).

FASHION

Salarymen on the subway with fluoro socks and elaborately designed shoes. Kids on the streets of Harajuku in Tokyo in over-the-top styles. Chic women with angular haircuts wearing layers of linen. Genderless outfits, simplicity, a mash-up of seemingly disparate items. It's all found on the streets of Japan.

Tokyo is the fashion capital, with many one-off stores selling boutique items, but there are brilliant stores all over the country. If you're not sure where to start, head to one of the big department stores to get your bearings. International brands create special items for the hungry Japanese market. Stores curate stock for each location, so if you see something you like in one city, chances are it won't be in the next place you visit.

Sizes run small in Japan. With women's fashion there is often just one size: F or free size. Men's clothing usually comes in medium and large. Remember to try everything on – you may be a small in your own country and find yourself fitting a large in Japan. Accessories like scarves, bags, umbrellas, wallets and socks will Japanify your wardrobe and have everyone asking 'Where did you buy that?!'

——— Japan has a unique take on fashion and as a consequence has been a destination for many fashion-, design- or art-conscious travellers over the years. It's difficult to put a finger on why fashion is so distinctive in Japan. Is it their history of kimono with unusual colour theories and shapes; is it connected to technology, new fabrics and techniques to make everyday items like jeans or seasonal wear; or is it connected to the way creativity is integrated into regular life? Perhaps it's all of these things and more, and it doesn't really matter – all we know is Japanese fashion showcases the future unlike that of any other country; shop design and displays are art-gallery worthy; and what you see on the streets of Japan may not make sense in the West for years to come.

ACCESSORIES

- Porter (Tokyo, Kantō; Osaka, Kansai)
- Postalco (Tokyo, Kantō)
  postalco.net
- Tabio (all over Japan)
  tabio.com/jp

BRANDS WITH STORES JAPAN-WIDE

- Beams
  beams.co.jp
- Tomorrowland
  tomorrowland.jp
- United Arrows
  united-arrows.co.jp

CHIC

- Biotop (Tokyo, Kantō; Osaka, Kansai)
  www.biotop.jp
- Evam Eva (Tokyo, Kantō; Kyoto, Kansai)
  evameva.com
- Fog Linen Work (Tokyo, Kantō)
  foglinenwork.com/en
- ILDK Apartments (Tokyo, Kantō)
  1ldkshop.com

DEPARTMENT STORES OR SHOPPING CENTRES

- Fuji Daimaru (Kyoto, Kansai; p. 238)
  fujiidaimaru.co.jp/fg_tax_ekc
- Hankyu Department Store (Osaka, Kansai; p. 254)
  hankyu-dept.co.jp/fl/english/honten
- Isetan (all over Japan)
- Parco (all over Japan)
  www.parco.co.jp/sp/en/about/store
- Takashimaya (all over Japan)
  takashimaya-global.com

GEEK (OTAKU) FASHION

- Akihabara and Ikebukuro (Tokyo, Kantō; p. 170)
- Nipponbashi, Den Den Town (Osaka, Kansai)

MINIMALISM & INNOVATION

- Arts & Science (Tokyo, Kantō; Kyoto, Kansai)
  arts-science.com
- Centre for Cosmic Wonder (Tokyo, Kantō)
  cosmicwonder.com/center
- Muji Labo (inside larger Muji stores all over Japan)
  muji.com/us/mujilabo
- Okura (Tokyo, Kantō)
  www.hrm.co.jp/okura
- Studious (Tokyo, Kantō)
  studious.co.jp

MODERN KIMONO

- Otsuka Gofukuten (Kyoto, Kansai)
  otsuka-gofukuten.jp
- Robe Japonica (Tokyo, Kantō)
  robe-japonica.jp
- The Yard (Sendai, Tōhoku; Tokyo, Kantō)
  the-yard.jp

SHOPPING AREAS

- Ginza and Daikanyama (Tokyo, Kantō; pp. 166, 174)
- Shijō Dōri (Kyoto, Kansai; p. 238)
- Shinsaibashi-Suji Street and Orange Street (Osaka, Kansai; p. 252)

STREETWEAR & CASUAL

- C.E (Tokyo, Kantō)
  cavempt.com
- Nanamica (Tokyo, Kantō; Kobe, Kansai; Fukuoka, Kyūshū)
  nanamica.com
- Undercover (all over Japan)
  undercoverism.com

SUPERSTAR DESIGNERS

- Issey Miyake
  isseymiyake.com
- Rei Kawakubo (Comme des Garçons)
  comme-des-garcons.com
- Yohji Yamamoto
  theshopyohjiyamamoto.com

TEXTILES

- Minä Perhonen (Tokyo, Kantō; Kyoto, Kansai; Matsumoto, Chūbu)
  mina-perhonen.jp
- Sou Sou (Kyoto, Kansai)
  sousou.co.jp
- Tsumori Chisato (all over Japan)
  en.tsumorichisato.com

TRAINERS

Shibuya and Harajuku (both p. 165) are the home of trainers in Tokyo. You'll find Atmos, Onitsuka Tiger, RFW Tokyo, Hender Scheme, ABC Mart, Worm Tokyo and Japan-only versions of Converse, Puma and Nike.

YOUTH FASHION HOTSPOTS

TOKYO, KANTŌ

- 109 Building (Shibuya)
  shibuya109.jp
- Laforet (Harajuku)
  laforet.ne.jp
- Shopping areas: Omotesandō Dōri, around Yoyogi Park on weekends (Harajuku); vintage street style (Shimokitazawa and Kōenji; p. 173)
- Takashita Dōri (Harajuku)
  takeshita-street.com

OSAKA, KANSAI

- Around Namba Hatch on weekends
- Vintage street style (Amemura, Nakazakichō; p. 255)

OPPOSITE PAGE & ABOVE: Tokyo and Kyoto fashion moments

MUSIC

———— The Japanese are passionate about music and have a long history of traditional musical styles leading up to a mid-century fascination with jazz and American rock'n'roll. They became leaders in experimental electronica in the 1970s and 1980s, and developed an obsession with homegrown pop music in the 1990s and Korean pop (K-pop) after that. Indie music, twee, experimental and metal are not only popular, they can often be combined into one band's sound. From the ethereal sounds of *Noh* theatre (p. 363) and the meditative plucking of early instruments to the *kawaii* girls belting out dark tunes with Babymetal or Kyary Pamyu Pamyu's irresistible quirky pop, Japanese music is fascinating, challenging, diverse and exciting.

BELOW: Our friend Shoko Seko with some of her vintage vinyl

TRADITIONAL

The earliest Japanese music can be traced to *shōmyō* (the chanting and singing of the monks) and *gagaku*, which accompanied theatrical performances at the Imperial Court. *Jōruri* was a style of folk music made by the general population who lacked access to the courts and couldn't partake of monk chants. *Hyōshigi* is an ambient, tonal sound made by two wooden boards or sticks striking each other – a recognisable part of Japanese spiritual or meditative music that you'll still hear in *Noh* theatre (p. 363) and at temples.

TRADITIONAL INSTRUMENTS

- *Biwa* (lute)
- *Fue* (flute)
- *Kokyū* (bowed string instrument)
- *Koto* (zither)
- *Shakuhachi* (bamboo flute)
- *Shamisen* (three-stringed lute used in *Jōruri*)
- *Wadaiko* (taiko)/*odaiko*/*tzusumi* – (drums)

ENKA

Enka preceded contemporary music. It began as musical political messages, sentimental, melancholy songs with vocal flourishes and vibrato that formed the basis of sorts for Japanese contemporary pop. Misora Hibari's impassioned serenade 'Kawa no Nagare no Yō ni' ('Like the Flow of the River') is still frequently voted the best Japanese song of all time.

THE NEW AGE

The influence of America on twentieth-century music was huge – 1950s rock'n'roll, jazz and Hawaiian music took over the public consciousness, and remain popular to this day. Japan remains obsessed with jazz; go into most bars and cafés, and you'll hear it playing.

ROCK BANDS

Indie rock, punk and 1960s-inspired rock still influence many Japanese bands. Check out:

- 5.6.7.8's
- Glay
- Maximum the Hormone
- Mono
- ONE OK ROCK
- Shonen Knife
- Snail Ramp
- Thee Michelle Gun Elephant
- X Japan

EXPERIMENTAL

Japan had its own Kraftwerk in the form of Ryuichi Sakamoto's Yellow Magic Orchestra – listen to 'Computer Game (Theme from the Circus)' (1978). Japan was fast becoming one of the most technologically advanced countries in the world, and this was reflected in its music. Electronic experimentation was a staple of both regular music releases and avant-garde performances, and this aesthetic remains strong today – listen to ' Audio Architecture' by Cornelius (2018).

Japanese experimentation is also reflected in its soundscapes – experimental or meditative music and sounds that waft through landscapes, city buildings and galleries, even department stores. Soundscapes can be natural (rivers, birdsong, rustling trees), historical (church bells, the sounds of crafting woodwork, textiles and ceramics) and spiritual (temple bells and chimes, monk prayers). Japan voted the 'Drift ice in the Sea of Okhotsk' its number one sound.

EXPERIMENTAL BANDS

- Cornelius
- Fantastic Plastic Machine
- Lullatone
- Pizzicato Five
- Ryuichi Sakamoto
- Yellow Magic Orchestra

J-POP & THE IDOL WARS

It's the 1990s and Japan has discovered what will become an undying love for cute pop music. Modern J-pop is born (the name first covered all types of pop music), and it storms the charts. J-pop began with the Beach Boys and the Beatles as models – classic pop-song structures and feel. Now it's chart candy-floss with catchy melodies and trite lyrics, nearly always accompanied by highly choreographed dances. More recently, J-pop has been influenced by K-pop (although it is more chaste) and has taken in elements of rap and R'n'B.

Pop idol bands have become big business since the 2000s. *Idol sengoku jida* ('idol war age') is the term the Japanese give to the J-pop era. Bands like AKB48 were moulded by mega-producer Yasushi Akimoto, who put together a girl group with their own performance space (in Akihabara; p. 170) to do shows and meet the obsessive fans. They have reigned over the pop charts for ten years. Fans at concerts are known to wave glowsticks, chant and dance, a bit like a rave, in a practice called *wotagei* (obsessive J-pop fans are called *wota* – pronounced 'oh-ta', an offshoot of *otaku*, meaning obsessives or nerds). →

J-POP BANDS & SINGERS

- AKB48
- Babymetal
- B'z
- Exile
- Hey! Say! JUMP
- Kyary Pamyu Pamyu
- Perfume
- Scandal
- SMAP

LIVE HOUSES, VENUES & ARENAS

If you want to experience Japanese music for yourself, one of the best ways is to head down to a live house. Any space that can fit a (tiny) stage and a bar can become a live house – they're often small, dank basements, obscure back-alley dives, or rooms on the top floor of office blocks. Expect to see a bunch of people onstage playing thrash, experimental jazz, jangly twee pop, 1960s surf, heavy metal, prog and psychedelia ... and when that band finishes, an acid house band will probably come on. From young kids taking their first tentative music steps to 40-plus-year-old office workers and hobbyists who should be playing at Carnegie Hall, live houses take you on a wonderful journey through the Japanese musical underground. Shows often start as early as 6 pm, and despite a line-up of four or five bands you'll still get the last train home.

As you'd expect, Japan is also full of spectacular arenas and many mid-sized venues that host gigs from bands from all over the world and all genres of music. The Nippon Budokan is a famous arena in Japan, once the hallowed ground for martial arts, which made the Beatles gig there in 1966 somewhat controversial. Cheap

Trick released 'Live at the Budokan' in 1979, bringing the venue's name to a world audience.

Expect early starts – forget about a band going on at any time from 9 to 11 pm; in Japan they can go on as early as 6 or 7 pm. You could be in bed by eight. Very respectable! Always check times so you don't miss out. Also expect polite crowds – you might be used to unbridled enthusiasm from a live crowd and copious amount of booze, but the Japanese keep it classy. Until recently, there was often respectful silence during a song and then a burst of applause later. We've been to seated gigs where people actually *remained seated* for the whole performance (a few rebels stood up and swayed during some songs). It's a bit different now – there'll be cheering and the occasional '*Dai suki*' ('I like it/you very much'), but it will still be pleasantly less chaotic. You'll often have to pay a 'venue surcharge' when you arrive, which comes with a drink ticket. It's a way to force you to buy at least one drink so the venue can make money on top of their meagre ticket takings, which might mostly go to the promotor. Roll with it and get a loosen-up drink for the gig. You'll need it with all those well-mannered gig-goers and the 8–9 pm late night you're about to have!

LIVE HOUSES

TOKYO, KANTŌ

· Ikebukuro: ADM Live Garage, Apple Jump
· Kōenji: Knock, 20,000 Den-atsu, Penguin House, SUBstore, Muryoko Muzenji, Jirokichi, Kōenji Alone, BnA Hotel
· Shibuya: Aoyama Hachi, 7th Floor
· Shimokitazawa: Live Holic, Shelter, 440, Garage, Drum Song, Mosaic
· Shinjuku: 21st century, ACB Hall

VENUES

· Club Quattro (Tokyo, Kantō; Hiroshima Parco, Hiroshima, Chūgoku; Umeda, Osaka, Kansai)
· Metro (Kyoto, Kansai)
· Muse (Osaka, Kansai)
· Nippon Budokan (Tokyo, Kantō)
· Saitama Super Arena (Tokyo, Kantō)
· Shidax Hall (Tokyo, Kantō)
· Sone (Kobe, Kansai)
· Shinikaba Studio Coast (Tokyo, Kantō)
· Tokyo Dome (Tokyo, Kantō)

VINYL-HUNTING IN JAPAN

The Japanese are vintage obsessed and when it comes to music they love to do a bit of crate-digging to add to their vinyl collections. As far as record stores go, Japan is high on the list when it comes to rarities, quality, ultra-cool stores and Japan-only special releases. Big cities are the place to be, but some stores exist in out-of-the-way towns and hidden destinations as well.

TOKYO, KANTŌ
· Be-In Record (Kōenji)
· Big Love (Harajuku)
· Coconuts Disk (Ikebura)
· Disc Union (Shinjuku, Shibuya)
· Flash Disc Ranch (Shimokitazawa)
· HMV (Shibuya)
· Jet Set (Shimokitazawa)
· Manhattan Records (Shibuya)
· Nat Records (Shinjuku)

OSAKA, KANSAI
· Compufunk Records (Kitahamahigashi)
· Disc Union (Amemura)
· King Kong (Shinsaibashi)
· Rare Groove (Shinsaibashi)
· Time Bomb Records (Amemura)

KYOTO, KANSAI
· 100000t Alone Toko
· Bootsy's
· Happy Jack
· Jet Set
· Joe's Garage
· Parallax Records
· Pocoapoco
· Prototype
· Workshop Records

OTHERS
· Hakata/Fukuoka, Kyūshū: Ticro Market, Jungle Exotica, Groovin
· Hiroshima, Chūgoku: Dumd Records, Hiroshima Will Burn (Disc Union)
· Kanazawa, Chūbu: Record Jungle
· Kagoshima, Kyūshū: Sunrise, Gadget
· Matsumoto, Chūbu: Beatniks Records
· Morioka, Tōhoku: Disknote, Neat Records, Knowledge Records, SoundChannel
· Sapporo, Hokkaidō: Beat Records, Takechas
· Takamatsu, Shikoku: Mushroom Records

Thank you to our amazing publisher and friend, Mary Small. Thank you for believing in us, for your insight, care and inspirational way of taking an idea and making it into something so much more than we ever thought possible.

To Clare Marshall, our perfect project manager and editor. For your passion, way with words and keen eye for perfection. Thank you for travelling to Japan with us, for the 15-hour days, for modelling on the pages and for having the perfect *onsen* etiquette. Thanks also to Nina for your art direction and tips on adding more cats to the pages.

To Jane Winning, such an important part of the Plum family, for all your support for our Japan books over the years.

To Armelle Habib, for travelling with us and taking the perfect images of our Japan. Your ability to capture people and places is awe-inspiring. Thank you for 15-hour days, and for knowing we needed ALL the *ekiben* shots.

Thank you to Heather Menzies for typesetting skills that go above and beyond. Thank you for carrying on under extraordinary circumstances with a sunny disposition and immaculate handiwork.

Thank you to Nicola Young for your smart and speedy editing skills, for your patience on such a large project and for your help shaping this book.

Thank you to Hiki and Ryo Komura for sharing Mashiko with us. And a huge thank-you to Hiki for checking the Japanese text on the pages, and for your craft consultancy, friendship and incredible support.

Thank you to Coco Tashima for all your help, support and kindness during the making of this book. To both Hiki and Coco, thank you for sharing your Japan with us over so many years, for answering all of our cultural questions, and for giving us a deeper understanding of your beautiful country.

Thank you to our Insiders: Makiko Sugita, Flora Waycott, Beth Kempton, Trisha Garner, Ryoko Tashima, Sarah Richmond and Taka Tsubata, for sharing your passion for Japan with us and our readers. Thank you to Makiko for showing us the beauty of Morioka and for making us fall in love with the north.

A huge thanks to Keitaro Osajima from the Kyushu Railway Company (Seven Stars in Kyushu), Matsuda Takeyoshi from Reversible Destiny Lofts Mitaka and Keisuke Matsumiya from Hiroshi Nakamura & NAP Co., Ltd. Thanks also to Hiroki Osaki and Nobuko Ohara from Nacasa & Partners Inc., Aki Yamada from the Toyo Ito Museum of Architecture, Yuko Fujii from Gunma Prefectural Government, Yusuke Harada from Hoshino Resorts Inc and the wonderful staff at HOSHINOYA Kyoto.

Thank you to our supportive families: Margaret and Barry, Chris, Heather, Tracy, Marlene, Carolyn and Andrew and families. And to our absent fathers, David and Neil, who would have loved to see this book published.

Thanks to ALL our amazing friends and work colleagues for their unwavering love and support, and for sharing with us and listening patiently to all our Japan travel stories.

Steve and Michelle xxx

INDEX

A

Abashiri 288
accommodation 86–95
Adachi Museum Garden 275
Ainu people 14, 282
Airbnb 93
Akihabara 170
Akita City 194
Akita Kantō Matsuri 211
Akita Prefecture 148, 194, 196
Ando, Tadao 261, 292, 293, 303, 304, 353
animal cafés 168, 169
Anpanman Train 104
antique markets 373
Aomori 59, 116, 198–9, 361
Aomori Prefecture 198
Aoshima (Cat Island) 296
Aoyama 165
Arashiyama 95, 245–7, 315
arcade games 168, 169
architects, contemporary 92, 100, 261, 292, 293, 303, 304, 311, 352–5
architecture, by period 15, 17, 22, 29
Arima Onsen 260
Arita 310
art & artists, contemporary 374–5
art & craft 181, 182–3, 299, 310, 322, 329, 356, 366–9
    by period 15, 17, 18, 21, 22, 29, 33, 38, 43, 47
    map 370–2
art islands 292, 295
art stays 93
Asahikawa 74, 287, 315
Asakusa 172
Ashikaga shogunate 22
Astro Boy 50, 100
Atami 226
autumn 64–9, 70
    experiences 68–9
    festivals 66–7
    trains 105
    autumn leaves 68, 350
Azuchi-Momoyama period (1573–1600) 22–5, 347

B

beer 62, 145, 149, 153, 217, 227, 283
beliefs and religion 332
    see also Buddhism/Buddhist temples;
    Shinto/Shinto shrines
bentō 78, 97, 98–9
Beppu 316–19
    onsen 318
Biei 287, 299, 316
Bonin Islands 181

bonsai 350
Book Nerd 202, 203
boro 367
brewery tastings and tours 148–9
Buddhism/Buddhist temples 61, 75, 177, 189, 237, 240, 243, 251, 256, 259, 287, 329, 332, 336–7, 347
buildings
    by period 18, 21, 30, 34, 41, 44, 48, 342–3
    see also temples and shrines;
    tiered pagodas
Bukko-ji, the Temple of Buddha's Light 237
Byakue Daikannon (White-robed Buddha) 189

C

capsule hotels 90
capsule toys 169
castles 22, 181, 210, 216, 242, 256, 266, 268, 289, 302, 329, 344–5
cherry blossom (sakura) 36, 70, 83
    trains 83, 106
    viewing 83–5, 175, 177, 207, 210, 216, 218, 221, 266, 289, 309
Chiba Prefecture 161
Chibiko Ninja Mura (Kids' Ninja Village) 78
Chichu Art Museum 293
Chikubu Island 256
Chūbu 109, 158, 159, 212–31, 267
    adventures 226–7
    regional food and drink 118, 119, 121, 124, 136, 145, 147
Chūgoku 109, 158, 159, 262–75
    adventures 274–5
    regional food and drink 125, 145
Churaumi Aquarium 78, 327
cities and regions 158, 159
clothing 89, 376–7
    to pack 70
coffee 152
Comico Art Museum 311
craft beer 145, 149, 173, 217, 227
cultural icons 338–41
culture, by period 15, 18, 21, 24, 29, 33, 38, 43, 47
Cup Noodles Museum 191, 361
cycling adventures 314–15

D

Daikanyama 174
Daisetsuzan National Park 287
dango 128, 140
Danjiri Matsuri (Cart-pulling festivals) 67
Danjō-garan 259
daruma (dolls) 83, 339

deer feeding 78, 250, 272
Demchiyanagi 240
Doai Station, Minakami 100
Dōgo Onsen 302, 303
Domo-kun 50
Dōtonbori 255
drinks 144–53
    see also under specific towns and regions
D.T. Suzuki Museum 217, 361

E

early Japan 14
Earthquake Museum 261
Ebisu 149
Edo period (1603–1868) 24, 28–31, 342, 343, 349
Ehime Prefecture 302
Eighty-eight Temple Pilgrimage Trail 229, 303
Eizan Railway to Kurama Maple Leaf Tunnel 105
ekiben (train bentō) 78, 97, 99
Engaku-ji (Zen temple) 177
enka 379
Enoden (retro train) 105, 177
Enoshima 177
Enoshima Sea Candle 105, 176
eras of Japan 13–49
experimental bands/music 379

F

fashion 26–7, 376–7
festivals 163, 199, 210, 246, 255, 271, 309
    by season 58–63, 66–7, 74–5, 82–3
film and television 47
flea markets 373
flowers 287, 299, 309, 315, 349
    festivals 68
food 6, 111–43, 153
    see also under seasons; specific regions and towns
food markets 154–5, 216, 238, 283, 309, 322
Fuji art 222
Fuji Excursion Train 107
Fuji Fives Lakes 221, 349
Fukui Prefectural Dinosaur Museum 361
Fukuoka 308–9
Fukuoka Buddha 337
Fukuoka Prefecture 308
Fukushima Castle 289
Furano 287, 299, 315, 349
Furano Biei Norokko Train (Lavender Express) 105
Fushimi Inari shrine 243, 334
Futago-ji 329
Futenma Shrine 334

G

gardens/garden styles 163, 236, 240, 253, 275, 301, 336, 346–51
  by period 16, 18, 24, 29, 33, 349
Gasshō-style Minka farm houses 343
Gegege No Kitaro (train) 104
geisha 17
  in Gion 238
Ghibli Museum 175, 361
giant Buddhas (Daibutsu) 177, 251, 337
Gifu Prefecture 224, 227
Ginkaku-ji (Silver Pavilion) 22, 337, 348
ginkgo trees 68
Ginza 166
Ginzan Onsen 208
Gion 238
Gion Matsuri (Kyoto) 59
Gion Yamakasa Matsuri 309
glamping/yurting 88
Godzilla 50
gohan (rice) 115
Gōjo Dōri 237
Gokayama 181, 225
'Golden Week' 83
Gono Line, Akita 108
Gotemba 149
gourd (hyōtan) 36
Gozan No Okuribi Daimonji Festival (Fire Mountain Send-off Festival) 59
Great Daibutsu 177
greenhouses 350
Gunkanjima Island 329
Gunma Prefecture 161, 184, 188
  onsen 184–5
gyōza 116

H

Hakata 116, 308
Hakodate 116, 278
  Asaichi Morning Market 154, 278
Hakone 184–5
  Jinja Shrine 334
Hakusan 361
Hanamaki 211
Hanamaki Onsen 211
Hanamikoji 238
Hanayome Noren (train) 106
hanbāgu (hamburger) 138
Hannō 78
Hanwa Line 106
Harajuku 165
Harajuku-Omotesandō Genki Matsuri Super Yosakoi (Traditional Dance Festival) 58
Hatsumōde 75
hayashi rice (beef and rice) 138
Heian period (794–1185) 17–19, 26, 347
Heisei/Reiwa era (1989–ongoing) 46–9
Hello Kitty 50, 78, 104
Hida Folk Village 224, 225
Higashi Hongan-ji 237
Higashiyama 238, 239
Hikone Castle 256

Himeji 260
Himeji Castle 181, 345
Himi Line (Toyama) 105
Hina Matsuri (Doll's Day/Girls' Day) 82
Hirosaki Castle 211
Hiroshi Nakamura & NAP 354
Hiroshima 148, 264–6
  Genbaku (Atomic Bomb) Dome 181, 265
  Peace Memorial Park and Museum 265, 361
Hiroshima Castle 266
Hiroshima Prefecture 264, 272
Hisatsu Line 105
historical building sites 18, 21, 30, 34, 41, 44, 48, 342–3
Hita 148
hobbyists 169
Hojusanrishaku-ji 206, 299
Hokkaidō 09, 158, 159, 267, 276–88
  adventures 286–9
  regional food and drink 118, 121, 122, 125, 131, 132, 145, 147
Hokkaidō Shrine 284
homestays 91
Honshū 158, 159, 161, 193, 213, 233
Hōryū-ji 337
Hoshi Onsen Chōkukan 185
HOSHINOYA brand 88
Hoshokan Museum 249
hostels 91
hot springs 317, 329
hotels 90, 91, 93
Hozuki-ichi (Lantern Plant Festival) 58

I

Ibaraki Prefecture 149, 161
Iburi Subprefecture 279, 280
Ibusuki 329
Ichinoseki 211
Ikaho Onsen 187
ikebana 350, 369
Ikebukuro 170
Imabari 305
Imari 310
Inujima 295
Inuyama Castle 345
Isamu Noguchi Garden Museum 301
Ise Jingū shrine 334
Ise-Shima 260, 335
Ishikari Subprefecture 281
Ishikawa Insect Museum 361
islands 158, 181, 261, 272–3, 292–8, 299, 326–7
Isozaki, Arata 355
Itami Juzo Museum 361
Ito 226
Ito, Toyo 354
Itsukushima-jinja 181, 273, 334
Iwami Ginzan Silver Mine 181, 275
Iya Valley 304
izakaya 117
Izu Peninsula 226
Izumo 67, 271, 335
Izumo Taisha 271, 335

J

J-pop 379
Japan, life in 357, 365
Japanese arts 363
Japanese Folk Toys Museum 269
Jidai Matsuri 66
Jigokudani 280
Jigokudani Monkey Park 78
Jimbōchō 175
Jindai-ji Yakuyoke Ganzan Jie Daishi Sai (Daruma Doll Fair) 83
Jizō (Ojizo-sama) 339
Jōmon period (1000–300 BC) 14, 342
Jōshin'etsu-kōgen National Park 187
Jozankei Onsen 287
JR Rikuu-to Line 105

K

Kabuki theatre 363
Kaga Onsen 227
Kagawa Prefecture 292, 301
Kagoshima 320–3
Kagoshima Prefecture 148, 151, 299, 320, 324
Kai brand 88
kaiseki ryōri 127
Kakunodate Fire and Snow Festival 75
Kamakura (city) 177
Kamakura (snow igloos) 343
Kamakura Daibutsu 337
Kamakura period (1185–1333) 20–1, 24, 348
Kamiari Festival 67
Kanagawa Prefecture 161, 185
Kanamara Penis Festivals 83
Kanazawa 116, 148, 154, 214–17, 361
Kanazawa Castle 216, 345
Kannawa 318
Kansai 109, 124, 125, 130–1, 158, 159, 232–61, 267
  adventures 260–1
  regional food and drink 119, 121, 123, 124, 125, 130–1, 132, 136, 145, 146, 147
Kantō 109, 158, 159, 160–91, 267
  adventures 190–1
  regional food and drink 118, 119, 121, 123, 125, 130, 132, 145, 147
karaage (fried chicken) 118
karaoke 168, 169
Karatsu 154
kare (curry) 138
Kasugayama Primeval Forest 251
Katsuyama City 361
Kawaguchiko Music Forest 361
Keio Takaosanguchi Station, Tokyo 100
Kichijōji 175
kids' Japan 78
Kii Mountains and Sacred Sites Pilgrimage 181, 230
Kimba the White Lion 50
kimchi nabe 119
Kinkaku-ji (Golden Pavilion) 22, 240, 337
Kinosaki 261

Kinosaki Onsen 261
Kintetsu Ikoma Cable Line (dog, cat and cake carriages) 104
kintsugi 368
Kirishima 324
kitsune 339
Kiyomizu-dera 239
    Seiryu-e Dragon Festival 66
Kizukuri Station, Aomori 101
Kobe 148, 261
Koenji 173
koi 340
Koinobori Festivals (Children's Day koi streamers) 83
kokedama 351
kokeshi 340
Kominato Railway 106
Konagai 329
Kōraku-en 268
Kubota Itchiku Art Museum 221
Kuma, Kengo 100, 311, 353
Kumamon Train 104
Kumamoto 329
Kumamoto Castle 329, 345
Kumano Kodō Trail 261
Kura warehouses with namako walls 342
Kurama No Hi Matsuri (Fire Festival) 66
Kurashiki 269
Kurobe Gorge 105
Kurokawa 299, 313
Kurokawa, Kisho 354
Kurokawa Onsen 299, 313
Kuromon Market, Osaka 154
Kusama, Yayoi 219, 375
Kusatsu Onsen 187
Kushiro 288
Kyo Train Garaku 106
Kyorinbo Temple 256
Kyoto 169, 181, 234–5, 315
    areas 236–43
    arts and crafts 236
    festivals 59, 66, 246
    gardens and parks 236, 240
    markets 154
    museums and galleries 236, 361
    omiyage 235
    regional food and drink 116, 148, 235
    sights 235
    temples and shrines 235, 335, 337
Kyoto Imperial Palace Gardens 240
Kyoto International Manga Museum 361
Kyoto Prefecture 234, 245
Kyoto Station 236
Kyūshū 109, 158, 159, 267, 306–29
    adventures 328–9
    regional food and drink 118, 119, 123, 132, 145, 146, 147

L

Lake Ashi 184, 185
Lake Biwa 105, 256–7
Lake Chūzenji 179, 315

Lake Kawaguchiko 221
Lake Mashū 288
Lake Motosuko 221
Lake Saiko ('Lake of the Maiden') 221
Lake Shojiko 221
Lake Towada 211
Lake Tōya 279
Lake Yamanakako 221
lavender 287
legendary creatures 341
Legoland Japan Resort 78
libraries 358
Limited Express Aso Boy 104
Limited Express Sonic (883 and 885 series) 106
Limited Express Spacia 107
Limited Express Umisachi Yamasachi 106
Limited Express Yufuin No Mori 105
literature 207, 215, 236, 249, 251, 259
    by period 15, 16, 17, 18, 21, 24, 29, 34, 38, 44, 47
lotus (rōtasu) 36
love hotels 93
luxury special-occasion experiences 88, 103, 106

M

Machiya houses 342
maneki neko 340
manhole art 356
Manza Onsen 187
maple leaves (momiji) 37
maps 158–9
Maruoka Castle 345
Mashiko 148, 182–3, 299
Matsue Castle 275, 345
Matsumae 289
Matsumoto 219, 299
Matsumoto Castle 219, 345
Matsuyama 302–3, 361
Matsuyama Castle 302
Media Arts Festival 59
Meguro 174
Meiji era (1868–1912) 27, 32–5
mentaiko pasta 138
Meoto Iwa (Wedded Rocks) 260, 335
Mie Prefecture 260
Miho Museum 257, 299
Miraikan 361
Miyagi Prefecture 59, 195, 204
Miyajima Island 272–3, 335
Moerenuma Park 284
Moominvalley Park 78
Morioka 200–3
moss 351
Mount Daisen 274
Mount Fuji 105, 181, 221, 222–3, 227
Mount Hakusan 217
Mount Kōya 91, 259, 337
Mount Misen 273
Mount Nasu 191
Mount Takao 176, 340

Mount Tengu 340
Murakami, Takashi 375
Muromachi period (1338–1573) 22–5, 24, 348
museums 16, 18, 21, 24, 30, 34, 41, 44, 48, 163, 236, 293, 359–61
    see also specific museums, e.g. Ghibli Museum
music 16, 18, 21, 24, 30, 34, 41, 44, 48, 378–9
    festivals 62
    live houses, venues and arenas 380
    vinyl-hunting 381

N

nabe 119
Nachi-Katsuura 337
Naga 148
Nagano Prefecture 218
Nagasaki 329, 335
Nagasaki Peace Park 329
Nagoya 78
Naha 78, 327
Nakasendō Way 231
Nambu Tekki ironware 202
Nanzen-ji 337
Naoshima 292–8
    Art House Project 293
    food and drink 293, 297
    museums and galleries 293
    natural occurrences 297
    onsen 297
Nara 181, 250–1, 315, 337
Nara Daibutsu 337
Nara Park 250
Nara period (710–794) 14–15, 26
Nara Prefecture 250
Naruko Onsen 204–5, 299
Nasu 191
national symbols 36
Nawa, Kohei 375
Nebuta Matsuri 59, 199
Nebuta Museum Wa-Rasse 198, 199, 361
Nemuro 288
New Age (music) 379
New Financial and School Year 83
New Year's Eve decorations 77
Niigata Prefecture 226
Nijō Castle 242, 345
Nijo Market, Sapporo 154, 283
Nikkō 178–9, 181
    Tōshō-gū shrine 178, 335
Nishi-Ogikubo 173
Nishiki Market, Kyoto 154, 249
Nishizawa, Ryue 355
Noboribetsu 280–1
Noguchi sculptures 284
Noh theatre 363
nomimono (drinks) 144–53
noodles 120–4, 153
Noto Peninsula 226
Nyūtō Onsen 196–7

O

Obanazawa 208
Obon (Festival of the Dead) 59
   Ōita 61
Odaiba 171
Ogasawara Islands 181
oishi (savoury food) 114–38
Ōita City 61, 329, 337
Ōita Prefecture 316
Oka Castle 345
okashi (sweets) 139–43
Okayama 268
Okayama Castle 268
Okayama Prefecture 268
Okinawa 326–7
   beaches 327
   regional food 118, 125, 131, 327
okonomiyaki 125, 266
Okunoin Temple 259
Ōkunoshima (Rabbit Island) 78, 296
Omicho Market, Kanazawa 154, 216
omiyage (regional souvenirs) 109, 163,
   235, 253
omuraisu (omelette rice) 138
onsen 87
   day-rate 93
   see also specific onsen,
     e.g. Kurokawa Onsen
Ontayaki pottery village 329
Osaka 154, 169, 252–5
   arts and crafts 255
   festivals 255
   gardens and parks 253
   markets 154
   omiyage 253
   regional food and drink 149, 253, 255
   sights 253
   temples and shrines 253
Osaka Prefecture 252
Oshima Subprefecture 278
Oshino Hakkai 221
Otaru 149, 287

P

pachinko 168, 169
packing (travel) 70–1
paradise gardens 347
playtime 168–9
plum blossom (ume) 37, 70
Pokémon 50, 104
pop culture icons 50–1
pottery 182, 183, 299, 310, 322, 329
'Power Spots' (spirituality) 267
prefectures by region 159

R

rainy season 57, 70
ramen 122–3, 135, 153, 261, 278, 322
Randen-Arashiyama Station, Kyoto 100
Reihokan Museum 259
Reversible Destiny Lofts 92
rice 115, 153, 217

rock bands 379
Romancecar (train) 107
Roppongi 167
Rurikō-ji 275
ryokan 87, 95

S

sacred sites & pilgrimage trails 181, 228–31
Saihō-ji 337
Saitama Prefecture 149, 161
Sakai 345
sake 62, 146, 148, 153
sakura see cherry blossom
sakura mochi 85
Sakurajima (active volcano) 320
samurai 22, 26, 30, 198, 214, 329, 349
SANAA architects 292, 293, 355
sand dunes 275, 299
Sannai-Maruyama Historical Site 199
Sanrio Puroland 78
Sapporo 67, 74, 149, 154, 281–5
Sasaguri Kyudai Forest 329
sashimi 130–1, 153
savoury food (oishi) 114–38
seafood 130–1, 132, 154, 278, 283, 288,
   303, 309, 322
seasons 53–85
Seiganto-ji 261
Sejima, Kazuyo 355
Sendai 195, 337
Sendai Tanabata Matsuri 59
Seto Inland Sea 292, 294–5, 303, 304
Setouchi Retreat Aonagi 91, 303, 304
Setsubun (spring eve) 74
Seven Stars in Kyushu (train) 88, 103, 106
shibori 368
Shibuya 165
Shiga Prefecture 256, 299
Shijō Dōri 238
Shiki-shima (train) 106
Shikoku 109, 158, 159, 267, 290–305
   adventures 304–5
   Eighty-eight Temple Pilgrimage Trail
     229, 303
   onsen 304
   regional food and drink 119, 124, 146
Shikotsu-Toya National Park 279
Shima Onsen 187
Shimame Prefecture 271, 275
Shimanami Kaidō Bridge 296
Shimokitazawa 173
Shinden gardens 347
Shinjō (Matsuri) 211
Shinjuku 165
Shinsekai 255
Shinto/Shinto shrines 75, 185, 227, 240,
   260, 271, 273, 332, 333–5, 351
Shirahama 261
Shirakawa-go 181, 224–5
Shirogane Blue Pond 287, 315
Shiroishi 78
Shitamachi Tanabata Matsuri
   (Star Festival) 58

Shizuoka Prefecture 151, 227
shōchū 147, 148, 153
Shodō 336
Shoji Ueda Museum of Photography 274
shōjin ryōri 126, 133, 135
Shorinzan Daruma-ji Temple 189
Shōwa Daibutsu 337
Shōwa era 27, 42–5
skiing 209, 226, 287, 288, 340
SL Ginga (train) 107
Snow Crystal Museum 287
Snow Festival 74
snow season 70, 72–3
soba noodles 121
Sounkyo Gorge 285, 287
spring 70, 80–1
   events 83–5
   festivals 82–3
   foods 85
   trains 106
station stamps 356
street food 128–9
strolling gardens 349
Sumidagawa Hanabi Taikai
   (Sumida River Fireworks Festival) 58
summer 54–7, 70
   experiences 62
   festivals 58–63
   food and drink 56
   trains 105
sumo 363
Sunrise Izumo (train) 106
Sunrise Seto (train) 106
super sentō 93
superstar architect hotels 91
sushi 130–1, 153
Suwa Shrine 335
sweets (okashi) 139–43, 217, 303

T

taco rice 138, 327
Taishō era (1912–1926) 27, 38–41
taiyaki 128
Takadanobaba Station, Tokyo 100
Takamatsu 293, 295, 301
Takaragawa Onsen Osenkaku 187
Takasaki 188–9
Takayama 67, 224–5
   Morning Markets 154
Takeda Castle ruins 345
takoyaki 128
Tamaden train 261
Tange, Kenzō 245, 353
tanuki 341
tea 150–1, 153, 249, 309, 322
tea gardens 347
temple stays 91
temples and shrines 189, 275, 299
   by period 4, 21, 24, 30, 34, 41, 484
   see also Buddhism/Buddhist temples;
     Shinto/Shinto shrines
tempura 132
Tendo Ningen Shōgi 210

tengu 341
Teshima 293, 295
themed hotels 91
tiered pagodas (Tō or Buttō) 250, 256, 261, 275, 309, 337
Tochigi City 66
Tochigi Prefecture 161, 178, 183, 191, 334
Todai-ji 251
tofu 133
Tōfuku-ji (Zen temple) 243
Tōhoku 109, 158, 159, 192–211, 267
    adventures 210–11
    regional food and drink 131, 136, 145, 147
Tōhoku Emotion (train) 106
Tōhoku Shinkansen Gran Class (train) 106
Tokugawa Ieyasu 28
Tokugawa shogunate 22
Tokyo 162–3
    areas 164–7
    cycling 315
    festivals 58, 163
    food and drink 148, 149
    gardens and parks 78, 163
    markets 154
    museums and galleries 163, 361
    near Tokyo 176–7
    old-world charm 172
    omiyage 163
    sights 163
    toys, tech and games 169, 170–1
    train daytrips 107
    vending machines 175
    views 163
    vintage 173
    weekends 174–5
Tokyo Prefecture 161, 162
Tomioka Silk Mills 181
Tomogashima Islands 261
tonkatsu 136
Toto Museum 361
Totoro 50
    bus stops 78
Tottori 275, 299
Towada-Hachimantai National Park 196
Toyama 226
Toyo Ito Museum of Architecture 303, 305
Toyotomi Hideyoshi 22, 36
toys, tech and games 169, 170–1, 269, 339, 340

traditional music 379
train journeys 5, 88–9, 100
    character trains 104
    cherry blossom (sakura-viewing) 83, 106
    ekiben 78, 97, 99
    express trains 101
    glamorous and high-end experiences 88, 103, 106
    landscape and nature trains 105
    local trains 101
    seasonal trains 105–6
    Shinkansen (bullet trains) 101, 107
    stations 97, 100–1
    stylish and designer trains 106–7
    Tokyo daytrip romance 107
    traditional culture 106
    train passes 100–1
tsuboniwa 351
Tsukiji Fish Market, Tokyo 154
Tsukimi Moon-viewing Festival 67
Tsurunoyu Onsen 197
Twilight Express Mizukaze 106
typhoon season 57, 70

U
Uchiko-za 305
udon noodles 124
Ueno Park 172
Uji 151, 249, 334
Ukiyo-e Museum 219
umeshu 146
UNESCO World Heritage Sites 181, 225, 230, 261, 273, 275, 337
Urasu Naked Man Pushing Festival 75
Utsonomiya 116, 191

V
Valley Gallery 293, 353
vegan/vegetarian food 134–5
vending machines 175

W
wagashi 140, 142–3, 217
Wakayama Electric Railway 104, 107
Wakayama Prefecture 261
Wakayama ramen taxis 123, 261
Wakkanai 288

whisky 147, 149, 153
Wide View Hida Train 105, 106
winter 70, 72–3
    experiences 77
    festivals 74–5
    food and drink 76, 77
    trains 106

Y
Yaeyama Islands 327
yaki imo 128
yaki tomorokoshi 128
yakisoba 128
yakitori 128, 137
Yakushima 181, 299, 325
Yamadera 206–7, 299
Yamagata Prefecture 206, 208, 299
Yamaguchi 275
Yamanashi Prefecture 149, 221
Yamanouchi 227
Yamanouchi Onsen 227
Yanagibashi Fish Market 309
Yanaka 172
Yasugi 275
Yayoi period (1000 BC–30 AD) 14
    reconstructed houses 342
Yobuko Morning Market, Karatsu 154
yōgashi 141
Yokaichi Old Town 305
Yokohama 191, 361
Yokote Kamakura Festival 75
Yonago 274
yorishiro 351
yōshoku 138
Yudanaka 78
Yufuin 311
yukata 89
Yukizuri ropes 351

Z
Zaō Kitsune Mura (Fox Village) 78
Zaō Onsen 209
Zaō Snow Monster Festival 75
Zen gardens 336, 348
Zen meditation 337
Zuikoyama Kiyomizu-dera 275

Pan Macmillan acknowledges the Traditional Custodians of Country throughout Australia and their connections to lands, waters and communities. We pay our respect to Elders past and present and extend that respect to all Aboriginal and Torres Strait Islander peoples today. We honour more than sixty thousand years of storytelling, art and culture.

A Plum book

First published in 2022 by
Pan Macmillan Australia Pty Limited
Level 25, 1 Market Street,
Sydney, NSW 2000, Australia

Level 3, 112 Wellington Parade,
East Melbourne, VIC 3002, Australia

Design by Michelle Mackintosh

Edited by Nicola Young

Index by Max McMaster

Photography by Michelle Mackintosh and Steve Wide, with additional photography as listed

Typeset by Heather Menzies and Michelle Mackintosh

Colour reproduction by Splitting Image Colour Studio

Printed and bound in China by 1010 Printing International Limited

A CIP catalogue record for this book is available from the National Library of Australia.